D1687419

EXPERIMENT AND DESIGN
Archaeological Studies in honour of John Coles

Experiment and Design

Archaeological Studies in Honour of John Coles

Edited by A. F. Harding

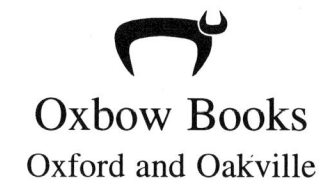

Oxbow Books
Oxford and Oakville

Published by
Oxbow Books, Park End Place, Oxford OX1 1HN

© Oxbow Books and the individual authors, 1999

ISBN 1 900188 76 7

This book is available direct from

Oxbow Books, Park End Place, Oxford OX1 1HN
(Phone: 01865–241249; Fax: 01865–794449)

and

The David Brown Book Company
PO Box 511, Oakville, CT 06779, USA
(Phone: 860–945–9329; Fax: 860–945–9468)

or from our website

www.oxbowbooks.com

*Cover: John Coles and Don Allan illustrating the techniques of Bronze Age Combat.
Photograph by Ralph Crane, 1963. © Time/Life*

*Printed in Great Britain at
The Short Run Press
Exeter*

Contents

Foreword vi
Introduction, *by Bo Gräslund* vii

PALAEOLITHIC ARCHAEOLOGY
1. Radiocarbon dating and the origins of anatomically modern populations in Europe,
   by Paul Mellars 1
2. The Chauvet Cave dates, *by Jean Clottes* 13

THE ARCHAEOLOGY OF SCOTLAND
3. A hidden landscape: the Neolithic of Tayside, *by Gordon J. Barclay* 20
4. The stony limits – rock carvings in passage graves and in the open air, *by Richard Bradley* ... 30
5. Evidence, North and South, in the earlier Neolithic, *by R.J. Mercer* 37
6. The birth of the Scottish Bronze Age, *by J.N. Graham Ritchie* 41
7. Drinking, driving, death and display: Scottish Bronze Age artefact studies since Coles,
   by Alison Sheridan 49

BRONZE AGE ARCHAEOLOGY
8. Bronze Age landscapes in Southern Europe, *by Graeme Barker* 60
9. From Skåne to Scotstown: some notes on amber in Bronze Age Ireland, *by George Eogan* 75
10. Swords, shields and scholars: Bronze Age warfare, past and present, *by Anthony Harding* ... 87
11. The Bronze Age hoards of Hampshire, *by Andrew J. Lawson* 94
12. Gold reflections, *by Joan J. Taylor* 108
13. Rise and fall: the deposition of Bronze Age weapons in the Thames Valley and the Fenland,
    by Roger Thomas 116
14. Bronze Age settlement in South Scandinavia – territoriality and organisation,
    by Henrik Thrane 123

EXPERIMENTAL ARCHAEOLOGY
15. Getting to grips with music's prehistory: experimental approaches to function,
    design and operational wear in excavated musical instruments, *by Graeme Lawson* 133
16. Experimental ship archaeology in Denmark, *by Ole Crumlin-Pedersen* 139
17. Wood-tar and pitch experiments at Biskupin Museum, *by Wojciech Piotrowski* 148
18. The nature of experiment in archaeology, *by Peter J. Reynolds* 156

WETLAND ARCHAEOLOGY
19. Somerset and the Sweet Conundrum, *by Bryony Coles* 163
20. Paths, tracks and roads in Early Ireland: viewing the people rather than the trees,
    by Barry Raftery 170
21. Underwater medieval sites on Lake Paladru (Isère, France):
    from rescue excavations to cultural project, *by Michel Colardelle & Eric Verdel* 183

Epilogue: Of weapons and wetlands, *by Timothy Champion* 191
J.M. Coles – a Bibliography 194

Foreword

The idea for a Conference and *Festschrift* for John Coles emanated from a group of his friends and colleagues in 1995. The immediate problem they faced was that he had already passed his 65th birthday, and waiting until his 70th seemed too long. Why, you may ask, did we not remember his approaching 65th birthday earlier? The answer is simple: none of us (with one obvious exception!) could quite believe that John had actually achieved this milestone. His undiminished energy, formidable work-rate, and ever-youthful appearance seemed to give the lie to the notion that John could ever become – except in academic status – a 'senior citizen'. However, the bald facts of chronology cannot be denied: John Coles was born in Woodstock, Ontario in March 1930. After graduating from the University of Toronto he arrived in Britain in 1955 to study for the Diploma in Prehistoric Archaeology at Cambridge with Grahame Clark and Charles McBurney. In 1957 he went to Edinburgh to undertake his PhD with Stuart Piggott; typically, he was ready to submit it in 1959, before the regulations actually allowed him to do so! For the academic year 1959–60 he held a Carnegie Scholarship, and late in 1960 he moved back to Cambridge, initially as Assistant Lecturer, later as Lecturer, Reader, and finally Professor. Leaving Cambridge in 1986 he moved to Exeter, where he and Bryony made their home in the beautiful Devon countryside at Fursdon Mill. The word 'retirement' does not appear in John's vocabulary, so he is constantly busy with projects of his own and with advice and help to others. Wherever wetland archaeology is practised, John is asked to come and offer his thoughts – which are invariably wise, concise and to the point: he is or has been Chairman of numerous wetland projects. He is also kept extremely busy by his work for the Royal Commission on the Ancient and Historical Monuments of Scotland, and for the Heritage Lottery Fund. In spite of this, he maintains a flow of publications (as the Bibliography on p. 194 indicates) that relate both to his own academic interests and to public archaeology in general.

The meeting which underlies this book took place in Exeter in April 1997 under the title 'From Somerset to Simris', having been enthusiastically adopted by the Prehistoric Society for its Spring Conference that year. Not all the contributors were able to be present, and time did not permit others to be invited to speak; in particular, other commitments meant that Dr Clottes and Professor Mellars were on the other side of the Atlantic, so there was no Palaeolithic section. Since John is co-author of a text-book on the Palaeolithic, it is fitting that we have been able to include such a section here. The summarising conclusion has been provided by Tim Champion, at the time President of the Prehistoric Society, standing in at the last minute for Derek Simpson, who attended the Conference but was taken ill before giving his concluding remarks, and whose health since has unfortunately not permitted him to make a contribution here. The problem faced at the time, repeated in spades here, is that John's interests are so broad it is hard to get all of them into a single book. The separate and distinct themes of Scotland, the Bronze Age, experimental archaeology, rock art, and wetlands, to all of which he has made major contributions, are only the most obvious. It was a striking, and typical, feature of John that when a contributor to the rock art section of the conference dropped out at the last minute he himself stepped in to give a paper – a paper whose detailed knowledge, coupled with breadth and vision, could not have been matched by anyone else in Britain; arguably not in the world. In this book, the rock art section has been merged with other groups of papers, but in other respects the order follows chronologically that in which John Coles has engaged in the various subjects.

Much help has been received in the preparation of this volume from John and Bryony Coles themselves. English Heritage generously supported the Conference, and help in kind has been received from other organisations. Thanks are also due to David Brown of Oxbow Books for undertaking the publication of this volume, which all the contributors hope John Coles will enjoy.

Anthony Harding

Introductory address

Bo Gräslund

Dear John, Dear colleagues,

During the few days I have been in Britain, I have found that strange things are happening here. Recently Dolly, the Easter Lamb, revealed itself through a virgin birth at the Roslin Institute. Then came the large comet with its glittering tail, which can now be seen in the firmament in the north-west. Add to this the fact that the river Thames has suddenly run dry, and that we are close to the turn of a new millennium. I cannot see all this other than as heralding this unique conference in honour of John Coles.

Since John does not like too much fuss about his person, and since I don't want to see him sitting here covering his ears with his hands, I will not review his achievements as an archaeologist in too much detail or try to present a full scholarly biography. Besides, it is difficult to know where to stop, as John is like a never-ending eruption of new publications and achievements. I bet he finished a fresh article this morning. Instead, I will confine myself to some general comments and personal reflections.

The various sections of this conference neatly summarize John's research interests and highlight the unusual diversity of his main areas of activity: the Bronze Age, rock art, Scotland, experimental archaeology, and wetland archaeology. To this could be added much more, like the Early Stone Age, or popular archaeology. Any other normal archaeologist would have been satisfied with a few of these topics. But John has made impressive and lasting contributions to all of them. The participants in this conference will no doubt in various ways, directly or indirectly, bear witness to the extraordinary importance of John's collected works.

I made John's acquaintance some thirty years ago. While writing a couple of articles on Bronze Age shields, I had been impressed by his experiments with bronze and leather shields and by his treatment of European Bronze Age shields in general. I sent him offprints, maybe with a short letter – but that might be a rationalization. Anyway, the shields were the contact, and John immediately sent a kind, typically Coles-ish reply, together with offprints. Those who know my disability as a letter-writer will understand who has kept this relationship going. Over the years a friendship has developed, which has meant very much to me personally.

John is probably one of the most productive letter-writers in the history of archaeology. Sticking to pencil and typewriter, he spurts out thousands rather than hundreds of letters in a single year. I suppose many of you get them, written in his stenographic short-grammar style, which nobody can imitate. They are not only a pleasure to receive but they also represent a remnant of a several thousand year-old cultural tradition, which the rest of us now threaten with extinction. But John's letter-writing is also an important functional element of his archaeology.

Having accepted the kind invitation to give this speech, the more I thought about it, the more I became aware of that I had very little competence to assess John's works. I am very well aware that I myself would never have been able to achieve what he has achieved, and to write what he has written. Aware that Nature has deprived me of some qualifications useful to a normal archaeologist, I prefer to do my archaeology in my arm-chair or in the cosy corner of a café. At the time when I got to know John better, I was interested in the way the old Germanic peoples gave names to their children. They believed that a certain name could represent only one soul at the same time within the family, and that it would create severe problems if the same name was given to different persons in two generations. With this in mind, it suddenly appeared to me that it was only to be expected that I lacked these properties: John, as a bit older, had already grabbed them, they were occupied. It may sound ridiculous, but it was all like a message from our prehistoric forefathers, and it helped me to get some distance from things and concentrate more on the matters I had some talent for. But the key factor, which explains how this metaphor could appear to me at all, was the very modest and humorous way in which John himself expressed his own outstanding qualities.

Author's Address: Bo Gräslund, Department of Archaeology, University of Uppsala, Sweden

What I have just said illustrates a characteristic feature of archaeology compared to many other fields of research. The archaeological source material and, as a consequence, the range and variation of possible problems and questions, are so complex and rich that there is free scope for almost any kind of intellectual type and personal temperament. However different we are, we can all find a niche which suits us and still make an important contribution to the solution of our common problems. Some may object that this also explains why there are so many odd and eccentric personalities in archaeology. Maybe this is the case, but thank Heaven for that. Just imagine the opposite.

I think that this scientific complexity of archaeology also explains to some extent why archaeologists often feel more at home in the atmosphere of an institute for natural sciences rather than in that of many institutes of traditional humanistic and social studies. The reason is that natural scientists often have similar social and scholarly experiences and needs to archaeologists; a combination of the handling of material data, intellectual work indoors and practical fieldwork out of doors. There is probably also a selection of similar personal characteristics in operation.

Pure chance and elderly colleagues may influence our first steps as scholars, our first choice of problems, periods, type of data and printed articles, and to some extent they also put their stamp on us methodologically and theoretically. Nevertheless, good scholars would not become good scholars if they followed a particular line or tradition just because they were expected to, or because they wished to make a career in it. They become good scholars primarily because, like John, they make their personal intellectual temperament and disposition clearly felt in their research.

John is not that easy to define as an archaeologist. Even though there is a strong empirical component in his research, his archaeology is so much more than that. It is as personal as his spoken and written English, which, as far as I can understand, does not follow any known linguistic tradition.

Our primate genes can be blamed for some hierarchical tendencies in human behaviour which no doubt also act as the ultimate mechanism behind many of our scholarly strivings. But for the same reason, we are also by nature highly social beings. In my opinion, social competence ought to be better acknowledged as a positive force behind archaeological research, and that kind of humour which allows for a long view of ourselves and of others, in turn making good scholarship even better. There is in fact an increasing appreciation of the role of personalities in research, reflected by the growing number of professional biographies of scholars, and of conferences specially aimed at the art of writing such biographies.

Thus, archaeology is a social science not only in terms of its goals but also because it is hardly possible to produce good empirical archaeology without an element of social co-operation, whereas this is fully possible in many other humanistic fields. We cannot carry out much fieldwork or organize excursions, get analyses done, receive technical help, have drawings made or get access to our colleagues' unpublished excavation data, without some social efforts and talents. Thus positive social relationships are probably more necessary in archaeology than in many other areas of the humanities.

In the prefaces and notes to his hundreds of printed works, John has thanked thousands of people of every possible speciality, position inside or outside the archaeological community, age, citizenship and colour. The complete list of persons with whom he has co-operated during his career is probably one of the longest in the history of archaeology. His unusual position in the international archaeological community, and his remarkable achievements as an archaeologist, illustrate my thesis about the importance of personality in scholarship. The key factor in this connection, however, is John's personal modesty and generous consideration of other peoples' contributions whatever their position, in combination with his distanced perspective on the fussy world around him. It is that personal integrity which can be felt when one reads any publication of John's.

During the last thirty years, archaeology has undergone a profound theoretical development. But theoretical archaeology seems to be like modern fiction: after some years much of it has withered away and only a few pieces survive to be re-read. However, since the mid-1990s, archaeological theory seems to have come to something like a stand-still. Much of the debate has faded out, and prominent theorists have become silent or turned to traditional empiricism. In this situation, it is important not to forget the good lessons we have learnt, first and foremost a better awareness of our lack of awareness and of our subjectivity. It also affords us an excellent opportunity to sum up and to evaluate.

Earlier generations of archaeologists could be irritatingly cautious in, for instance, their social interpretations. But this often had its background in an awareness of the subjectivity of our interpretations. It was also due to a general lack of understanding of the analogies for archaeological interpretations, which are to a large extent non-archaeological in nature. However, this general weakness is also shared by modern theory. Thus there has been very little systematic, critical evaluation of the nature of those frames of reference on which archaeological interpretation is to a large extent based.

The proximate aim of theory is to discuss, at the level of principles, how to think and act in order to produce good archaeology. Its ultimate goal is to apply this theory in interpretation, whether at our desk, during field-work, or in the laboratory. However, theoretical argumentation does not always imply theoretical awareness. At the same time, the lack of an explicit theoretical discussion does not necessarily reflect the absence of theoretical considerations. The history of archaeology gives clear evidence that much of the writing of earlier generations demonstrates a substantial amount of theoretical awareness, even if it is mostly between the lines.

This also holds for John's works. He does not regard

himself as a theorist and he does not normally take part in public theoretical discussions. Nevertheless, as I understand it, many of his works are imbued with a deep understanding of the complexity of archaeological thinking. Like many other empiricists, he implicitly, sometimes also explicitly, expresses a profound insight into fundamental theoretical problems. This is indirectly exemplified by, for instance, his experimental works. Meaningful scientific experiments simply cannot be performed and evaluated without some talent for theoretical thinking. John's experimental works reflect a deep awareness of the subjective element in archaeological research, strongly underlining that element in archaeological interpretation. He teaches us that there are no truths, and that "archaeologists can do nothing except deal with opinions". Almost like a devoted post-processualist, but long before any post-modernism, he compared the interpretation of archaeological data with reading a text, asserting that we, while reading, create prehistory.

John has little talent for a life of sitting still. He is a great traveller. He is also a welcome guest. John seems to differ from many other people in that he doesn't travel around in order to promote himself, but to learn, to work, and to meet people. He is genuinely interested in other countries' archaeological conditions, traditions and writings. He also always tries to give due attention to works published in languages which he does not have a command of, or only partially.

All over the world, archaeology is suffering from a chronic endemic disease – the never finished excavation report. The effect of this is that enormous investments in money and human work never bear fruit, and huge quantities of archaeological data and knowledge are lost for ever. John is probably one of the few archaeologists, at least north of Tierra del Fuego, dead or alive, who can go to bed any night without being stricken by bad conscience about reports which should have been written long ago. Imagine if every archaeologist was organized as a joint-stock company – which God forbid – and regularly assessed by the market with respect to the relation between invested capital and production. We all know colleagues whose shares we would not dare to buy. Maybe we would not even buy our own. But without hesitation we would all buy the shares of John Coles Ltd. In a way, John embodies, not so say outshines, the principle of perpetual motion: his total archaeological output always seems to be greater than the input, at least as represented by material resources, money or consumed food.

Archaeology has had a long-standing interest in experimental work. However, for a very long time experimental archaeology was given little space in university circles, and was to a large extent performed by amateurs. John was in fact the first established academic who had the foresight and the courage to point out the necessity for and the possibilities of systematic experiments, and to argue for a professional experimental archaeology. By doing experiments himself, by setting up sound methodological and theoretical rules for experimental work, and by summarizing experimental archaeology in books published and distributed all over the world, he gave experimental archaeology an academic face. His books *Archaeology by Experiment* (1973) and *Experimental Archaeology* (1979) are classics of their kind. Their indirect influence has probably been even greater: they released an explosion of systematic experimental work around the world, even in universities. Even though John did not dwell much in them on stone technology, the general example of his books also helped to establish academically systematic experimental stone technology in many parts of the world.

One of archaeology's great drawbacks is that our data stem to such a great extent from the inorganic world, which no doubt only represents a fragment of the total material culture of prehistoric societies. This means an enormous lack of insight into a rich and complex world, necessary for a high quality understanding of the social life, ideology, art and technology of prehistoric society. Although we have known about the archaeological potential of wetlands for centuries, the logical consequences of this knowledge have seldom been followed up. In 1981, I wrote an official report on the future of Swedish archaeology, underlining, no doubt inspired by John's works, the necessity of a systematic wetland archaeology based on inventories of potential sites for preservation and future excavation. This plea was completely ignored and nothing has happened since except an accelerating destruction of sites. I haven't done anything myself. Instead, look at John. Without unnecessary talk he walked straight out into the Somerset wetlands in 1963 to show what could be achieved, thanks to a plain philosophy, an outstanding methodology and the swift reporting and publishing of his findings. Apart from magnificent archaeological results, John and Bryony's works in the Somerset wetlands and other parts of Britain have set a worthy example for us. Their wetland programme has influenced the international archaeological community in a way which cannot be overestimated.

In 1979, John and Anthony Harding published their monumental book *The Bronze Age in Europe*, a splendid attempt to summarize this enormous topic, in fact one of the few ever made. John's excellent overview in this book of the Bronze Age of the northern countries was actually the first since 1935, and it is still the most recent. This book has had an enormous importance, not least in academic education.

John's commitment to the Scandinavian Bronze Age led him across to the study and documentation of Scandinavian rock art. This is an extensive project, which has for many years brought him over to Scandinavia once or twice a year. Oddly enough, there is at present little other ongoing large-scale academic research on Swedish rock art. There is hardly any other living archaeologist with such a detailed knowledge of the total collection of Scandinavian rock art, based on his own direct studies. It should also be noted that he has carried this out in parallel with his large wetland projects and an endless number of other commissions.

John's feeling of responsibility to the archaeological

heritage is more genuine than that of most of us. This is reflected not only by his swift publication record but also by his commitments to the problem of preservation of the archaeological heritage in Britain, Scandinavia and elsewhere. More than anyone else, he has helped to rouse the authorities in Sweden from their deep antiquarian slumber in order to start taking measures against the rapid deterioration of rock art through acid rain and direct damage. It is also characteristic that the only existing modern guide books for the two most important rock-carving areas in Sweden have been written by John Coles, and are published in three languages.

Since John has never followed any trends just because they are new, he will never be untrendy. His works are based on so much scholarly professionalism, wisdom, experience, intelligence, methodological insight and awareness of the conditions and possibilities of archaeology, that when the archaeology of our time is looked back on in retrospect some hundred years ahead, he will be one of the few who will still be reckoned with and whose influence will still be felt.

Uppsala University is quite restrictive in appointing honorary doctors. Among British archaeologists, only Grahame Clark has previously been appointed. It is an honour for me to announce that Uppsala University has decided to appoint John Coles an honorary doctor, for his outstanding scholarship and for the excellent services he has rendered Swedish and Scandinavian Archaeology.

As a practice for the solemnities of the promotion of the 30th May 1997, I will now hand over to John an artefact which I have kept for some time as a memory of his work on Swedish rock-carving sites. It seems to have passed through the whole process from a purely functional to a mainly symbolic implement. It is almost worn down to the marrow, there are only a few bristles left, and the handle has been repainted several times. I will in any case give it back to John as I suspect he might still find it useful. This brush can be seen as the very incarnation of John Coles' famous laboratory, almost fully equipped. It says something fundamental about John: don't wait, do things now, do it yourself, do it cheap, do it simple, do it thoroughly, and do it well.

1. Radiocarbon dating and the origins of anatomically modern populations in Europe

Paul Mellars

Abstract: The aim of this paper is to illustrate the critical importance of time control in studying the currently topical issue of the origin and dispersal of anatomically and behaviourally modern populations across Europe. A second aim is to highlight some of the current problems inherent in most of the current dating methods available for this time range – and especially those of the radiocarbon method. A third aim is to try to identify some of the strategies we might adopt to get better control over some of the inherent ambiguities and uncertainties in current applications of radiocarbon dating over this period.

We should never underestimate the importance of dating in archaeology. Archaeology is by essence a historical discipline, and time is the primary dimension in all of our research. The importance of time lies not only in documenting the relative and absolute sequence of events in different times and places but, above all perhaps, in formulating and testing alternative *explanations* for the events and patterns we observe. One of the few philosophical statements we can make with absolute certainty about explanations in prehistory is that a 'cause' must invariably precede an 'effect'. Imagine the plight of an historian attempting to explain developments in eighteenth century France without knowing whether the building of Versailles preceded or followed the French Revolution!

Current models of the origin and dispersal of modern humans

After almost a century of debate there is now an increasing consensus among both archaeologists and specialists in hominid evolution that the appearance of fully anatomically modern populations in Europe – and the associated disappearance of the preceding Neanderthal populations – almost certainly reflects a major episode of population dispersal across the continent (see for example papers in Aitken *et al.* 1992; Nitecki & Nitecki 1994; Akazawa *et al.* 1998 etc.). Many discoveries over the past decade have served to reinforce this model: the spate of studies of both mitochondrial and nuclear DNA in present-day world populations, which point repeatedly to a relatively recent (most probably African) origin of the modern human genotype (e.g. Stoneking *et al.* 1992; Harpending *et al.* 1993; Lahr & Foley 1994; Cann *et al.* 1994; Rogers & Jorde 1995; Tishkoff *et al* 1996); the clear evidence that essentially modern anatomical forms were present in both the Middle East and parts of Africa from a least 100,000 years ago – at least 50,000 years before their first appearance in Europe (Stringer & McKie 1996; Bar-Yosef 1996); the equally clear evidence for the survival of essentially 'classic' Neanderthal forms in Europe until at least 35,000 years ago, and their apparently abrupt replacement by equally classic 'Cro-Magnon' forms (Stringer & McKie 1996; Hublin *et al.* 1996; Mercier *et al.* 1991); and (arguably most significant) the recent demonstration that the mitochondrial DNA pattern recovered from the original Neanderthal skeleton from the type-site in Germany was sufficiently different from that of all modern human populations to suggest a period of evolutionary and genetic separation of the two lineages over a period of at least 300,000, if not closer to 600,000 years (Krings *et al.* 1997).

Author's Address: Paul Mellars, Department of Archaeology, Downing Street, Cambridge, CB2 3DZ

In earlier papers I and several other workers have argued that equally strong evidence for a process of population dispersal and replacement in Europe can be documented in the archaeological data (Mellars 1989, 1992, 1996a,b, 1998; Allsworth-Jones 1989; Hublin 1990; Kozłowski 1988, 1992, 1993, 1996; Djindjian 1993; Broglio 1996 etc.). The evidence in this case lies not only in the dramatic nature of the contrast between typically Middle as opposed to Upper Palaeolithic behavioural patterns (i.e. the sudden appearance of both portable and cave art; complex, highly shaped bone, antler and ivory tools; a proliferation of 'personal ornaments' and far-travelled sea shells; unambiguous musical instruments; apparent numerical notation systems etc.) but also in the seemingly very sudden and abrupt way in which these behavioural innovations appear in the archaeological records in many different regions of Europe.

When we examine the archaeological records of this transition in detail, two major patterns seem to emerge. One is the widespread distribution of one specific archaeological entity – the so-called Aurignacian – distributed over a zone extending from Israel and Afghanistan to the Atlantic coasts of western Europe, and clearly associated in several contexts with characteristic (if 'robust') forms of anatomically modern hominids (Mellars 1992, 1996a; Djindjian 1993; Kozłowski 1993; Gambier 1989, 1993; Olszewski & Dibble 1994). When examined in detail, the uniformity of the Aurignacian is perhaps not quite as monolithic as some earlier studies have implied. We can now see that there were at least two major variants of the earliest so-called Aurignacian – a distinctive southern or Mediterranean facies, extending esssentially from the Adriatic coast to the northern coasts of Spain, and characterized predominantly by a range of distinctive retouched bladelet forms of so-called 'Dufour' and 'Font-Yves' types. And a more 'classic' form of carinate-scraper dominated Aurignacian, distributed mainly through central and eastern Europe, but extending into the classic south-west French region and to at least some Spanish sites such as El Castillo and El Pendo (Djindjian 1993; Kozłowski 1993). Despite this apparent dichotomy – apparently reflecting two separate routes of dispersal of early anatomically modern populations across Europe – there are sufficient highly distinctive continuities in these early Aurignacian technologies (such as the occurrence of typical split-base bone point forms in areas ranging from northern Spain to northern Israel, and the similar distribution of equally distinctive 'El Wad' and 'Font-Yves' bladelet forms) to support the notion of a major population dispersal across this broad geographical zone. Recent discoveries confirm that the earliest occurrences of all of the classically Upper Palaeolithic cultural features (cave and mobiliary art, bone tools, pendants, perforated shells, flutes etc.) are associated specifically with these Aurignacian occupations (Mellars 1992; Clottes 1996). There is a further recent suggestion that this process of population dispersal may have been associated closely with a period of major climatic warming, which carried essentially Mediterranean-type scattered woodland over large areas of southern Europe (Mellars 1996a, 1998; Van Andel & Tzedakis 1996).

The second equally intriguing phenomenon is the apparent evidence for various forms of contact, interaction, and apparently 'acculturation' between these dispersing Aurignacian communities and the pre-existing Neanderthal populations in several different regions of Europe. At present by far the clearest evidence for this is embodied in the French Châtelperronian industries, which have been found in association with characteristically Neanderthal skeletal remains in at least two sites (Saint-Césaire and Arcy-sur-Cure) (Harrold 1989; Mellars 1989; Hublin *et al.* 1996). In other parts of Europe the same phenomenon is probably reflected in industries such as the central European Szeletian, the Italian Uluzzian, and some other broadly analogous industries in eastern and south-east Europe (Allsworth-Jones 1989; Kozłowski 1988, 1996; Mussi 1992). The presence of these Neanderthal/Modern 'contact' phenomena is arguably not only unsurprising, but essentially predictable, if we accept the current population-dispersal scenario for the spread of anatomically modern populations across Europe. It would clearly be difficult to imagine how any process of population dispersal of this kind could occur without some degree of chronological overlap, social contact, and potentially various forms of behavioural interaction between the two populations – just as observed in all the historically documented situations of modern European expansion into areas ranging from Australia to the Americas.

The purpose of this brief review of the archaeological evidence is to highlight how critically dependent all of the preceding models are on our understanding and control of the relevant chronological frameworks. There are at least three components of the models outlined above which ultimately stand or fall on the basis of the chronological data:–

1. The assumption that there was a clear east-to-west chronological cline in the appearance of the earliest fully 'modern' technologies, and associated anatomically modern populations, across the different regions of Europe (see Fig. 1.1);
2. The assumption that the apparent archaeological reflections of interaction and acculturation between the expanding anatomically modern and resident Neanderthal populations did indeed occur *after* the arrival of the modern populations within the adjacent areas of Europe, and not *prior* to the dispersal of the new populations; and,
3. If we are to argue that this process of population dispersal was in some way associated directly with a period of rapid climatic amelioration (Mellars 1996a; Van Andel & Tzedakis 1996), we must be able to demonstrate a very close correspondence between the relevant archaeological and climatic records.

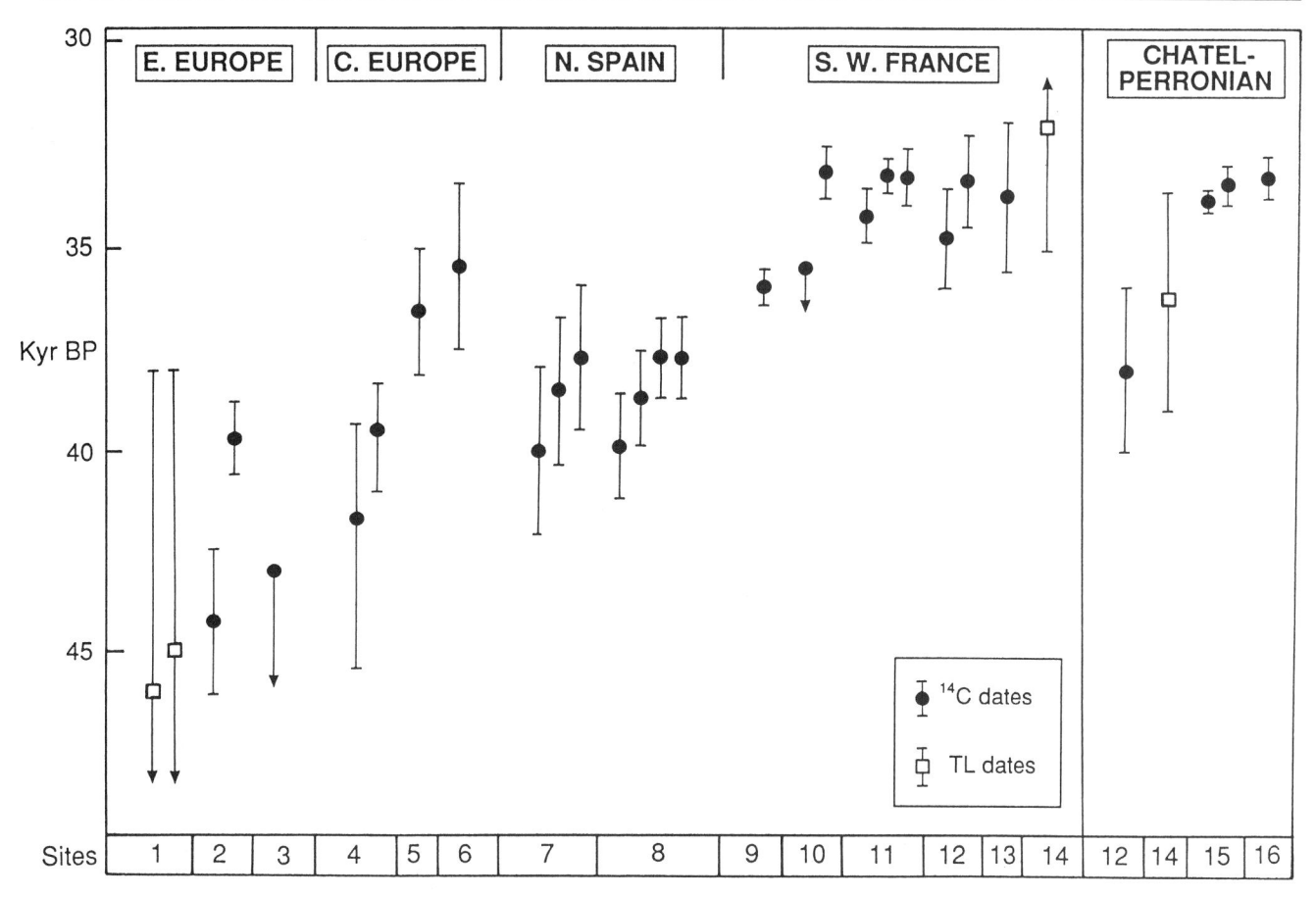

Fig. 1.1. Absolute age measurements for early Aurignacian industries in eastern, central and western Europe, and for Châtelperronian industries in France. For the radiocarbon dates (indicated by circles) the graph includes only the oldest dates from each region, on the assumption that these are likely to show patterns least affected by contamination with more recent, intrusive carbon. From Mellars 1992, Fig. 2.

The reliability of chronological frameworks over the Neanderthal-Modern human transition

Even a cursory review of the literature will show how heavily dependent we are on radiocarbon dating for virtually the whole of our current understanding of archaeological patterns over the period of the Neanderthal to Modern human transition. There is an increasing and crucially important number of sites where the results of radiocarbon dating have been supplemented by other dating methods (such as thermoluminescence, electron-spin-resonance, or uranium-series), but for most of the critical, wide-ranging chronological comparisons we are still perilously dependent on the radiocarbon method. As we shall see later, most of the other techniques employed in this time range are not without their own problems (Aitken 1990). But for the core of the present discussion I will focus primarily on the problems raised by a heavy reliance on the radiocarbon technique. For simplicity, the issues can be summarized under three principal headings.

1. The first and no doubt most obvious problem in the case of radiocarbon and no doubt most other dating techniques is that of demonstrating close chronological synchroneity between the samples submitted for dating and the precise archaeological horizons they are supposed to date. Although these stratigraphic problems have been clearly set out in the literature (e.g. Barton 1987; Hahn 1988) they are all too easy to forget in our enthusiasm to compile long and impressive lists of dates. The problems arise not only from the inescapable stratigraphic uncertainties in even the most meticulously controlled excavation (where critical stratigraphic boundaries can often be highly unclear) but also from the well-documented distortions of these boundaries through a variety of complex site formation processes, ranging from climatically induced solifluction or cryoturbation phenomena to the effects of both human and animal (e.g. cave bear) disturbance in the sites. Several studies based on the direct refitting of lithic artefacts have demonstrated how individual objects can sometimes be displaced through vertical distances of 30 cm or more (Hahn 1988; Villa 1983; Barton 1987). Some of the ways in which the effects of these stratigraphic distortions can be mitigated are discussed

below, but in many cases we must accept that it is virtually impossible to be absolutely certain on stratigraphic grounds that a particular object (such as an animal bone or charcoal fragment) derives from a specific archaeological occupation horizon, as opposed to an immediately underlying or overlying level.

2. The second, and in my own view by far the most serious source of ambiguity in current radiocarbon dating over the Middle/Early Upper Palaeolithic time range stems from the profound problems of contamination by intrusive, more recent carbon, in dated samples. There is hardly space here to provide more than a brief review of these problems, but the essential factors to keep in mind are as follows:

(a) The effects of contamination by even miniscule quantities of intrusive, more recent carbon in this age range can be dramatic (see Mook & Waterbolk 1985; Aitken 1990; Bowman 1990; Waterbolk 1971 etc.). As shown in Table 1.1, contamination by as little as 1 percent of isotopically modern carbon would reduce the measured age of a radiocarbon sample from 40,000 years to less than 34,000. On a sample 50,000 years in age the effect of the same degree of contamination would reduce the age of the sample by around 14,000 years (Aitken 1990, 85). Contamination of this kind can arise from a number of sources, depending on the nature of the site itself (and its subsequent geological history) and the nature of the samples dated. In most cases however contamination by humic acids and other chemicals dissolved in percolating ground water is likely to to be the most serious source of intrusive carbon in samples of both animal bone and charcoal (Mook & Waterbolk 1985; Aitken 1990; Van Klinken *et al.* 1994). Even with the most stringent of chemical pre-treatment procedures there can hardly be any theoretical certainty that all of the intrusive carbon has been removed. The effects of contamination by intrusive *older* carbon, by contrast, is almost negligable. Even 10 percent of contamination by isotopically 'dead' carbon would add only *ca.* 850 years to the measured age of a sample dated to *ca.* 40,000 years – or indeed to samples of any radiocarbon age! (Mook 1971; Mook & Waterbolk 1985; Aitken 1990).

(b) The reality of this kind of contamination by intrusive younger carbon can be documented by numerous past applications of ^{14}C dating to samples in the early Upper Palaeolithic time range. In one controlled dating study

True age of sample	Reduction of measured ^{14}C age by 1% of modern carbon
12,000 BP	270 years
24,000 BP	1400 years
34,000 BP	*ca.* 4000 years
50,000 BP	*ca.* 14,000 years

Table 1.1. *Effects of contamination by 1 percent of 'isotopically modern'* ^{14}C *on radiocarbon samples of different ages. From Waterbolk 1971, 18 and Aitken 1990, 85.*

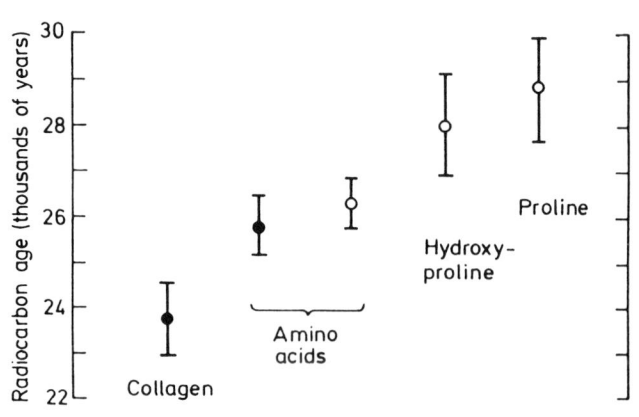

Fig. 1.2. *Radiocarbon dates for different chemical fractions from a mid-last-glacial rhinoceros bone. Open symbols indicate radiocarbon-accelerator dates by the Oxford laboratory, and closed symbols conventional dates by the British Museum laboratory. The older ages given by the proline and hydroxyproline factions, which are amino acids generally specific to bone, suggest contamination by intrusive amino acids in the other fractions. After Aitken 1990, Fig. 4.4.*

of bone collagen from a mid-last-glacial rhinoceros bone from near Northampton, the Oxford radiocarbon laboratory secured first a 'conventional' radiocarbon measurement on a sample of total collagen from the bone, followed by three radiocarbon-accelerator measurements based respectively on the combined amino-acid fraction of the sample, and then on two specific amino-acids (hydroxy-proline and proline) extracted from the collagen component (Aitken 1990, 88). As shown in Fig. 1.2, the measured ages of the different fractions increased progressively from *ca.* 24,000 to almost 29,000 BP as increasingly selective chemical components of the sample – assumed to be increasingly free from intrusive carbon – were measured. More recently the same laboratory has been experimenting with a range of 'tripeptide' extraction techniques on bone collagen, which are again believed to provide chemical fractions increasingly immune from the effects of contamination by percolating humic acids or other contaminants (Van Klinken *et al.* 1994). Preliminary results of measurements of early Upper Palaeolithic samples from the site of Combe Sauniere in southwest France have yielded dates from these tripeptide fractions which in some cases differ only slightly from those of conventional extraction techniques, but in other cases yield dates up to 2–3,000 years older than the conventionally measured ages (R. Hedges & P. Pettitt, personal communication). Similar levels of residual contamination in samples of 40,000 years in age would of course yield much more serious errors of perhaps 5–6,000 years younger than the true age of the samples. Purely on the basis of these controlled studies, therefore, there is inescapable

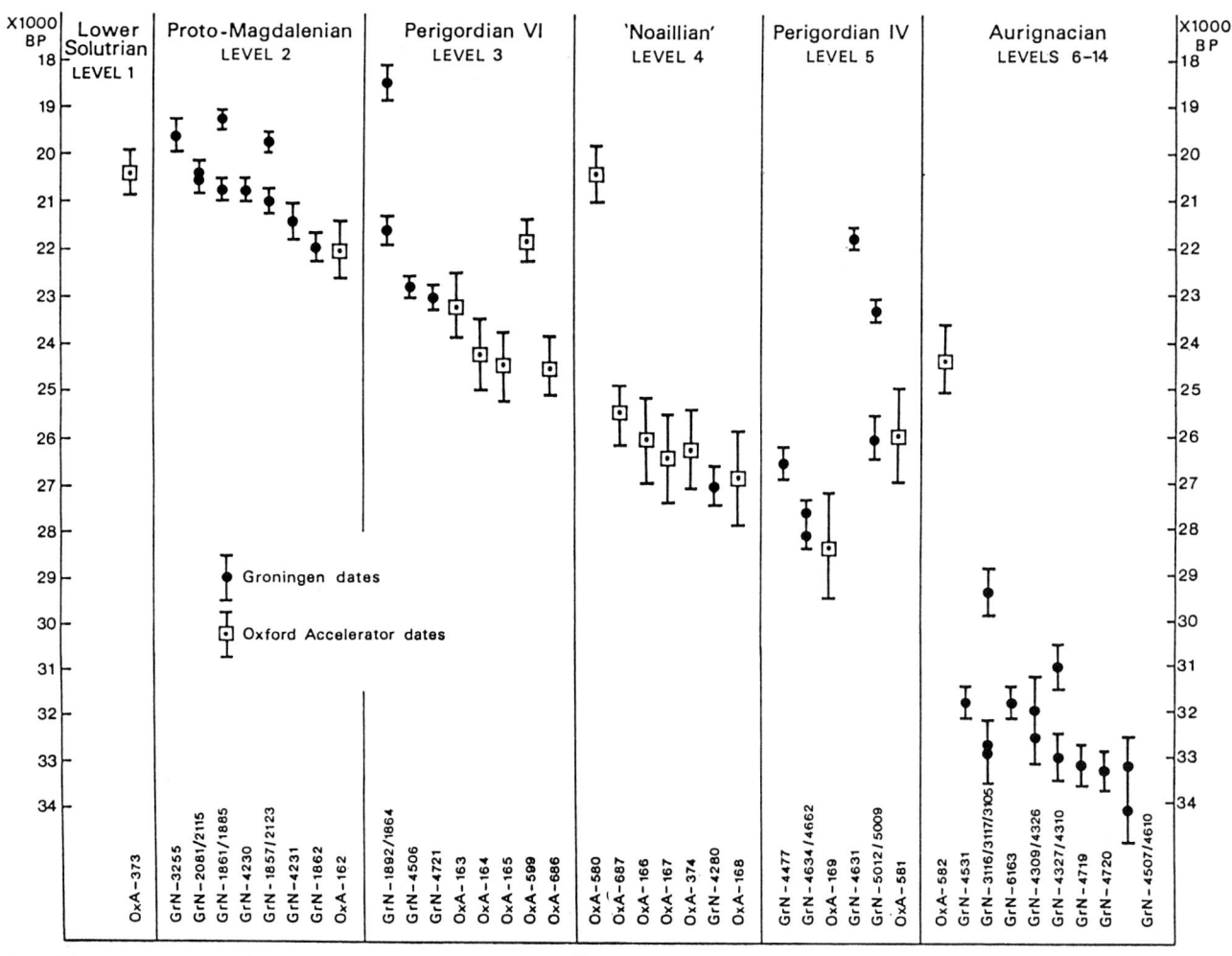

Fig. 1.3. Comparison of conventional and accelerator ^{14}C dates through the long Upper Palaeolithic sequence at the Abri Pataud, south-west France. Note how all the dates which diverge from the general age/depth regression line are on the young side of the line. From Mellars et al. 1987.

evidence that many of the conventional methods of preparing and pre-treating archaeological bone samples in the 30–40,000 year age range will be likely to yield dates several thousand years younger than the real age of the samples.

(c) Further depressingly clear illustrations of the same contamination effects can be seen in many of the long sequences of radiocarbon dates from Upper Palaeolithic sites secured over the past 20 years. In the impressively long sequence of both conventional and AMS dates from the Abri Pataud, for example, it can be seen immediately that all of the measurements which diverge significantly from the general linear trend of the measurements through the deposits are invariably on the younger side of the age/depth regression line, with dates for at least 10 samples demonstrably between 2000 and 6000 years younger than the expected age (see Fig. 1.3; Mellars et al. 1987). Once again, if the same implied levels of contamination were applied to samples around 40,000 years in age, the measured age reduction of the samples could easily lie between 5000 and even 10,000 years. One of the most alarming illustrations of similar contamination effects was documented at the nearby site of La Ferrassie, where the original series of measurements by the Gif-sur-Yvette laboratory yielded a pattern of dates which bore little relationship to the stratigraphic sequence of the samples, and diverged by up to 8000 years from the subsequent dating of the same levels – involving more stringent pre-treatment methods – by the Groningen and Oxford laboratories (see Fig. 1.4: Mellars et al. 1987; Delporte 1984).

A further, highly instructive comparison emerged from the recent dating of early Aurignacian levels in the Riparo Fumane site in northern Italy, by the Utrecht AMS laboratory (Broglio 1996). Here, samples of charcoal were submitted for dating from the same archaeological levels both within and outside the area of the rock overhang of the rock shelter. As shown in Fig. 1.5, the results showed major discrepancies between

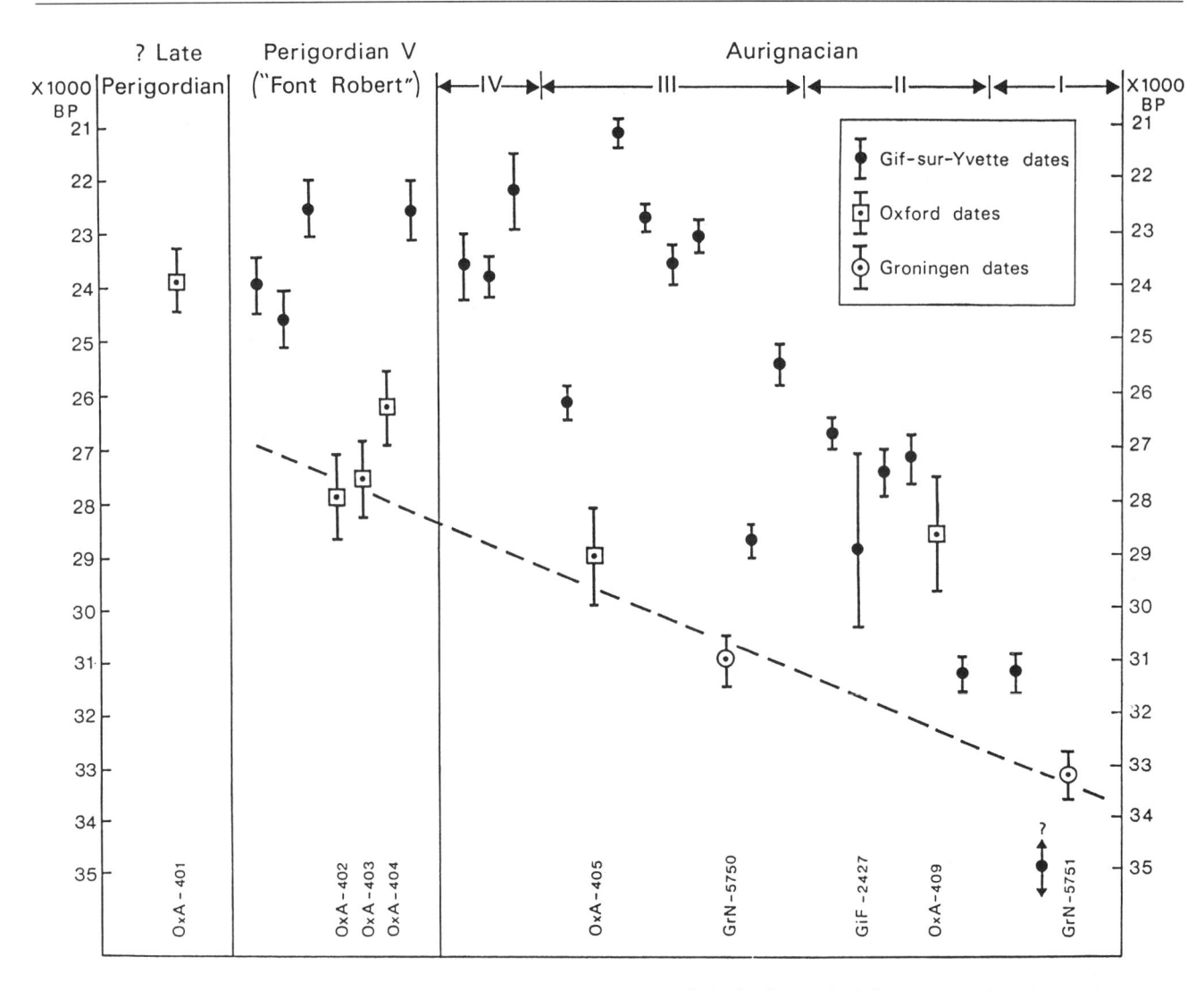

Fig. 1.4. Radiocarbon dates by the Gif-sur-Yvette, Groningen and Oxford (AMS) laboratories for the early Upper Palaeolithic sequence at La Ferrassie, south-west France. From Mellars et al. 1987; Delporte 1984.

the samples collected from the two areas of the site, with the dates from outside the shelter being around 3000–5000 years younger than those from the more protected interior of the site. The most likely explanation for this discrepancy would appear to be that the deposits exposed to rainfall in the outer part of the shelter had been subjected to much greater percolation by water action than those in the sheltered interior of the cave, with correspondingly much greater opportunities for the movement of humic acids and other chemicals down the profile. This example certainly seems to demonstrate that even in the dating of charcoal samples, current methods of cleaning and pre-treatment of the samples cannot be guaranteed to remove all traces of contamination from the dated fractions (Mook & Waterbolk 1985).

3. The final issue relates to the increasing evidence for a major divergence between the radiocarbon timescale and that of other absolute dating methods in the period prior to *ca.* 20,000 BP. The first indications of this came from the studies of Bard *et al.* (1990) on the combined radiocarbon and uranium-series dating of a series of coral samples from Barbados reef formations, which initially suggested a divergence of around 3000 years between the radiocarbon and U-series time scales at around 30,000 BP. Since then there have been a number of other studies involving both further direct comparisons of radiocarbon and other dating methods (Bischoff *et al.* 1994), and estimations of the likely effects on the radiocarbon concentration in the atmosphere arising from major variations in the earth's magnetic field (Laj *et al.* 1996; Van Andel 1998). The latter studies suggest that the maximum divergence of the radiocarbon timescale is likely to have occurred at between 20,000 and 30,000 years, with radiocarbon dates at this time up to 3–4000 years younger than true (calendrical) dates (see Fig. 1.6). On present evidence it appears that radiocarbon measurements

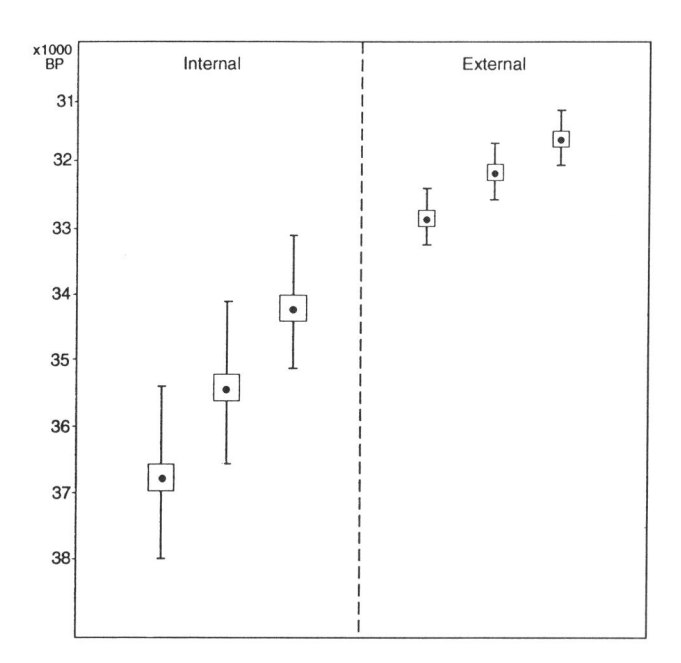

Fig. 1.5. Comparison of radiocarbon-accelerator dates on charcoal samples collected from the same stratigraphic level (layer A2, early Aurignacian) inside and outside the area of the rock overhang in the Riparo Fumane rock-shelter, north-east Italy. After Broglio 1996.

may revert to 'true' levels at around 50,000 BP.

Obviously, the major impact of this calibration arises where the results of radiocarbon dating are being compared with those of other 'absolute' dating methods, such as thermoluminescence, electron-spin-resonance or uranium-series, either in particular archaeological sites, or for dating particular cultural or technological horizons between sites. So long as comparisons between different sites are made purely on the basis of radiocarbon measurements, the effect of these calibration factors are relatively insignificant – at least in terms of the *relative* ordering of the sites. What we must keep in mind, however, is that the shape of the calibration curve over this time range has the effect of significantly stretching the radiocarbon timescale between 30,000 and 50,000 BP, so that an actual time-span of, say, 8,000 years is represented in radiocarbon terms by more than 10,000 (see Fig. 1.6; Laj *et al.* 1996). We should certainly keep this in mind when considering the possible rates of dispersal of anatomically modern populations across Europe, or the overall period of coexistence of anatomically modern and Neanderthal populations. What could be much more serious is the possible existence of major 'wiggles' in the radiocarbon calibration curve over this period, which could potentially lead to some significant reversals in radiocarbon

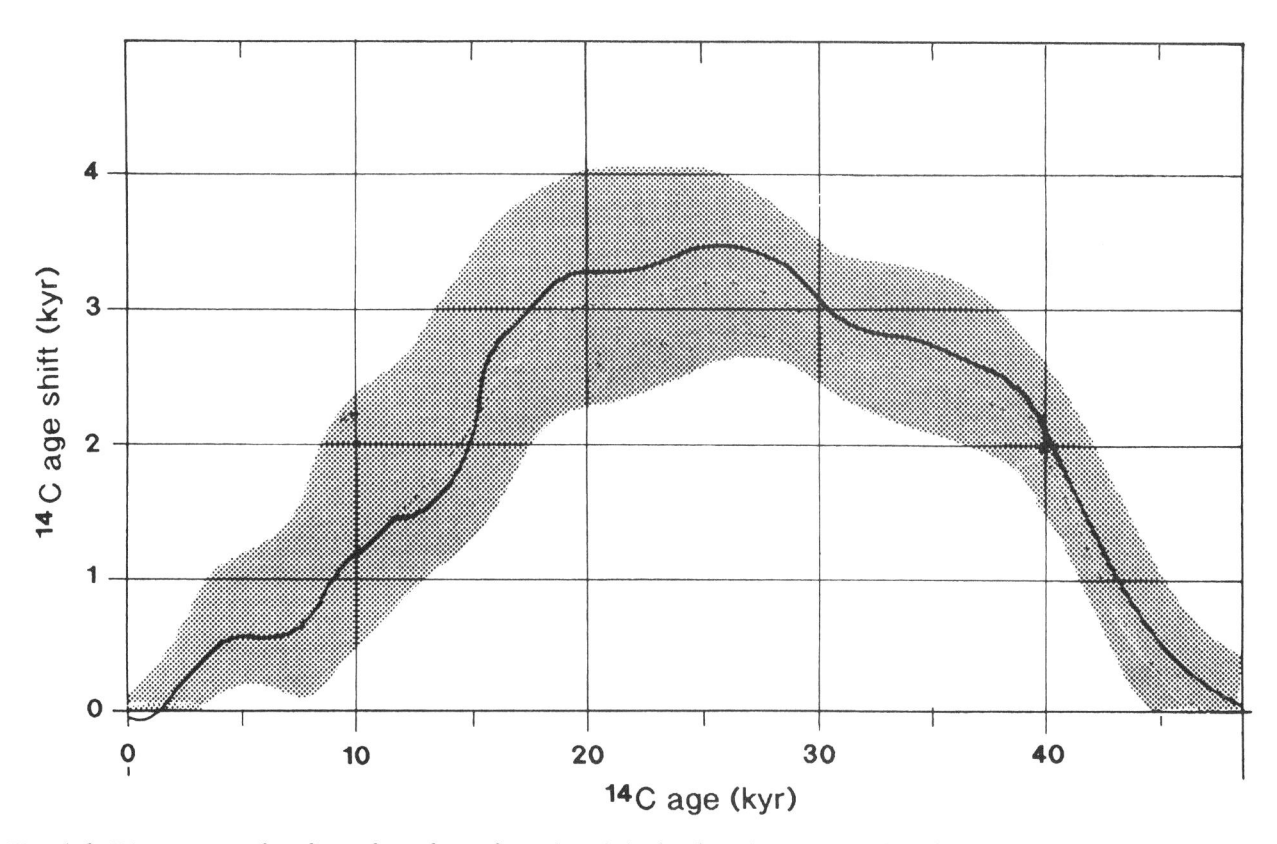

Fig. 1.6. Divergence of radiocarbon dates from 'true' (calendrical) ages, predicted from variations in the earth's geomagnetic field – showing the extent to which radiocarbon dates are estimated to be younger than the true age of the samples. The shaded area indicates the confidence limits on the measurements. After Van Andel 1998; Laj et al. 1996.

dates between different levels in the same stratigraphic sequence, or between different sites. Studies of these divergences between the radiocarbon and absolute time scales however are still at an early stage, and it is likely to be some time before we have access to a fully detailed and reliable calibration curve over this time range.

What can be done?

Having documented in rather depressing detail some of the inherent ambiguities and uncertainties of current applications of radiocarbon dating in the critical early Upper Palaeolithic time range, the question arises as to what strategies we might adopt to overcome – or at least mitigate – the effects of these uncertainties in our future assessments of the radiocarbon evidence. While there are clearly no easy, 'quick-fix' solutions to many of the problems, it is possible to suggest a number of reasonably secure, and essentially common-sense strategies, which can, one hopes, allow us to work more constructively with the available sample of dates.

1. One obvious strategy is to secure wherever possible not only multiple dates based on separate samples from the same occupation horizon but – equally if not much more important – to secure long *stratified* series of dates from the same stratigraphic section. As discussed above, the notion of precise stratigraphic contemporaneity in a strictly chronological sense is almost meaningless in any archaeological excavation. The best we can hope to show is that a given radiocarbon sample is *to all appearances* stratigraphically equivalent to a specific occupation horizon. But in most cases the best we can hope to demonstrate with complete confidence is that a particular sample is demonstrably *older* or *younger* than a particular occupation level, in stratigraphic terms. In this context, long, closely stratified sequences of samples of the kind dated at the Abri Pataud (Fig. 1.3) provide the best possible chronological control over the sequence of occupation horizons as a whole. The other great advantage of long stratified series of samples is that we can usually recognize immediately when any individual radiocarbon result is clearly anomalous (as the sequence at the Abri Pataud clearly revealed: see Fig. 1.3) and with luck identify some coherent and mutually consistent pattern in the dating trend over the sequence as a whole. If the dates are based on different samples of material which can be directly compared (such as charcoal and bone), so much the better.

2. A second obvious strategy is to attempt wherever possible to date samples of material which can be shown beyond reasonable doubt to relate directly to actual episodes of human occupation in a site, as opposed to samples which could potentially derive from non-human activities on the site. The latter is especially critical in the dating of bone samples from cave sites which are likely to have been used, if only sporadically, as carnivore dens. In these cases much of the faunal material is likely to date from episodes of carnivore activity in the sites *between* the main periods of human occupation – and which of course in some cases could be substantially older or younger than the intervening occupation horizons. In this case the dating of either obvious bone or antler artefacts, or at least bones with clear signs of human butchery marks, is far preferable to the dating of non-modified bones. One could also argue that charcoal (especially in cave or rock-shelter sites) is likely in most cases to relate directly to periods of human occupation on the site, but it is only when the charcoal derives from well defined hearth features (as for example in the case of the large sample from layer 11 in the Bacho Kiro cave dated by the Groningen laboratory: Mook 1982; Kozłowski 1982) that one can be absolutely certain of this association. The dating of individual specimens of typologically distinctive bone or antler artefacts (such as split-base bone/antler points) is another obvious strategy, so long as the problems of potential contamination can be overcome in the pretreatment of the generally very small samples which can be removed from valuable museum specimens.

3. The third, and in my view most important, strategy in the interpretation of radiocarbon dates in the early Upper Palaeolithic time range is to recognize that *all* samples of dated material are likely to include *some* component of intrusive, more recent carbon, and to acknowledge that this will have the effect in the great majority of cases of yielding dates which are significantly younger than the true age of the samples. This point was stressed repeatedly by the Groningen laboratory in their large-scale programme of dating Palaeolithic samples in the 1960s (e.g. Vogel & Waterbolk 1963, 1967; Waterbolk 1971, 17) but has rarely been stressed as a routine precaution by other dating laboratories. As noted earlier, the point is simply that while it is virtually impossible for a radiocarbon date to emerge as significantly *older* than the true age of the sample, it is highly possible for dates to be substantially too young. As Waterbolk stressed clearly in 1971, it is therefore the pattern of the *oldest* dates secured for particular archaeological horizons (or individual levels in sites) which is likely to provide the most reliable guide in constructing radiocarbon chronologies – so long, of course, as the stratigraphic provenance of the samples and their association with specific occupation horizons is secure.

4. Most of the other strategies for the improvement of future radiocarbon chronologies for the early Upper Palaeolithic lie in the strictly technical sphere of the radiocarbon laboratories themselves (Mook & Waterbolk 1985; Aitken 1990). Clearly, more research needs to be done to compare the methods of both

pre-treatment and measurement of samples in different laboratories, to be sure that inter-laboratory results are truly comparable. Equally, more research needs to be done on the comparison of dating of different materials from specific contexts (such as bone and charcoal) to see whether the inherent susceptibility of different materials to contamination are significantly different, and to devise the best methods for pre-treatment of the different materials. In the dating of bone, the selective extraction of specific chemical components of collagen, such as individual amino acids (Fig. 1.2) or separate tripeptide fractions, clearly offers the best prospect for identifying and eliminating contamination by later, intrusive carbon – though of course these procedures can be expensive in terms of the time and laboratory procedures involved, and often require the processing of large samples (Van Klinken *et al*. 1994, with references). My own view is that the radiocarbon laboratories should be encouraged to concentrate not only on trying to devise the best possible laboratory treatment procedures but – equally if not more important – to devise some explicit research strategies to estimate exactly how efficient these different cleaning and pre-treatment procedures are in eliminating all possible contaminants. In other words we need not only to be assured that the laboratories have 'done their best' in the processing of samples, but to have some form of controlled evaluation of exactly how effective these cleaning strategies are.

5. The final strategy is perhaps the most obvious. Clearly, wherever possible we should date sites by two or preferably more independent dating methods, not only to achieve the maximum chronological control over the dated horizons, but to evaluate the mutual comparability and congruence of the different techniques (e.g. Bischoff *et al*. 1994). Combined with this of course we urgently need more detailed control over the calibration of the radiocarbon timescale (whether from studies of the effects of geomagnetic fluctuations on the atmospheric ^{14}C content, or from closely matched series of dating by radiocarbon and other dating methods) to discover more about the potential extent of radiocarbon aberrations, and associated major 'wiggles' or 'plateaux' in the radiocarbon record (Fig. 1.6).

Conclusions

Finally, if we return to the principal archaeological issues defined in the earlier part of the paper, what conclusions *can* we legitimately draw from the available radiocarbon and associated dating evidence, making due allowance for the various caveats and reservations voiced above? Briefly, I would suggest that the following conclusions can be drawn with a fair degree of confidence:

1. First, there seems little doubt the the earliest occurrences of fully 'Upper Palaeolithic' technology (in the sense of well developed blade production, associated with relatively abundant and typical specimens of both end-scrapers and burins) can be dated significantly earlier in some Middle Eastern and south-east European sites than in western and central Europe. Three sites are especially critical in this context: Boker Tachtit in southern Israel, where the earliest Upper Palaeolithic levels are dated on the basis of apparently closely associated charcoal samples to around 47,000 BP (Marks 1983); Ksar Akil in the Lebanon, where a combination of radiocarbon dates and extrapolated sedimentation rates suggests a broadly similar date for the earliest so-called 'Emiran' or 'Transitional' industries (Mellars & Tixier 1989); and Bacho Kiro in Bulgaria, where a large charcoal sample collected from a well defined hearth in the lowermost 'Proto-Aurignacian/Bacho-Kirian' levels was dated by the Groningen laboratory to > 43,000 BP – with the suggestion that the *actual* date might be closer to 47,000 (Mook 1982; Kozłowski 1982). Further support for this dating may perhaps be provided by the date of 44,300±1900 BP (GrN-4659) reported for the lowermost Aurignacian level (with typical split-base bone points) at the Istallosko cave in Hungary (Allsworth-Jones 1986) – though in this case it would be important to confirm that the dated bone sample was indeed associated directly with the Aurignacian occupation, and could not derive from a closely underlying level of cave-bear occupation in the site.

2. In western Europe the earliest securely dated occurrences of Upper Palaeolithic technology – in the form of the early Aurignacian industries – seem to date from around 40,000 BP in radiocarbon terms (see Fig. 1.1). The most significant sites in this context are those of l'Arbreda in Catalonia (north-east Spain) and El Castillo in Cantabria, for both of which we have multiple, stratified series of dates based on AMS dating of charcoal samples, evidently associated directly with the early Aurignacian occupations (Cabrera-Valdés & Bischoff 1989; Bischoff *et al*. 1989; Mellars 1994; Cabrera-Valdés *et al*. 1996). There are similar results for a thin level of bladelet Aurignacian (apparently closely similar to that from the nearby site of l'Arbreda) from the site of Abric Romani in Catalonia (Bischoff *et al*. 1994) and a more tentative date of *ca*. 40,000 BP (though with a large standard deviation) for a similar bladelet Aurignacian industry from layer A2 in the Riparo Fumane rock-shelter in north-east Italy (Broglio 1996).

Interestingly, there are at present no clear indications that Aurignacian industries were being produced by this early date in the classic region of southwestern France. Despite radiocarbon dating of many early Aurignacian levels, the oldest radiocarbon dates so far secured for these levels cluster between ca. 34,000 and 36,000 BP (notably at the Abri Pataud, Roc de Combe, La Rochette, La Ferrassie, Le Flagéolet and in recent unpublished dates for the Abri Castanet and Abri Caminade – with two exceptions all based on bone samples: Mellars et al. 1987; Mellars 1990; Valladas, pers. comm). Whether some of the currently undated levels of 'bladelet' Aurignacian reported from sites such as Le Piage (Lot) and Font-Yves (Corrèze) may date from significantly earlier than these sites is a critical question which still remains to be resolved (Champagne & Espitalié 1981; de Sonneville-Bordes 1960).

3. The totality of the radiocarbon and other dating evidence leaves little doubt that some substantial overlap can be documented between the earliest Aurignacian industries in western Europe and the time range of the typically 'Châtelperronian' industries – now generally seen (as discussed earlier) as some form of 'contact' phenomenon between the final Neanderthal and earliest anatomically modern populations, and associated at two sites (Saint-Césaire and Arcy-sur-Cure) with apparently typical Neanderthal skeletal remains (Harrold 1989; Lévêque & Vandermeersch 1980; Hublin et al. 1996). The critical point to emphasize in this context is that at present we have no securely dated occurrences of typically Châtelperronian industries in France earlier than ca. 38,000 BP in radiocarbon terms – i.e. substantially later than the earliest dated occurrences of typically Aurignacian industries in the north-Spanish sites discussed above (see Fig. 1.1). This pattern is reinforced by the fact that in the long succession in the lower shelter at Le Moustier, several levels of characteristic late Mousterian industries, clearly underlying a Châtelperronian level, were dated by thermoluminescence to ca. 40–42,000 BP (Valladas et al. 1986) – which, allowing for calibration, probably equates to a radiocarbon age of ca. 38.000 BP (Laj et al. 1996). Unless this pattern is seriously disrupted by subsequent dating of Châtelperronian levels, this clearly adds strong support to the hypothesis that the appearance of distinctively Upper Palaeolithic features (typical blades, end-scrapers and burins, and sporadic bone artefacts and perforated animal teeth) in these Châtelperronian industries can be attributed much more economically to some kind of interaction or exchange mechanisms between the two populations than to an independent 'invention' of Upper Palaeolithic technology by the final Neanderthal populations themselves (Mellars 1989; Hublin et al. 1996). In Italy it is debatable whether any of the published radiocarbon dates for the Uluzzian industries are sufficiently secure to draw firm conclusions, but on the available indications these industries seem in general to be substantially younger than 40,000 BP (Mussi 1992) – as in the case of the French Châtelperronian. In central Europe the dating of 'Bohunician' industries to around 40–43,000 BP may provide a further example of Neanderthal/modern acculturation industries rather earlier than that in western Europe, but still broadly contemporaneous with the earliest occurrences of local Aurignacian or Proto-Aurignacian technologies in adjacent areas (Allsworth Jones 1989; Oliva 1993; Kozłowski 1996).

4. Finally we should at present be rather cautious about making close correlations between the archaeological and palaeoclimatic records over the final Mousterian/ early Upper Palaeolithic time range. Recent research, especially in the Greenland ice cores, has shown that that climatic oscillations over this period were highly complex, with temperature shifts of up to 8–10°C in several cases occurring at intervals of only 1000–2000 years (Dansgaard et al. 1993; Bond et al. 1993; Van Andel & Tzedakis 1996; Van Andel 1998). Clearly, correlations with rapid and closely-spaced climatic oscillations of this kind put massive demands on the accuracy and time resolution of current dating methods. Indeed, leaving aside the problems of archaeological dating, there are some real problems at present in correlating and synchronising many of the key climatic sequences themselves, over this time range (Van Andel & Tzedakis 1996).

Provisionally however there do seem to be some fairly strong and mutually reinforcing indications of a more prolonged period of climatic amelioration dated approximately (in radiocarbon terms) to around 40,000 BP, possibly equivalent to the so-called 'Hengelo interstadial' as originally defined in the Netherlands (Dansgaard et al. 1993). As discussed elsewhere (Mellars 1996a, 1998) it may well be that the occurrence of this major climatic amelioration – and the associated spread of scattered woodland across large areas of southern Europe – was one of the key factors in facilitating the territorial expansion of anatomically modern populations from east to west across Europe.

But to press these correlations further and produce the kind of aggregated distribution chart of radiocarbon-dated archaeological levels of the kind published recently by Van Andel (1998) may perhaps be pushing the evidence too far. If we accept all the caveats concerning the inherent limitations and inevitable contamination effects of radiocarbon dating in this time range, there must be serious doubt as to what proportion of these dates can be accepted as more than essentially *minimum* estimates for the ages of the levels in question. If many or most of the available ^{14}C dates are in fact under-estimates of the true ages by a factor of several thousand years – as most of the current evidence suggests – then this could be sufficient to shift the major peaks and troughs of the aggregated distribution curve through a whole climatic cycle – i.e. with the peaks in the distribution correponding with inferred cold stages, and the troughs in the same curve coinciding with warm stages. This may perhaps be carrying the role of Devil's advocate too far, but in my own view there are sufficient, well-documented ambiguities in the current radiocarbon dating evidence to call for a great deal of caution in any exercise of this kind.

Acknowledgements

I am greatly indebted to Martin Aitken and Tjeerd Van Andel for permission to reproduce Figs 1.2 and 1.6 respectively, and to Robert Hedges, Paul Pettitt, Hélène Valladas and Tjeerd Van Andel for stimulating discussions of some of the issues raised in this paper – though their opinions should not necessarily be assumed to coincide with mine.

Bibliography

Aitken, M.J. 1990. *Science-Based Dating in Archaeology*. London: Longman.

Aitken, M., Stringer, C. & Mellars, P. (eds) 1992. *The Origin of Modern Humans and the Impact of Chronometric Dating*. London: Royal Society (Philosophical Transactions of the Royal Society, series B, 337, no. 1280)

Akazawa, T., Aoki, K. & Bar-Yosef, O. (eds) 1998. *Neandertals and Modern Humans in Western Asia*. New York: Plenum (in press).

Allsworth-Jones, P. 1986. *The Szeletian and the Transition from Middle to Upper Palaeolithic in Central Europe*. Oxford: Oxford University Press.

Allsworth-Jones, P. 1990. The Szeletian and the stratigraphic succession in Central Europe and adjacent areas: main trends, recent results, and problems for solution. In P. Mellars (ed.) *The Emergence of Modern Humans: an archaeological perspective*, 160–243. Edinburgh: Edinburgh University Press.

Bar-Yosef, O. 1994. The contribution of south-west Asia to the study of the origins of modern humans. In M.T. Nitecki & D.V. Nitecki (eds) *Origins of Anatomically Modern Humans*, 23–66. New York: Plenum Press.

Bar-Yosef, O. 1996. Modern humans, Neanderthals and the Middle/Upper Palaeolithic transition in western Asia. In M. Piperno (ed.) *The Lower and Middle Palaeolithic: Colloquia*, 175–90. Forlì: XIII International Congress of Prehistoric and Protohistoric Sciences.

Bard, E., Hamelin, B., Fairbanks, R.G. & Zindler, A. 1990. Calibration of the ^{14}C timescale over the past 30,000 years using mass spectrometric U-Th ages from Barbados corals, *Nature* 354, 405–10.

Barton, N. 1987. Vertical distribution of artefacts and some post-depositional factors affecting site formation. In P. Rowley-Conwy, M. Zvelebil & H.-P. Blankholm (eds) *The Mesolithic of Northwest Europe: recent trends*, 55–62. Sheffield: J.R. Collis publications.

Bischoff, J.L., Ludwig, K., Garcia, J.F., Carbonell, E., Vaquero, M., Stafford, T. & Jull, A. 1994. Dating of the basal Aurignacian sandwich at Abric Romani (Catalunya, Spain) by radiocarbon and uranium-series, *J. Archaeol. Science* 21, 541–51.

Bischoff, J.L., Soler, N., Maroto, J. & Julia, R. 1989. Abrupt Mousterian/Aurignacian boundary at *ca.* 40 ka bp: accelerator 14C dates from l'Arbreda Cave (Catalunya, Spain), *J. Archaeol. Science* 16, 563–76.

Bond, G., Broeker, W., Johnsen, S., McManus, J., Labeyrie, L., Jouzel, J. & Bonani, G. 1993. Correlations between climatic records from North Atlantic sediments and Greenland ice, *Nature* 365, 143–7.

Bowman, S.G.E. 1990. *Radiocarbon Dating*. London: British Museum.

Bräuer, G., Yokoyama, Y, Falgueres, C. & Mbua, E. 1997. Modern human origins backdated, *Nature* 386, 337.

Broglio, A. 1996. The appearance of modern humans in Europe: the archaeological evidence from the Mediterranean regions. In M. Piperno (ed.) *The Lower and Middle Palaeolithic: Colloquia*, 237–49. Forlì: XIII International Congress of Prehistoric and Protohistoric Sciences.

Cabrera-Valdés, V. & Bischoff, J.L. 1989. Accelerator ^{14}C dates for early Upper Palaeolithic (basal Aurignacian) at El Castillo Cave (Spain), *J. Archaeol. Science* 16, 577–84.

Cabrera-Valdés, V., Valladas, H., Bernaldo de Quiros, F. & Gomez, M.H. 1996. La transition Paléolithique moyen-Paléolithique supiérieur a El Castillo (Cantabrie): nouvelles datations par le carbone-14, *Comptes Rendus de l'Académie des Sciences de Paris* 322 (Ser. IIa) 1093–8.

Cann, R.L., Rickards, O. & Koji Lum, J. 1994. Mitochondrial DNA and human evolution: our one lucky mother. In M.H. Nitecki and D.V. Nitecki (eds.) *Origins of Anatomically Modern Humans*, 135–48. New York: Plenum Press.

Champagne, F. & Espitalié, R. 1981. *Le Piage, site Préhistorique du Lot*. Paris: Mémoires de la Société Préhistorique Française.

Clottes, J. 1996. Recent studies on Palaeolithic art, *Cambridge Archaeol. J.* 6, 179–89.

Dansgaard, W., Johnsen, S.J., Clausen, H.B., Dahl-Jensen, D., Gundestrup, N.S., Hammer, C.U., Hvidberg, C.S., Steffensen, J.P., Sveinbjornsdottir, A.E., Jouzel, J., & Bond, G. 1993. Evidence for general instability of past climate from a 250-kyr ice-core record, *Nature* 364, 218–20.

Delporte, H. 1984. *Le Grand Abri de la Ferrassie: Fouilles 1968–1973*. Paris: Institut de Paléontologie Humaine.

Djindjian, F. 1993. Les origines du peuplement Aurignacien en Europe. In L. Banesz & J.K. Kozłowski (eds.) *Aurignacien en Europe et au Proche Orient*, 136–54. Bratislava: Acts of 12th International Congress of Prehistoric and Protohistoric Sciences.

Gambier, D. 1989. Fossil hominids from the early Upper Palaeolithic (Aurignacian) of France. In P. Mellars & C. Stringer (eds.) *The Human Revolution: behavioural and biological perspectives on the origins of modern humans*, 194–211. Princeton: Princeton University Press.

Gambier, D. 1993. Les hommes modernes du debut du Paléolithique supérieur en France: bilan des données anthropologiques et perspectives. In V. Cabrera Valdés (ed.) *El Origen del Hombre Moderno en el Suroeste de Europa*, 409–30. Madrid: Universidad Nacional de Educacion a Distancia.

Hahn, J. 1988. *Die Geissenklösterle-Höhle in Achtal bei Blaubeuren I*. Forschungen und Berichte zur Vor- und Frühgeschichte in Baden-Württemberg 26. Stuttgart: Theiss.

Harpending, H., Sherry, S., Rogers, A. & Stoneking, M. 1993. The genetic structure of ancient human populations, *Current Anthropology* 34, 483–96.

Harrold, F.B., 1989. Mousterian, Châtelperronian, and Early Aurignacian in Western Europe: continuity or discontinuity?. In P. Mellars & C. Stringer (eds.) *The Human Revolution: behavioural and biological perspectives on the origins of modern humans*, 677–713. Princeton: Princeton University Press.

Hublin, J.-J., 1990. Les peuplements paléolithiques de l'Europe: un point de vue géographique. In C. Farizy (ed.) *Paléolithique Moyen Récent et Paléolithique Supérieur Ancien en Europe*, 29–37. Nemours: Mémoires du Musée de Préhistoire d'Ile de France No. 3.

Hublin, J.-J., Spoor, F., Braun, M., Zonneveld, F. & Condemi, S. 1996. A late Neanderthal associated with Upper Palaeolithic artefacts, *Nature* 381, 224–6.

Knecht, H., Pike-Tay, A. & White, R. (eds.) 1993. *Before Lascaux:*

the complex record of the early Upper Paleolithic. Boca Raton: CRC Press.

Kozłowski, J.K. (ed.) 1982. *Excavation in the Bacho Kiro Cave: final report.* Warsaw: Polish Scientific Publishers.

Kozłowski, J.K. 1988. Transition from the Middle to the early Upper Paleolithic in Central Europe and the Balkans. In J.F. Hoffecker & C.A. Wolf (eds) *The Early Upper Paleolithic: Evidence from Europe and the Near East,* 193–236. Oxford: British Archaeological Reports International Series 437.

Kozłowski, J.K. 1992. The Balkans in the Middle and Upper Palaeolithic: the gateway to Europe or a cul de sac? *Proc. Prehist. Soc.* 58, 1–20.

Kozłowski, J.K. 1993. L'Aurignacien en Europe et au Proche Orient. In L. Banesz & J.K. Kozłowski (eds) *Aurignacien en Europe et au Proche Orient,* 283–91. Bratislava: Acts of 12th International Congress of Prehistoric and Protohistoric Sciences.

Kozłowski, J.K. 1996. Cultural context of the last Neanderthals and early modern humans in central-eastern Europe. In M. Piperno (ed.) *The Lower and Middle Palaeolithic: Colloquia,* 205–18. Forli: XIII International Congress of Prehistoric and Protohistoric Sciences.

Krings, M., Stone, A., Schmitz, R.W., Krainitzki, H., Stoneking, M. & Paabo, S. 1997. Neandertal DNA sequences and the origin of modern humans, *Cell* 90, 19–30.

Lahr, M.M. & Foley, R. 1994. Multiple dispersals and modern human origins, *Evolutionary Anthropology* 3, 48–60.

Laj, C., Mazaud, A. & Duplessy, J.-C. 1996. Geomagnetic intensity and ^{14}C abundance in the atmosphere and ocean during the past 50 kyr, *Geophysical Research Letters* 23, 2045–8.

Marks, A.E. 1983. The Middle-Upper Palaeolithic transition in the Levant. In F. Wendorf & A.E. Close (eds) *Advances in World Archaeology* 2, 51–98. Orlando: Academic Press.

Mellars, P.A. 1973. The character of the Middle-Upper Palaeolithic transition in south-west France. In C. Renfrew (ed.) *The Explanation of Culture Change: Models in Prehistory,* 255–76. London: Duckworth.

Mellars, P.A. 1989. Major issues in the emergence of modern humans, *Current Anthropology* 30, 349–85.

Mellars, P.A. 1990. Radiocarbon dating of Roc de Combe, *Archaeometry* 32, 101–2.

Mellars, P.A. 1992. Archaeology and the population-dispersal hypothesis of modern human origins in Europe. In M.J. Aitken, C.B. Stringer, & P.A. Mellars (eds) *The Origin of Modern Humans and the Impact of Chronometric Dating,* 225–34. London: Royal Society (Philosophical Transactions of the Royal Society, series B, 337, no. 1280).

Mellars, P.A. 1994. Radiocarbon accelerator dates for El Castillo (Spain), Riparo Mochi (Italy) and Bacho Kiro (Bulgaria), *Archaeometry* 36, 345–8.

Mellars, P.A. 1996a. Models for the dispersal of anatomically modern populations across Europe: theoretical and archaeological perspectives. In M. Piperno (ed.) *The Lower and Middle Palaeolithic: Colloquia,* 225–37. Forli: XIII International Congress of Prehistoric and Protohistoric Sciences.

Mellars, P.A. 1996b. *The Neanderthal Legacy: an archaeological perspective from Western Europe.* Princeton: Princeton University Press.

Mellars, P.A. 1998. The impact of climatic changes on the demography of late Neanderthal and early anatomically modern populations in Europe. In T. Akazawa, K. Aoki & O. Bar-Yosef (eds) *Neandertals and Modern Humans in Western Asia.* New York: Plenum (in press).

Mellars, P.A., Bricker, H.M., Gowlett, J.A.J., & Hedges, R.E.M. 1987. Radiocarbon accelerator dating of French Upper Palaeolithic sites, *Current Anthropology* 28, 128–33.

Mercier, N., Valladas, H., Joron, J.-L., Reyss, J.-L., Lévêque, F. & Vandermeersch, B. 1991. Thermoluminescence dating of the late Neanderthal remains from Saint-Césaire, *Nature* 351, 737–9.

Mook, W. 1982. Radiocarbon dating. In J.K. Kozłowski (ed.) *Excavation in the Bacho Kiro Cave: final report.* Warsaw: Polish Scientific Publishers.

Mook, W.G. & Waterbolk, H.T. 1985. *Radiocarbon Dating.* Strasbourg: European Science Foundation, Handbooks in Archaeology.

Mussi, M. 1992. *Popoli e Civiltà dell'Italia Antica: Volume Decimo: Il Paleolitico e il Mesolitico in Italia.* Bologna (Italy): Biblioteca di Storia Patria.

Nitecki, M.H. & Nitecki, D.V. (eds.) 1994. *Origins of Anatomically Modern Humans.* New York: Plenum Press.

Oliva, M. 1993. The Aurignacian in Czechoslovakia. In H. Knecht, A. Pike-Tay & R. White (eds) *Before Lascaux: the complex record of the early Upper Paleolithic.* Boca Raton: CRC Press.

Olszewski, D.I. & Dibble, H.L. 1994. The Zagros Aurignacian, *Current Anthropology* 35, 68–75

Rogers, A.R. & Jorde, L.B. 1995. Genetic evidence on modern human origins, *Human Biology* 67, 1–36.

Sonneville-Bordes, D. de. 1960. *Le Paléolithique Supérieur en Périgord.* Bordeaux: Delmas.

Stoneking, M., Sherry, S.T., Redd, A.J. & Vigilant, L. 1992. New approaches to dating suggest a recent age for the human DNA ancestor. In M. Aitken, C.B. Stringer & P.A. Mellars (eds.) *The Origin of Modern Humans and the Impact of Chronometric Dating.,* 167–76. London: Royal Society (Philosophical Transactions of the Royal Society, series B, 337, no. 1280).

Stringer, C.B. & McKie, R. 1996. *African Exodus: the origins of modern humanity.* London: Jonathan Cape.

Tishkoff, S.A., Dietzsch, E., Speed, W., Pakstis, A.J., Kidd, J.R., Cheung, K., Bonné Tamir, B., Santachiara-Benerecetti, A.S., Moral, P., Krings, M., Paabo, S., Watson, E., Risch, N., Jenkins, T. & Kidd, K.K.. 1996. Global patterns of linkage disequilibrium at the CD4 locus and modern human origins, *Science* 271, 1380–7.

Valladas, H., Geneste, J.-M., Joron, J.-L. & Chadelle, J.-P. 1986. Thermoluminescence dating of Le Moustier (Dordogne, France), *Nature* 322, 452–4.

Van Andel, T. H., & Tzedakis, P. C. 1996. Palaeolithic landscapes of Europe and environs, 150,000–25,000 years ago, *Quaternary Science Reviews* 15, 481–500.

Van Andel, T.H. 1998. Middle and Upper Palaeolithic environments and the calibration of ^{14}C dates beyond 10,000 BP, *Antiquity* 72, 26–33.

Van Klinken, G.J., Bowles, A.D. & Hedges, R.E.M. 1994. Radiocarbon dating of peptides isolated from contaminated fossil bone collagen by collagenase digestion and reversed-phase chromatography, *Geochimica et Cosmochimica Acta* 58 (11), 2543–51.

Villa, P. 1983. Terra Amata and the Middle Pleistocene archaeological record of Southern France, *University of California Publications in Anthropology* 13, 1–303.

Vogel, J.C. & Waterbolk, H.T. 1963. Groningen radiocarbon dates IV, *Radiocarbon* 5, 163–202.

Vogel, J.C. & Waterbolk, H.T. 1967. Groningen radiocarbon dates VII, *Radiocarbon* 9, 107–55.

Waterbolk, H.T. 1971. Working with radiocarbon dates, *Proc. Prehist. Soc.* 37, 15–33.

2. The Chauvet Cave Dates

Jean Clottes

Abstract: The paper reviews the AMS dates from the Chauvet Cave, considering them in the context of the art represented and comparing the results with finds from other European sites. A critique of the views of other scholars is presented, the conclusion being that the early dates from Chauvet Cave are valid.

Each time a new Palaeolithic painted or engraved cave is discovered in Europe (generally in Spain or in France), one or several specialists are asked to go and visit them in order to give a preliminary appraisal as to their authenticity and possible date(s). Analyses, whenever possible, come later and may or may not corroborate the provisional assessment. When the discovery is particularly spectacular and original, and in particular when it gets into the media, there may be polemics about the primary expertise and its results, generally with some other specialists doubting the authenticity of the works of art. This is what happened in the case of Altamira from 1879 to 1902, and more recently for Rouffignac and for the Cosquer Cave (for the whole story of the latter, see Clottes & Courtin 1994: 23–31).[1]

With the Chauvet Cave, discovered on 18 December 1994, no archaeologist expressed any doubt about the genuineness of its art, perhaps because of the then quite recent Cosquer controversy and its result. However, opinions varied greatly as to the chronology of the Chauvet images. In various public conferences, Jean Combier expressed his view that they could be Magdalenian, and in a public exhibition on the site at Vallon-Pont-d'Arc in which he participated as a scientific adviser, the Chauvet cave was placed right at the end of the Upper Palaeolithic in the chronological scale.[2]

After my first visit to the Chauvet Cave, I wrote that "a tentative bracket between 17,000 and 21,000 years ago or earlier was considered plausible" (Clottes 1996c, 121), in other words, I cautiously ascribed it to the Solutrean (Clottes 1995, 1). My opinion was based on a stylistic analysis supported by the following arguments. First, it seemed likely that the paintings and engravings were not made by successive cultures that were widely separated in time, because of their numerous similarities irrespective of the technique used: the same themes rare elsewhere (rhinos (Fig. 2.1); lions, bears), the body shading; the same way of drawing the animals (small ears on the rhinos, horns in twisted perspective for the bison, etc.). Second, except for a few details which were reminiscent of Lascaux (which is why for the lower end of the bracket I tentatively set a date of around 17,000 BP – the date supposed to be that of Lascaux, even though some of the Lascaux art could be older), most other observations pointed to a pre-Lascaux period: clouds of big red dots, hand stencils and handprints, S-shaped horns for aurochs and horseshoe-shaped bellies of the mammoths (in some Ardèche caves supposed to be Solutrean), and comparisons with some of the well-dated (around 19,000 BP) Cosquer representations, in particular the spindly bison legs in the form of a Y.

Obviously, stylistic comparisons – which are unavoidable and to which all specialists without exception resort all over the world – can only take into account what is known at the time. That is to say, they may lead to errors either when the supposedly well-known caves turn out to be not that well-dated after all, for various reasons (in

---

Author's Address: Jean Clottes, 11, rue du Fourcat, 09000 Foix, France

Lascaux, for example, it has so far been impossible to get one single direct radiocarbon date for the art because the black paintings were made with manganese and not with charcoal), or again when a new discovery is profoundly original and without close parallels, despite all our efforts to find some.

The dates obtained for the Chauvet Cave

Three samples that I lifted from so many animal paintings were dated by AMS, with the following results (Clottes *et al.* 1995): 30,940 ± 610 BP (GifA 95126) for one of a couple of rhinos; 30,790 ± 600 BP (GifA 95133) and 32,410 ± 720 BP (GifA 95132) for the other rhino; 30,340 ± 570 BP (GifA 95128) for a bison in a different chamber. In addition, a torch mark on the Panel of Horses was dated to 26,120 ± 400 BP (GifA 95127). Two pieces of charcoal fallen from a torch in another chamber gave identical results: 26,980 ± 410 BP (GifA 95129) and 26,980 ± 420 (GifA 95130). Three different charcoal pieces picked straight from the ground without any excavation, one in front of the Panel of Reindeer and the others near or in the end chamber, were respectively dated to 24,770 ± 780 BP (Lyon-118/OxA), 22,800 ± 400 BP (Ly. 6879) and 29,000 ± 400 BP (Ly. 6878).

If there had just been one date in the 30,000s, no one would have believed it and it would have been widely considered to be a laboratory freak or mistake, even though laboratory experts refuse now to accept that "one date is no date" (Evin 1996, 109). However the results obtained at Chauvet are coherent. With a two-sigma bracket the four direct dates for the three animals and one date from a charcoal piece on the ground (Ly. 6878) fall within the same range. This would be enough to support credence in the credibility of these results. But there are two more arguments.

The torch marks on the Panel of Horses were made on top of a thin layer of calcite covering some earlier paintings. There was thus a real stratigraphy. As these torch marks were not calcited over, we had no means of telling at first whether they had been made many millennia ago or in recent times. This is why I also lifted another sample from charcoal fallen from identical torch marks in a different chamber, as corroboration. Both dated samples were fairly close together, between 26,000 and 27,000 BP: they could have been made at the same time. However, their dates are far enough from those of the painted animals to be beyond even two sigma, which is consistent with the depositing of a layer of calcite over the earlier paintings. People therefore came into the cave a long time after the first paintings had been made, and the dates obtained for their torch marks are in keeping with the dates for the early paintings, which are thus strengthened.

The second argument in support of the very early dates obtained at Chauvet is the comparison between the wall art there and the portable art found in the Swabian Jura in

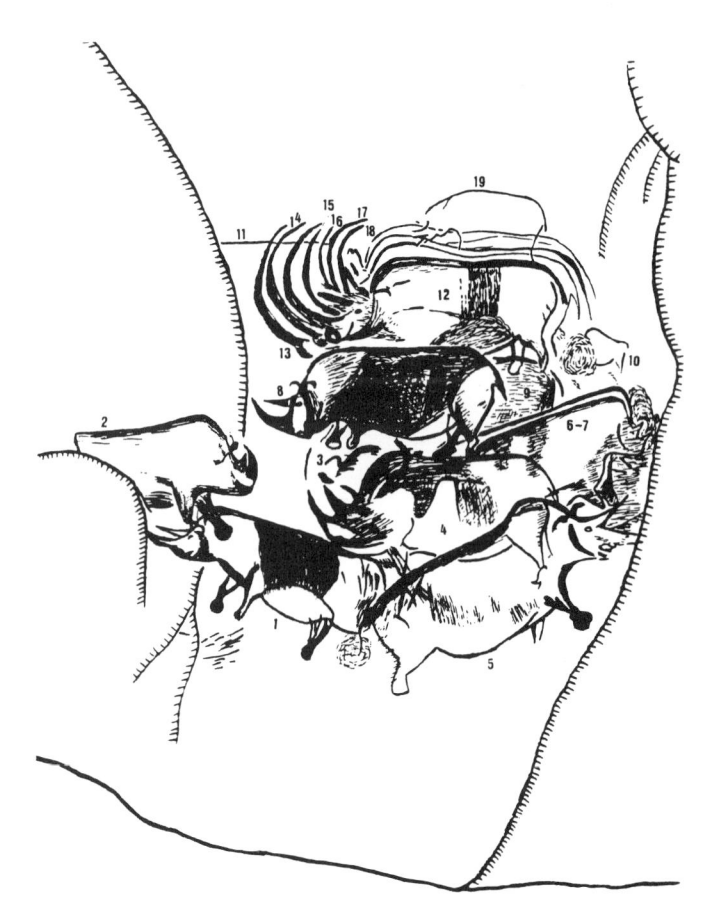

Fig. 2.1. On this panel of the Chauvet Cave, at least 17 rhinoceroses (plus two indeterminate figures) have been painted, all in black. Ears and body shading – in particular with a middle band – are very similar from one animal to the next. Rhinos are very rarely represented in Palaeolithic caves. Preliminary tracing from a photo (J. Clottes).

south-western Germany, where seventeen ivory statuettes were discovered in three Aurignacian shelters (Hohlenstein-Stadel, Geissenklosterle and Vogelherd) (Hahn 1986; Kozlowski 1992), each with dates around 30,000 BP (Bandi 1996, 104). The aesthetic quality of these figurines (Fig. 2.2) had long been noticed as they testified to the existence of fully developed artistic feelings and techniques as early as the Aurignacian, at least in the realm of portable art (Sieveking 1979, 204; Marshack 1985, 8; Marshack 1990, 141). That they were also expressed in parietal art at about the same dates should not therefore be such a surprise. Another corroboration came with a comparison of the themes represented in both cases. Hahn (1986, 222; 1990) had noticed that the species represented on the German statuettes were the biggest, the most powerful and the most dangerous. It is no coincidence that the same can be said of the animals drawn on the walls of the Chauvet Cave: the most numerous are rhinoceroses (20%); if one adds the mammoths (14%), lions (13.7%) and bears (5.7%), plus one panther and a possible hyena, one reaches a total of 60.8%.[3] An examination of the existing evidence in the

Fig. 2.2. Ivory horse carving from the Vogelherd shelter in Germany. Photo: Unrath, Urgeschichte, University of Tübingen.

Dordogne and elsewhere has shown that the animal themes in the Aurignacian differed significantly from those chosen at later periods (Clottes 1996b). Apparently the change in themes took place during the Gravettian in western Europe and much later in central and eastern Europe. In addition to the similarities between the animals represented at Chauvet and on the German figurines, there is another common element: at Hohlenstein-Stadel an ivory statuette representing a human with the head of a lion was found (Fig. 2.3), while at Chauvet a composite creature was painted, the lower half human and the upper half a bison (Fig. 2.4). Since the discovery of the Hohlenstein-Stadel figurine it had been known that composite creatures were Aurignacian concepts. The Chauvet example constitutes another link with the German Aurignacian sites.

Reactions to the Chauvet dates

I must confess that my initial "gut" reaction was one of scepticism when I was apprised of the laboratory dates, even though I had contemplated (and written) that the art could be earlier than my cautious estimate (Clottes 1996c, 121), which I had stated clearly was provisional while waiting for radiocarbon datings to "provide a more solid base" (Clottes 1995, 1).[4] Those early dates ran counter to many long-established ideas about "early art" and to paradigms about its development from crude beginnings in the Aurignacian to greater and greater progress and achievements over the following millenia, culminating in Lascaux. However, after the first shock, the above-mentioned arguments made me realize that the Chauvet dates had to be accepted whatever the consequences. Most

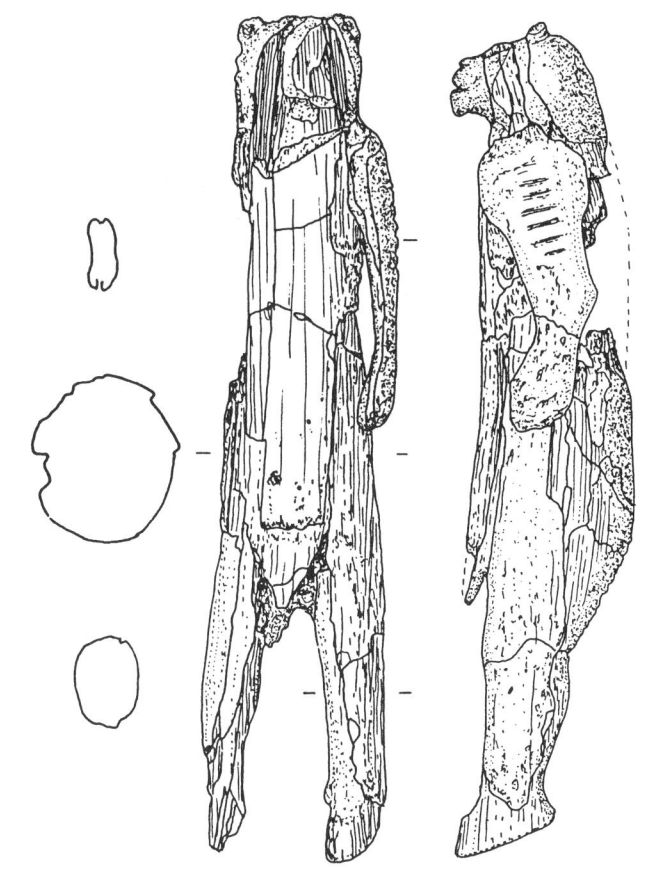

Fig. 2.3. Ivory figurine representing a human with a lion's head, from the Hohlenstein-Stadel shelter in Germany. Drawing by J. Hahn, University of Tübingen.

specialists were equally convinced "despite the universal amazement" (Bahn & Vertut 1997, 76). Most but not all.

More than a year after the Chauvet dates had been published (Clottes *et al*. 1995), Brigitte and Gilles Delluc gave a paper at the UISPP 1996 Conference in Forlì about the earliest European cave art. Their theories about Palaeolithic art in Europe had always closely followed Leroi-Gourhan's scheme: the beginnings of art are clumsy and the animal silhouettes are very poor, 'frozen' (Delluc & Delluc 1991, 342) because animation is absent from the Aurignacian. According to them no difference is made between foreground and background before the Solutrean, and there is neither perspective nor infill in what they call 'archaic art' (Leroi-Gourhan called it the 'primitive period' (see Clottes 1996b, 278). Archaic art always occurred in the open.

As the characteristics of the Chauvet Cave contradict all these observations based on the Aurignacian rock shelters in the Dordogne, one expected one of two possible attitudes: either the Dellucs would challenge the Chauvet dates and argue why they should not be taken into account, or they would re-examine the validity of traditional conceptions of the origins and development of cave art, as

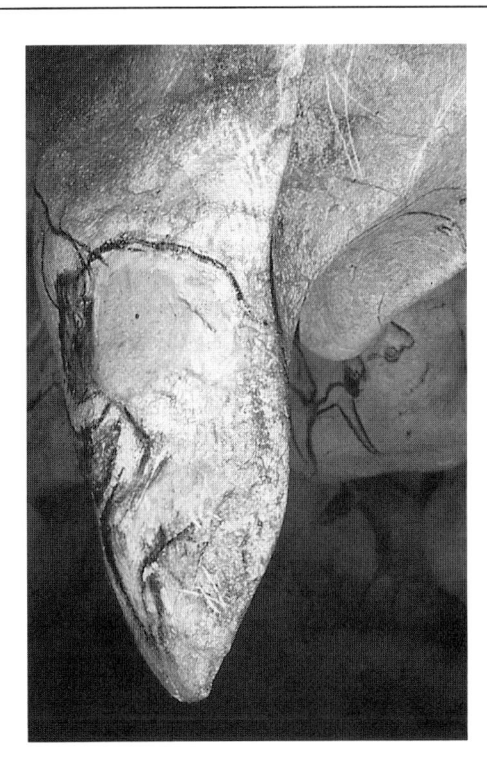

Fig. 2.4. Composite creature in the Chauvet Cave: a standing human with the head and hump of a bison. Photo J. Clottes.

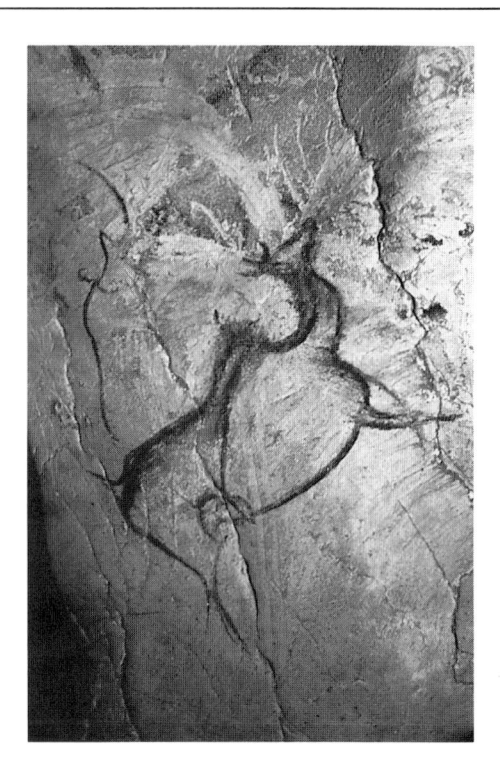

Fig. 2.5. Chauvet Cave. A megaloceros with body shading, identifiable by its huge hump. On top of it, on the left, one can see the body outline of a vertical rhinoceros, recognizable because of its two horns; also notice its characteristic small ears. Photo J. Clottes.

well as of several of its stylistic conventions. Amazingly, they did neither, and gave (and published) their paper without changing anything in their pre-Chauvet discovery theories and schemes, and without discussing the Chauvet dates. They just remarked that for Chauvet "the dates obtained contrast with the characteristics of the paintings and engravings, topographically well organized and graphically very sophisticated: those dates are notably more ancient than is indicated by the stylistic analysis of the works of art" (Delluc & Delluc 1996, 90). This is a classical example of evidence which is set aside undiscussed because it does not fit with a theory elaborated many years before, and as a consequence based on insufficient and incomplete data.

Combier (1995) challenged the Chauvet dates obliquely. While admitting that the art is clearly pre-Magdalenian, he stressed some themes (megaloceros) and several peculiar features which are to be found in Gravettian and Solutrean art, particularly in the Ardèche Solutrean, and he wondered whether Chauvet was homogeneous.

So far as we know the only specialist who explicitly challenged the Chauvet dates with concrete arguments in support of his scepticism is Christian Züchner (1996). In his opinion, the red figures are obviously Gravettian and Early Solutrean, whereas the black ones are Late Solutrean and Early Magdalenian, and contemporary with Lascaux and Gabillou. He bases his opinion on two lines of reasoning. The first one is finding individual comparisons between some animals or signs represented in the Chauvet Cave and similar ones from other caves dated to later periods: for example, the megaloceros in Chauvet (Fig. 2.5) "are comparable only with those of the Cosquer Cave belonging to the Upper Solutrean – Early Magdalenian period.... Owls are rare in Palaeolithic art. But they occur at Trois-Frères, Le Portel and La Viña near Oviedo (Magdalenian IV)". His second broad argument is that some animals and techniques are either restricted to one period or do not appear before a particular period: for example, "handprints belong to the Gravettian (cf Gargas etc.)"; for horses, "the manner heads, bodies and movement are treated in that cave was unknown before the Early Magdalenian". To explain the discrepancy between the radiocarbon dates and his chronological attributions, he speculates that the Magdalenian artists in Chauvet may have "collected fossil wood from the gravel of the Ardèche or somewhere else to prepare their black colour". In addition, "the charcoal left in the cave by Gravettian people who created the red signs and drawings was still available" and it could have been used by them or by anybody else (Züchner 1996, 25–26).

None of these arguments can be accepted (Clottes 1996a). I sampled three different animal drawings from two separate chambers and their dates were coherent. As a consequence Züchner implies that all black paintings were made with fossil wood, which in itself is rather difficult to believe. But even if we did, his hypothesis would still leave unexplained the dates for the torch marks, which would also have had to be made with fossil wood that by coincidence would happen to be later by several millennia than the fossil wood used for the paintings. As to the art in Chauvet, it seems difficult to separate a supposedly older red phase from a more recent black phase. The same animals, elsewhere rare (lions, rhinos, bears), have been represented in black and in red (or engraved), and what is more, by using the same techniques (shading) and conventions, even down to minute details such as the strange ears of the rhinos (figs. 2.1, 2.5). In fact, distinct similarities can be found which blur the differences between red and black figures. Even if red animals are rarely found with black ones and vice versa, they do occur (a black horse with red stencils; a red rhino on the black Panel of Horses, etc.). To a black rhino in the last chamber was added red paint for the horns and the 'breath'. Three lions were drawn in perspective with parallel lines, one red between two black ones; finally, on the main panel, also in the last chamber, black paintings were superimposed on older red figures and signs. This shows that occasionally red and black were used before or after each other, and at times together. It is not surprising then to notice that stump drawing, so prevalent with the black animals, is also present – albeit more discreetly – with a few red ones (see the bears in Chauvet *et al.* 1995, figs. 20, 21). All in all, Chauvet looks like a fairly homogeneous ensemble.

The main postulate on which Züchner's argument rests is the overriding value of stylistic criteria. For stylistic criteria to provide an infallible diagnostic tool one must assume that we know the essentials of Palaeolithic art, and that nothing drastically new can ever crop up. For example, we should have to know the first time that such and such a technique (or theme) was used, its precise duration and geographical spread. Now, each major new discovery brings new information and compels us to readjust our conceptions (cf the discovery in the past few years of a very important series of open air Palaeolithic art sites in Portugal and Spain). It is therefore impossible to follow Züchner when he considers that some particular theme or other did not exist before a particular period or culture (Clottes 1996a). We just have no idea how long exactly they lasted, and we must always be ready to update our knowledge.

On the other hand, the discrepancy between the early guesses about the art of Chauvet and the results of direct radiocarbon dating were quoted as still more evidence of the inanity and imprudence of stylistic evaluations (Bednarik 1995, 1996; Lorblanchet 1995). In fact, taking into account the originality of the cave, the possibility of surprises had explicitly been mentioned (Clottes 1996c, 121). It would have been much stranger and contrary to the initial stylistic analysis of the paintings if they had yielded Magdalenian dates. Bednarik also stressed these and other unexpected results in the direct dating of several sites, to conclude that stylistic datings "appear to be totally random and irrelevant, offering no redeeming feature at all" (Bednarik 1995, 100) and even that Chauvet "makes a mockery of stylistic perceptions of Palaeolithic art specialists generally" (Bednarik 1996, 11). In his opinion, specialists "cannot produce consistently valid predictions" i.e. "predictions that are found to agree consistently with scientific dating estimates" (Bednarik 1995, 100), and he publishes a diagram supposed to demonstrate that there is no correlation between stylistic guesses and direct datings (Bednarik 1995, 100, fig. 12). That diagram and Bednarik's conclusions are flawed for two reasons: he just picked four examples of dated art out of the nine then available (Niaux, Portel, Altamira, Castillo, Covaciella, Cosquer, Chauvet, Cougnac, Pech-Merle), and whenever there was a controversy (Cosquer, Zubialde) he chose to quote the opinion of the people who had initially misinterpreted the art and not the assessment of those who had been right from the first. For the nine caves mentioned above, the results broadly fitted with expectations for Niaux, Portel, Altamira, Castillo, Covaciella, Cosquer, Pech-Merle (seven out of nine), which is not such a bad result (Clottes 1998).

After the Chauvet dates

As regards the Chauvet Cave itself, the dates obtained are just a first step. After all, there probably are more than 400 animal figures and we have direct dates for only three of them. In the years to come we shall try to have many more dated if at all possible. Even if it is likely that many if not most representations are closely akin and likely to be contemporaneous, it is still obvious that different persons with different degrees of expertise painted and/or engraved various animals. We have seen that the torch marks were several millennia later than the paintings dated: did their users make some paintings of their own? It cannot be ruled out. We have also seen that two pieces of charcoal picked from the ground yielded still later dates and the same question applies for those who left them.

However, the validity of the very early dates now seems securely established, which entails the following observations and remarks and raises a number of problems (for more details, see Clottes, in print):

1. Sophisticated techniques for wall art were invented by Aurignacians, i.e. far earlier than had been surmised, and they occasionally achieved an art of the highest aesthetic quality.
2. This means that instead of a steady linear development over millennia, as had so long been assumed, there must have been many heydays and many declines for the art, as some researchers had guessed long ago (Ucko & Rosenfeld 1967; Ucko 1987). It also means that one cannot assume that the same quality should be expected everywhere at the same time. The notions

of 'archaic' or 'evolved' are equally devoid of meaning. As a consequence, Leroi-Gourhan's evolutionary scheme has now become obsolete.

3. A surprise of the magnitude of that brought about by the Chauvet dates is chastening. It should incite specialists to be cautious about the major caves where the art has not yet been directly dated, like Lascaux[5] and many others in France and Spain. This particularly applies with the older art as Magdalenian art seems rather well-known, and the latest analyses have confirmed what had been assumed about its date from stylistic evaluation (Clottes 1998).

4. Was the mastery of the Chauvet art preceded by thousands of years of trials and errors, i.e. is the old idea of a gradual evolution and progress still tenable (after all, when the Chauvet Cave was painted, Aurignacians had already been in Western Europe for at least 6,000 or 7,000 years), or is it due to some artistic genius? For the development of art, the current paradigm had for decades applied to humankind as a whole the model of the development of artistic feelings and expertise with children. In fact, progress could have been very swift.

5. On the other hand, since *Homo Sapiens sapiens* has been found in the Middle East more than 90,000 years ago, elaborate forms of art may have been created long before the Upper Palaeolithic and not yet been discovered because of taphonomical problems (Bednarik 1994).

One should therefore expect new discoveries and great advances in our knowledge as direct AMS dating of the art becomes generalized. The next few years should be quite exciting!

Notes

1 Later on, after controversies have petered out, there may be a tendency to re-write their history in a more favourable way. After expressing his initial doubts about the Cosquer Cave images in a newspaper article (Bahn 1992), Paul Bahn blandly stated that "it was scientific analysis which brought firm and final proof of the authenticity of Cosquer Cave, over which there were initial doubts, thanks to poor press pictures and to the recent Zubialde fiasco" (Bahn & Vertut 1997, 82). None of these statements is true. The authenticity of the Cosquer Cave had been firmly established (and published) months before the C14 analyses were available (see Clottes *et al.* 1992); the "initial doubts" were certainly not raised because of poor photographs, as those published in the press were excellent; while the polemics about the authenticity of Cosquer started in November 1991, the Zubialde fiasco was exposed in August 1992 in a report by our Spanish colleagues; before, doubts had been expressed – including by myself – but there had been no certainty one way or the other.

2 At the end of 1997 the error had not yet been rectified.

3 The figures quoted are provisional as we are far from knowing the exact number of animal representations in the Chauvet Cave. However, as they are based on a total of 263, they should give a fair statistical basis.

4 Detractors of the use of stylistic methods consistently forgot to cite those precautions and precisions (Lorblanchet 1995, 19; Bednarik 1995, 881).

5 Without however going to some extremes like attributing some of the most prominent figures in Lascaux to the Holocene (Bahn 1994).

Bibliography

Bahn, P.G. 1992. Prehistoric wonder or a mammoth red herring? *The Independent on Sunday*, 12.1.92, 47.

Bahn, P.G. 1994. Lascaux: composition or accumulation, *Zephyrus* 47, 3–13.

Bahn, P.G. & Vertut, J. 1997. *Journey through the Ice Age*. London: Weidenfeld & Nicolson.

Bandi, H.-G. 1996. Ice Age art of Central Europe. In Beltrán, A. & Vigliardi, A. (eds.), *Art in the Palaeolithic and Mesolithic*, Colloquium 8, XIII International Congress of Prehistoric and Protohistoric Sciences, Forlì (Italy), 8–14 Sept. 1996, 101–107.

Bednarik, R.-G. 1994. A taphonomy of palaeoart, *Antiquity* 68, 68–74.

Bednarik, R.-G. 1995. The Côa petroglyphs: an obituary to the stylistic dating of Palaeolithic rock art, *Antiquity* 69, 877–83.

Bednarik, R. 1996. 'Incongruities' in palaeoart, *Pictogram* (8), 2, 9–12.

Chauvet, J.M., Brunel-Deschamps, E., Hillaire, C. 1996. *Chauvet Cave. The discovery of the world's oldest paintings*. London: Thames & Hudson.

Clottes, J. 1995. The Chauvet Cave, at Combe d'Arc in the Ardèche, France. *INORA* 10, 1.

Clottes, J. 1996a. The Chauvet Cave dates implausible? *INORA* 13, 27–29.

Clottes, J. 1996b. Thematic changes in Upper Palaeolithic art: a view from the Grotte Chauvet, *Antiquity* 70, 276–88.

Clottes, J. 1996c. Epilogue: Chauvet Cave today. In Chauvet, J.M., Brunel-Deschamps, E., Hillaire, C. *Chauvet Cave. The discovery of the world's oldest paintings*, 89–128. London: Thames & Hudson.

Clottes, J. 1998. The 'Three C's': fresh avenues towards European Palaeolithic art. In Chippindale, C. & Taçon, P (eds), *The Archaeology of Rock Art*, 112–29. Cambridge: Cambridge University Press.

Clottes, J. in press. Twenty thousand years of Palaeolithic cave art in southern France. In Coles, J.M., Bewley, R. and Mellars, P. (eds) *World Prehistory. Studies in Memory of Grahame Clark*. Memoirs of the British Academy.

Clottes, J., Chauvet, J.-M., Brunel-Deschamps, E., Hillaire, C., Daugas, J.-P., Arnold, M., Cachier, H., Evin, J., Fortin, P., Oberlin, C., Tisnerat, N. and Valladas, H. 1995. Les peintures paléolithiques de la Grotte Chauvet-Pont-d'Arc, à Vallon-Pont-d'Arc (Ardèche, France): datations directes et indirectes par la méthode du radiocarbone, *Comptes-rendus de l'Académie des Sciences de Paris*, 320, IIa, 1133–40.

Clottes, J., Beltrán, A., Courtin, J., Cosquer, H. 1992. La Grotte Cosquer (Cap Morgiou, Marseille), *Bull. Soc. Préhist. Française* 89, 4, 98–128.

Clottes, J. & Courtin, J. 1994. *La Grotte Cosquer. Peintures et gravures de la caverne engloutie*. Paris: Le Seuil.

Combier, J. 1995. Les grottes ornées de l'Ardèche, *L'art préhistorique* (Dossiers d'Archéologie 209), 66–85.

Delluc, B. & Delluc, G. 1991. *L'art pariétal archaïque en Aquitaine*. Gallia Préhistoire, supplement 28. Paris: Editions du CNRS.

Delluc, B. & Delluc, G. 1996. L'art paléolithique archaïque en France. In Beltrán, A. & Vigliardi, A. (eds), *Art in the Palaeolithic and Mesolithic*, 87–90. XIII International Congress of Prehistoric and Protohistoric Sciences, Forlì, Italy.

Evin, J. 1996. La datation des peintures pariétales par le radiocarbone, *Techne* 3, 98–107.

Hahn, J. 1986. *Kraft und Aggression. Die Botschaft der Eiszeitkunst im Aurignacien Süddeutschlands?* Tübingen: Institut für Urgeschichte der Universität Tübingen / Verlag Archaeologica Venatoria.

Hahn, J. 1990. Fonction et signification des statuettes du Paléolithique supérieur européen. In Clottes, J. (ed) *L'Art des Objets au Paléolithique, t. 2: Les Voies de la Recherche*, 173–83.

Kozłowski, J.K. 1992. *L'art de la Préhistoire en Europe orientale*. Paris: CNRS.

Lorblanchet, M. 1994. La datation de l'art pariétal paléolithique, *Bull. Soc. Etudes Littéraires, Scientifiques et Historiques du Lot*, 115, 3, 161–82.

Lorblanchet, M. 1995. La datation de l'art pariétal paléolithique. Etat de la question (juin 1995), *L'art préhistorique* (Dossiers d'Archéologie 209), 18–19.

Marshack A. 1985. *Hierarchical evolution of the human capacity: the Paleolithic evidence*. New York: American Museum of Natural History.

Marshack A. 1990. L'évolution et la transformation du décor du début de l'Aurignacien au Magdalénien final. In Clottes J. (ed.), *L'Art des Objets au Paléolithique, 2: les Voies de la Recherche*, 139–162.

Sieveking, A. 1979. *The Cave Artists*. London: Thames & Hudson.

Ucko P.J. 1987. Débuts illusoires dans l'étude de la tradition artistique, *Bull. Soc. Préhist. Ariège-Pyrénées* 42, 15–81.

Ucko, P.J. & Rosenfeld, A. 1967. *L'art paléolithique*. Paris: Hachette, Collection L'univers des Connaissances 9.

Züchner, C. 1996. La Grotte Chauvet. Radiocarbone contre Archéologie, *INORA* 13, 25–27.

3. A Hidden Landscape: the Neolithic of Tayside[1]

Gordon J Barclay

Abstract: Coles and Simpson (with Piggott), were responsible for a brief, but important, upsurge in interest in the Neolithic of Perthshire in the 1960s. Since then aerial and ground survey and excavation have transformed our knowledge of the period in Tayside, showing it to have a very high density of sites. The Pitnacree Neolithic round barrow can now be seen as part of a distinct regional tradition, linked also to long mound and cursus traditions, through the Cleaven Dyke sequence – round barrow, long barrow, bank barrow/cursus. It can also be seen as the precursor of large barrows covering (?high status) individual burials.

Introduction

John Coles unwittingly played a significant part in my development as a prehistorian through his part-excavation with Derek Simpson of the round barrow at Pitnacree, in Perthshire in 1965 (Coles & Simpson 1965) (Fig. 3.1). While I was still an undergraduate in the early 1970s this site fascinated me, in its complexity and in its seeming isolation from, although having familiar features of, the Wessex-based British prehistory then universally taught. When I in my turn was faced with the complete excavation of another, even larger Perthshire round mound, at North Mains in 1978 (Barclay 1983), I turned first to Pitnacree for inspiration. From that time on, while I have been paid to undertake archaeological work all over Scotland, it is to the archaeology of Perthshire that I turn always in my own time. I think I have Pitnacree and John and Derek to thank for sowing that seed.

The landscape of Tayside, used here to encompass the old counties of Perthshire and Angus, is very varied: broad rolling fluvio-glacial gravels, forming one of the largest areas of prime agricultural land in Scotland, backed by the foothills of the Grampians, in which sheltered valleys offer different, but also good, land for settlement. The wealth of settlement, from prehistory to the present day, testifies to the nature of the soil and environment.

The story of the Neolithic of Tayside is one of the emergence of a rich archaeological landscape, which until recently has been physically hidden or has lain unrecognised.

The understanding of the Neolithic (particularly the earlier part of it) in this area of the lowlands has developed through a formative period in Scottish prehistoric studies in general. One of the main issues to emerge is regionality, in two senses – regional variation in the past, and the development of regionally-based interpretative models rather than inappropriate ones erected in distant and different areas (Barclay 1995). The journey for me starts with Pitnacree over 30 years ago, and ends, for the time being, with current research on the Cleaven Dyke with Gordon Maxwell (Barclay *et al.* 1995; Barclay & Maxwell 1998). That Gordon Maxwell, one of Scotland's foremost aerial photographers, and I are doing this work together is particularly appropriate, as the most important determinant in the development of prehistoric studies in Scotland in recent decades, particularly in Tayside, is aerial photography. We have rehearsed this argument before (Maxwell 1983; Barclay 1992; 1995) but its substance bears repetition.

The history of the development of aerial photography in Scotland is important to any understanding of how archaeology as a whole in the country developed after the last World War. Aerial survey began to have an impact on

Author's Address: Gordon J Barclay, Historic Scotland, Longmore House, Salisbury Place, Edinburgh, EH9 1SH

Fig. 3.1. The Neolithic round barrow at Pitnacree, Perthshire. Photo: RCAHMS.

the prehistory of the southern part of Britain before the Second World War. In contrast it is only since the early 1970s that there has been any serious Scottish-based aerial photography programme, where the results could be accessed locally. In Britain as a whole, from the mid 1940s onwards there was an upsurge in archaeology and the study of prehistory. In southern England in particular, we can see that cropmark archaeology was assimilated into the improving picture of that region's past; it was already a picture in which earthen monuments were familiar, if not the norm (RCHME 1960). In Scotland the parallel upsurge in archaeology and the improved understanding of prehistory took place with no major cropmark contribution, and to a great extent the perception of Scotland's surviving archaeology as predominantly stone or upland, a picture built up through the extensive antiquarian activity in the 19th and earlier 20th centuries, was reinforced. Earthen monuments of a kind common elsewhere in Britain were just not going to be recognised in this context – for example a prominent earthen barrow, discovered only in 1989, lies less than 100 m from the Corrimony cairn, excavated in the 1950s (Piggott 1956) and subsequently publicly displayed as a Guardianship monument. In this landscape archaeologists, even someone like Stuart Piggott, to whom barrows were familiar, expected to see stone, not earthen, monuments. Areas like Tayside were seen to have only relatively sparse distributions of monuments, and those of kinds with few characteristics to encourage classification or further study (Coutts 1971).

There are interesting parallels between this archaeological perception and the perception of the Scottish landscape in general, particularly as expressed in landscape painting. To quote:

> "During the nineteenth century the popular image of Scotland was created by the painters of the vast panoramic landscapes which filled the walls of the Academies and Institutes in London, Edinburgh and Glasgow. They conformed with, and encouraged, the romantic notions of the Highlands evoked in a populace brought up on the novels of Sir Walter Scott and his imitators, where the noble stag was master of all he surveyed, and the climate veered uncontrollably between storms of hail and snow and livid sunsets reflected in the surface of disquieting lochs. Farms and cottages...were shown derelict and broken down. That hypothetical visitor from outer space could be readily forgiven if, through knowledge of these paintings alone, he assumed that Scotland was entirely populated by sheep, woolly cattle and antlered beasts who stood proud against the snow, rain and fiery sun of this mountainous land" (Billcliffe 1987).

Where the life of the people was shown, it was that of the picturesque Highlander, not the prosperous lowland farmer. This concern with rainy highland and windswept island may be said to continue to haunt much of Scotland's modern archaeological endeavour – the lowlands have, in recent decades, singularly failed to attract as much university-based research as the northern and western isles (Barclay 1997b).

We may contrast this Victorian view of landscape with reality, for the most heavily populated areas of Scotland – the landscape of the lowlands, particularly in the work of the artist, James McIntosh Patrick, who "expressed more interest in a landscape which has offered man an opportunity to co-exist, a countryside that has not spurned his husbandry, but which has openly responded to his care and his exploitation of its contour ..." (Billcliffe 1987).

This landscape has seen little research into that past co-existence, particularly in contrast to the area immediately to the north, the new local authority area of Aberdeenshire, which, as the pages of the *Proceedings of the Society of Antiquaries of Scotland* testify, was one of the most intensively studied areas in Scotland in the 19th century. The excellent summary of antiquarian and early archaeological activity in south-east Perthshire provided by the Scottish Royal Commission in their 1994 survey (RCAHMS 1994b), is necessarily brief; earlier prehistory had received little attention, past antiquaries had been very much drawn to the wealth of Roman remains in the area – the legionary fortress at Inchtuthil, the Gask Ridge frontier system, the temporary camps and the roads.

The first substantial review of the prehistory of the area, and then only a small part of it, was in 1961, when Margaret Stewart published an account of upper Strathtay in the Neolithic and Early Bronze Age (Stewart 1958–59). The number of sites known was limited, to say the least – a scatter of chambered cairns, cists, stone circles, and artefacts, and some round mounds like Pitnacree, which were attributed (inevitably at that time) to an intrusive Early Bronze Age culture penetrating inland from the east coast.

Some of the chambered cairns had been excavated to a very limited degree since the Second World War, but in the early to mid 1960s there was a flurry of activity in the same area of upper Strathtay – John Coles, Stuart Piggott and Derek Simpson, in different combinations, excavated a handful of sites, including Pitnacree and the Croft Moraig stone circle, which were both published promptly, and in the *Proceedings of the Prehistoric Society*, giving Scottish material a wider audience than often hitherto (Coles & Simpson 1965; Piggott & Simpson 1971).

At Croft Moraig Piggott and Simpson (1971) discovered that the monument had three phases, beginning with a penannular setting of posts with outliers, and a slight ditch associated with early Neolithic pottery, and developing through complex stone settings. It was inevitable that, in the then current models of prehistoric interpretation, the excavators interpreted the timber structure below the Croft Moraig stone circle as a '*provincial* version' [my italics] of the structures being discovered at Durrington Walls (Wainwright & Longworth 1971). Pitnacree, as we know of course, emerged as a complex Early Neolithic mound, dating to around 3500 BC, incorporating a variant on the familiar linear zone type of Neolithic mortuary structure (Kinnes 1979; Scott 1992).

In the Pitnacree report, Coles and Simpson presented a distribution map (based largely on Stewart 1958–59, fig. 8) showing 21 apparently similar mounds, offering the possibility of a remarkably dense survival of possibly Neolithic mortuary monuments. There had been interestingly varied responses in Scottish archaeology to Stewart's map of the round mounds – the Inspectorate of Ancient Monuments had proceeded urgently with the scheduling of round mounds in Perthshire and Angus. However, there was resistance in the Ordnance Survey Archaeology Division to interpreting many of them as anything but natural glacial mounds. Indeed, the view that most were natural, despite their scheduled status, was made very clear on the OS cards until after the excavation of the North Mains mound in 1978–79: for example, the Little Trochry mound (scheduled in 1960), was still firmly identified as a glacial hillock on the OS monument cards in 1975, and was only reconsidered after the excavation of the North Mains mound in 1978–9. There is now no doubt about the interpretation of the round mounds, but problems of identification are still with us in lowland Scotland, as I will mention later.

After the mid 1960s, little work on sites of the period was undertaken in the area for over a decade. When the North Mains mound, 5.5 m high and 40 m across, came under threat, Pitnacree was the obvious parallel to draw. However, the mound revealed a different but equally complex history, from pre-barrow cultivation, through complex timber settings, through a ring bank and finally to a capping of turf and stones. It had also been built around a thousand years after Pitnacree (Barclay 1983).

At about the same time, the rescue excavation undertaken on a pit-defined site at Douglasmuir in Angus in 1979 and 1980 revealed it to be a complex palisaded enclosure radiocarbon-dated to the mid-4th millennium cal BC. In pits close by, an assemblage of Early Neolithic pottery was discovered (Kendrick 1995).

Since the mid-1970s, aerial photography and intensive ground survey by RCAHMS has placed our knowledge of the distribution of monuments, and indeed landscape fragments, of many periods on a completely different footing from that known to Margaret Stewart in the 1950s. Tayside as a whole has had the benefit of five major episodes of RCAHMS or RCAHMS-sponsored terrestrial survey (RCAHMS 1978; 1983; 1990; 1994a; 1994b). While the effect of the terrestrial survey has been felt most strongly in later prehistory, there have also been major effects on the distribution of Neolithic monuments.

The effects of aerial survey can be seen most clearly in the way that the distribution of hengiform monuments has changed from the late 1960s, when Burl (1969) and Wainwright (1969) mapped sixteen or seventeen examples in Scotland, to more recently, when over 70 henges and small hengiform enclosures have been identified (Barclay 1997a; forthcoming).

Cursus monument and bank barrow distribution has also changed radically through the effects of aerial reconnaissance. Only a handful of these sites have been located by terrestrial survey and none, apart from the Cleaven Dyke and one other, were known before the mid 1970s. Brophy has listed over 40 in Scotland (Brophy forthcoming), based on the results of aerial survey (Fig. 3.2).

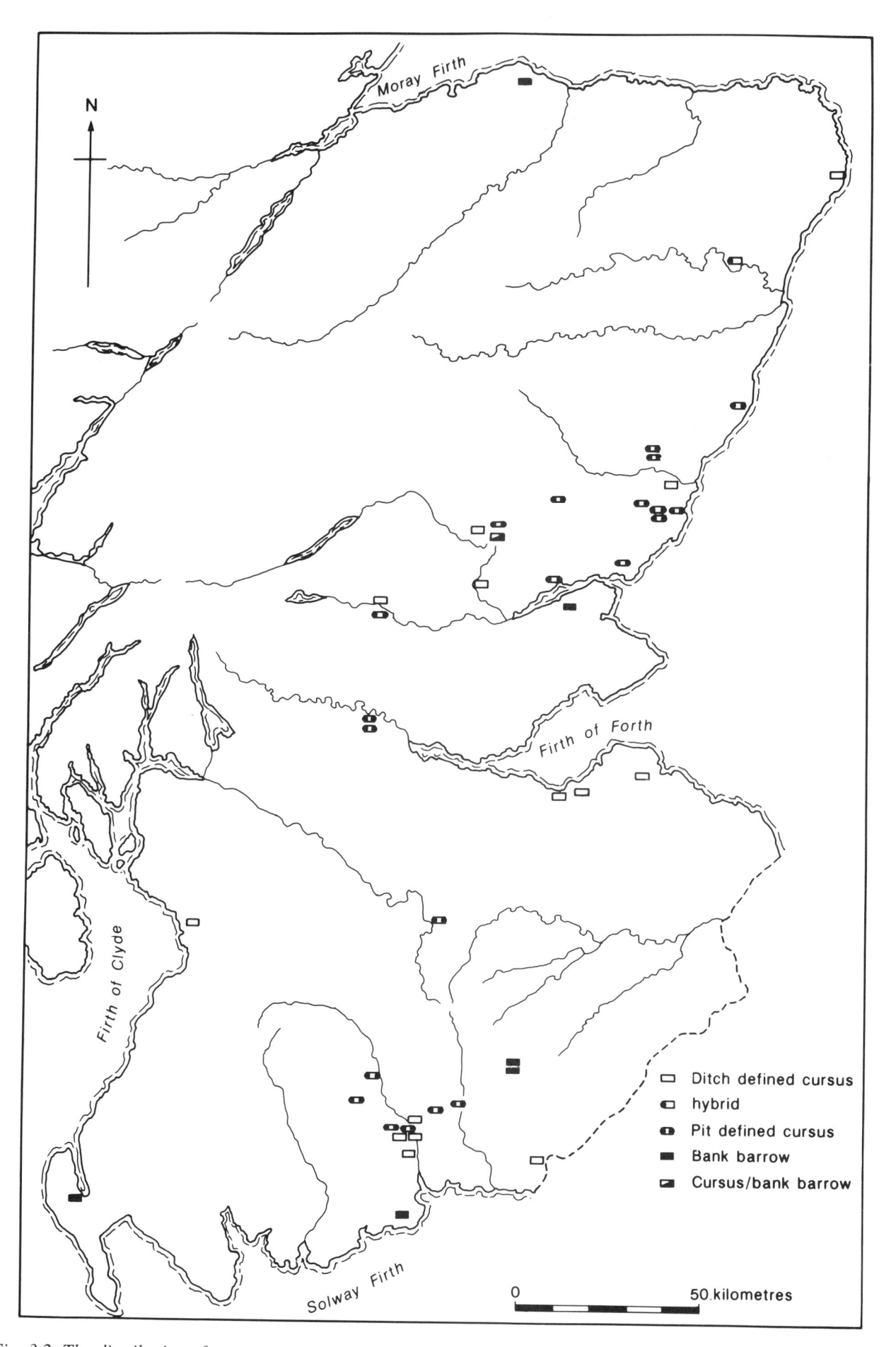

Fig. 3.2. The distribution of cursus monuments and bank barrows in Scotland, from information provided by Kenneth Brophy. The 'Cursus/bank barrow' is the Cleaven Dyke. Since this map was prepared a further probable pit-defined cursus has been found in the Kilmartin Valley, Argyll (Discovery and Excavation in Scotland 1997, *19–21*).

The high density of monuments in Tayside and Dumfries and Galloway is striking.

Round Barrows

A paradox of the situation in Tayside in the last 20 years, as this denser distribution of Neolithic sites has developed, has been the way in which the burial mound at Pitnacree has remained geographically isolated. The most recent overall consideration of round barrows in the Neolithic of Britain is that of Kinnes (1979). In common with more recent regional studies of these sites (RCAHMS 1994b), the implications of Pitnacree do not seem to be adequately addressed. In an area containing many mounds on the same scale as Pitnacree, to publish distribution maps which show Pitnacree as the sole Neolithic round barrow in Tayside (Kinnes 1979, fig. 4.1; RCAHMS 1994b, fig. 37a) is perhaps misleading. The Royal Commission specifically resisted "the temptation to assume that many of the large lowland round barrows [were] of Neolithic date" (RCAHMS 1994b, 38); however, to give the clear impression through the distribution map that *none* was, and then to discuss the meaning of the limited distribution of Neolithic burial mounds, is surely even less appropriate.

The Pitnacree mound was 27.5 m by 23.5 m across and *ca.* 2 m high (a height to diameter ratio (using the average diameter) of *ca.* 12.7:1). Another excavated and published round barrow of the period, at Fochabers in Moray, measured *ca.* 14 m in diameter by 1 m high (Burl 1984). Both were low, flattish mounds. North Mains, in contrast, was 40 m in diameter and 5.5 m high (a ratio of 7.3:1), and had the traditional pudding-bowl shape of a Bronze Age mound. In the field, I have observed that individual round barrows in Perthshire, Angus and Fife (where they have escaped mutilation) seem to fall into one class or the other – broad and low, like Pitnacree, or high and bowl-shaped, like North Mains. Taking the measurement data of apparently undisturbed mounds in the NMRS records and trying to separate the two possible types only shows up the unreliability of many measurements, particularly of height (which seems to have been 'rounded' to an unacceptable degree); any profound statistical approach would be misleading until better data are available. However, as an interim measure a distribution has been prepared of 'low flat' mounds which have a diameter of 20 m or more and a diameter to height ratio of 12:1 or more (given the doubts about the rounding of heights, a fairly conservative ratio). While to attempt this separation on crude morphological

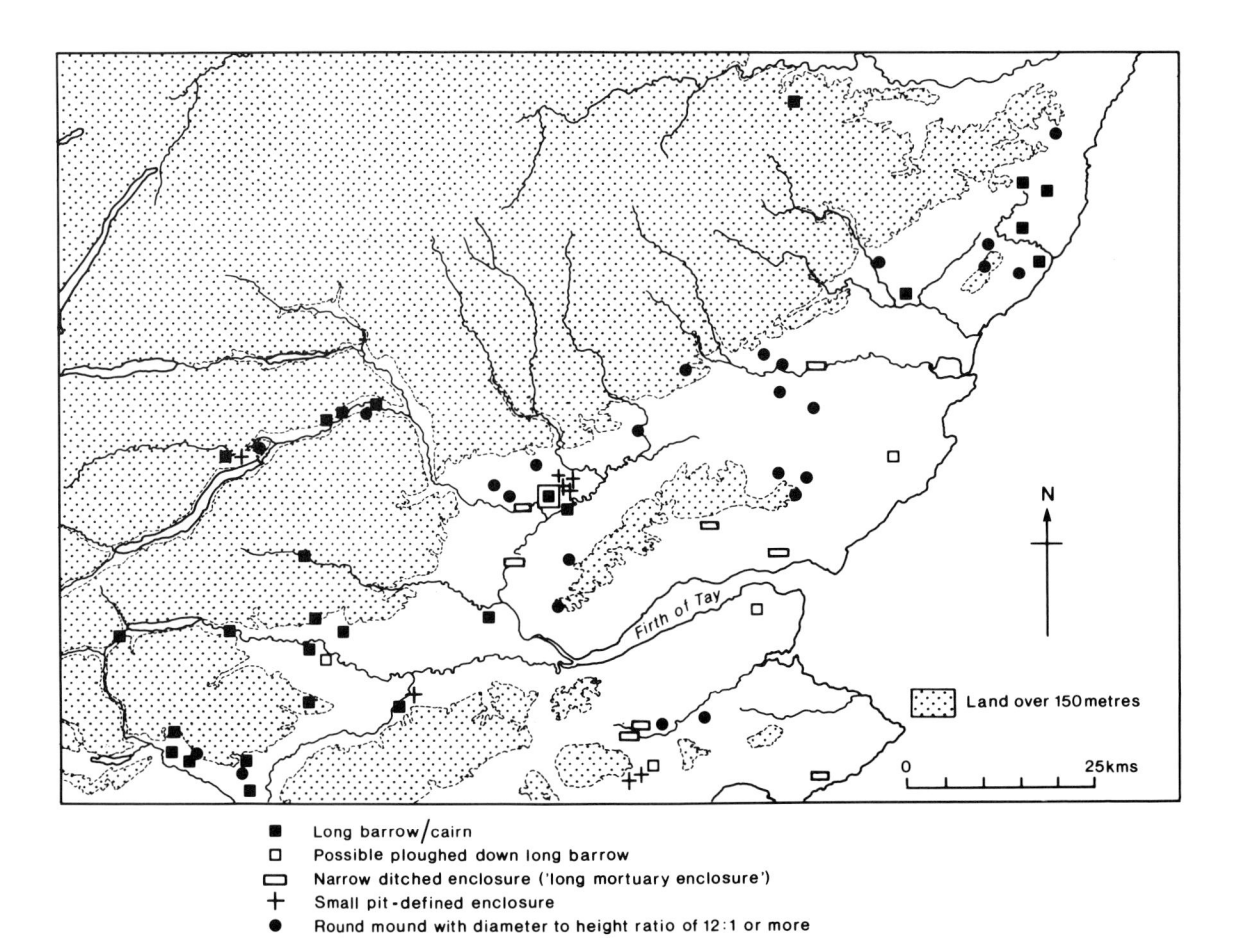

Fig. 3.3. Distribution in Tayside and north Fife of certain and possible funerary monuments: long barrows/cairns, 'long mortuary enclosures', small pit-defined enclosures, and round barrows over 20 m in diameter with a diameter to height ratio of 12:1 or more. The rectangular symbol near the centre of the map marks the Cleaven Dyke.

grounds is risky, the attempt is itself informative and the result of the experiment is, I believe, no more misleading than the minimalist approaches of Kinnes and RCAHMS (Fig. 3.3).

Even the crude distribution of round mounds must also be treated as provisional, as these densely populated arable lowlands still have the capacity to reveal unknown burial mounds over 20 m diameter and 1–2 m high. Two substantial tree-covered burial mounds of similar proportions to Pitnacree have been located in the last decade in arable areas of Perthshire, one on the outskirts of the village of Dunning, the other within sight of the Perth-Crieff main road (*Discovery and Excavation in Scotland 1991*, 73).

Regional Variation

The distribution of the low, flat (Pitnacree-type) and the higher, bowl-shaped (North Mains-type) mounds is regionally restricted, as the map shows: round mounds of this scale are rarer elsewhere in the lowlands. The eastern lowlands also provide an even more striking example of regional variation, in the apparently almost exclusive distribution of henges and recumbent stone circles – monuments believed to be broadly contemporary (Fig. 3.4). While henges, the supposed product of large-scale communal effort, are relatively sparsely distributed, the recumbent stone circles, perhaps the products of individual farming settlements, are so densely distributed that they are frequently intervisible.

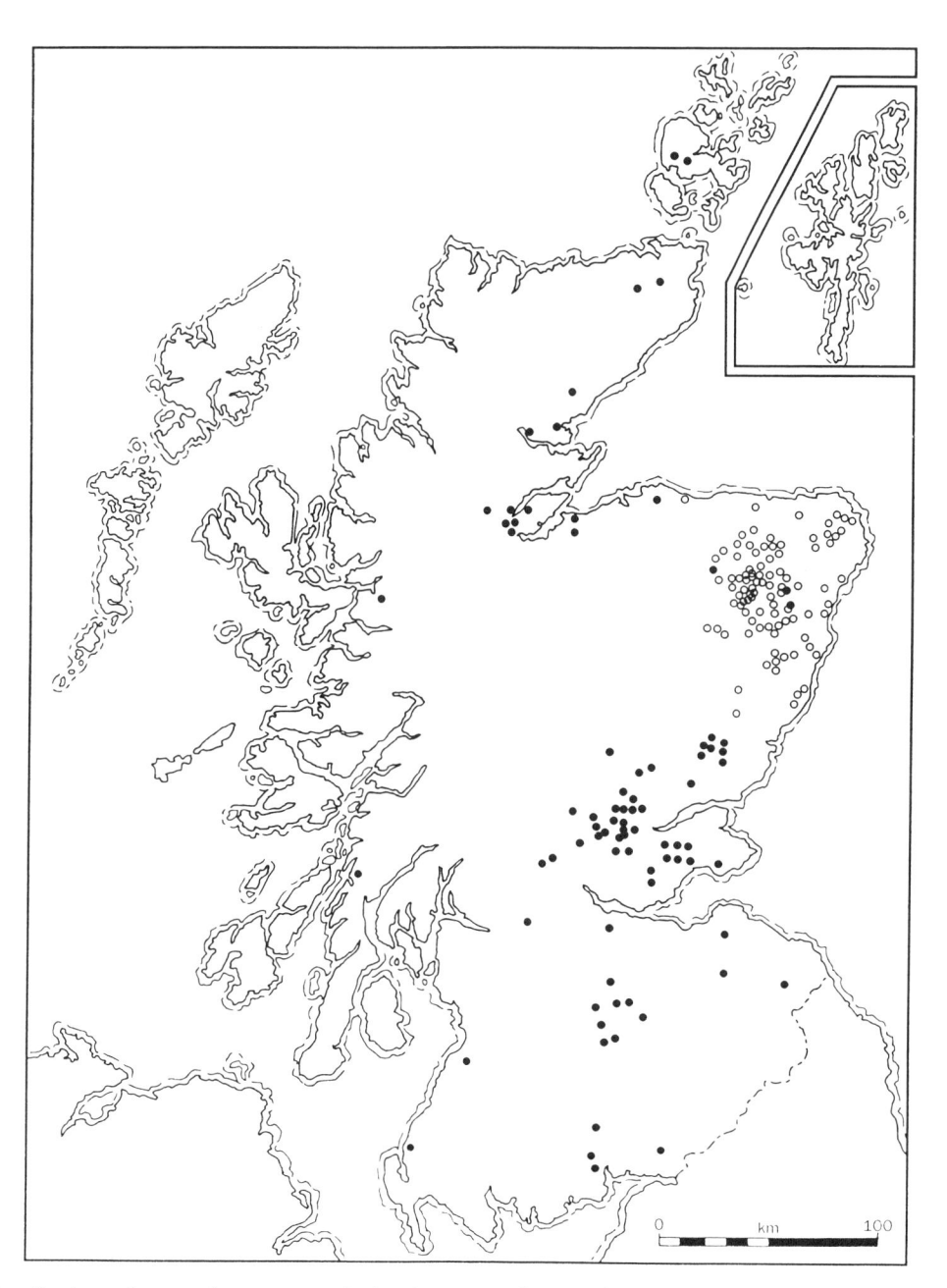

Fig. 3.4. The distribution of recumbent stone circles (open circles) and possible and certain henges and hengiform enclosures (filled circles). RSC distribution after Burl.

The distribution of carved stone balls, normally also interpreted as later Neolithic prestige items, is also concentrated in the north-east of Scotland (Edmonds 1992).

Kinnes, in his perceptive review of the Neolithic in Scotland, commented that there was no such thing as a 'Scottish Neolithic', only a range of regionally distinct Neolithics (Kinnes 1985). To get to this point we have had to move from the position where Croft Moraig could be described as a 'provincial version' of a Wessex monument, but we have also had to work to balance the place Orkney has come to play in the way that other regional Neolithics in northern Britain are interpreted. The prehistory of Scotland and the rest of Britain is diverse, and we all suffer from the importation of perhaps inappropriate models erected on fuller but possibly irrelevant data sets elsewhere (Barclay 1995; Cooney 1997).

The Cleaven Dyke

Investigations into the earlier Neolithic in Tayside and adjacent areas have not been numerous, and our knowledge through excavation of the various classes of monuments now known as a result of aerial and ground survey is limited.

The 1998 National Museums of Scotland project of survey and excavation at the axe quarrying site at Craig na Caillich has provided valuable information on the processes of stone extraction (Edmonds *et al.* 1992). In 1994 Richard Bradley undertook a study of rock art and lithic scatter distribution in upper Strathtay, indicating that the complex markings may have followed or even marked the outer limits of settled land. The project also resulted in the discovery of a hitherto unsuspected quartz industry in the area (Bradley 1994).

The most recent research project on the Neolithic of the area is that undertaken by Gordon Maxwell and myself on the Cleaven Dyke, a monument broadly contemporary with Pitnacree (Barclay *et al.* 1995; Barclay & Maxwell 1998; Barclay & Maxwell forthcoming). The Cleaven Dyke comprises a pair of ditches between 38 m and 50 m apart (Fig. 3.5). Roughly centrally between them lies a bank, varying between 7 m and 15 m across and up to *ca.* 1.7 m high. The bank of the Dyke survives for 1.8 km as an upstanding earthwork, mainly in woodland. The swollen north-western terminal lies just within the wood. To the south-east of the upstanding portion of the Dyke the ditches have been detected on aerial photographs for a further *ca.* 380 m. Interestingly, the tail of a nearby long barrow points at the hill on which the Cleaven Dyke appears to end: this mound, the Herald Hill, was also until recently interpreted as a natural feature – recent trial excavation has proven otherwise (*Discovery and Excavation in Scotland 1997*, 62). Although the Cleaven Dyke keeps to a fairly straight course, it varies in height, width and direction to a greater or lesser extent. There are four breaks in the line of the bank (W to Z on Fig. 3.5), all of which seem to be part of the original construction. Recent survey and excavation has shown that within these larger sections, the mound is built in smaller segments, which are visible both on the surface and on excavation.

Radiocarbon dating suggests that the monument was built in the late 5th to mid/late 4th millennium cal BC, that is, broadly similar to Pitnacree and Douglasmuir.

Palaeoenvironmental studies suggest that the Dyke was built through a landscape of mixed hazel/birch woodland and rough heath and grass (Edwards & Whittington 1998a; b; Simpson & Davidson 1998). The possibility is that this was secondary woodland forming after clearing – an area under some, but not intense, grazing pressure.

The Dyke has been excavated on three previous occasions – in the first years of the century by Abercromby (Abercromby *et al.* 1902), and in 1939 by Richmond (1940), in both cases in relation to work on the nearby Roman installations, for the Dyke had been interpreted as a Roman work for over two centuries. Richmond vigorously promoted the Roman interpretation in his paper, suggesting that it was a political boundary related to the fortress at Inchtuthil, running many kilometres from the Isla to the foothills of the Grampian mountains. The basis of evidence upon which the complex argument rested was, unfortunately, slight. His arguments were refuted in detail by Pitts and St Joseph in the report on the Inchtuthil excavations (1985).

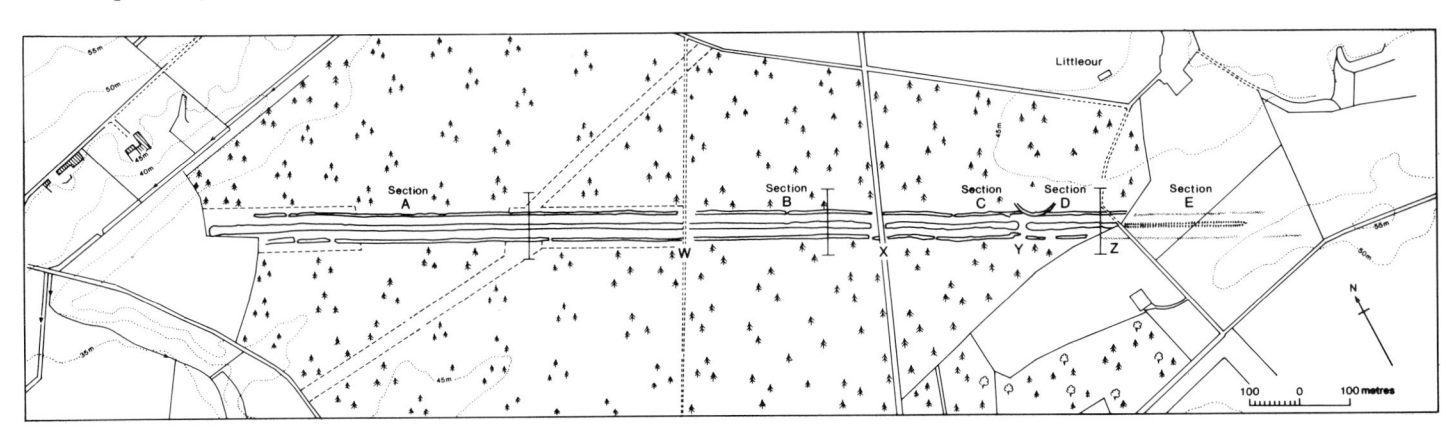

Fig. 3.5. The Cleaven Dyke, showing the five sections in which it was built.

It is at this point that the reader will, I hope, begin to see the relationship between Pitnacree, with which I started this paper, and the broadly contemporary Cleaven Dyke.

In 1975 Helen Adamson undertook a limited rescue excavation just beyond the visible north-west terminal of the Dyke (Adamson & Gallagher 1986). A long narrow trench was cut NE to SW across the projected line of the Dyke, just beyond the boundary fence of the wood. Unfortunately, in the final publication the location of the trench, and the features it contained, seems to have been accidentally transposed over 8 m to the north. As a result important (and accurate) observations and interpretations put forward in the site archive and the published interim report (Adamson 1979) were omitted from the final one.

On the publication plan the bank in the excavated area is shown as continuing the line of the bank in the adjacent wood (Fig. 3.6). Adamson located two ditches, one to the north of the upstanding adjacent bank section, the other cutting the edge of the bank, although it does not appear to on the published plan. However, the site archive and the interim report both make it clear that the trench and the features it contained lay *ca.* 8.5 m further to the south: in the interim report Adamson noted in particular that the mound she detected "was not on the line of the adjacent upstanding bank", but to the south.

As part of the overall study of the monument Chris Burgess has undertaken a contour survey of the whole upstanding length (Burgess 1998). If the plan of the north-west terminal is combined with a correctly positioned plan of Adamson's trench, a complex story emerges.

First, we suggest that the primary monument at the terminal is an oval mound similar in size and proportions, and probably in date, to Pitnacree. The mound, whose edge may be marked by the contour has an east-west axis. Adamson's trench seems to have cut across the north-west corner of this mound.

Second, the oval mound has what seems to be a long barrow attached to it; this mound is *not* associated with the cursus-type ditches of the Dyke, which only start some 60 m to the south-east. The two ditches Adamson located, when positioned correctly on the plan, seem to closely parallel the main bank of the Dyke in the woodland, and it seems likely that, as Adamson noted that the southern ditch cut the revetment of the possible oval mound, the ditches she located were the north-western ends of the quarry ditches of this long mound.

It is only at the end of the *ca.* 90 m long mound that the pattern of the Cleaven Dyke proper is established, with its widely-spaced cursus-like ditches. From that point it seems to be built in over thirty clearly-defined segments, suggesting perhaps prolonged construction. While most cursus monuments are considered as unitary structures designed to act in their final elongated form, the Dyke, and other monuments of the class, may have

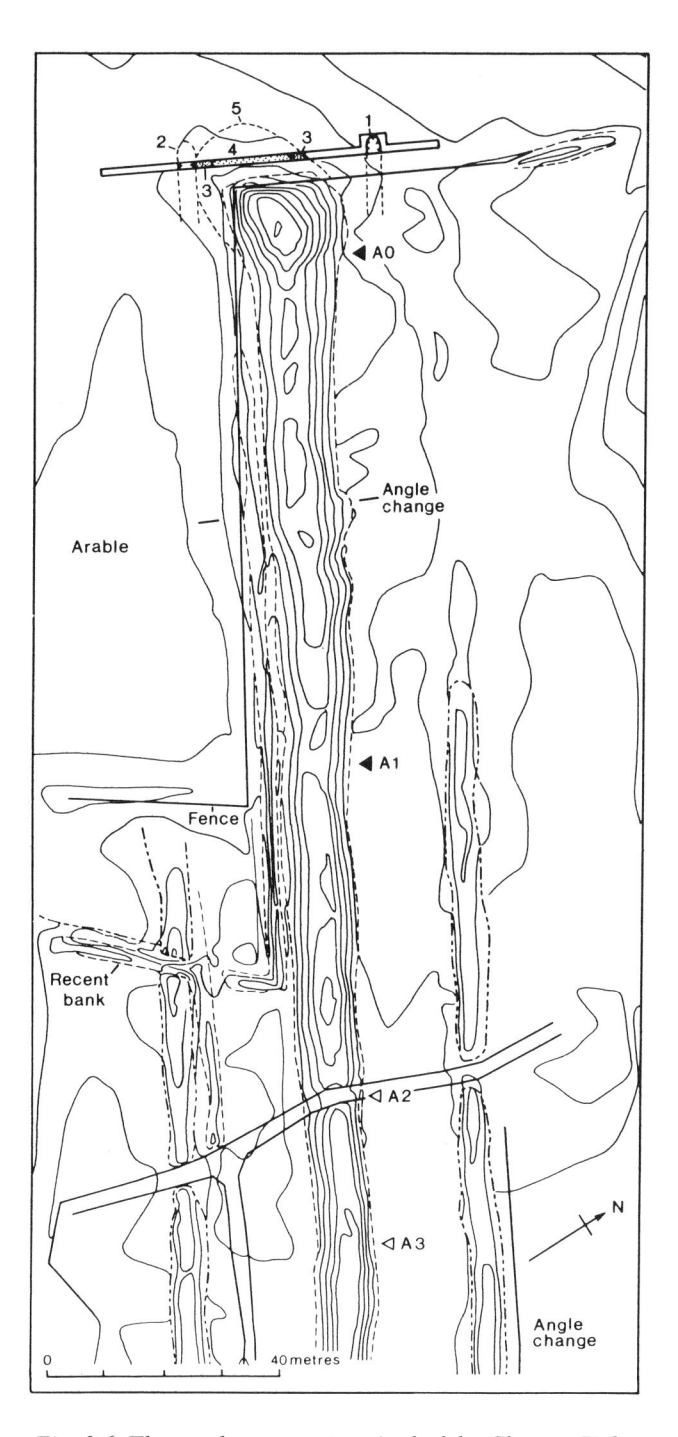

Fig. 3.6. The north-western terminal of the Cleaven Dyke, with Adamson's trench in its correct location (see text). 1 & 2 = the ditches located by Adamson; 3 = the 'turf toeing' of the gravel mound; 4 = the gravel mound, distinctly offset from the bank in the wood; 5 = the estimated boundary of the primary oval barrow. As ditch 2 cuts the mound, the ditches are interpreted as the flanking ditches for the long barrow (which runs from A0 to A1) attached to the primary oval barrow; the 'angle change' within the long barrow may indicate more than one phase of construction. The Cleaven Dyke proper commences at A1; the open triangles labelled A2 and A3 mark the first visible segment boundaries in the bank.

Fig. 3.7. The 350 m long cairn at Auchenlaich, Callander. The main chamber lies at the top left end. The cairn now ends at the clump of trees at the bottom right. Photo: RCAHMS.

had different functions. These matters are discussed further elsewhere (Barclay & Maxwell 1998; forthcoming).

That a round or oval barrow has an unusually long mound attached to it is not unexpected. Henshall has noted a similar pattern with peculiarly long cairns in Caithness and Sutherland, suggesting indeed that in cairns more than 60 m long, single phase construction is the exception rather than the rule (Henshall 1972). Closer to the Dyke a similar pattern can be seen in some of the north-eastern monuments, as at Longmanhill, Banffshire. Parallels can also be drawn with the extraordinarily long cairn at Auchenlaich; in particular, it has some of the same patterns of irregularity in plan as Cleaven Dyke (Fig. 3.7). Interestingly, this monument too was interpreted as a natural feature, with cists built into it, until in 1991 the perceptive Local Authority archaeologist, Lorna Main, recognised it for

what it was (Foster & Stevenson in prep). This is really where we came in, with the Perthshire round mounds, and the problems of their identification.

Conclusion

This paper has taken a brief journey over 30 years, from a time when Coles and Simpson's excavation at Pitnacree was a very isolated discovery of Neolithic burial and ceremonial activity, to a time when Tayside has been transformed by extensive survey, and some, but perhaps as yet not nearly enough, other fieldwork, into an area with a diverse distribution of monuments, which has the potential to answer many questions about the nature and development of the Neolithic in eastern Scotland, and possibly in eastern Britain. John and Derek, in their work in Strathtay in the 1960s, were amongst the first to push at that door which others have since opened a little wider.

Notes

1 This paper is largely as given at the conference in 1997. Elements of it have been incorporated into the final publication of the Cleaven Dyke project (Barclay & Maxwell 1998).

Bibliography

Abercromby, J., Ross, T. & Anderson, J. 1902. Account of the excavation of the Roman station at Inchtuthil, Perthshire, undertaken by the Society of Antiquaries of Scotland in 1901, *Proc. Soc. Antiq. Scotland* 36, 182–242.

Adamson, H. 1979. Cleaven Dyke [Interim Report]. In D.J. Breeze (ed) *Roman Scotland: Some Recent Excavations*, 45. Edinburgh: Inspectorate of Ancient Monuments.

Adamson, H.C. & Gallagher, D.B. 1986. Excavations at the Cleaven Dyke, Perthshire, 1975. *Glasgow Archaeol. J.* 13, 63–8.

Barclay, G.J. 1983. Sites of the third millennium bc to the first millennium ad at North Mains, Strathallan, Perthshire, *Proc. Soc. Antiq. Scotland* 113, 122–281.

Barclay, G.J. 1992. The Scottish gravels: a neglected resource? In M. Fulford & E. Nichols (eds), *Developing Landscapes of Lowland Britain. The Archaeology of the British Gravels: A Review*, 106–24. London: Society of Antiquaries.

Barclay, G.J. 1995. What's new in Scottish prehistory? *Scottish Archaeol. Review* 9/10, 3–14.

Barclay, G.J. 1996. Neolithic buildings in Scotland. In T. Darvill & J. Thomas (eds), *Neolithic Houses in Northwest Europe and Beyond*, 61–75. Oxford: Oxbow.

Barclay, G.J. 1997a. The Neolithic. In K.J. Edwards & I.B.M. Ralston (eds), *Scotland: Environment and Archaeology, 8000 BC – AD 1000*, 127–49. Chichester: Wiley.

Barclay, G.J. (ed.) 1997b. *State-funded Rescue Archaeology in Scotland: Past, Present and Future*. Edinburgh: Historic Scotland.

Barclay, G.J. forthcoming. Cairnpapple revisited: 1948–1998, *Proc. Prehist. Soc.*

Barclay, G.J. & Maxwell, G.S. 1998. *The Cleaven Dyke and Littleour: monuments in the Neolithic of Perthshire*. Edinburgh: Society of Antiquaries of Scotland.

Barclay, G.J. & Maxwell, G.S. forthcoming. The Cleaven Dyke: survey and excavation 1993–1996: an interim account. In A. Barclay & J. Harding (eds), *Pathways and Ceremonies: the cursus monuments of Britain and Ireland*. Oxford: Oxbow.

Barclay, G.J., Maxwell, G.S., Simpson, I.A. & Davidson, D.A. 1995. The Cleaven Dyke: a Neolithic cursus monument/bank barrow in Scotland, *Antiquity* 69, 317–26.

Billcliffe, R. 1987. *James McIntosh Patrick*. London: The Fine Art Society.

Bradley, R. 1994. *Strath Tay Field Survey, 1994. Interim report*. Privately circulated paper.

Brophy, K. forthcoming. The cursus monuments of Scotland. In A. Barclay & J. Harding (eds), *Pathways and Ceremonies: the cursus monuments of Britain and Ireland*. Oxford: Oxbow.

Burgess, C. 1998. Contour models and digital terrain modelling in archaeological survey: the development of approaches to the Cleaven Dyke. In G.J. Barclay & G.S. Maxwell (eds), 74–76.

Burl, A. 1969. Henges: internal structures and regional groups, *Archaeol. J.* 126, 1–28.

Burl, H.A.W. 1984. Report on the excavation of a Neolithic mound at Boghead, Speymouth Forest, Fochabers, Moray, 1972 and 1974, *Proc. Soc. Antiq. Scotland* 114, 35–73.

Coles, J.M. & Simpson, D.D.A. 1965. The excavation of a Neolithic round barrow at Pitnacree, Perthshire, Scotland, *Proc. Prehist. Soc.* 31, 34–57.

Cooney, G. 1997. Images of settlement and the landscape in the Neolithic. In P. Topping (ed), *Neolithic Landscapes*, 23–31. Oxford: Oxbow.

Coutts, H. 1971. *Tayside Before History*. Dundee: Dundee Museum and Art Gallery.

Edmonds, M. 1992. "Their use is wholly unknown". In N. Sharples & A. Sheridan (eds), *Vessels for the Ancestors*, 179–193. Edinburgh: Edinburgh University Press.

Edmonds, M., Sheridan, A. & Tipping, R. 1992. Survey and excavation at Creag na Caillich, Killin, Perthshire, *Proc. Soc. Antiq. Scotland* 122, 77–112.

Edwards, K. & Whittington, G. 1998 a. The palaeoenvironmental background: pollen studies at Rae Loch. In G.J. Barclay & G.S. Maxwell (eds), 5–12.

Edwards, K. & Whittington, G. 1998 b. Soil pollen beneath the Cleaven Dyke. In G.J. Barclay & G.S. Maxwell forthcoming.

Henshall, A.S. 1972. *The Chambered Tombs of Scotland. Vol. II.* Edinburgh: Edinburgh University Press.

Kendrick, J. 1995. Excavation of a Neolithic enclosure and an Iron Age settlement at Douglasmuir, Angus, *Proc. Soc. Antiq. Scotland* 125, 29–67.

Kinnes, I. 1979. *Round Barrows and Ring-ditches in the British Neolithic*. London: British Museum Occasional Paper, 7.

Kinnes, I. 1985. Circumstance not context: the Neolithic of Scotland as seen from the outside, *Proc. Soc. Antiq. Scotland* 115, 15–57.

Maxwell, G.S. 1983. Recent aerial survey in Scotland. In G.S. Maxwell (ed), *The Impact of of Aerial Reconnaissance on Archaeology*, 27–40. London: CBA Research Report 49.

Piggott, S. 1954–55 [1956]. Excavations in passage-graves and ring cairns of the Clava group, 1952–3, *Proc. Soc. Antiq. Scotland* 88, 173–207.

Piggott, S. & Simpson, D.D.A. 1971. Excavation of a stone circle at Croft Moraig, Perthshire, Scotland, *Proc. Prehist. Soc.* 37, 1–15.

Pitts, L.F. & St Joseph, J.K. 1985. *Inchtuthil: the Roman Legionary Fortress excavations 1962–65*. London: Society for the Promotion of Roman Studies.

RCAHMS 1978. *Lunan Valley*. Edinburgh: RCAHMS (The Archaeological Sites and Monuments Series, 4).

RCAHMS 1983. *Central Angus*. Edinburgh: RCAHMS (The Archaeological Sites and Monuments Series, 18).

RCAHMS 1990. *North east Perth: an archaeological landscape*. Edinburgh: HMSO.

RCAHMS 1994a. *Braes of Doune: an archaeological survey*. Edinburgh: RCAHMS.

RCAHMS 1994b. *South east Perth: an archaeological landscape*. Edinburgh: HMSO.

RCHME 1960. *A Matter of Time*. London: HMSO.

Richmond, I.A. 1940. Excavations on the estate of Meikleour, Perthshire, 1939, *Proc. Soc. Antiq. Scotland* 74, 37–48.

Scott, J.G. 1992. Mortuary structures and megaliths. In N. Sharples & A. Sheridan (eds), *Vessels for the Ancestors*, 104–19. Edinburgh: Edinburgh University Press.

Simpson, I. & Davidson, D. 1998. Palaeosols of the Cleaven Dyke. In G.J. Barclay & G.S Maxwell (eds), 36–42.

Stewart, M.E.C. 1958–59 [1961]. Strath Tay in the second millennium BC – a field survey, *Proc. Soc. Antiq. Scotland* 92, 71–84.

Wainwright, G.J. 1969. A review of henge monuments in the light of recent research, *Proc. Prehist. Soc.* 35, 112–133.

Wainwright, G.J. & Longworth, I.A. 1971. *Durrington Walls: Excavations 1966–1968*. London: Society of Antiquaries.

4. The stony limits – rock carvings in passage graves and in the open air

Richard Bradley

Abstract: This paper considers two different ways of approaching prehistoric rock art. One is by the well-established methods of stylistic analysis. The other approach can best be described as 'contextual'. It reviews a single body of material and compares those approaches with one another. As the title suggests, the subject of this article is the rock art found in megalithic tombs and its counterparts in the open air. It does not consider those cases in which carved stones made the transition between these two domains, like the re-used menhirs in Breton passage graves, nor does it investigate the evidence from Northern Europe. Instead, it is concerned with what has become known as passage tomb art and with its relationship to the images created on natural surfaces. Although its starting point is in Iberia, its main concern will be with Ireland and Britain.

Introduction

'Stony limits' is the title of a poem by Hugh MacDiarmid. I have used it for this article because it is a phrase that seems to epitomise the character of rock art research. The stony limits are those boundaries in the landscape that were embellished by paintings and carvings, but they are also the limits in our own thinking when we try to interpret that evidence. John Coles has never suffered from these inhibitions. His approach to the study of rock art is more ambitious and more broad-minded. It is an example that I shall try to emulate.

It is important to distinguish between two different approaches to the evidence. In Spain and Portugal megalithic art occurs in two distinct media – painting and carving – and the same is true of the open-air rock art found in both those countries. Each has been considered separately, so that there are studies of tomb decoration and detailed documentation of the images in the open air. There is little cross-reference between them, except where the passage graves provide some dating evidence. There is rather more of an overlap between these two groups than is commonly supposed. Although many of the paintings and carvings found inside passage graves consist of abstract motifs, there are more naturalistic images – humans and animals in particular – that are shared with the widely distributed tradition of Schematic Art. This is the conventional name applied to a style of abstract and naturalistic images, both paintings and carvings, found over most parts of the Iberian Peninsula and created over a lengthy period extending from the early Neolithic to the Early Bronze Age. In addition, cup marks are associated with these tombs but have not attracted much attention until recently (Bueno & Balbín 1992).

There is a real need to document the character of both styles of rock art, but it is just as important to study the contexts in which they are found. Bueno and Balbín have commented on the spatial relationship between these two groups of images (1992, 529). Their analysis has important lessons for work in other areas of Europe. Discussing the megalithic art of the Meseta and north-west Iberia, they observe that the human figures are usually located in the chamber and especially towards its rear; they are less common in the passage and occur very rarely on the capstone where cup marks appear instead. Although they do not say so, the same distinction between these different images can be found on natural surfaces in the countryside

Author's Address: Richard Bradley, Department of Archaeology, University of Reading, Whiteknights, Reading, RG2 2AA

where cup marks are widely distributed and are readily accessible, whilst the more complex motifs that are shared with Schematic Art may be found in remote and dangerous positions on the margins of the settled landscape. These include cliffs, caves and rock shelters, and on some sites the more complex panels of paintings are the most difficult to reach of all (Bradley and Fábregas 1998). It seems as if particularly significant motifs were shared between the chambers and special places in the landscape, whilst cup marks were also located at accessible points in the surrounding country. This is particularly true at El Pedroso in Zamora, where the entrance to a decorated cave is marked by panels of cup marks, whilst drawings of human figures are confined to the interior (Esparza 1977).

Britain and Ireland

Britain and Ireland provide another region in which decorated tombs occur together with open-air sites, although they are rarely found in close proximity to one another. Again the main emphasis has been on studies of style. One group characterises the carvings found in passage graves, whilst the other consists of the abstract motifs found on natural surfaces in the landscape (Simpson and Thawley 1972; Shee Twohig 1981).

The relationship between the two groups has always been controversial, and opinion has fluctuated over the years. It was in his Presidential Lecture to the Prehistoric Society of East Anglia that the Abbé Breuil (1934) suggested that both groups had a common source; in his opinion they originated in Iberia and were conceived as depictions of the human figure. Later writers from MacWhite (1946) onwards have rejected this view, contending that the two styles really were distinct from one another, and this line has been followed for the most part by Shee Twohig (1981) in her study of megalithic art and by Simpson and Thawley (1972) in their review of open-air rock art. When it has been questioned, as it has by Johnston (1993), the debate is still conducted in terms of individual motifs and the extent to which they overlap between these groups.

In terms of technique and typology, the traditional view wins the day. The two groups of carvings are made in rather different ways, and the open-air sites very rarely posses the sculptural quality of the 'public' art of the Boyne Valley. In the same way, few motifs take quite the same form in these two groups, and the repertoire of open-air rock art is much more restricted than the vocabulary of passage grave art: any connections are limited to the curvilinear motifs, as geometric designs such as lozenges or triangles are virtually unknown in the open air (Bradley 1997, chapter 3). More important, the individual design elements are organised according to quite different conventions in these two styles. In the tombs they float free of one another or they coalesce into complex compositions (Shee Twohig 1981, chapter 4). On open-air sites the different designs may be connected to one another in

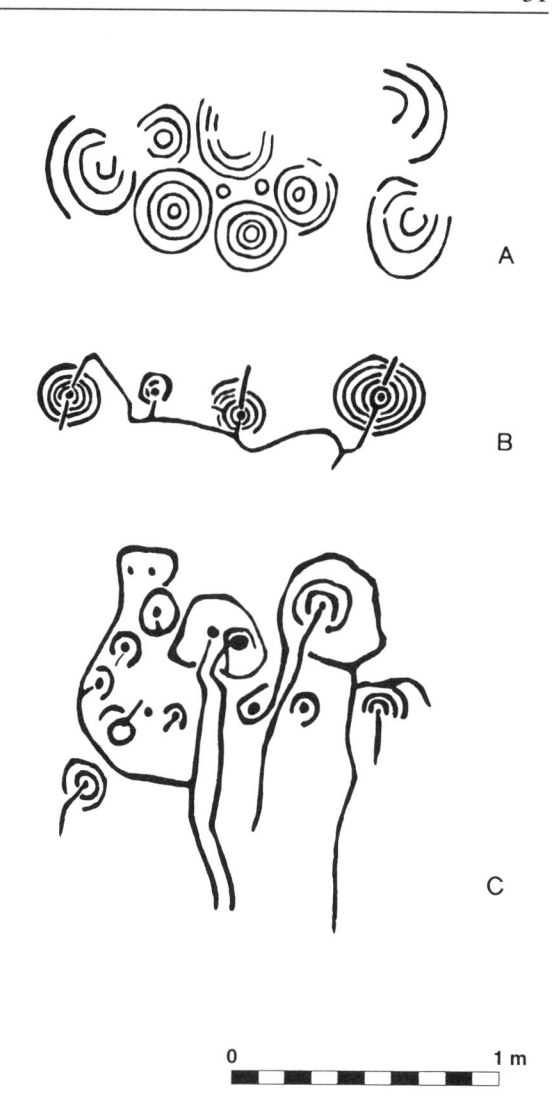

Fig. 4.1. Contrasting compositions in passage grave art and open-air rock art. A: kerbstone at Knowth (after Eogan 1986); B: rock carving at Buttony, Northumberland (after Beckensall 1991); C: rock carving at Horton, Northumberland (after Beckensall 1991)

'chains' (Bradley 1997, chapter 3; Fig. 4.1). To use a linguistic analogy, even where the words are much the same, the grammar is very different.

The chronology of the two groups reveals further differences still. There is some overlap between the motifs found in both these styles, but there seems little doubt that passage grave art did not extend long after about 3000 BC, when the largest tombs in the Boyne Valley were constructed. On the other hand, cup and ring carvings were still employed in burial monuments dating from the Early Bronze Age (Bradley 1997, 57–66). Although some of the carved stones were perhaps being reused, there are a number of monuments where this does not seem likely. In any event it is clear that considerable importance still attached to these motifs, even if their original significance had changed.

These differences are important, but some problems

still remain. There does seem to be a certain overlap between the motifs found in both of these styles. That is not the usual situation with rock art in Atlantic Europe. Such links are hardly found in France, and even in Iberia such connections are the exception rather than the rule (Shee Twohig 1981; Bueno and Balbín 1992). Even if megalithic art and open-air rock art can be considered as separate styles, the reasons for that overlap have to be discussed. The requirement is to adopt the right framework for analysis. If studies of style and technique point in one direction, what can be learnt by studying the art in its wider context? Might the British and Irish rock art form part of a more complex system, like the drawings of people and animals in the Iberian peninsula?

The context of megalithic art

The best starting point for this discussion is Irish megalithic art. Its style has been well documented and so have its possible relationships with tomb decoration in other regions, but this method of analysis has tended to overshadow its quite exceptional character (Shee Twohig 1981; Eogan 1986, chapters 7 and 8). When we consider the range of variation exhibited by passage grave art over a wider area, this becomes apparent in a number of ways.

The first point to make is that outside Ireland decoration is usually confined to the interior of these monuments. It is generally found in the chamber and less often in the passage. In many cases the most complex decoration is at the rear of the chamber, and it is quite unusual for the decoration in the passage to extend as far as the entrance. It seems as if the art had an incremental character in which the imagery increased in complexity towards the centre of the monument.

That is not surprising, for the structure of many of these tombs placed little emphasis on the exterior. Some of the most important monuments were bounded by dry stone walls, and impressive kerbs like those found in Ireland are not particularly common on the Continent. Indeed, there are many sites where it is difficult to recognise any formal limit to the covering mound or cairn. At one level this might seem to explain why all the decoration was inside the monument, but practical arguments of this kind miss the point. The outside of these monuments was never the focus of attention; the interior space was what mattered most.

In fact the Irish tombs may originally have had a rather similar emphasis. Their internal chronology is not well defined, but two of the most useful analyses agree on certain key points. Sheridan's study of their architectural evolution would place the decorated tombs at Loughcrew earlier than the major monuments of the Boyne Valley (Sheridan 1987) and this would agree with the sequence of decorative styles postulated by O'Sullivan (1986). He has identified a number of instances in which stones that were originally decorated in the style typical of Loughcrew were reworked in a more formal style of composition which found its fullest expression at Newgrange and Knowth.

This sequence is significant because it suggests that megalithic art changed its contexts over time. In the earlier phase, typified by many of the carvings at Loughcrew, the motifs were confined to the interior of the monuments. This is important, for these particular cairns were provided with external kerbs, yet only three of the kerbstones bear any decoration, compared with almost one hundred in the chambers and passages (Shee Twohig 1981, 205–20). This contrasts very sharply with the situation at Newgrange where almost the same number of surfaces in the chamber and passage have carved decoration; in this case the same process extended to no fewer than 48 of the kerbstones (O'Kelly 1982, 146–85). This suggests a growing emphasis on the perimeter of these tombs (Fig. 4.2). The same idea is illustrated by Bergh's observation that quartz was used to enhance the exterior of the later megalithic tombs in Ireland. In the earlier monuments it was deposited mainly inside them (Bergh 1995, 196).

There are other indications of a changing emphasis in the design of passage graves. The later tombs include a number of sites where the monument was enclosed by an earthwork, and at some sites the external area is associated with specialised structures, including settings of pebbles, stone-built hearths and circles of posts (Bradley 1998, chapter 7). There are considerable deposits of cultural material beyond the kerbs at Newgrange and Knowth, and in Orkney Sharples argues that it is only the later tombs where artefacts are commonly found outside the monuments (1985, 69). It seems as if the nature of public ritual may have been extending from the restricted number of people who could enter the tomb to the much larger congregations that could gather around its limits.

That emphasis on larger gatherings may help to explain one further feature which distinguishes megalithic art in Britain and Ireland from that found in most parts of Europe. That is the occurrence of its characteristic imagery on a small number of stone circles: monuments which were entirely open. The main evidence comes from Cumbria, where several sites are decorated with spirals and other motifs with close counterparts in the Irish tombs (Beckensall 1992). These sites include the outlying monolith at Long Meg and her Daughters, and the recently discovered carving at Castlerigg (Frodsham 1996, 112). Another link may be between the Irish tombs and the spiral carved on the Temple Wood stone circle in western Scotland (Scott 1989). Thus the British and Irish monuments have a rather unusual history., compared with those in Continental Europe. The distinctive character of the passage graves is illustrated by the use of decorated kerbs. It is equally unusual to find the same motifs shared between megaliths and other stone-built monuments.

Such observations are important as they help to account for a number of observations made during excavations in the Boyne Valley. Eogan (1986) has identified a broad division in the art of Newgrange and Knowth between

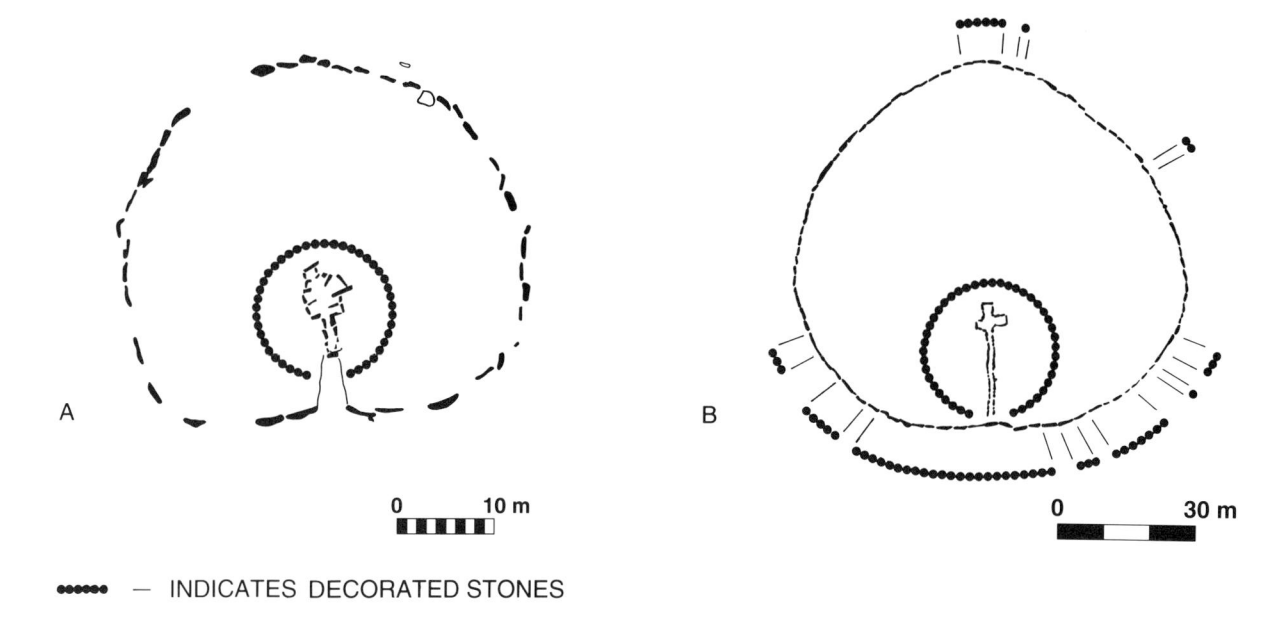

Fig. 4.2. The distributions of decorated stones at (A) Loughcrew Cairn L and (B) Newgrange

curvilinear motifs, which tend to be found on the kerbstones and at the entrance(s), and angular motifs which are more common inside these monuments. This is intriguing as it suggests that the elements that show the greatest resemblance to the open-air carvings are found on the *exterior*: the part that faces into the wider landscape. Again these links are very general ones and the motifs in these two styles are not the same. Even so, the pattern is striking. Figures kindly provided by Dr Muiris O'Sullivan show that at Newgrange cup marks and circles occur on 55% of the decorated kerbstones, compared with only 12% of those inside the monument. His figures for Knowth show a similar pattern. Cups and circles are represented on 20% of the decorated kerbstones but on only 5% of the decorated stones in each of the chambers and passages. There is the same contrast at Dowth where the sample is much smaller (O'Sullivan pers. comm.).

These observations identify a series of important contrasts in the rock art of Britain and Ireland. It was in the Irish passage graves, where the exterior of those monuments was embellished, that the motifs employed in the tombs resemble those in the wider landscape; this does not happen in other parts of Europe. In that case it seems as if the closest links between megalithic art and open-air rock art involve the stones that were exposed to view on the kerbs of passage graves. The decoration found *inside* these monuments has much less in common with the designs found in the wider landscape. At the same time, that emphasis on the outside of the monument was a relatively late development. It may have happened at a time when stone circles were first being built at Newgrange and other sites, and that may be why some of the designs on the kerbstones are shared with such monuments in England and Scotland.

From monuments to natural places

So far the discussion has been conducted at a rather general level. Now we must consider some of these issues in more detail. It is worth drawing attention to two of the best known images from Newgrange, the entrance stone and the decorated kerbstone on the opposite side of the monument (O'Kelly 1982, 154 and 158). These not only exemplify most of the key elements of megalithic art, they help to identify the differences between this style and the carvings in the wider landscape.

The entrance stone is notable for its complex array of spirals (Fig. 4.3). Motifs of this kind seem to be associated with the position of the passage. An attractive interpretation is that this particular image not only represents the path leading into the tomb but also evokes the sensation of entering a kind of tunnel or vortex often reported in states of altered consciousness (Dronfield 1996). This may explain why motifs of this kind are so common in societies where shamans play an important role.

Such spirals are not a common feature of open-air rock art, and even when this type of motif is found it forms part of a much less elaborate design. Instead, one of the commonest motifs is a cup mark enclosed by a series of concentric rings. Often that central cup is linked to surrounding area by a radial line (Fig. 4.1). This motif is rarely found in megalithic art. At first sight the two designs are not related to one another, but at a different level a quite different interpretation suggests itself. Perhaps both motifs represent the *sensation* of entering the solid rock through a tunnel so common in trance experience (Lewis-Williams & Dowson 1990). Where the decoration formed part of a megalithic tomb, there would be no need to depict the path leading down that vortex, for the monument itself

Fig. 4.3. The entrance stone (A) and kerbstone 52 (B) at Newgrange (after O'Kelly 1982)

was equipped with an entrance passage. Where the same idea was represented on a natural outcrop, the cup mark and radial line might be used to suggest a structure of the same kind. In other words, the key images in both these styles may take different forms, but each may have been intended to evoke the same basic idea. That may be why a number of the spirals identified in England and Scotland seem to have been equipped with tails (Van Hoek 1993). This allowed them to conform to the prevailing tradition of representation.

There is no doubt that megalithic art has a more varied vocabulary than the rock carvings in the open air. That is because the curvilinear designs are supplemented by an equally varied range of angular motifs, including lozenges and triangles. Both groups of images come together on the kerbstone directly opposite the entrance to Newgrange (Fig. 4.3). The stone is divided in half by a vertical line. This separates one group of carvings that typify the normal repertoire of Boyne Valley art from another series of less standard motifs. On the left hand side of that division there are triangles, lozenges and spirals, and on the right is an unusual group of circular and oval motifs, including rings with central basins or cup marks and another group of curvilinear enclosures, each of them broken by an entrance. The distinction between these two panels was clearly considered significant, for they are separated from one another by the line that cuts the kerbstone in half. The left hand group includes some of the most striking images associated with passage tombs, and also a number of the images that are shared between megalithic art and Grooved Ware. The right hand group has much more in common with the kinds of enclosure found in open-air rock art.

The equation is not exact, but the pairing of the two groups of motifs is enough to suggest that their similarities and differences were considered to be significant.

Although there are important contrasts between the two styles, there are also cases in which they overlap. In particular, there are sites where passage grave motifs are found in open-air rock art. Here the main examples are spirals, stars and rings without a central cup. Such motifs are not very common in open-air rock art and where they are found together with the normal range of designs they are often associated with the more complex decorated panels: surfaces on which the cup marks are enclosed by several concentric rings and where these different elements are joined together in 'chains'. This suggests that these panels were recognised as somehow exceptional. In Argyll, for example, these motifs are limited to sites on which the cup marks may be enclosed by four or more rings (Bradley 1997, 76–7). Although there are certain exceptions, the same pattern is found in south-west Scotland. A further characteristic of these spirals has been identified by Frodsham (1996), for not only are many of these motifs associated with the more complex panels of rock art, they also exhibit a striking preference for surfaces that are coloured red. Such sites are sometimes found close to henges or stone circles (Bradley 1997, chapter 7).

In other cases it is the passage grave motifs that are more common in open-air carvings. When this happens there are further indications that their special significance was recognised. There is sometimes a preference for locating these images on vertical or steeply sloping surfaces, and the most striking examples of all are located on prominent cliffs (Bradley 1997, 132). The most extensive of these sites is at Ballochmyle in Ayrshire, which includes both spirals and stars (Stevenson 1993). This site contains a profusion of cups and rings, but they are not organised according to the usual conventions. Although there are numerous concentric rings, hardly any have radial lines and very few of the motifs are joined together, although the circles may abut one another (Fig. 4.4). This is the way in which passage graves were decorated.

It was only towards the end of the period in which cup and ring marks were in use that these motifs were employed in burials (Bradley 1997, chapter 9). In one case they seem to have been located according to similar conventions to those used in megalithic art many centuries before. This evidence is confined to the Clava Cairns. Although these include a number of passage graves, there is no evidence that they were built until the Early Bronze Age (Bradley 1999). It is usually supposed that the only decoration found on these particular monuments consists of the ubiquitous cup marks, but this is not quite true. Both the passage graves at Balnuaran of Clava incorporate cup and ring carvings. In one case these were created on one of the kerbstones, but in a position that would have been masked when a platform was built against the monument soon after the construction of the cairn. In the other instance, one of the orthostats in the central chamber is lavishly decorated.

This is situated where the chamber meets the passage, and ever since the work of Simpson 130 years ago this has been described as a cup-marked stone (Simpson 1867, plate x). In fact it is nothing of the sort, for the decoration includes a number of circular motifs. It continues to the base of the stone, which would have been concealed once the chamber was built (Figure 4.5). There is a stone with very similar decoration on a natural surface just outside the Clava cemetery, emphasising the point that these designs are the same as those in the surrounding landscape. The passage graves at Balnuaran of Clava share another striking feature too, for their corbelled chambers incorporate a significant number of cup-marked slabs of red sandstone. Whatever their explanation, these can be compared with the 'hidden' art of the Irish passage graves which is so much earlier in date. The main group at Clava are on the rear wall of the chamber where it is illuminated by the rays of the midwinter sun.

Conclusions

Such evidence suggests a number of conclusions. There may have been certain links between the designs applied to the exterior of Irish passage tombs and those found on natural surfaces in the countryside. Although one group is undoubtedly more informal than the other, it seems as if the special significance of those monuments extended to the features of the wider landscape. This happened at just the point when the audience for public ritual was changing and new kinds of monuments such as stone circles were coming into use. Open-air rock art remained important for a long time afterwards. Where the vocabulary of megalithic art was employed on natural surfaces those images were often treated in a special way. The same is true where cup marks and cups and rings were employed in the last Scottish passage graves. All these images may be variations on a common theme, and this is most clearly represented by the tunnel imagery associated with the entrances to the Boyne tombs.

There are certain similarities between the two styles, but resemblance is not identity. There is no need to question the careful work of classification on which this account has been based. The evidence is so confusing that it is easy to lose direction, yet John Coles has taught us that there is much to be gained from an approach which considers rock art in its wider context. When we do that, a quite new prospect appears. In time we may

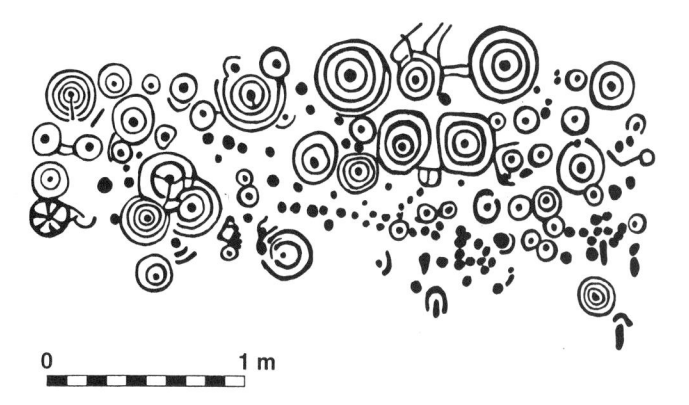

Fig. 4.4. Part of the decorated cliff at Ballochmyle, Ayrshire (after Stevenson 1993)

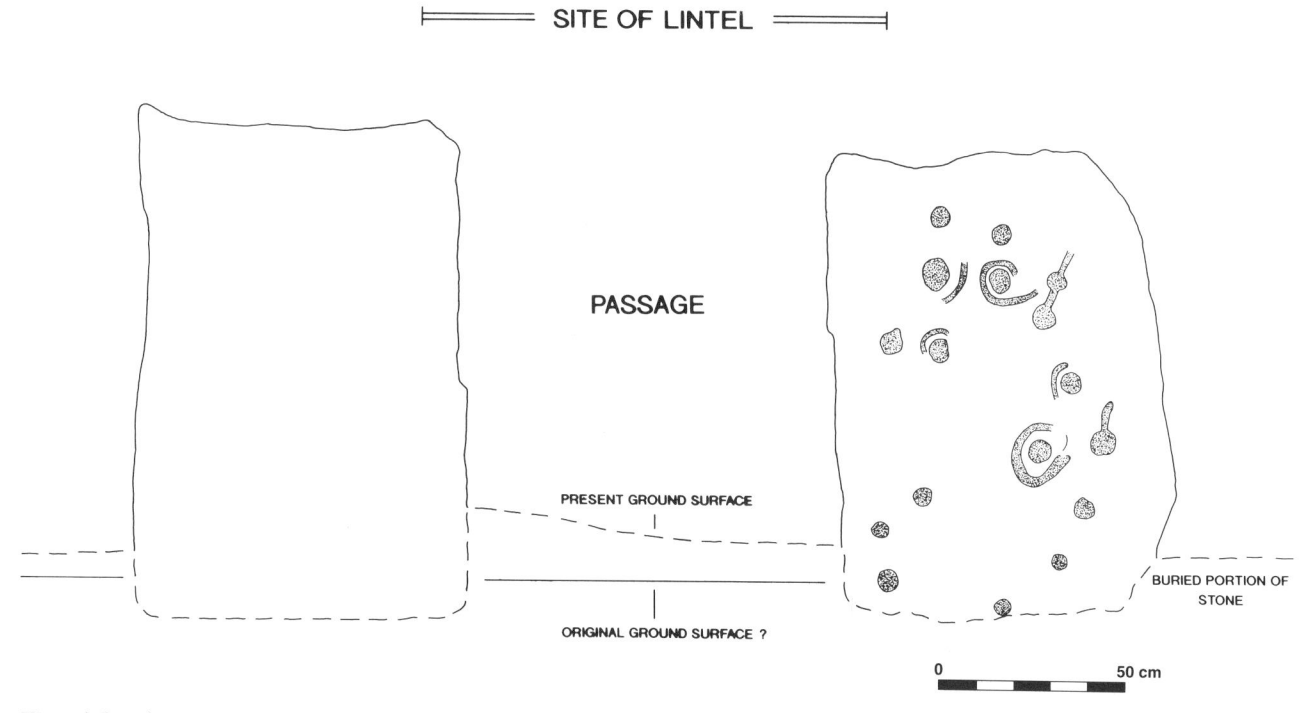

Fig. 4.5. The entrance between the central chamber and the passage in the south-western cairn at Balnuaran of Clava

breach the stony limits altogether. We face the same challenge as those shamans who must pass through the solid rock if they are to communicate with the dead.

Acknowledgements

I am most grateful to Muiris O'Sullivan for information on the motifs in the Boyne Valley tombs and to Jason Walker for preparing the figure drawings.

Bibliography

Beckensall, S. 1991. *Prehistoric Rock Motifs of Northumberland, volume 1*. Hexham: privately published.

Beckensall, S. 1992. *Cumbrian Prehistoric Rock Art*. Hexham: privately published.

Bergh, S. 1995. *Landscape of the Monuments*. Stockholm: Riksantikvarieämbet Arkeologiska Undersökningar.

Bradley, R. 1997. *Rock Art and the Prehistory of Atlantic Europe*. London: Routledge.

Bradley, R. 1998. *The Significance of Monuments*. London: Routledge.

Bradley, R. 1999. *The Good Stones. A New Investigation of the Clava Cairns*. Edinburgh: Society of Antiquaries of Scotland.

Bradley, R. and Fábregas Valcarce, R. 1998. Crossing the border: contrasting style of rock art in the prehistory of north-west Iberia, *Oxford J. Archaeology* 17, 287–308.

Breuil, H. 1934. Presidential address, *Proc. Prehist. Soc. East Anglia* 7, 289–322.

Bueno Ramirez, P. and Balbín Behrmann, R. 1992. L'art mégalithique dans la péninsule Iberique: une vue d'ensemble, *L'Anthropologie* 96, 499–572.

Dronfield, J. 1996. Entering alternative realities: cognition, art and architecture in Irish passage tombs, *Cambridge Archaeol. J.* 6, 37–72.

Eogan, G. 1986. *Knowth and the Passage-tombs of Ireland*. London: Thames and Hudson.

Esparza Arroyo, A. 1977. El castro zamorana de El Pedroso y sus insculturas, *Boletin del Seminario de Estudios de Arte y Arqueología, Valladolid* 43, 27–39.

Frodsham, P. 1996. Spirals in time: Morwick Mill and the spiral in Northern British rock art, *Northern Archaeology* 13/14, 101–38.

Johnston, S. 1993. The relationship between prehistoric Irish rock art and Irish passage tomb art, *Oxford J. Archaeology* 12, 257–79.

Lewis-Williams, D. and Dowson, T. 1990. Through the veil: San rock paintings and the rock face, *South African Archaeol. Bulletin* 45, 5–16.

MacWhite, E. 1946. A new view on Irish Bronze Age rock-scribings, *J. Royal Soc. Antiqs Ireland* 76, 59–80.

O'Kelly, M. 1982. *Newgrange. Archaeology, Art and Legend*. London: Thames and Hudson.

O'Sullivan, M. 1986. Approaches to passage tomb art, *J. Royal Soc. Antiqs Ireland* 116, 68–83.

Scott, J. 1989. The stone circles at Temple Wood, Kilmartin, Argyll, *Glasgow Archaeol. J.* 15, 53–124.

Sharples, N. 1985. Individual and community: the changing role of megaliths in the Orcadian Neolithic, *Proc. Prehist. Soc.* 51, 59–74.

Shee Twohig, E. 1981. *The Megalithic Art of Western Europe*. Oxford: Clarendon Press.

Sheridan, A. 1987. Megaliths and megalomania. An account, and interpretation, of the development of passage tombs in Ireland, *J. Irish Archaeology* 2, 229–65.

Simpson, D. and Thawley, J. 1972. Single grave art in Britain, *Scottish Archaeol. Forum* 4, 81–104.

Simpson, J. 1867. *On Ancient Sculpturings of Cup and Concentric Rings, etc*. Edinburgh: Society of Antiquaries of Scotland.

Stevenson, J. 1993. Cup and ring markings at Ballochmyle, Ayrshire, *Glasgow Archaeol. J.* 11, 33–40.

Van Hoek, M. 1993. The spiral in British and Irish rock art, *Glasgow Archaeol. J.* 18, 11–32.

5. Evidence, North and South, in the earlier Neolithic

R. J. Mercer

Abstract: The paper reviews the nature of the evidence for early farming communities in Britain, contrasting Wessex with the north of Scotland, considering what archaeological traces such communities might have left in the landscapes of those two areas and what this implies for the wider use of archaeological evidence.

My rôle as chairman, at a conference which will always remain in my memory for the sparkling quality of its atmosphere, whether academic or social, was to introduce three first rate contributions in an area where John Coles commenced his British career – Scottish archaeology. Having graduated in the fens, John, with that acumen for which he is so admired, chose to study for his doctorate at the University of Edinburgh under Stuart Piggott. The product of that study was prodigious, trend-setting on a British (and wider) scale and has established a bench-mark for Scottish prehistoric studies that we in Scotland have sought to emulate ever since (Coles 1959–60, 1963–64, 1968–69). To have studied under both Grahame Clark and Stuart Piggott must, in itself, be something of a distinction (I think unique, actually) and that distinction has lent itself to all of John's many achievements ever since. I salute those achievements and look forward to many more. John's return to Scotland in 1992 as a Commissioner for RCAHMS was widely welcomed and his contribution in this sphere, as in so many others, has been enormous.

Scotland is a country that can be compared closely with England in the extraordinary variety of its landscape and the division of that landscape into a highland and lowland zone. That division, first mooted in archaeological terms by Fox (1923), has traditionally been seen as one of relative poverty *versus* prosperity. To Fox, his thoughts dominated by the Invasion Hypothesis (Clark 1966) and, like Erskine Childers (1903), with a 'neurosis' focused upon the east, withdrawal into a twilight zone in the west emphasising its poverty was the model. Now we perhaps see the western and northern margins of Britain as areas of unique attraction to early farming communities with their light calcareous soils and ubiquitous fresh and saltwater resources.

Like England, Scotland has also endured a partial and, perhaps, self-indulgent imbalance in the geographical disposition of prehistoric archaeological investigation. In England the imbalance has been self-perpetuating since the early seventeenth century as the monumentality of Wessex archaeology has been analysed and interpreted by Inigo Jones and his successors. There, from the earliest times, monumentality, and individual (or perceived individual) burial with its (by British standards) great wealth has created a sustained image of a chronologically perspectiveless hierarchical society that has proved easy to assimilate. That image has lasted more or less unbroken to the present day through Stonehenge's Druids (Stukeley 1740), and Colt Hoare's (1812) view of the societies with which he felt he was dealing, to Piggott's immigrant warriors (Piggott 1938) and Renfrew's emergent chiefdoms (Renfrew 1979).

In Scotland the story is deceptively similar, but actually rather different. The lands set on either side of the Pentland Firth, Caithness and Orkney, have, like Wesssex, been long admired for the monumentality of sites of all ages. The Rev George Barry (1805) saw brochs and chambered

Author's Address: R. J. Mercer, Royal Commission on the Ancient and Historical Monuments of Scotland, John Sinclair House, 16 Bernard Terrace, Edinburgh, EH8 9NX

tombs ('Pict's Houses') as Pictish – equating them, as Stukeley had before him, to the earliest cultural horizon evidenced (sketchily) in the written record. It was not until Daniel Wilson (1863) brought Science to bear that a comparison with (principally) Scandinavian material saw at least the stone circles/settings and chambered tombs allocated to the Neolithic. And from the 1850s with Rhind and Anderson (1886) and later Tress Barry in Caithness and then in Orkney George Petrie, further knowledge and understanding of these northern sites grew. A second, golden age of investigation began in the 1920s with Childe's excavations at Skara Brae (beginning in 1927), at Rinyo on Rousay, as well as his series of excavations on Rousay chambered cairns (Childe & Grant 1939; Childe 1942).

A third period of extraordinarily intense and methodologically advanced activity began in the early seventies with excavation at Skara Brae (Clarke & Sharples 1985), Stenness (Ritchie 1976) and Quanterness (Renfrew 1979). So intensive was the activity that the archipelago was termed a 'laboratory'. Sadly it is not for the archaeologist to choose his laboratory, although s/he can of course choose which part of it to work in. To use Orkney as a 'think tank', or Wessex, was to court problems that have, I believe, bedevilled Neolithic and Bronze Age studies for half a century. Both areas are untypical in a whole gamut of ways:–

a) The field archaeology of both areas is 'site-exaggerated'. Sites, by virtue of their often indestructable stature remain as divorced 'islands' within a landscape effectively levelled by successive agricultural activity over five millennia.
b) The landscape that might serve to mediate between these sites is absent to surface view. In Wessex aerial photography has served to assist in a largely undifferentiated way with the 'filling' of the intermediate zones but has not, prior to late prehistory (late Bronze Age and Iron Age), brought about any real articulation of the sites.
c) In both landscapes, fieldwork undertaken to assist directly with the process of articulation is, and has been, rare. Important exceptions exist – for example the work of Julian Richards in the Stonehenge area and Colin Richards on Mainland Orkney – in both cases methodologically exemplary but not (so far) followed up.
d) In Wessex fieldwork is assisted (although evaluation is still in its infancy) by the ubiquitous presence of easily recognisable and classified struck flint. This ubiquity is revealed by the current prevalent regime of agriculture that favours arable, by no means typically in England – and barely significant in Orkney (as a proportion of total land surface), where flint is anyway so rare that sites as rich and fully excavated as Knap of Howar produce relatively tiny amounts (which nevertheless includes one fragmentary leaf arrowhead – that classic British early Neolithic type). The quartzite industries that dominate the North and West of Scotland defy easy categorisation or even, in the eye of the unskilled, recognition. As for field collection, in a land where arable production is a minority pursuit, where field walking is an eccentricity, and where the objective is barely recognisable, there is little tradition of activity.
e) Pottery is plentiful on sites in Orkney. Of a minimum of 78 pots present at the Knap of Howar settlement site, some 40 comprise vessels of a plain-bowl form with no, or only very minimal, decoration that would not look out of place, even in terms of fabric, at Carn Brea in Cornwall. Per square metre excavated, the quantities recovered resembled closely those at Carn Brea, but this density is not replicated (per area excavated) at any of the monumental sites of Wessex or at any of the chambered tombs in Orkney.
f) In one other regard does the evidential spectrum from the North and South coincide – in the frequent presence of animal bone in well preserved condition. At the Knap of Howar in Orkney, on the basis of the minimum number of individual animals calculated as present (Noddle, in Ritchie 1983) the proportion of 50% sheep, 40% cattle, 9% pig and 1% 'other' has a remarkably close relationship with the proportions among the species at Hambledon Hill and other contemporary sites in Wessex. In the south, of course, the relationship between sheep and cattle is reversed (as one might expect anyway), but the near absence of wild species on these early Neolithic sites and the low presence of pig suggest an economy that is broadly similar in its inspiration.
g) Both Orkney and Wessex offer significant difficulties for the palaeoenvironmentalist. In Orkney a wide range of materials for study exist in a variety of environments. Yet the key issue that determines (or at present would appear to determine) the impact of man on a landscape – the degree of clearance – is uncertainly divided between anthropogenic considerations and those more closely related to the unusual situation of the archipelago. In Wessex the information that we have relating to palaeoenvironment is even less satisfactory. The sources of information are limited, and hopelessly biased, with the result that our understanding of the nature of the landscape in Neolithic and Bronze Age in Wessex is flawed despite the pioneering efforts of Bob Smith (1984).

Absence of evidence has tacitly been construed as evidence of absence and 'partial evidence for' construed as 'evidence of'. As a consequence our perception of Neolithic and Bronze Age society in Britain has become one dominated by monumental conceptions framed in a misunderstood landscape. This misunderstanding has fuelled a desire, anyway inherent in a culture cowering in the face of the unacceptable costs of agricultural intensification, of minimal agricultural activity in what has become known as a 'ritual landscape'.

The difficulty lies in the absence of evidence. Many of the 'monumental' structures (with labour inputs in the 10–100K man-hour range) produce the earliest dates (Kinnes 1988) for the Neolithic in Wessex. It has therefore been concluded that monumentalisation was a conceptual process that created a medium within which intensified farming could eventually, but by no means immediately, emerge (Thomas 1991, 180–84).

In Orkney it is, if in a completely different setting, broadly similar. Here radiocarbon dating once again places us *in medias res* in the development of a seemingly mature monumental architectural tradition with little by way of prologue to allow the emergence of any appropriate economic infra-structure. In Orkney, however, settlements apparently contemporary (on C14 grounds) and apparently closely linked socially (on ceramic grounds) occur, notably the settlement at Knap of Howar (Ritchie 1983).

With obvious and acceptable stylistic and environmental differentiation the 'package' recovered by Anna Ritchie at Knap of Howar is very similar to and contemporary with that recovered at Hambledon Hill in Dorset (Mercer 1988). Viewed on the European spectrum the cultural and economic aspect of both sites as archaeologically expressed is very similar – amazingly so given the difference of their respective surroundings.

How do we visualise this happening? Do we really see people moving very rapidly over a six hundred mile stretch of the Atlantic facade, with an infinitely adjustable capacity for variation to deal with circumstances – and yet with the 'cultural will' to retain detailed aspects of lithic, ceramic and other technology, solely in order to construct 'ritual landscapes' that symbolise changed priorities and approaches? Why must our interpretation of our insular Neolithic be so very insular?

Rapid transmission of cultural innovation into distant locations whence complex and variant cultural development occurs is, from the advent of LBK culture in Europe, a well established model of the advent and development of farming culture. It is based upon a relatively well understood sequence from detectable and clearly related origins and frequently finds itself challenged, but not unseated, by specific palaeo-environmental evidence in individual locations. In Britain we suffer one intellectually overwhelming problem. We do not understand the origins of our first farming culture and when we do first encounter it it appears, in insular terms, to be 'eclectic' (an adjective used by generations of scholars), as though someone had taken a shopping-trolley on an impulse-buying spree from Iberia to Poland. Whether at the Knap of Howar or at Carn Brea (Mercer 1981) or at Hambledon Hill (Mercer 1988) they appear in fully developed and often monumentalised form. Furthermore the immensely impressive and ubiquitous artillery of palaeo-environmental investigation that is brought up in support seems to be of little assistance. There are 'straws in the wind' (Edwards & Ralston 1984), as soon gathered together as blown away by those who wish to develop the model before we have cracked the problem.

We must ask if pollen analysis is likely to detect the first clearings in an already variegated landscape – and one already 'broken' by Mesolithic groups – especially if the majority of palynological studies have been undertaken in locations that must rank as marginal by early farming standards. But more importantly we must question whether archaeologists have even been trying to dig in the right places to achieve a balanced resolution of the nature and development of our earliest farming societies.

Where then are we to seek this earliest occupation? – a question which relates as much to the northern part of Britain as any other. For any area the answer must lie in seaward or riverine settings where woodland margins, already contracted, offered hospitable and seaward tenure. In the north of Britain isostatic recovery offers considerable possibilities for the location and investigation of such sites that sadly are unlikely to be available in southern Britain. Sites like Morton, in Fife (Coles 1971, 1983) may well conceal other components that might relate to an earlier, so far undocumented, period of farming exploitation that established the societies that were able to create an 'economic landscape' within which monumentalism came to have an important rôle to play.

It is no coincidence that this very short contribution ends with reference to John Coles. John has never contented himself with the further exploration of the already well-known. Morton represented a revolutionary approach in Scotland in the 1960s, and the 1970s and 80s saw the Coles's brilliant exploration in other *terra incognita* – recovering the astounding archaeology (much of it related to our early Neolithic) of the Somerset Levels (Coles & Coles 1986)

We will not solve this fundamental problem of British later prehistory unless we adapt our strategies to looking in the right place. Until we have undertaken that necessary labour we should, perhaps, not seek to apply universal explanations on the basis of biased, incomplete and misinformative data sets.

Bibliography

Anderson, J. 1886. *Scotland in Pagan Times: the Bronze and Stone Ages* (Rhind Lectures in Archaeology for 1882). Edinburgh: Douglas.

Barry, Rev. G. 1805. *The History of the Orkney Islands*. Edinburgh: privately published.

Childe, V.G. 1942. The chambered cairns of Rousay, *Antiq. J.* 22, 139–42.

Childe V.G. and Grant W.G. 1938–39. A stone age settlement at the Braes of Rinyo, Rousay, Orkney (First Report), *Proc. Soc. Antiq. Scotland* 73, 6–31.

Childers, E. 1903. *The Riddle of the Sands. A record of secret service recently achieved.* London: Smith, Elder & Co.

Clark, J.G.D. 1966. The invasion hypothesis in British prehistory, *Antiquity* 49, 172–89.

Clarke, D.V. and Sharples, N. 1985. Settlements and subsistence in the third millennium BC. In C. Renfrew (ed) *The Prehistory of Orkney*, 54–82. Edinburgh: Edinburgh University Press.

Coles, B. and J. 1986. *Sweet Track to Glastonbury*. London: Thames and Hudson.

Coles, J.M. 1959–60 [1962]. Scottish Late Bronze Age metalwork, *Proc. Soc. Antiq. Scotland* 93, 16–134.

Coles, J.M. 1963–64 [1966]. Scottish Middle Bronze Age metalwork, *Proc. Soc. Antiq. Scotland* 97, 82–156.

Coles, J.M. 1968–69 [1970]. Scottish Early Bronze Age metalwork, *Proc. Soc. Antiq. Scotland* 101, 1–110.

Coles, J.M. 1971. The early settlement of Scotland: excavations at Morton, Fife, *Proc. Prehist. Soc.* 37, 284–366.

Coles, J.M. 1983. Morton revisited. In A. O'Connor and D.V. Clarke (eds.) *From the Stone Age to the 'Forty-five*, 9–18. Edinburgh: John Donald.

Colt Hoare, R. 1812. *Ancient History of Wiltshire*. London: W. Miller.

Edwards, K.J. and Ralston, I.B.M. 1984. Post-glacial hunter-gatherers and vegetational history in Scotland, *Proc. Soc. Antiq. Scotland* 114, 15–34.

Fox, C. 1932. *The Personality of Britain*. Cardiff: National Museum of Wales.

Kinnes, I. 1988. The Cattleship Potemkin: reflections on the first Neolithic in Britain. In Barrett J.C. and Kinnes I. (eds) *The Archaeology of Context in the Neolithic and Bronze Age: Recent Trends*, 2–8. Sheffield: Department of Prehistory and Archaeology, University of Sheffield.

Mercer, R.J. 1981. *Excavations at Carn Brea, Illogan, Cornwall 1970–73 – a Neolithic fortified complex of the third millennium bc*. [Exeter]: Cornwall Archaeological Society.

Mercer, R.J. 1988. Hambledon Hill, Dorset, England. In C. Burgess, P. Topping, C. Mordant and M. Maddison (eds), *Enclosures and Defences in the Neolithic of Western Europe*, 89–106. Oxford: British Archaeol. Reports Int. Series 403.

Piggott, S. 1938. The Early Bronze Age in Wessex, *Proc. Prehist. Soc.* 4, 52–106.

Renfrew, A.C. 1979. *Investigations in Orkney*. London: Society of Antiquaries Research Report 38.

Ritchie, A. 1983. Excavation of a Neolithic farmstead at Knap of Howar, Papa Westray, Orkney, *Proc. Soc. Antiq. Scotland* 113, 40–121.

Ritchie, J.N.G. 1976. The Stones of Stenness, Orkney, *Proc. Soc. Antiq. Scotland* 107, 1–60.

Smith, R.W. 1984. The ecology of Neolithic farming systems as exemplified by the Avebury region of Wiltshire, *Proc. Prehist. Soc.* 50, 99–120.

Stukeley, W. 1740. *Stonehenge: A Temple Restored to the British Druids*.

Thomas, J. 1991. *Rethinking the Neolithic*. Cambridge: Cambridge University Press.

Wilson, D. 1863. *Prehistoric Annals of Scotland*. London: Macmillan.

6. The Birth of the Scottish Bronze Age

J.N. Graham Ritchie

Abstract: The concept of the Scottish Bronze Age as set out by Victorian scholars has proved to be very resistant to change in popular perceptions of archaeology. The various strands of archaeological evidence available at the first stages of writing about the Scottish Bronze Age are explored, including burials and associated pottery, monuments and bronzework. Fieldwork and excavation have radically changed archaeological perceptions and approaches to the presentation of "Bronze Age" Britain, as for example in the recent travelling Council of Europe Exhibition, but there has been less success in redefining the popular view of the ways in which this particular slice of time might be seen. The particular contribution of Joseph Anderson, Keeper of the National Museum of Antiquities of Scotland, in codifying Scotland in Pagan Times is considered, as well as the role that modern survey methods have had in widening our understanding of the prehistoric landscape.

Bronze Age Research

John Coles has played a crucial role in how we classify bronzework in Scotland today in a series of papers that have set the pattern for research (1959–60, 1963–64, 1968–69). With Professor Stuart Piggott as supervisor, this work included a trip around north-east Scottish museums that took them to Elgin, where an unmarked array of bronzes was proudly taken off display for study. "But none of these bronzes has any identifying markings", they cried. "Aye", said the curator, "but I've got all the labels that were with them", he said, brandishing a Food Vessel with some yellowing museum labels sticking out. But which were which? John Coles successfully managed to make sense of this unsatisfactory body of material, as he has done since in so many different fields.

John Coles is a Commissioner on the Royal Commission on the Ancient and Historical Monuments of Scotland, the body charged with the survey of archaeological sites (and buildings and industrial monuments), as well as the presentation of the results both through the national archive, the National Monuments Record of Scotland, and through publications. Since the creation of the Royal Commission in 1908, the publication of the fruits of survey has taken the form of site by site descriptions with an introductory essay. In musing about a suitable topic on which to record his gratitude to the contribution of John Coles to the archaeology of Scotland, the present writer recalled that one of his own first duties within the Royal Commission was to compile the List of Bronze Age Pottery and Metalwork found in Kintyre for the first volume of the *Inventory of Argyll*, and the preparation of the distribution map of Bronze Age artefacts, with Bronzes – Early, Middle, and Late, and pottery – Beakers, Food Vessels and Cinerary Urns. It was in the days when archaeologists *knew* what the Bronze Age was, and, like all good stories, it had a beginning, a middle and an end. Such a list had first been published in the Roxburgh *Inventory* in 1956 to show that the Royal Commission understood that the recording of archaeology went beyond the field monuments of any area. The list format was to continue throughout the *Argyll* series of *Inventory* volumes till 1988, and it certainly had its uses in flagging settlement sites in sand-dunes, for which there were no visible remains.

Author's Address: J.N. Graham Ritchie, 50/1 Spylaw Road, Edinburgh, EH10 5BL

Fig. 6.1. Flesh-fork, Killeonan, Kintyre, Argyll. Inveraray Castle Collections. Crown Copyright: Royal Commission on the Ancient and Historical Monuments of Scotland. Scale 1:4.

Bronzes – Late had been tidied up by John Coles in the *Proceedings of the Society of Antiquaries of Scotland* of 1959–60, Bronzes – Middle in 1963–4, and Bronzes – Early in 1968–9. The *Inventory* listing produced one piece of archaeologically important information, which was that the flesh-fork in Inveraray Castle (Fig. 6.1), published by Coles (1959–60, 25, 91), had certainly been the second part of a discovery at Killeonan, in Kintyre, in 1908 and was not unlocated as had previously been thought; the papers in the Kintyre Antiquarian Society archive in Campbeltown Museum, unavailable to Coles, left no doubt about the provenance of this exciting object (NGR: NR *ca.* 684188). The earlier discovery at Killeonan, in 1884, comprised five swords, a chape, a spearhead and eleven flint flakes (Coles 1959–60, 103–4; RCAHMS 1971, 12,14), drawings of these bronzes having been exhibited to the Society of Antiquaries of Scotland by Lady Constance Campbell.[1] In the present contribution the flesh-fork is also illustrated as an icon of the Late Bronze Age in a comparatively isolated part of the west coast of Scotland; we can see that there was Late Bronze Age activity, but we do not understand the framework of sites within which it is taking place.

The neatness of the *Inventory* lists and maps belied a very limited understanding of this period on the ground. The differing approaches to linking artefactual evidence to that of field recording is a theme that will be explored later.

The museum accession number was a vital part of the information that had to be prepared, and the economy of the system used by the National Museum of Antiquities of Scotland was intriguing, the neat DC 39 or DE 11. The system had clearly been worked out during the Keepership of Joseph Anderson (Fig. 6.2), and it was used in the National Museum of Antiquities of Scotland *Catalogue* of 1892. Anderson's role in creating a Bronze Age for Scotland was very positive, but field-survey and excavation have provided new perspectives. Yet the late Victorian picture of the Bronze Age is difficult to budge from popular understanding, even in the light of modern research. Joseph Anderson was not the first to write an overview of the Scottish Bronze Age. The pioneer was Daniel Wilson in 1851 and 1863, who in scientific spirit looked into the composition of copper and bronze artefacts. "The works of the Bronze Period possess an entirely new and distinct source of interest from those which preceded them, in so far as they exhibit not only the skill and ingenuity which is prompted by necessity, but also the graceful form and decoration which give evidence of the pleasurable exercise of thought and fancy" (Wilson 1851, 250). He follows Worsaae in thinking that an entirely new race of people must be represented. "We must look, indeed, upon this whole period, as upon the early years of an intelligent child: rich with the freshness, the originality, and the unconscious simplicity of youth" (Wilson 1863, 489).

Joseph Anderson's Rhind Lectures

The Rhind Lectures are among the most prestigious, perhaps the most ancient, lecture series north of the

Fig. 6.2. Joseph Anderson, by Henry Wright Kerr. Scottish National Portrait Gallery. Reproduced by kind permission of the National Galleries of Scotland.

Border – memorably delivered by John and Bryony Coles on Wetland Archaeology in 1995. Joseph Anderson delivered four series in a row between 1879–82, and he set the framework for the periodization of Scottish archaeology.

> "In view of their delivery to a popular audience, it seemed", he said, "desirable to make the systematic nature of the investigation a matter of continuous demonstration. Regarding the historical method of dealing with prehistoric materials as wholly inapplicable to them, it behoved me to adopt and substitute a purely scientific method. Instead of commencing with the story of primeval man, and leading the narration downwards (as if drawing it from a record), it was necessary to select a starting-place in the region of history bordering on the prehistoric, from which by tracing upwards, through the unrecorded ages, the interlinked succession of types and systems, I might penetrate as far towards the primitive conditions of human life in Scotland as the materials might serve to carry the investigation" (1886, v–vi).

The three lectures on the Age of Bronze cover *Bronze Age Burials, Circles, and Settings of Standing Stones*, and *Weapons, Implements, etc., of the Bronze Age*.

> "The Age of Bronze has been defined to be that stage of progress towards the existing culture and civilisation which manifested itself in the construction of cutting tools and weapons of bronze" (1886, 2).

Anderson also distinguished between the styles of ornamentation in the Bronze and Iron Ages. In the Iron Age the system was one of curvilinear decoration – the curves not being parts of circles. In the Bronze Age, however, he identified a "rectilinear decoration associated with occasional circles or parts of circles. Again this distinctive system of ornamentation of the Bronze Age is associated with a very remarkable development of sepulchral pottery, the entire absence of which was found to be one of the most striking features of the Iron Age deposits of Scotland, so far as they are yet known" (1886, 3).

At the risk of labouring the point, it is important to stress the systematic nature of Anderson's work, which still sees expression in the Museum Accession number EQ for items found together in Cists, Graves, or Cemeteries, chiefly of the Early Bronze Age, underlining the essential concept of thinking about groups of objects found together, and in comparable contexts. Association was certainly his major methodological tool: gold lunulae could be ascribed to the Bronze Age because of their association at Padstow, in Cornwall, with flat axe-heads of bronze.

Cist burials associated round cairns with such funerary vessels (some even with axe-markings on the slabs), as well as cup-and ring markings as at Nether Largie North or Caerlowrie, and linked stone circles, sites that are now described as henge monuments (such as the Ring of Brodgar, Orkney) and stone rows into the framework. Such monumental structures were associated with the burial traditions of the Bronze Age by the discovery of Cinerary Urns, and indeed a cremation within the stone circle at Balbirnie, in Fife, was associated with several fragments of a thin blade of bronze. He had created a Bronze Age of grand monuments.

Yet of settlement sites there was no evidence:

> "Although we know nothing whatever of their household arrangements, or the manners and customs of their domestic life, seeing that not a trace or a dwelling or site of a settlement of the Bronze Age has been discovered in Scotland, yet we are not without evidence of an indirect nature to indicate that they could not have been wholly destitute of the comforts and conveniences of life" (1886, 227).

What Anderson was able to evoke from the Bronze Age of his vision was a

> "people who supplied themselves with implements and weapons in this capable and cultured way, also used gold occasionally in the mounting of their weapons, and most lavishly in personal adornment.... If life with them was a struggle for existence, we look in vain for its memorials; but there is no wide district of the country in which the memorials of their dead are not prominent, picturesque and familiar features. In this, no less than in the varied phenomena of their burial customs, the preparation of the funeral pile, the fabrication of the finely ornamented urns, and the costly dedications of articles of use or adornment, freely renounced by the survivors, and set apart from the inheritance of the living as grave-goods for the dead, we realise the intensity of their devotion to filial memories and family ties, to hereditary honour and ancestral tradition" (1886, 227).

This is heady Victorian prose, but it demonstrates Anderson's sense of respect and very personal evocation of the people represented by the objects of his study.

A.O. Curle and J. Graham Callander

Curle's work as Secretary to the Royal Commission on the Ancient and Historical Monuments of Scotland led to the identification of many new archaeological sites in the field, particularly in Caithness and Sutherland, hut-circles and small cairns among others, but their date remained uncertain. Excavations at Muirkirk, Ayrshire, led to the association of this class of monument with Beaker pottery, the pottery being written up by Curle, who was by 1913 Director of the National Museum of Antiquities of Scotland (Baird 1913–14). His successor as Director, John Graham Callander, made many notable contributions to Scottish archaeology; the three collected volumes of his papers contain ninety-one individual pieces, including a systematic examination of Bronze Age hoards (1922–23) and jet necklaces (1915–16). He had for a short period been Archaeologist to the Royal Commission and his approach to field monuments was one that today's field surveyor readily recognises. In a lecture to the Dumfriesshire and Galloway Natural History and Antiquarian Society in March 1924 he said

> "We have seen that no dwelling sites of the Stone Age have been recorded in the county, and although none has actually been proved as belonging to the Bronze Age, there is good reason to believe that the small hut-circles found in juxta-position to the small cairns which occur in groups in many parts of our area, belong to this period. Three of these structures in Ayrshire have yielded pottery belonging to this time. Groups of small cairns and accompanying hut-circles are found in profusion in many parts of Scotland, usually at an elevation of 700 to 900 feet above sea level, and frequently they occur in the neighbourhood of un-doubted Bronze Age cairns and stone circles" (1923–24, 103).

V. Gordon Childe

Gordon Childe expressed his admiration of Joseph Anderson's work, writing in *The Prehistory of Scotland* that he "had sketched the essential outlines of Scottish prehistory in a comprehensive and scientific study such as then existed in no other country" (1935, xi). Childe (Fig. 6.3) reviewed a similar range of material to that examined by Anderson, with the benefit of Lord Abercromby's work on Beaker pottery, and the first chapter of this section is titled 'The Round-headed Invasions'. Perhaps a trailer title for an *X-Files* plot.

"To-day," he wrote, "it is generally admitted that independent landings may have taken place at several points along the east coast of Scotland as well as of England" (1935, 81). Among settlements he was prepared to cite Skara Brae, which he had originally published as Pictish and which is now known to be Neolithic. With Jarlshof in Shetland he was on firmer ground – and it remains one of the few sites where metal-working is firmly associated with a settlement, though the smith was using an already existing building.

Childe envisaged Early Bronze Age communities as "exceedingly small and far from rooted in the soil.... The impression of semi-nomadism is enhanced by the few glimpses of habitation available – a few middens near the coast and isolated hut-circles on a hillside. Tillage was undoubtedly practised, but it need have been no more than the cultivation with a digging stick or foot-plough of a small plot which was abandoned after a few seasons. Life would have been to an extent nomadic and largely dependent on pastoralism and hunting for which Scotland was so well fitted. If this is correct, the total population, considering the restrictions imposed by mountains, forests, and swamps, may have been quite small" (1935, 122). A very different impression to that offered by Anderson, where family ties and hereditary honour would surely have transcended the swampiness of the surroundings!

Excavation and radiocarbon dating has changed our perceptions about stone circles and henges, and we are more aware of the length of time over which a monument may have undergone construction and reconstruction. Finds from secondary cists have no place in the dating of the original construction.

Henges and stone circles are now known to be Neolithic in origin. Stuart Piggott's excavation at Dalladies, in Kincardineshire, showed that the tradition of cupmarks was equally early (1971–2, 45). Jack Scott's excavations at Temple Wood in Argyll have underlined the Neolithic date for stone circles and have offered a fascinating sequence of construction and reconstruction throughout the third and second millennia BC (1988–9). The old Bronze Age was looking a bit thin.

Fig. 6.3. Gordon Childe. Crown Copyright: Royal Commission on the Ancient and Historical Monuments of Scotland.

Current Approaches to Field Survey

But it is fieldwork coupled with excavation and a greater understanding of the environmental framework that has provided the bulk of the evidence for settlement sites and field systems, and a completely new Bronze Age has emerged, with the bronzes sitting uncertainly within an entirely different set of monuments. The realization that the field boundary emerging from the original ground surface beneath the peat covering the Moss of Achnacree must be of early date prompted small-scale excavation in 1969 and 1971 (Ritchie *et al.* 1974). The only comparable site that had previously been reported was at Cul a'Bhaile, on Jura, where a hut-circle with a surrounding field-wall

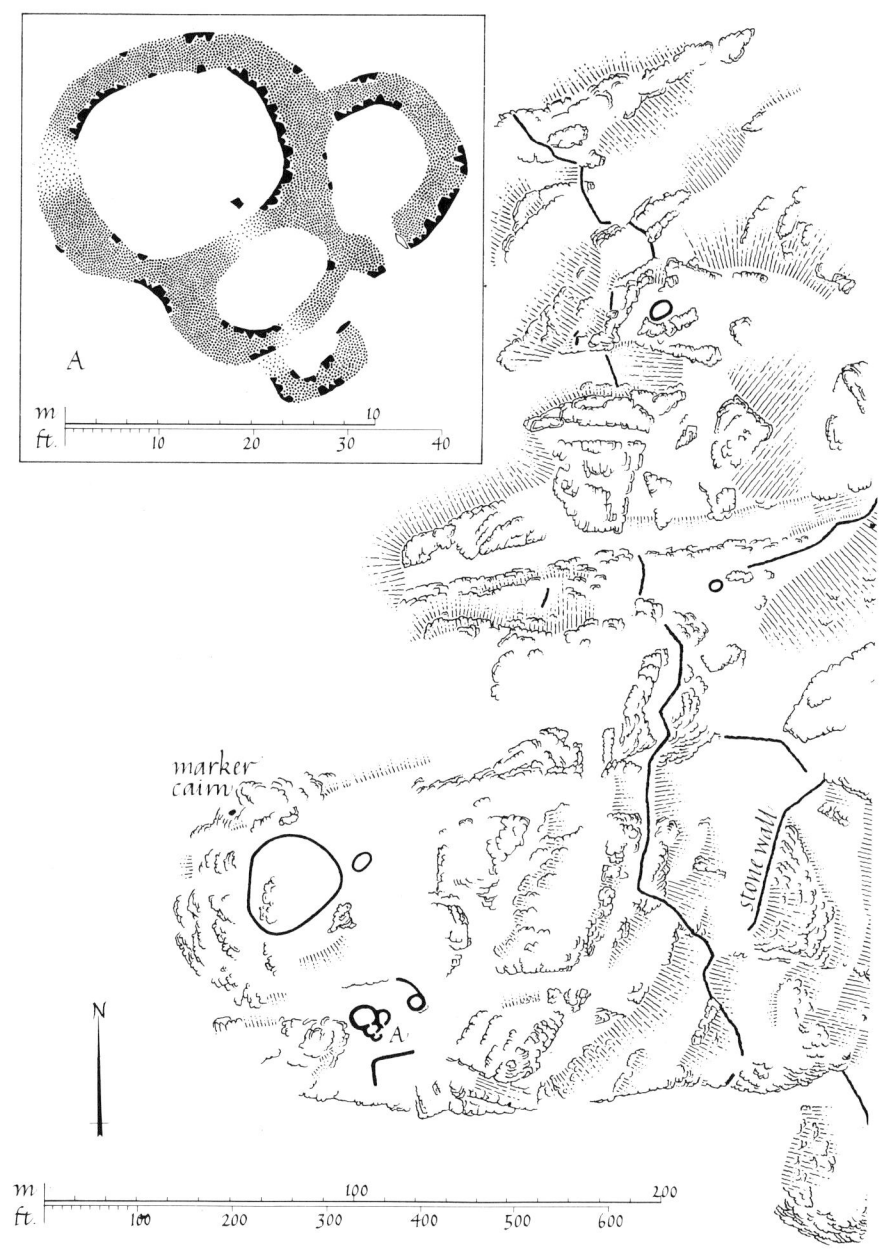

Fig. 6.4. Beinn Arnicil, Colonsay, Argyll, hut-circle and field-system. Crown Copyright: Royal Commission on the Ancient and Historical Monuments of Scotland.

appearing from below a covering of peat had been noted by Marion Campbell of Kilberry and Mary Sandeman.[2] The hut-circle was to be the subject of excavation by my colleague Jack Stevenson (1984). Survey work by Roger Mercer on Arran, followed up by excavation by John Barber, was by the 1970s at last creating a later third and second millennium landscape for Scotland, a landscape that could be recorded with greater insight than ever before (outlined by Cowie & Shepherd 1997, 158–65). The planning of hut-circles with associated field-systems and groups of small cairns became the staple fare of the highland archaeologist, together with the slotting of the fragments of environmental evidence into any local framework.

It would be wrong not to mention burnt mounds, for John Hedges' work in Orkney and John Barber's on Islay flagged a class of monument that has now been identified whenever fieldwork has been undertaken. The sites are often located in situations beside streams and in damp patches. Unenclosed platform settlements are now seen to belong to the second millennium BC (Cowie & Shepherd 1997, 158–9). It is difficult now to evoke the reluctance of many archaeologists in the 1970s to accept the notion that such field boundaries, hut-circles, and small cairns mattered (they would be horrified by the care now taken in plotting burnt mounds). But it may be that it was a residue of the "prominent, picturesque and familiar" vision of Anderson and the sophistication of bronze

Fig. 6.5. An Sithean, Islay, Argyll, hut-circles and field-system. Crown Copyright: Royal Commission on the Ancient and Historical Monuments of Scotland.

technology (particularly Late Bronze Age technology) that helped to reinforce the sense of disbelief.

The planning of the Bronze Age landscape is one of these areas where technological advance came along at just the right time. Plane-table survey, single monument survey, was overtaken first by the Self-Reducing Alidade (SRA) and then by the Electronic Distance Measurer (EDM), which allowed the distributions of houses, field-systems and small cairns to be mapped readily and economically. The technological developments are fully explained by Halliday and Stevenson (1991, 133–4). The contribution of the former Archaeology Division of the Ordnance Survey in illustrating this shift of emphasis was outlined by Feachem (1973). The countryside cried out to be surveyed; nothing less would do. The vision had changed. And of course this was not just happening in Scotland, nor indeed first in Scotland. Nor just for the Bronze Age. Once an idea becomes a picture it is much more difficult to sweep aside. Childe's "isolated hut-circle on a hill-side" became a pattern of houses and fields in a landscape, graphically illustrated by the survey of North-East Perth (RCAHMS 1990).

From a personal point of view, the catalyst was Beinn Arnicil, on Colonsay (Fig. 6.4), where we tried to survey a hillside over several periods of fieldwork with a simple plane-table and tape, and we failed to capture what we saw. Then we got an SRA and did not look back. The single, rather complex, hut-circle – once considered to be too well-preserved to be prehistoric – could be set within its field-system of little walls edging the rocky ridges of the hillside (RCAHMS 1984, 130–1, No. 244). The cairns and systems on Druim Mor, Oronsay, "surely quite recent", could be captured on plan with a hut-circle, surely prehistoric! (RCAHMS 1984, 135–6, No. 257). The hut-circles on An Sithean, Islay, were initially dismissed as sheilings of comparatively recent date until their form was properly understood (Fig. 6.5) (RCAHMS 1984, 123–6, No. 237).

If the bronzes have still rarely been associated with settlement sites, pottery has fared rather better. So much more is known about the settlement sites of the makers of Beaker pottery with excavations such as those of John Barber on Arran and Derek Simpson at Northton, on Harris. Though hardly typical, the excavations at Ardnave, on Islay, provided evidence of a settlement site associated with a classic Food Vessel, and overlying middens offered an important range of later ceramic styles, some with Irish parallels, in a settlement context.

The burial traditions of the later second millennium and earlier first millennium BC are also more fully documented with small cairns such as Claggan, Morvern, Argyll, representing comparatively simple cremations, but this was doubtless a sequence of ritual acts, which are difficult to disentangle from the surviving archaeological evidence.

But where do the spectacular and warlike Late Bronze Age objects that began this consideration fit into this comparatively domestic and agricultural picture?

For if we believe that we are beginning to understand the landscape, and the gaps in the tapestry are beginning to fill up for the first millennium AD and for early medieval Scotland, we must make some suggestions for the Bronze Age. Clearly the flesh-fork and hoard of swords, the symbols of the Late Bronze Age invoked at the beginning of this paper, betoken something new in the archaeological record. But it is hard to imagine the flesh-fork beside the trough of a burnt mound. There is the suspicion that many of the hill-top enclosures may have an earlier origin than is usually considered. Crucibles of Late Bronze Age date have been identified from Eildon Hill North, Traprain and Green Castle, Portknockie (Spearman, in Rideout et al. 1992, 46), though there is as yet no evidence from limited number of excavations in the West.

Anderson had a fine peroration to his final Bronze Age lecture:

"But we attain to this realisation [of respect for Bronze Age people] only by patient investigation, and after a long course of sustained and laborious effort to gather and preserve the mutilated relics and memorials of the piety and industry, the culture and civilisation, of our Bronze Age ancestors. For in our ironshod progress we trample out the footmarks of those who thus travelled before us. We demolish their monuments, we plough their graves, we scatter their bones. We do this as if it were a necessity of civilisation, and we do it with the less compunction that we call them savages" (1886, 228).

Acknowledgements

The advice of Dr Alison Sheridan and Dr David Clarke, Royal Museum of Scotland, and Dr Anna Ritchie is gratefully acknowledged.

Notes

1 *Proc. Soc. Antiq. Scotland* 19, 1884–85, 12–14.
2 *Discovery and Excavation in Scotland in 1966*, 9.

Bibliography

Anderson, J. 1886. *Scotland in Pagan Times: the Bronze and Stone Ages* (Rhind Lectures in Archaeology for 1882). Edinburgh: Douglas.

Baird, J.G.A. 1913–14. Account of the excavation of two hut-circles of the Bronze Age, in the parish of Muirkirk, Ayrshire, *Proc. Soc. Antiq. Scotland* 48, 373–81.

Callander, J.G. 1915–16. Notice of a jet necklace found in a cist in a Bronze Age cemetery, discovered on Burgie Lodge, Morayshire, with notes on Scottish prehistoric jet ornaments, *Proc. Soc. Antiq. Scotland* 50, 201–40.

Callander, J.G. 1922–3. Scottish Bronze Age hoards, *Proc. Soc. Antiq. Scotland* 57, 123–66.

Callander, J.G. 1923–4. Dumfriesshire in the Stone, Bronze and Early Iron Ages, *Trans. Dumfriesshire & Galloway Natural History and Antiq. Soc.*, 3rd series 11, 97–119.

Childe, V.G. 1935. *The Prehistory of Scotland*. London: Kegan Paul, Trench, Trubner.

Coles, J.M. 1959–60 [1962]. Scottish Late Bronze Age metalwork: typology, distribution and chronology, *Proc. Soc. Antiq. Scotland* 93, 16–134.

Coles, J.M. 1963–4 [1966]. Scottish Middle Bronze Age metalwork, *Proc. Soc. Antiq. Scotland* 97, 82–156.

Coles, J.M. 1968–9 [1970]. Scottish Early Bronze Age metalwork, *Proc. Soc. Antiq. Scotland* 101, 1–110.

Cowie, T.G. and Shepherd, I.A.G. 1997. The Bronze Age. In Edwards, K.J. and Ralston, I.B.M. (eds) *Scotland: Environment and Archaeology, 800BC–AD1000*, 151–68. Chichester: Wiley.

Feachem, R.W. 1973. Ancient agriculture in the highland of Britain, *Proc. Prehist. Soc.* 39, 332–53.

Halliday, S.P. and Stevenson, J.B. 1991. Surveying for the future: RCAHMS Archaeological Survey 1908–1990. In Hanson, W.S. and Slater, E.A. (eds) *Scottish Archaeology: New Perceptions*, 129–39. Aberdeen: Aberdeen University Press.

Piggott, S. 1971–2 [1974]. Excavation of the Dalladies long barrow, Fettercairn, Kincardineshire, *Proc. Soc. Antiq. Scotland* 104, 23–47.

Rideout, J.S., Owen, O.A. and Halpin, E 1992. *Hillforts of Southern Scotland*. Historic Scotland, Monograph 1. Edinburgh: AOC (Scotland).

Ritchie, A., Ritchie, J.N.G., Whittington, G. and Soulsby, J. 1974. A prehistoric field-boundary from the Black Crofts, North Connel, Argyll, *Glasgow Archaeol. J.* 3, 66–70.

RCAHMS 1971. *Argyll: an Inventory of the Monuments, Kintyre*. Edinburgh: HMSO.

RCAHMS 1984. *Argyll: an Inventory of the Monuments, Islay,*

Jura, Colonsay and Oronsay. Edinburgh: HMSO.

RCAHMS 1990. *North- east Perth: an archaeological survey*. Edinburgh: HMSO.

Scott, J.G. 1988–9. The stone circles at Temple Wood, Kilmartin, Argyll, *Glasgow Archaeol. J.* 15, 53–124.

Stevenson, J.B. 1984. The excavation of a hut-circle at Cùl a'Bhaile, *Proc. Soc. Antiq. Scotland*, 114, 127–60.

Wilson, D. 1851. *The Archaeology and Prehistoric Annals of Scotland*. Edinburgh: Sutherland & Knox.

Wilson, D. 1863. *Prehistoric Annals of Scotland*. London: Macmillan.

Abbreviation

RCAHMS: Royal Commission on the Ancient and Historical Monuments of Scotland.

7. Drinking, driving, death and display: Scottish Bronze Age artefact studies since Coles

Alison Sheridan

Abstract: This chapter reviews developments in Scottish Bronze Age artefact studies since the publication of John Coles' papers on Scottish metalwork in the 1960s. New discoveries and new approaches are discussed, and their impact on our understanding of Scottish Bronze Age societies and economy is considered.

"During one of my visits to an archaeological and natural historical museum in east-central Scotland, one socketed axe was discovered lodged in a crocodile mouth in a corner of the disarrayed collection..." (Coles 1984, 421)

Introduction

In common with some of the contributors to this volume, I had the immense pleasure of being taught by John Coles, and the rather more questionable pleasure of being one of his *viva voce* examinees. There are also fond memories of excavating frozen peat, with a plastic spatula, lying on my belly, under John and Bryony's watchful eyes. Still, time is a great healer... and so this article is offered with gratitude and best wishes to John for having made archaeology not only thrilling but also *fun*.

John's contribution to Scottish Bronze Age artefact studies during the 1960s was not simply as the 'Crocodile Dundee' of axehead typology. His was the first serious attempt at a systematic collation of data on Bronze Age metal artefacts. Having listed them, he also placed them in a chronological framework (at a time when radiocarbon dates were not abundant); sought to define industrial traditions (using the recently-obtained results of the Stuttgart-based SAM metal analysis programme); and highlighted imports and influences from outside Scotland.

Furthermore, his experimental work (Coles 1973) dramatically demonstrated that certain bronze artefacts – the superbly crafted sheet bronze shields – were "for display purposes only", being part of a range of Late Bronze Age prestige possessions, used by a competitive and image-conscious elite.

The suite of articles about Scottish Bronze Age metalwork (Coles 1958–59; 1959–60; 1963–64; 1968–69) remains the bedrock of our understanding, and although subsequent work has led to a re-evaluation of some of the arguments, many others have been vindicated by the advances of the last three decades.

This paper begins by outlining the main developments in the study of Scottish Bronze Age metalwork since John's departure for balmy Cambridge, then broadens to consider other aspects of Bronze Age artefact studies which have helped to flesh out and modify the social and economic model implicit in his papers in the *Proceedings of the Society of Antiquaries of Scotland*.

Metalwork studies: striking it rich

Five developments have helped to broaden and deepen our understanding of Scottish Bronze Age metalwork: new descriptive and typological work; new artefact discoveries; further metallurgical analysis; refinement of chronology; and use-wear analysis.

Author's Address: Alison Sheridan, Department of Archaeology, National Museums of Scotland, Chambers Street, Edinburgh EH1 1JF

Descriptive and typological work

Several corpora featuring or encompassing Scottish Bronze Age metal artefacts have appeared since 1970. Prominent among these are the volumes in the *Prähistorische Bronzefunde* series, on axeheads (Schmidt & Burgess 1981), daggers (Gerloff 1975), dirks and rapiers (Burgess & Gerloff 1981) and swords (Colquhoun & Burgess 1988); Sabine Gerloff's forthcoming contribution on sheet bronze vessels will cover another key category of material. Gold artefacts are dealt with by Joan Taylor's *Prehistoric Goldwork of the British Isles* (1980) and George Eogan's *The Accomplished Art* (1994), while Brendan O'Connor's *Cross-Channel Relations in the Later Bronze Age* (1980) systematically reviews the evidence for Continental imports and influences. This tradition of scholarly documentation has been continued by Trevor Cowie's work on finds old and new (e.g. Cowie & Reid 1986; O'Connor & Cowie 1995; 1997), and on fakes – a topic to which John Coles drew attention, and which was taken up by Schmidt and Burgess (1981). While the creation of corpora is currently unfashionable in some quarters, and while the shortcomings of typology as a method of artefact study are well known (Coles 1984), nevertheless these databases are an invaluable source of 'raw' information for various types of research (e.g. studies of production and consumption patterns). Furthermore, the painstaking review of primary source material in Europe by Brendan O'Connor (1980) has permitted the deconstruction of a long-held idea of "settlers [arriving] from the north-west German plain" (Coles 1959–60, 54)

Fig. 7.1. Gold torc from the Minch. Reproduced courtesy of the Trustees of the National Museums of Scotland.

New artefact discoveries

Although metal detecting has increased the number of known Bronze Age objects, the most significant finds of the past three decades have, ironically, been purely serendipitous. The gold bar torc from the sea-bed off the Isle of Harris (Fig. 7.1; Cowie 1994) was an unexpected catch for a couple of clam dredgers – and one which nearly got away, as a tangled piece of old wire! This piece – whose watery grave suggests an act of ritual devotion, or a shipwreck, or perhaps a particularly unfortunate bout of sea-sickness – is the only extant example of its kind from Scotland, the previous three finds having been lost or melted down. It is an important piece of confirmatory evidence for contacts between Scotland and Ireland (or indeed southern England) around 1200–1000 BC.

Another watery context – albeit the humanly-made environment of a reservoir – yielded an even more surprising find, during an unusually dry spell in 1992. An Early Bronze Age cemetery on a natural knoll in West Water Reservoir, Peeblesshire, included one cist which had contained the crouched inhumation of an infant, around 3–6 years old. Around its neck was a two-strand necklace (Fig. 7.2), of which one was composed of 'ordinary' cannel coal disc beads, graded in size, and the other of unique, tiny, blobby beads of metallic lead (Hunter & Davis 1994). This

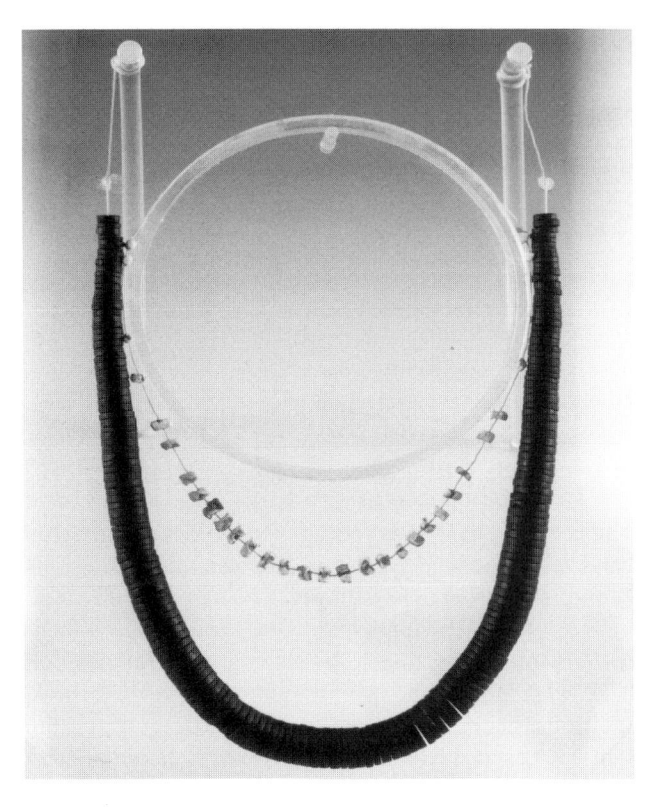

Fig. 7.2. Cannel coal and lead necklace, West Water Reservoir. Reproduced courtesy of the Trustees of the National Museums of Scotland.

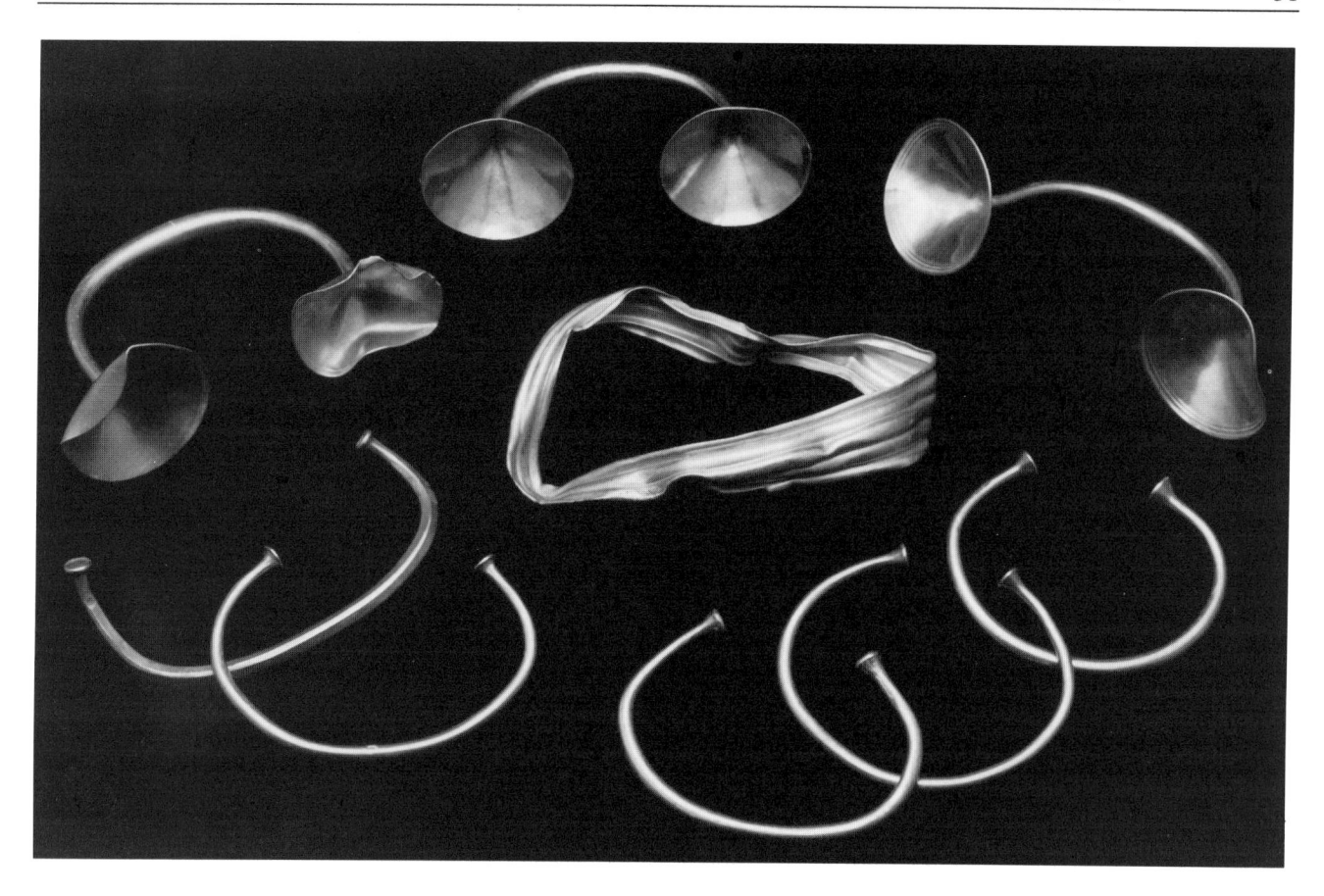

Fig. 7.3. Gold hoard, Heights of Brae. Reproduced courtesy of the Trustees of the National Museums of Scotland.

represents the earliest use of metallic lead in Britain and Ireland, predating the earliest regular use by several centuries; and while it may signify no more than the precocious use of a locally available resource, nevertheless its manufacture is a noteworthy event in the history of Scottish Bronze Age metallurgy.

Two discoveries from north-east Scotland have helped to deepen our understanding of the links between Scotland and Ireland at either end of the Bronze Age. These are the hoard of Late Bronze Age gold objects ploughed up at the Heights of Brae, Easter Ross (Fig. 7.3; Clarke & Kemp 1984), and the finds from a pair of unusual Early Bronze Age graves discovered during pre-building assessment at Seafield West, near Inverness (Cressey 1997). One grave contained a boat-shaped tree-trunk coffin, with the remains of an extended individual, buried with an early tin-bronze 'Type Butterwick' dagger in a hide sheath (Fig. 7.4); the other, adjacent grave, contained a box-like wooden coffin with an Irish Bowl Food Vessel and three flints. The discovery of this type of pot so far from the area of its design origin, and in virtual isolation from the other Scottish examples (which are mostly clustered in mid-Argyll), reminds us of the Irish involvement in the introduction of metal objects and metallurgy to Scotland. It has been persuasively argued (Cowie 1988) that the establishment of Scotland's earliest known native metal industry, the so-called 'Migdale' tradition in the North-East, owed much to contacts across the North Sea, whereas the west of Scotland seems to have received objects and know-how from Ireland. However, it is also clear that objects of Irish copper had already been reaching north-east Scotland (*ibid.*; Northover 1980) by the time that the skills of the central European copper alloy metalworking tradition were being adopted there.

The Easter Ross hoard, some thirteen hundred years or so younger, confirms the continuing importance of links with Ireland, and adds to a picture of complex Late Bronze Age connections. These linked Scotland not only to Ireland (where the gold items are likely to have been made), but also to Continental Europe, as finds such as the hoard from Balmashanner, Angus, indicate (Anderson 1892). It may be that Scotland played an important intermediary role in the flow of bronze from metal-rich Ireland to metal-poor northern Europe, and that the acquisition of valuable items from both areas was a dividend of this entrepreneurial activity. The presence of a single iron ring in the Balmashanner hoard – one of the earliest iron objects in Scotland, and probably originating in the eastern Alps – presaged a change in this privileged position, as iron became the metal of preference in Europe.

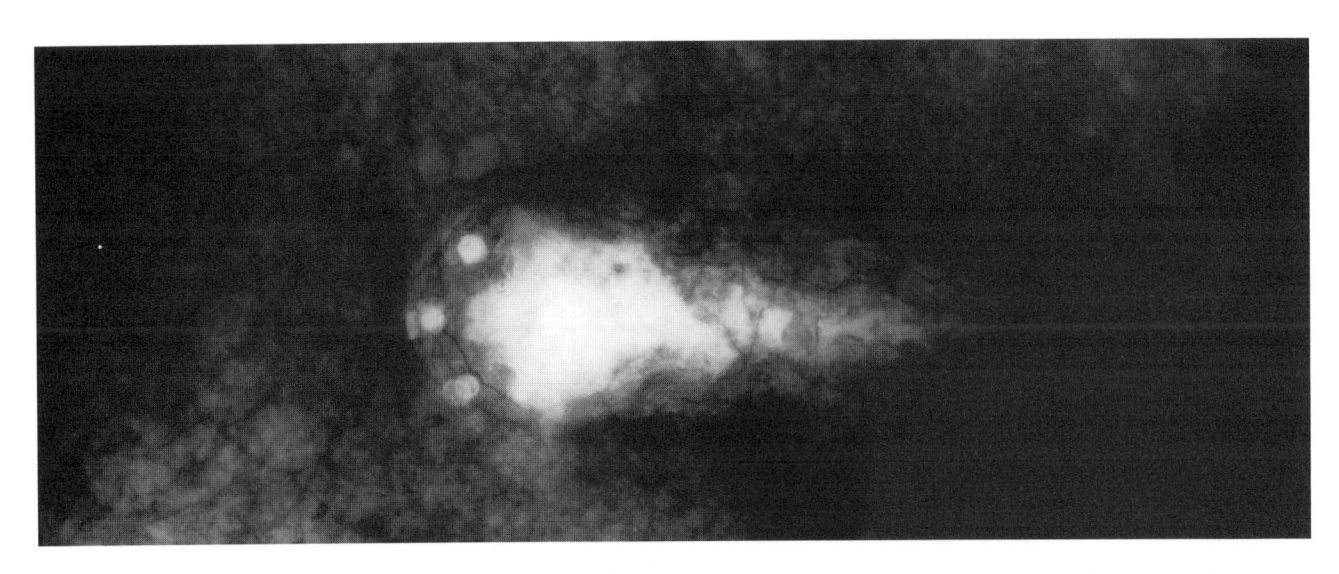

Fig. 7.4. X-ray image of dagger, Seafield West. Reproduced courtesy of the Trustees of the National Museums of Scotland.

Fig. 7.5. The St. Andrews Hoard. Reproduced courtesy of the Trustees of the National Museums of Scotland.

The fact that a large amount of bronze was removed from circulation, through votive deposits and hoarding, during the early first millennium BC in Britain, Ireland and northern Europe, has often been remarked upon (e.g. Bradley 1990; Eogan 1983). It has been suggested (Needham 1990) that an important contributory cause may have been the advent of iron metallurgy – so that as bronze may have become 'devalued' in comparison, the manipulation of supply maintained an element of exclusivity. Whatever the reasons, the pattern of recent finds has confirmed the phenomenon. In 1990, the largest surviving Late Bronze Age hoard to have been found in Scotland was discovered during house extension work at St Andrews, Fife (Fig. 7.5; Cowie *et al.* 1991; 1998). Over two hundred bronze items were present, comprising tools, weapons, pieces connected with horse-drawn transport and ornaments (including sixteen sunflower head pins – more than all the previous Scottish finds combined). It also included seven amber beads, three cannel coal bangles, and a significant amount of organic material: leather fragments, pieces of horn/antler handles and of wooden hafts/shafts, fragments of boars' tusks, pieces of thread (some linking bronze rings together), and over 80 textile fragments. The latter were of wool and linen or hemp, and they were in both coarse and fine weaves (Gabra-Sanders 1994).

A smaller, but nevertheless significant, Late Bronze Age hoard came to light in 1995, when a couple walking their dog over boggy ground at Corrymuckloch, Perthshire, spotted several bronze items in the upcast of a drainage channel (Cowie *et al.* 1996). This disturbed hoard comprised three socketed axeheads, pieces of a blade of a deliberately-destroyed leaf-shaped sword, and a unique, exotic-looking ladle (Fig. 7.6). The latter, a component of the Late Bronze Age feasting kit along with the cauldron, flesh-hook, bucket and fancy eating and drinking utensils, suggested long-distance movement of some kind across Europe. The nature of this movement is discussed below.

New analytical work

In common with Bronze Age metalwork studies elsewhere in Britain (e.g. in Needham 1990), the Scottish work of the last quarter century has been concerned with identifying metalworking practices and traditions; with the difficult task of sourcing metals; and with mapping the distribution of products from individual production areas. Credit for many of the advances goes to Peter Northover, who, in collaboration with Trevor Cowie and others, has undertaken programmes of compositional and metallographic research (e.g. Cowie *et al.* 1998).

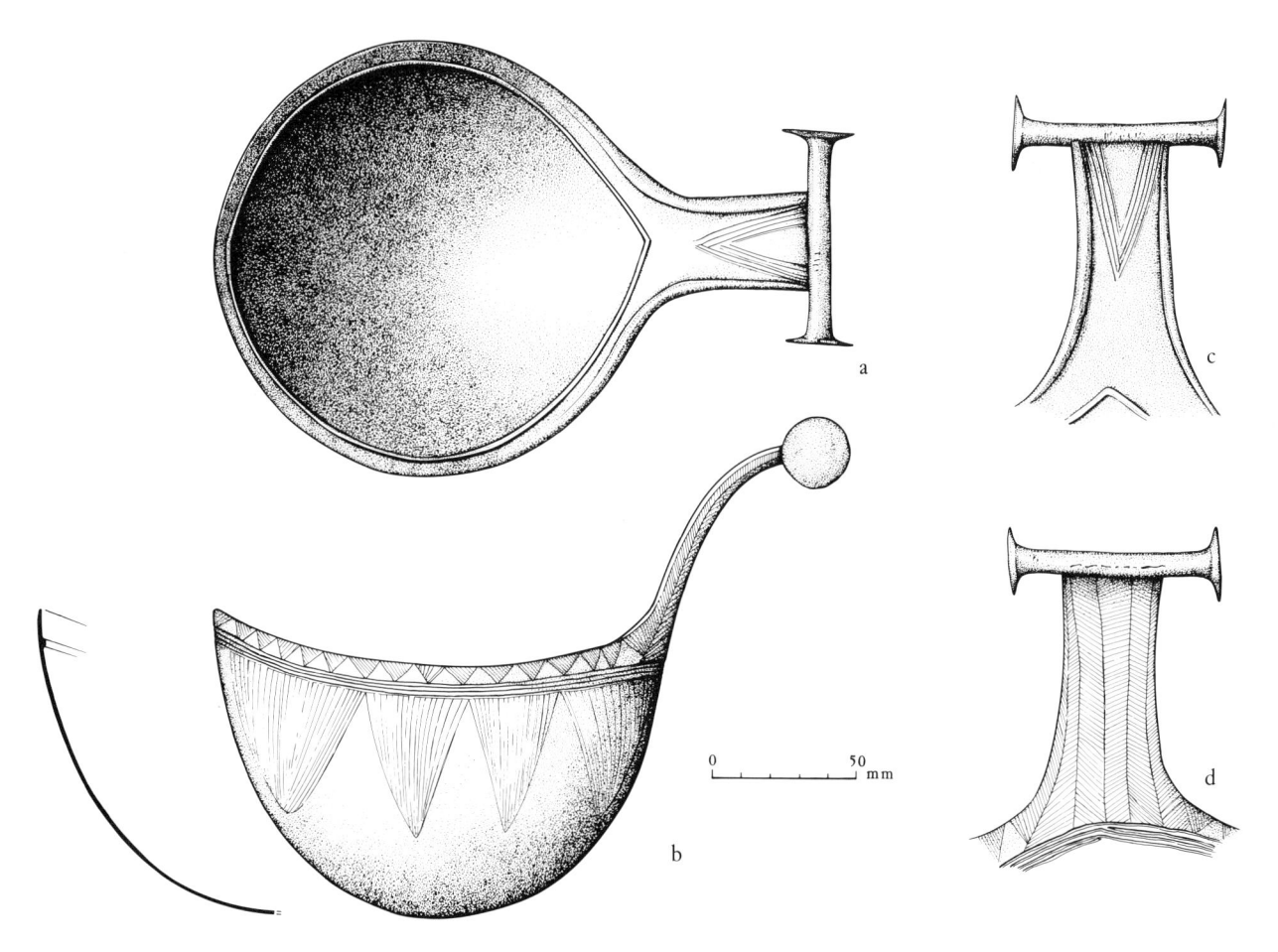

Fig. 7.6. The Corrymuckloch ladle. Drawing by Marion O'Neil.

The results of this work have confirmed earlier suspicions about the importance of Ireland as an early provider of prestigious metal objects (of gold, copper and bronze), and of the know-how required to make them. Decorated flat axeheads, for example, tend to have a distinctively Irish composition, as do copper objects (Northover 1980; 1987). The early development of a north-east Scottish tin-bronze industry, influenced from across the North Sea, is also borne out compositionally: the distinctive tinned axeheads of the 'Migdale' tradition have a composition which points towards their production around the Moray Firth (Northover 1987).

Northover's current project on Late Bronze Age Scottish metalwork (Cowie *et al.* 1998) has identified an overall compositional pattern for metalwork from the north of Britain, differing from that seen in south-west England and south-east Wales, but with points of similarity with the patterns seen in East Anglia and Ireland. This suggests the existence of zones, or networks of contacts, around which metal resources circulated. Against this background, his analysis of 77 objects from the St Andrews Hoard (*ibid.*) identified impurity patterns which suggested that some of the bracelets had a different manufacture history, based on a different supply of metal, from the rest of the hoard. These bracelets were compositionally comparable with metal from the Thames Estuary area, related to the so-called 'Carp's Tongue [Sword] Complex'. Furthermore, an ornament with ring-and-hook terminal from the hoard has a high lead content suggestive of an origin in south-eastern England or northern France.

Analysis of the Corrymuckloch hoard (*ibid*; Cowie *et al.* 1996) produced further intriguing results. Here, despite its exotic Continental appearance, the ladle proved compositionally to be consistent with bronzes made in northern Britain. This could, perhaps, mean that it was the design idea, rather than the finished object, which moved around Europe.

Refinement of chronology

The steady accumulation of radiocarbon and dendrochronological dates over the past two decades has permitted the formulation of a coherent typo-chronological model for British Bronze Age metalwork; here, the outstanding contribution of Stuart Needham should be acknowledged (Needham 1996). Needham's work has concentrated mainly on England and Wales, but the hitherto scanty dating record for Scotland is now being enhanced by the National Museums' of Scotland (NMS) ongoing radiocarbon dating project (Sheridan 1996). The results confirm what Needham (and indeed John Coles) had proposed. The date of 2204–1866 cal BC (OxA-4659) for a tubular bead core from the Migdale hoard is wholly in line with their predicted date for the Migdale industry, while that of 2316–1876 cal BC (OxA-4510) for ox-hairs from the sheath of the gold hilt-band dagger from Collessie, Fife, also accords with expectations. Welcome information about the currency of mid- and later Bronze Age artefact types is provided by dates of 1520–1260 cal BC (OxA-6041) for a spearshaft fragment from Arnicle, Argyll; of 1390–1010 cal BC (OxA-6040) for a socketed axe haft from near the River Kerrow, Inverness-shire (an early, but plausible date); and of 990–800 cal BC (OxA-6779) for a Ewart Park-style leaf-shaped sword made of yew from Grotstetter, Orkney.

The NMS project has not been limited to dating metal/metal-related objects. Its other Bronze Age results include three 'firsts' for Scotland, all connected with the 'driving' part of this chapter's title. The well-known disc wheel from Blair Drummond (Piggott 1956–57) turned out to constitute the earliest direct evidence for wheeled transport in Britain and Ireland, with its date range of 1255–815 cal BC (OxA-3538), while the Loch Nell ox yoke and the White Moss swingletree (used for pairs of traction animals) also proved to be the earliest examples of these artefact types from Britain and Ireland (with date ranges, respectively, of 1950–1525 cal BC, OxA-3541, and 1516–1253 cal BC, OxA-4507).

Use-wear analysis

The work of Sue Bridgford on Late Bronze Age swords (Bridgford 1997) is providing new insights into the length and kind of use experienced by individual items. The numerous examples of edge-damage relating to blade-on-blade strikes confirms that these swords were, indeed, used as weapons of war. Their prestige value is borne out by metallographic analysis, which demonstrates that these hard-to-cast items were consistently well made by specialist bronzeworkers; and their significance as symbolically-charged items is confirmed by Bridgford's observations on their patterns of deposition, with votive deposition in watery contexts, and the ritualised 'killing' of some swords by hacking up (and sometimes burning), featuring prominently. The extension of this kind of research to encompass other Bronze Age weapon types would be a useful next step.

Death: varied practices, varied approaches

The various advances in the study of metal objects outlined above have produced much new evidence which can be used to construct narratives of social and economic change during the Scottish Bronze Age. The study of funerary practices has also helped us gain a clearer picture, although little systematic research has been done. Jane Downes' 'Orkney Barrows Project' (Downes 1995; Downes & MacGregor 1995) is an honourable exception, building on past studies (e.g. Hedges 1980) and confirming the idiosyncratic nature of funerary traditions in the Northern Isles and parts of Caithness from the Early Bronze Age until the first millennium AD. Of greatest interest is the fact that radiocarbon dating at Linga Fold has shown that steatite urns were in use during the second millennium

BC (Downes pers. comm.), thus removing some of the uncertainty about the date of such objects (cf. Ritchie & Ritchie 1974, 35).

Other advances in our understanding of Bronze Age funerary traditions include the realisation that the deposition of 'floral tributes', mainly of meadowsweet, could have been a common (if seasonal) practice, along with the burial of pots containing ale, mead or gruel, in cist graves (Tipping 1994). Understanding of the pots themselves has been assisted by the publication of David Clarke's corpus of Beaker pottery (1970), by Ian Shepherd's reassessment of Beaker development in north-east Scotland (1986), and by Alexandra Shepherd's research into Beakers and gender differentiation (1989). Furthermore, despite the chronological conundrum posed by the British Museum's Beaker dating programme, which concluded that many Beaker styles could have had a long currency (Kinnes et al. 1991), it may eventually be possible to arrive at clearer, regional, sequences for Scotland through AMS dating of organic residues on the pots. The establishment of a systematic programme, covering Scottish Food Vessels as well as Beakers, should be an objective for the new millennium.

Two pieces of recently-obtained evidence help to confirm the date of Scotland's rare tree-trunk coffins. One is the discovery of the 'Type Butterwick' dagger in the previously mentioned Seafield West (possible) boat grave, which, by analogy with a recently-dated dagger from Gravelly Guy, Oxfordshire, should date to around 2200–2000 cal BC (Gerloff 1993). The other is the date of 2040–1740 cal BC (OxA-6813) obtained from a fragment of sewn birch-bark coffin cover from Dalrigh, near Oban. A currency of use within the late third-early second millennium BC accords with the picture obtained from analogous graves in England (e.g. Loose Howe, Yorkshire: Elgee & Elgee 1949), and also with the evidence from Barns Farm, Fife, where a coracle burial was found in an Early Bronze Age cemetery (Watkins 1982). Finally, Ian Shepherd's re-excavation of the Sculptor's Cave, Covesea (Shepherd & Shepherd 1979) has provided additional evidence confirming that Late Bronze Age funerary practices included the quasi-artefactual use of human remains for magical, symbolic purposes. Here, the discovery of several child mandibles on the floor of the cave confirmed what Sylvia Benton's excavations in the 1930s had indicated (Benton 1931): namely that the skulls of children aged 6–9 had been removed from their bodies and suspended from the roof of the cave. One may have been wearing a gold 'tress ring' in its hair. As Shepherd has argued (Society of Antiquaries of Scotland lecture), this use of human remains may have served to emphasise the special, liminal nature of this hard-of-access coastal cave, between the everyday world and the supernatural, watery 'underworld'. Whether these children had met a natural death, or – by analogy with some Late Bronze Age metalwork deposits, had been killed and presented as votive deposits to the deities of the 'underworld' – is not clear. However, the reported discovery of human bones along with animal bones and broken Late Bronze Age bronze artefacts in Duddingston Loch, Edinburgh, in 1775, offers a possible, if indirect, parallel (Chambers 1854).

Display: investigating the Bronze Age 'jet set' and their Wessex-orientated descendants

The use of funerary ceremonies as a platform for making statements about social status during the late third/early second millennium BC has long been recognised (e.g. Henshall 1968), and various discoveries over the last 25 years have confirmed this. Clearly, the use of jet and jet-like jewellery and dress accessories played an important role in expressing status, as finds such as the 31 V-perforated buttons, boat-shaped 'fastener' and pulley belt ring from a cist at Harehope, Peeblesshire, demonstrate (Fig. 7.7; Jobey 1980). Much useful work in cataloguing finds of Early Bronze Age 'jet' artefacts was done in the late 1960s/early 1970s, with Winifred Coutts' corpus of spacer-plate necklaces (1969) and Ian Shepherd's work on V-perforated buttons (1973); and further research by Ian Shepherd investigated manufacturing techniques (1981). However, opinions differed on the question of whether the black material genuinely was jet, imported from Whitby, or was a locally-obtained substance such as cannel coal, shale or lignite (compare Shepherd 1985 with Callander 1916). This question could not be addressed properly until a suitable technique of non-destructive analysis had been developed. Work by Gill Bussell on English 'jet' artefacts (Bussell 1976; Pollard et al. 1981) had demonstrated that X-ray fluorescence analysis had potential, and so in 1989 a programme of analysis was established by the author and Mary Davis. This evolved into a long-term, ongoing National Museums of Scotland project, which aims to produce a descriptive and analytical corpus of pre-Iron Age 'jet' artefacts in Scotland and Wales (Davis 1993; Sheridan & Davis 1995; 1998).

Space does not permit a full description of the project, but the results so far can be summarised. Ian Shepherd's view (1985) that specialist jet-workers around Whitby were producing jewellery and dress accessories for long-distance exchange is indeed supported by the evidence now available. That it was finished products, rather than raw materials, which were being exported to Scotland is indicated not only by the relative consistency of their design, but also by the decoration found on spacer-plate necklaces. As Shepherd has pointed out (1973, 66–75), this is closely comparable to designs which are a relatively common feature of Yorkshire Beakers, whilst bearing little resemblance to the decoration on the Food Vessels with which the necklaces are chiefly associated in Scotland. (Direct derivation, within Scotland, from the designs on lunulae was deemed unlikely by Shepherd because the lunula Beaker motifs are slightly different.)

This is not, however, the full story. What emerges

Fig. 7.7. Jet and jet-like dress accessories, Harehope. Reproduced courtesy of the Trustees of the National Museums of Scotland.

equally clearly is that local craft workers in Scotland were capable of making copies of these prestigious and valuable objects – even if the local jet substitutes lacked the magical, electrostatic properties of the real thing. In the assemblage of material from Harehope, for example, four of the buttons were found to have compositions suggestive of materials more akin to cannel coal and shaley cannel than to Whitby jet. Similarly, copies of jet pulley belt rings, made in local materials, are known (e.g. from Airngarth Hill, West Lothian). The same is also true of 'napkin rings' – items which may have served as 'eyelets' for a cloak drawstring, as the position of a recently-discovered jet pair at Camps Reservoir, Lanarkshire, has suggested.

With spacer-plate necklaces (and spacer-plate bracelets), locally-available jet substitutes were used in two ways. In many cases, they were used to provide replacements for individual components as they broke; but in a few cases entire necklaces (and possibly one bracelet) were made of the local material. Examples include those from Burgie Lodge Farm, Moray; 'Yirdies', Lanarkshire; and Inchmarnock, Bute. These locally made necklaces tend to have contained more strands of beads than 'standard' Whitby models: perhaps this 'gilding of the lily' represents an attempt to out-do the Whitby specialists.

Details have also emerged about the length of use of individual spacer-plate necklaces. In some cases (including locally-made ones), necklaces seem to have been buried when relatively new: the degree of wear on the beads and plates is not great, and there is little or no mixing of materials. In other cases, however, the necklaces have clearly seen a lot of use, perhaps being passed down over several generations as valuable heirlooms. In these cases, the presence of two or more materials is common; substantial wear may be present on the beads and plates; parts of more than one necklace may be present, with non-matching plates sometimes having been modified to fit (e.g. at Monybachach, Argyll); and often the necklaces were far from complete when buried. This variation in condition raises questions about how people chose *when* to bury a necklace: were the people who were buried with a relatively new necklace deemed to be more important than those with heirlooms – or did the latter gain in accumulated value as they grew older?

Disc-bead necklaces, in contrast to spacer-plate necklaces, seem mostly to have been made from non-jet materials; only one of the specimens analysed so far, from Cloburn Quarry, Lanarkshire, consists almost entirely of Whitby jet. Unfortunately, with cannel coal (the probable material for many necklaces), it can be impossible to pinpoint a specific source without undertaking destructive analysis. It is therefore unclear whether any centralised production occurred.

Finally, with disc-and-fusiform bead necklaces (and a unique belt from Culduthel, Inverness-shire), a mixture of materials and a variation in the degree of wear on individual beads is the norm. It is unclear whether disc-and-fusiform items were all just an amalgamation of parts of pre-existing disc bead and spacer-plate necklaces, or whether some were designed as mixed-bead items; but the analysed examples suggest that the former may be the case. In one of the necklaces from Almondbank, Perthshire, for example, a fastener made from an old, truncated spacer-plate was found, and three distinct groups of raw material were present – Whitby jet, represented in the fastener and four of the fusiform beads; one kind of cannel coal, represented in the other fusiform beads; and another cannel coal, represented in the disc beads (Wilthew & Davis 1997).

So much for the Early Bronze Age 'jet set'. At some point, probably during the 18th century BC, the fashion scene changed and the production of jet items declined. This change is undoubtedly due to the emergence of Wessex as a high-profile centre of power. For at least the next couple of centuries, the elite of Scotland adopted and adapted the fashions current in Wessex and other parts of southern England. This is seen most dramatically in the grave assemblage from the Knowes of Trotty, Orkney (Clarke *et al*. 1985, figs. 4.39, 5.44), with – amongst other items – its fragments of amber spacer-plate necklace and 11 amber prismatic V-bored buttons. It is also seen in items such as the handled pot from Balmuick, Perthshire, a copy of the gold cup from Rillaton (*ibid*., figs. 4.49, 4.44); in the Law Hill, Angus, skeuomorph of the Bush Barrow gold belt hook, made from local cannel coal or shale (*ibid*., fig. 5.47); and in the gold discs or 'button covers' from Barnhill, Angus, reminiscent of the gold-bound amber discs from Wilsford (*ibid*., figs. 4.31–32).

Faience beads are another example of a fashion idea which was almost certainly adopted from Wessex, along with the know-how for manufacturing them. A significant addition to the database was made with the discovery of a cordoned urn burial at Findhorn, Moray, in 1988 (Fig. 7.8; Shepherd & Shepherd 1989). Here, the cremated remains of a young adult female and neonate were found with one star-shaped and 21 segmented beads, and a secondary cremation deposit above the urn produced a further star-shaped bead and a quoit-shaped bead. All may have been slightly affected by heat, although none showed the extensive heat-damage of the recently-discovered beads from Stoneyburn, Lanarkshire (Sheridan 1995). Examination of the segmented beads confirmed that they had been made by wrapping paste around straw stalks, and compositional analysis of all the beads by Tony McDonald (1991) concluded that they had almost certainly been made in the area (Findhorn lies within one of the distributional concentrations of Scottish faience beads, around Culbin Sands; quartz sand would have been abundant, and the other constituent materials occur locally as well). The Findhorn discovery prompted moves to create a corpus of Scottish faience beads, and it is hoped that this will be published in 2000. This will feature the results of the earlier, extensive programme of analysis undertaken by Stanley Warren and Arnold Aspinall during the 1970s.

Conclusion

This brief review of developments in PC (post-Coles) Scottish artefact studies has, I hope, demonstrated the

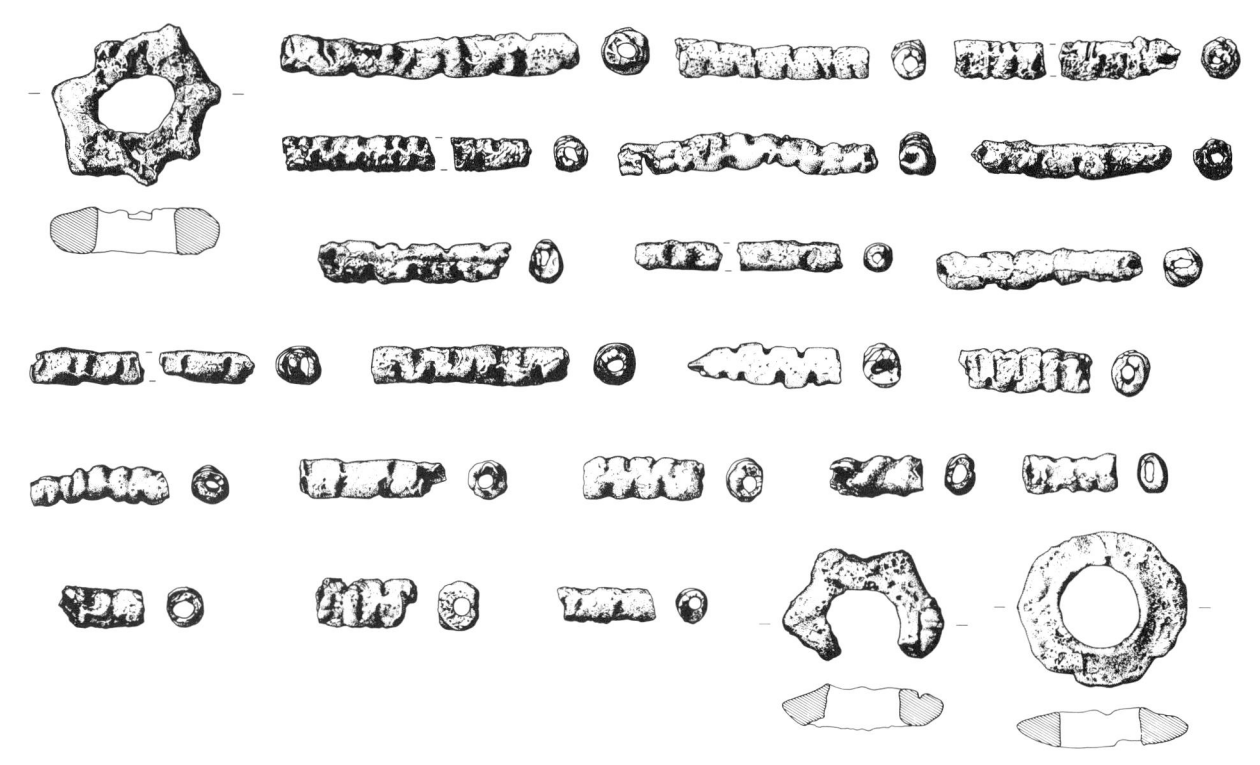

Fig. 7.8. Faience beads, Findhorn. Drawing by Helen Jackson. [Scale 1:1]

wealth, quality and variety of evidence now available. The task for the future is to pull the varied strands of this evidence together, along with the growing body of structural and palaeoenvironmental data, in order to construct coherent narratives of social and economic change.

Acknowledgements

Peter Northover and Stuart Needham are thanked for allowing me pre-publication access to key articles, and special thanks go to Trevor Cowie for this and for many other kindnesses.

Bibliography

Anderson, J. 1892. Notice of the discovery of a hoard of the Bronze age, consisting chiefly of personal ornaments of bronze, amber, and gold, at Balmashanner, near Forfar, *Proc. Soc. Antiq. Scotland* 26 (1891-2), 182-8.

Benton, S. 1931. The excavation of the Sculptor's Cave, Covesea, *Proc. Soc. Antiq. Scotland* 65, 177-216.

Bradley, R. 1990. *The Passage of Arms*. Cambridge: Cambridge University Press.

Bridgford, S. 1997. The first weapons devised only for war, *British Archaeology* March 1997, 7.

Burgess, C.B. & Gerloff, S. 1981. *The Dirks and Rapiers of Great Britain and Ireland*. Prähistorische Bronzefunde IV, 7. München: Beck.

Bussell, G.D. 1976. A Preliminary Neutron Activation Analysis of Ornaments of Jet and Similar Materials from Early Bronze Age sites in North Yorkshire and Derbyshire. Unpublished M.A. thesis, University of Bradford.

Callander, J.G. 1916. Notice of a jet necklace found in a cist in a Bronze Age cemetery, discovered on Burgie Lodge Farm, Morayshire, with notes on Scottish prehistoric jet ornaments, *Proc. Soc. Antiq. Scotland* 50, 201-40.

Chambers, R. 1854. On ancient terraces of cultivation, commonly called daisses, *Proc. Soc. Antiq. Scotland* 1, 127-33.

Clarke, D.L. 1970. *Beaker Pottery of Great Britain and Ireland*. Cambridge: Cambridge University Press.

Clarke, D.V., Cowie, T.G. and Foxon, A. 1985. *Symbols of Power at the Time of Stonehenge*. Edinburgh: Her Majesty's Stationery Office.

Clarke, D.V. & Kemp, M.M.B. 1984. A hoard of late Bronze Age gold objects from the Heights of Brae, Ross and Cromarty District, Highland Region, *Proc. Soc. Antiq. Scotland* 114, 189-98.

Coles, J.M. 1958-59 [1961]. Scottish swan's neck sunflower pins, *Proc. Soc. Antiq. Scotland* 92, 1-9.

Coles, J.M. 1959-60 [1962]. Scottish Late Bronze Age metalwork: typology, distributions and chronology, *Proc. Soc. Antiq. Scotland* 93, 16-134.

Coles, J.M. 1963-64 [1966]. Scottish Middle Bronze Age metalwork, *Proc. Soc. Antiq. Scotland* 97, 82-156.

Coles, J.M. 1968-69 [1970] Scottish Early Bronze Age metalwork, *Proc. Soc. Antiq. Scotland* 101, 1-110.

Coles, J.M. 1973. *Archaeology by Experiment*. London: Hutchinson.

Coles, J.M. 1984. Review of C.B. Burgess & S. Gerloff, *The Dirks and Rapiers of Great Britain and Ireland*, and of P.K. Schmidt & C.B. Burgess, *The Axes of Scotland and Northern England*, *Proc. Prehist. Soc.* 50, 420-1.

Colquhoun, I and Burgess, C 1988. *The Swords of Britain*. Prähistorische Bronzefunde, Abt. IV, 5. Munich: Beck.

Coutts, W. 1969. The Spacer-plate Necklaces of the British Bronze Age. Unpublished M.A. thesis, University of Edinburgh.

Cowie, T.G. 1994. A Bronze Age gold torc from the Minch, *Hebridean Naturalist* 12, 19-21.

Cowie, T.G. 1988. *Magic Metal: Early Metalworkers in the North-East*. Aberdeen: Anthropological Museum.

Cowie, T.G., Hall, M., O'Connor, B. & Tipping, R. 1996. The Late Bronze Age hoard from Corrymuckloch, near Amulree, Perthshire: an interim report, *Tayside and Fife Archaeological Journal*, 2, 60-69.

Cowie, T.G., Northover, P. & O'Connor, B. 1998. The St Andrews, Fife, hoard: context and chronology in the Scottish Late Bronze Age. In C. Mordant, M. Pernot & V. Rychner (eds), *L'Atelier du Bronzier: Élaboration, Transformation et Consommation du Bronze en Europe du XXe au VIIIe Siècle Avant Notre Ère*. Dijon: Université de Bourgogne, 141-54.

Cowie, T.G., O'Connor, B. & Proudfoot, E.V.W. 1991. A Late Bronze Age hoard from St Andrews, Fife, Scotland: a preliminary report. In C. Chevillot & A. Coffyn (eds) *Le Bronze Atlantique: Actes du colloque du Parc Archéologique du Beynac*, 49-58. Beynac: L'Association des Musées du Sarladais.

Cowie, T.G. and Reid, A. 1986. Some recent finds of Bronze Age metalwork from Perthshire, *Proc. Soc. Antiq. Scotland* 116, 69-88.

Cressey, M. 1997. *Archaeological Excavations of a Bronze Age Cemetery at Seafield West, Inverness, Highland Region*. Edinburgh: Centre for Field Archaeology Report 288.

Davis, M. 1993. The identification of various jet and jet-like materials used in the Early Bronze Age in Scotland, *The Conservator* 17, 11-18.

Downes, J. 1995. Linga Fold, *Current Archaeology* 142, 396-9.

Downes, J. and MacGregor, G. 1995. *Linga Fold, Sandwick, Orkney*. Glasgow: Glasgow University Archaeological Research Division Report 59.2.

Elgee, H.W. & the late F. 1949. An Early Bronze Age burial in a boat-shaped wooden coffin from North-East Yorkshire, *Proc. Prehist. Soc.* 15, 87-106.

Eogan, G. 1983. *Hoards of the Irish Later Bronze Age*. Dublin: Royal Irish Academy.

Eogan, G. 1994. *The Accomplished Art*. Oxford: Oxbow Monograph 42.

Gabra-Sanders, T. 1994. Textiles and fibres from the Late Bronze Age hoard from St Andrews, Fife, Scotland – a preliminary report. In G. Jaacks & K. Tidow (eds), *Archäologische Textilfunde – Archaeological Textiles. Textilsymposium Neumünster 4-7.5.1993*, 34-42. Neumünster: North European Symposium for Archaeological Textiles 5.

Gerloff, S. 1975. *The Early Bronze Age Daggers in Great Britain*. Prähistorische Bronzefunde VI, 2. München: Beck

Gerloff, S. 1993. Zu Fragen mittelmeerländischer Kontakte und absoluter Chronologie der Frühbronzezeit in Mittel- und Westeuropa, *Prähistorische Zeitschrift* 68(1), 58-102.

Hedges, J.W. 1980. Short cists recently excavated at Lower Ellibister and other locations in Orkney, *Proc. Soc. Antiq. Scotland* 110, 44-71.

Henshall, A.S. 1962-63 [1965]. A Bronze Age cist burial at Masterton, Pitreavie, Fife, *Proc. Soc. Antiq. Scotland* 96, 145-54.

Henshall, A.S. 1968. Scottish dagger graves. In J.M. Coles & D.D.A. Simpson (eds), *Studies in Ancient Europe*, 173-95. Leicester: Leicester University Press.

Hunter, F.J. & Davis, M. 1994. Early Bronze Age lead – a unique necklace from southeast Scotland, *Antiquity* 68, 824-30.

Jobey, G. 1980. Green Knowe unenclosed platform settlement and Harehope Cairn, Peeblesshire, *Proc. Soc. Antiq. Scotland* 110, 72-113.

Kinnes, I.A., Gibson, A., Ambers, J., Bowman, S., Leese, M. & Boast, R. 1991. Radiocarbon dating and British Beakers: the British Museum programme, *Scottish Archaeological Review* 8, 35–68.

McDonald, A. 1991. An Investigation into the Provenancing and Manufacture of an Assemblage of Faience Beads from Findhorn, Moray, using X-ray Fluorescence and Scanning Electron Microscopy. Unpublished M.Sc. thesis, University of Bradford.

Needham, S.P. 1990. *The Petters Late Bronze Age Metalwork*. London: British Museum Occasional Paper 70.

Needham, S.P. 1996. Chronology and periodisation in the British Bronze Age. In K. Randsborg (ed), *Absolute Chronology: Archaeological Europe 2500–500 BC*, 121–40 (Acta Archaeologica Supplementa Vol I). København: Munksgaard.

Northover, J.P. 1980. Bronze in the British Bronze Age. In W.A. Oddy (ed), *Aspects of Early Metallurgy*, 63–70. London: British Museum Occasional Paper 17.

Northover, J.P. 1987. Appendix: analysis of flat axe and dagger. In J.R. Watkin, Three finds of Bronze Age metalwork from the Vale of York, 496–7, *Proc. Prehist. Soc.* 53, 493–8.

O'Connor, B. 1980. *Cross-Channel Relations in the Later Bronze Age*. Oxford: British Archaeological Reports, International Series 91.

O'Connor, B. & Cowie, T.G. 1995. Middle Bronze Age dirks and rapiers from Scotland: some finds old and new, *Proc. Soc. Antiq. Scotland* 125, 345–67.

O'Connor, B. & Cowie, T.G. 1997. Bronze Age metalwork from Kinnoull, Perth, *Tayside and Fife Archaeological Journal* 3, 58–60.

Piggott, S. 1956–57 [1959] A tripartite disc wheel from Blair Drummond, Perthshire, *Proc. Soc. Antiq. Scotland* 90, 238–41.

Pollard, A.M., Bussell, G.D. & Baird, D.C. 1981. The analytical investigation of Early Bronze Age jet and jet-like material from the Devizes Museum, *Archaeometry* 29, 103–9.

Ritchie, G. & A. 1974. Excavation of a barrow at Queenafjold, Twatt, Orkney, *Proc. Soc. Antiq. Scotland* 105, 33–42.

Schmidt, P.K. & Burgess, C.B. 1981. *The Axes of Scotland and Northern Britain*. Prähistorische Bronzefunde IX, 7. München: Beck.

Shepherd, A.N. 1989. A note on the orientation of beaker burials in north-east Scotland. In M.K. Greig, C. Greig, A.N. Shepherd & I.A.G. Shepherd, A beaker cist at Chapeldon, Tore of Troup, Aberdour, Banff and Buchan District, with a note on the orientation of beaker burials in north-east Scotland, 79–80, *Proc. Soc. Antiq. Scotland* 119, 73–82.

Shepherd, I.A.G. 1973. The V-bored Buttons of Great Britain. Unpublished M.A. thesis, University of Edinburgh.

Shepherd, I.A.G. 1981. Bronze Age jet working in North Britain, *Scottish Archaeological Forum* 11, 43–51.

Shepherd, I.A.G. 1985. Jet and amber. In D.V. Clarke, T.G. Cowie & A. Foxon (eds), *Symbols of Power at the Time of Stonehenge*, 204–16. Edinburgh: Her Majesty's Stationery Office.

Shepherd, I.A.G. 1986. *Powerful Pots: Beakers in North-East Prehistory*. Aberdeen: Anthropological Museum, University of Aberdeen.

Shepherd, I.A.G. & A. 1979. The Sculptor's Cave, Covesea, Moray, *Discovery and Excavation in Scotland 1979*, 14–15.

Shepherd, I.A.G. & A. 1989. 102 Findhorn, *Discovery and Excavation in Scotland 1989*, 25.

Sheridan, J.A. 1995. The faience beads. In I. Banks, The excavation of three cairns at Stoneyburn Farm, Crawford, Lanarkshire, 1991, *Proc. Soc. Antiq. Scotland* 125, 289–343.

Sheridan, J.A. 1996. The oldest bow... and other objects, *Current Archaeology* 149, 188–90.

Sheridan, J.A. and Davis, M. 1995. The Poltalloch "jet" spacer plate necklace, *The Kist* 49, 1–9.

Sheridan, J.A. and Davis, M. 1998. The Welsh 'jet set' in prehistory: a case of Keeping Up with the Joneses? In A. Gibson & D.D.A. Simpson (eds.), *Prehistoric Ritual and Religion*, 148–62. Stroud: Sutton.

Taylor, J. 1980. *Prehistoric Goldwork of the British Isles*. Cambridge: Cambridge University Press.

Tipping, R. 1994. "Ritual" floral tributes in the Scottish Bronze Age – palynological evidence, *J. Archaeol. Science* 21, 133–9.

Watkins, T. 1982. The excavation of an Early Bronze Age cemetery at Barns Farm, Dalgety, Fife, *Proc. Soc. Antiq. Scotland* 112, 48–141.

Wilthew, P. and Davis, M. 1997. Analysis of the composition of the necklace from Cist VII. In the late M.E.C. Stewart and G.J. Barclay, Excavations in burial and ceremonial sites of the Bronze Age in Tayside, 28–9, *Tayside and Fife Archaeological Journal* 3, 22–54.

8. Bronze Age Landscapes in Southern Europe

Graeme Barker

Abstract: This chapter considers the profound changes that took place in the agricultural landscape of southern Europe during the second millennium BC. Over the past 25 years our understanding of Bronze Age agriculture has been transformed not only by excavations and by studies of the artefacts, animal bones and plant remains recovered from them, but also by inter-disciplinary work in landscape archaeology integrating regional field surveys with geomorphology and palaeoecology. A variety of regional trends in agricultural organization is emerging, reflecting not only adaptations to particular environments but also perceptions of the risks and opportunities presented by those environments, as well as different social structures and economic goals. Linking such variability, however, was the capacity of Bronze Age farmers to change the Mediterranean landscape in ways that in some respects mark the beginnings of the development of the agricultural landscape of today.

Introduction

It was a shock for me to realise, as it must have been for our editor, that the 'Somerset to Simris' conference in honour of John Coles was exactly 30 years after the two of us first began studying archaeology as undergraduates, and were introduced to the tantalizing charms of the European Bronze Age by John. Anthony Harding and I had started our undergraduate life at Cambridge together as classicists, but in 1967 we both switched degree courses halfway through, to prehistoric archaeology. In due course John Coles appeared before the five undergraduates studying the 'NBI' (Neolithic, Bronze and Iron Ages) course that year, to deliver his thoughts on the European Bronze Age, all in eight lectures. In preparing for the conference I found that I still had those lecture notes, and it was very revealing to see what John felt able to say about Bronze Age settlement and land use thirty years ago. Radiocarbon dating had still had little impact on Bronze Age studies in the late 1960s, and typological studies of artefacts dominated most scholarship in most regions of Europe – the most recent synthesis of the European Bronze Age was dominated by a bewildering succession of invasions and counter-invasions (Gimbutas 1965), and the first applications of archaeological science to the metal content of Bronze Age artefacts seemed to be producing some equally confusing scenarios of population movements (Junghans *et al.* 1960, 1968). Few Bronze Age settlements had been excavated on any scale to modern standards, and good analyses of animal bones or plant remains were fewer still. The single lecture we received on 'settlement and agriculture' had to weave a story using the very few good case studies available, such as the recently-published excavations of the Dutch settlement of Elp (Waterbolk 1964) and Charles Higham's analyses of faunal samples from Neolithic and Bronze Age sites in Switzerland (Higham 1967), alongside whatever could be gleaned from the rock art of northern Italy and Scandinavia.

I had taken a special subject with Eric Higgs on the early history of agriculture, and after graduation I went to the British School at Rome to prepare a PhD thesis under his supervision on the 'economic prehistory' of central Italy. The late 1960s were the heyday of Cambridge palaeoeconomy, with faunal studies and site catchment analysis the linked paths to the promised land, and for three years I wandered about the Apennines making my

Author's Address: Graeme Barker, School of Archaeological Studies, University of Leicester, Leicester LE1 7RH

one-hour and two-hour catchment maps to the puzzled amusement of scores of Italian farmers and shepherds, interspersed with weeks spent in dusty attics in Italian universities looking at faunal collections. Towards the end of this research I wrote my first paper, on the subsistence archaeology of the Bronze Age of central Italy. (I owe an immense debt of gratitude to John for the time he spent as editor of the *Proceedings* introducing a fledgling author to the editing and publication process, starting with "cut it down to half the size, then come back and we'll talk about it".) I am taking that paper (Barker 1972), and contemporary publications on other regions of southern Europe, as my starting point for a consideration of how our understanding of Bronze Age land use and landscapes in the Mediterranean has developed over the past 20–25 years.

In the 1972 paper, I addressed a debate about subsistence in the 'Apennine Bronze Age' of the Italian peninsula that had begun with a major study by Puglisi in 1959 arguing that most people at that time were transhumant pastoralists, moving with their animals (sheep and goats especially) between widely-separated winter lowland and summer upland pastures, in the manner of the transhumant shepherds of historical and recent times. There were three main planks to his argument: many Bronze Age sites were located at high altitudes in the Apennine mountains; many faunal samples seemed to be dominated by sheep and goat bones; and the ceramic assemblages from Apennine Bronze Age sites often included sherds from what looked like ceramic versions of the metal strainers and vessels used by modern Italian shepherds to boil sheep's milk to make *pecorino* and *ricotta* cheese. By contrast, Carl Östenberg (1965) had argued on the basis of his excavations of the lowland settlement of Luni sul Mignone that the Apennine Bronze Age was characterized by sedentary mixed farming, because his excavations had revealed substantial rock-cut houses, and the faunal sample included pigs as well as cattle, sheep and goats. In my paper, and in the extended paper I wrote for the second volume of papers on the Early History of Agriculture project edited by Eric Higgs (Barker 1975), I took an intermediate position, arguing that we could discern a mixture of activities from sedentary mixed farming to transhumant pastoralism in the earlier Bronze Age, with a decline in the latter in the later Bronze Age marked by a trend from seasonal to permanent settlements in the uplands.

For northern Italy at that time, there was evidence for mixed farming in the organically-rich lakeside Polada settlements along the northern edge of the Po plain, and on the *terramare* settlements of the southern Po plain, though little detailed understanding of the nature of these systems, how they functioned, and in the case of the *terramare*, whether agricultural failure was a factor in the abandonment of the settlements in the middle of the millennium (Barfield 1971). In the case of southern France, the apparent lack of Bronze Age settlement sites, but presence of megalithic tombs, contrasting with the rich settlement evidence of the Neolithic, had been used as evidence of a shift to pastoralism (Bailloud 1966). Higgs put forward rather similar arguments for the development of long-distance transhumant pastoralism in upland Spain, on the evidence of the perceived similarities between the distribution of megalithic tombs and the present-day drove-roads of transhumant shepherds (Higgs 1976), and similar systems were postulated for the arid regions of south-east Spain by Walker (1973), though Gilman (1976) argued that the complex societies of the Argaric Bronze Age here were characterized by sedentary agricultural systems involving far greater levels of investment and organisation, including the development of elements of Mediterranean polyculture, such as terraced olive cultivation.

Polyculture, particularly the exploitation of the olive and the vine, was also seen as the key to Bronze Age farming in Greece in the brilliant synthesis by Colin Renfrew (1972) of the evidence for the development of complex societies in the Aegean Early Bronze Age in the third millennium BC, and then of the Minoan and Mycenanean civilizations in the second millennium BC. On the basis of the storage facilities of the Minoan and Mycenaean palaces and the Linear B tablet archives, he argued that the palaces were the centres of a massive redistribution operation, with workers being required to reach production targets of foodstuffs such as cereals, wine and oil, and other agricultural products such as wool, in return for rations, the agricultural surplus feeding the palace communities and providing goods for overseas trade.

The following discussion does not pretend to be comprehensive, but I have tried to select a series of case studies to illustrate how our understanding of the Mediterranean landscape in the second millennium BC has developed from these studies, sometimes remarkably, in the ensuing 25 years.

The Western Mediterranean

South-east Spain is characterized by some of lowest and most irregular rainfall in Europe, making agriculture a high risk venture, yet the archaeological record of the Millaran Chalcolithic and Argaric Bronze Age makes it clear that the region supported complex societies characterized by marked differences in wealth, status and power (Chapman 1990; Mathers 1994). Whilst exchange and trade were critical to this process of emerging complexity, it is also clear that effective strategies were developed for farming this hostile landscape.

In the second millennium BC, as before and after, the prime settlement locations in the arid lowlands were beside springs and the main watercourse junctions, where the seasonal floodwaters would be most prolific. Early Argaric (*ca.* 2300–1800 BC) settlements here generally clustered together at such locations, whereas the better-watered uplands of the region supported more dispersed settlement systems (Fig. 8.1). Their inhabitants grew a range of cereals and legumes, and though sheep and goats remained the

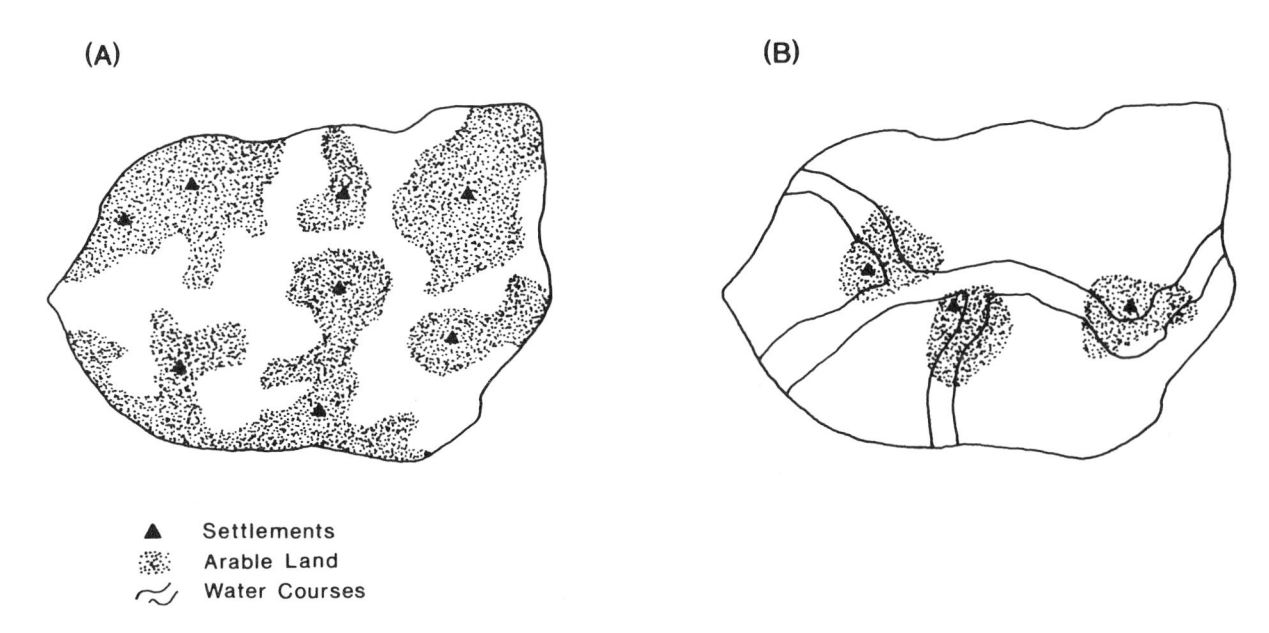

Fig. 8.1. Schematic representations of Bronze Age settlement distributions in the (A) humid upland and (B) semi-arid lowland zones of south-east Spain. After Mathers 1994.

principal stock as previously, there was an increasing emphasis on cattle and horses, the age structures of which suggest they were used respectively for ploughing and traction/draught (Driesch *et al.* 1985). It has been argued that primitive systems of floodwater farming were practised at this time, though there is as yet no indisputable evidence that the diversion walls and check dams in the vicinity of some of the settlements are definitely associated with them (Gilman & Thornes 1985). However, the presence on Later Argaric (1800–1600 BC) sites of moisture-demanding plants such as flax, and the construction of water storage facilities, as well as the location of sites by springs and watercourses, suggest that farmers had probably developed small-scale irrigation systems by the second millennium BC. Plant remains and wood charcoal indicate that olives and vines were cultivated (Gilman & Thornes 1985; Rivera Núñez & Walker 1989; Rodríguez & Vernet 1987, 1991), though it is not clear on what scale: although it is assumed that the increasing emphasis on raising cattle and horses for traction and/or draught indicates an expansion in the cultivated area, the first convincing evidence for terracing is not until the Late Bronze Age, whilst at the settlement of Gatas, although olives and vines were cultivated, barley was clearly the dominant species throughout the Chalcolithic and Bronze Age (Ruíz *et al.* 1992). The later second millennium also seems to have been marked by an increasing emphasis on sheep and goats, especially for milk and wool, on the evidence of the faunal samples from Cerro del Real and Cerro de la Encina (Chapman 1990; Harrison 1985).

The indications are, therefore, that Bronze Age farming in the arid lowlands of south-east Spain was an increasingly effective combination of small-scale irrigation horticulture adjacent to the settlements, arboriculture on the valley sides, and pastoralism on both local and more distant pastures exploited on a seasonal basis. In addition to this diversification at the household and settlement level, regional exchange systems were probably another important way of buffering against food shortages, allowing communities to convert craft objects into food. Regional variation in faunal data has been cited as evidence for such risk-avoidance exchange, though some of it may equally reflect the production of animals and animal products by peripheral communities to give as tribute to centres of Argaric power (Chapman 1996). In addition, the defensive site locations of many sites, and the military weaponry of the period, imply that risk-avoidance agricultural strategies do not seem to have been entirely effective, and in southern Almería in particular there is clear evidence for settlement abandonment and population decline. Evidence for the development of maquis and open evergreen woodland on the lowlands and *chaparral* in the mountains (López 1988; Rodríguez & Vernet 1991), and for episodes of erosion on hillslopes, and aggradation and delta formation on the coasts (Arteaga *et al.* 1986; Ruíz *et al.* 1992), suggest that Bronze Age farming severely degraded the landscape, perhaps lowering the water table. Comparable landcape transformations are indicated by pollen diagrams from El Acebron and the Laguna de las Madres, near Huelva in south-western Spain: between 2500 and 1600 BC there was a landscape of *dehesas*, open parkland managed for pasture, fuel, cork, wood, chestnuts, acorns and olives, but this was then subjected to drastic deforestation (Stevenson & Harrison 1992; Fig. 8.2). Such evidence can also be interpreted in terms of short-term climatic fluctuations (Fédéroff & Courty 1995), but whatever the agency – and it is likeliest that climate and human actions were both involved – the effects in such marginal and vulnerable landscapes could be equally catastrophic.

Information for much of the rest of Iberia is still very poor, beyond a general consensus that the development of mixed farming after the initial appearance of domesticates was generally a very long drawn-out process (Harrison 1994). One region that has been studied in some detail is La Mancha, an arid high plateau in central southern Spain – the name derives from the Arabic *ma' ancha*, meaning 'without water'. The region has traditionally supported a low-density population clustered into settlements near the few water sources. In the Bronze Age the people lived in widely-separated *motillas*, monumental dry-stone structures rather like the Balearic *talayots* and Sardinian *nuraghi*. Mixed farming was practised, but it is significant that there are indications of specialization within and between different *motillas* in terms of grain storage, livestock stabling, and cheese and wool production, and this variability, in combination with the hierarchy observable in the morphology of the *motillas*, has been used to suggest a regional system of agricultural organization controlled by the local elite. The arguments are much as for Bronze Age land use in south-east Spain (Chapman 1990), and rather similar hypotheses have been developed regarding the integration of regional exchange and agriculture in the west Mediterranean islands (Asole *et al.* 1995; Lewthwaite 1985).

There were also significant developments in the scale and complexity of land use in southern France during the second millennium BC, though agricultural technologies seem to have been fundamentally the same as those of the Neolithic and Chalcolithic until late in the Bronze Age (Gasco 1994). Many existing settlements remained in use, but there were numerous new foundations not only in the existing settlement enclaves but also in more marginal zones not much used for agricultural settlement hitherto, such as coastal lagoons and salt marshes, and the uplands. Parallel with the expansion in the settlement archaeology is the evidence in many pollen analyses and studies of charcoal from excavated sites for a progressive expansion of deforestation, with tree cover declining to as little as 10–20 per cent in some parts of southern France by the late second millennium BC (Guilaine *et al.* 1986; Laval & Médus 1994; Vernet 1991, 1995). In the Pyrenees, traces of burnt fields indicate the use of swidden farming (*essartage*), and there is similar evidence for burning vegetation off in the lowlands.

Numerous sites have produced evidence for the cultivation of cereals and legumes. The dominance of barley over wheat in the botanical samples is not surprising given its suitability for a wider variety of soil types. The grain was stored in ceramic vessels and pits or, occasionally, in raised granaries. Whilst sheep and goats are usually the dominant stock at most sites, there is much variation in the faunal samples, but it is difficult to know how much of this reflects preservation and recovery biases rather than real differences in husbandry strategies. However, one interesting trend is the increase of cheese-making equipment through the Bronze Age (Gasco 1988). Furthermore, many upland caves were certainly used for stabling sheep and goats on the evidence of the dung deposits they contain, and detailed phytolith studies of sediments at sites like the Abri de Font-Juvénal rock shelter near Carcassonne indicate that the site was used for the folding of sheep and goats on a seasonal basis. It therefore still seems likely that, as argued 25 years ago, one feature of Bronze Age land use in southern France was transhumant pastoralism linking mountains and lowlands, but it was integrated within a regional system of sedentary mixed farming. Both, too, were embedded within a wider economic system: the evidence for food storage and specialization is in parallel with other evidence for expanding exchange systems that included not only craft goods but also salt (Gasco 1994, 104).

There is also widespread evidence that the expansion and intensification in agricultural systems during the Bronze Age in southern France had an increasingly damaging impact on the landscape (Guilaine *et al.* 1986; Laval & Médus 1994; Vernet 1991, 1995). In addition to the evidence mentioned above for a systematic decline in the amount of woodland, anthracology (charcoal analysis) suggests the increased use of the practice of cultivation after scrub burning, which is particularly likely to cause local damage to slope stability. Sediment studies confirm the trend to increasingly severe hillslope erosion, an increase in stream sediment loads, and alluvial deposition on the plains (Provensal 1995). Within the woodland that remained, boxwood progressively replaced oak, and there are hints at the increasing management or protection of particular species that were valuable for human food such as walnuts, hazelnuts, and chestnuts. However, whilst the scale of land use and landscape degradation in the Bronze Age of southern France were very marked compared with preceding systems of land use, long-term regional studies here demonstrate that they were still very small in comparison with the economic systems and landscape transformations of the pre-Roman Iron Age and classical antiquity (Provensal 1995; Trément 1994).

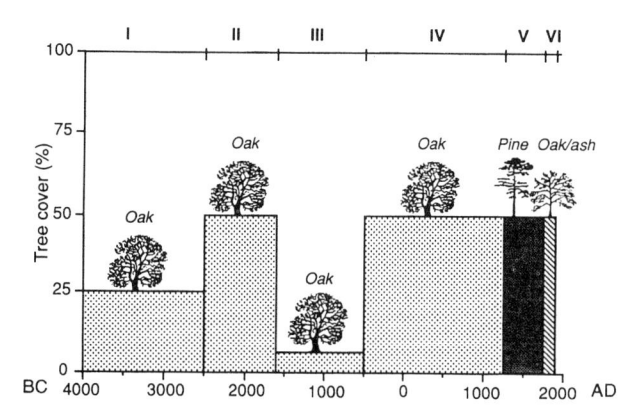

Fig. 8.2. Woodland development and dehesas *at El Acebrón and Laguna de las Madres. After Stevenson & Harrison 1992.*

The Central Mediterranean

The archaeological record for the Bronze Age of northern Italy is extraordinarily prolific especially because of the survival of numerous waterlogged settlements on the shores of the sub-Alpine lakes and along the southern side of the Po plain. Although many of these sites have been known for well over a century, it is only recently that detailed regional surveys and modern large-scale excavations are allowing us to move beyond generalizations regarding how these communities were organized and sustained. Air photography and ground surveys of the *terramare* of the southern Po plain indicate a remarkable density of settlement (Fig. 8.3) – sites are on average only six kilometres apart – and clear evidence of hierarchy, with sites dividing into large (7–11 ha), medium (2–3 ha) and small (1–1.5 ha) (Cardarelli 1989; Cremaschi 1997). Villages such as Fiavé in the north consisted of collections of wooden cabins laid out to a regular plan (Perini 1987), and the indications are that the *terramare* were much the same (Bernabó Brea *et al.* 1997). These communities raised a wide variety of plant foods, and kept livestock for milk products as well as meat, the evidence of the subsistence data being supported by an array of equipment such as ards, hoes, sickles, whisks, sieves, and churns (Bernabò Brea *et al.* 1997; Jones & Rowley-Conwy 1985). Faunal analyses suggest that animals and animal products were exchanged between lower-order settlements, and that by the end of the Bronze Age the larger settlements (which housed craft specialists working in pottery, textiles, metal and an array of prestige goods) were in part sustained by foodstuffs supplied by the sites in the hinterlands they controlled (Clark 1986). Further evidence for organizational complexity are the drainage ditches that had to be maintained around the *terramare* to keep them from flooding – some of them were quite elaborate, draining the waters away to neighbouring stream channels.

Cave excavations in the mountains adjacent to these major settlement zones provide further insights into the nature of pastoralism at this time. The cave of Arene Candide is best known for its long Palaeolithic and Neolithic sequence, but it was also occupied through the second millennium. The faunal sample indicates a remarkably stable system of animal management dominated by sheep and goat husbandry from the Early Neolithic, the animals exploited for their milk as well as their meat, but by the Bronze Age the system had become less intensive, with greater emphasis on meat (Rowley-Conwy 1997). The cave is only a short distance from the coastal plain, and earlier indications of seasonality of use suggested that it was probably used in the summer by shepherds belonging to nearby lowland settlements (Rowley-Conwy 1991). However, the final analysis of the faunal material, combined with other lines of evidence, makes it much more likely that the cave was in fact used throughout the year, perhaps by a specialized pastoral community on the fringe of the arable zone (Rowley-Conwy 1997).

Another settlement in the Ligurian Apennines, Castellaro di Uscio, at almost 750 metres above sea level, also has strong evidence for all-year-round occupation. The composition of its plant sample indicates that the cereals were being brought to the site rather than being grown around it, and its pottery was also imported, suggesting that this community, like that of Arene Candide, functioned by being embedded within a regional exchange system linking it with lowland communities. Microwear studies indicate that the community was producing (but rarely using) flint arrowheads, and also working bone, antler and hide, presumably to produce items for exchange (Maggi 1990). The site has also yielded the first clear evidence in the region for hillslope terracing by Bronze Age people. There is evidence for similar specialized settlements being established in the mountains of northern Italy during the Bronze Age (Maggi & Nisbet 1991), coinciding with numerous palaeoecological indicators for woodland clearance by fire and the development of hillslope erosion resulting in mineral inwash into lakes (Cruise 1991; Lowe 1991; Scaife 1991).

The widespread replacement of hoe agriculture by plough agriculture, and of small-scale animal husbandry by more specialized pastoralism, is assumed to have been characterized amongst most Bronze Age societies by transformations in status, power and social control, transformations that also imply a profound shift in gender relations – that is, the increasing dominance of males (Sherratt 1981). In northern Italy there is much evidence for such an increasing emphasis on adult male status in the grave-goods of burials, in statue menhirs showing individuals wearing the same daggers and axes found in the burials, and in the images of males bearing daggers and axes in the rock art of Monte Bégo and Val Camonica alongside many motifs of cattle and of ploughing with cattle-drawn ploughs. There are also images of what seem to be settlements as they would appear if viewed from the mountains (Barfield & Chippindale 1997; Fig. 8.4): solid rectangular areas (houses?), lines (paths?), and rectangular open areas (fields?) with larger (cattle?) and smaller (sheep?) dots within them. Looking down from his mountain viewpoint, the shepherd saw "a masculine world of adult male status, a declaration to the world, whether of gods or of fellow-men, of its achievements.... the plough and its private potentials left its mark on the people of Mediterranean and of Alpine Europe" (Barfield & Chippindale 1997, 124–5).

In the peninsula, as in northern Italy, the most striking feature of the settlement record is the evidence for exponential settlement growth during the second millennium. Several regional surveys have shown that the Apennine Bronze Age (*ca.* 1700–1300 BC) was invariably characterized by a consistent filling out of the landscape. On the western lowlands, numbers of sites increased dramatically at this time: in the Fiora and Albegna valleys, for example, most parts of the topography were used for settlement, but for the first time these included naturally defensible

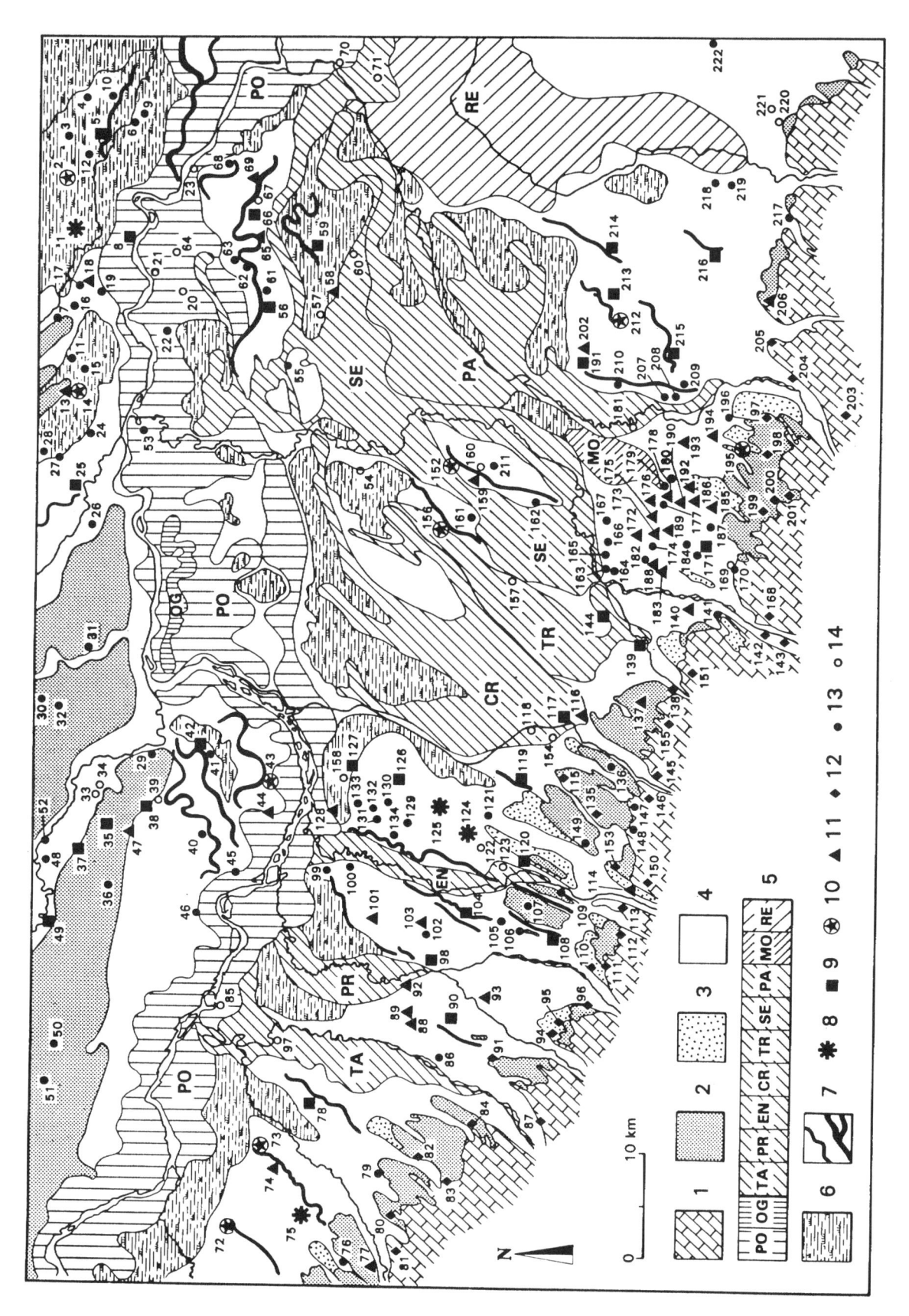

Fig. 8.3. Geomorphological map of part of the Po plain, showing the distribution of terramare sites. Key: 1. Pre- and Pleistocene marine deposits; 2. Pleistocene terraces; 3. Holocene fans; 4. Holocene alluvium, laid down before and up to the Bronze Age; 5. Holocene alluvium by major water channels, post-Bronze Age; 6. marshes drained in medieval and modern times; 7. Bronze Age palaeochannels. 8. terramare larger than 10 hectares; 9. 4–9 ha terramare; 10 2–3 ha terramare; 11. c.1 ha terramare; 12. hill sites; 13. terramare smaller than 1 ha; 14. burial sites. After Cremaschi 1997.

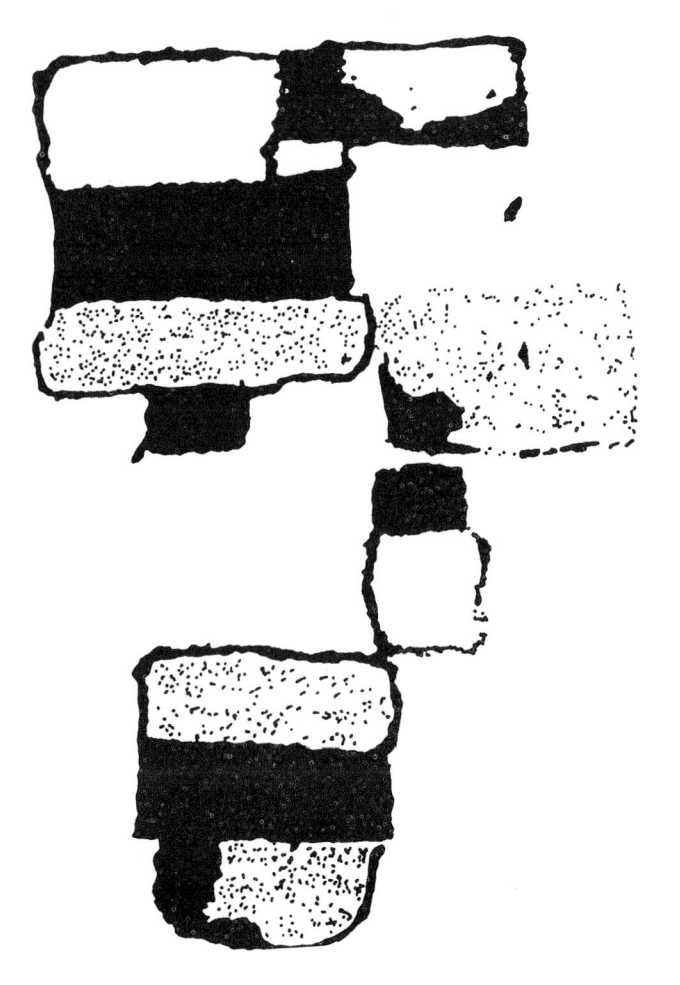

Fig. 8.4. Possible representations of settlement units depicted in the rock carvings of Monte Bégo. After Barfield & Chippindale 1997.

locations, and during the course of the Bronze Age, settlement increasingly concentrated on bluffs and hilltops overlooking the rivers, often narrow rock promontories that were easily defensible (Miari 1987). In the interior, the intermontane valleys and basins were now permanently occupied, some of them densely, settlement concentrating especially in lakeside locations (Balista *et al.* 1991–92; Barker *et al.* 1986; Malone & Stoddart 1994). On the eastern side of the Apennines, the Biferno valley survey found Apennine Bronze Age material at over 50 locations (Barker 1995; Fig. 8.5). The distributions indicate that the principal zone of permanent settlement extended from the lower to the middle valley during the course of the second millennium BC, with hunting and pastoral activities creating 'off-site' material from the mountains at the head of the valley, 2000 metres above sea level, down to the coast. The expansion of settlement throughout the peninsula is documented in increased evidence for clearance activities in the pollen record both on the lowlands and in the interior (Alessio *et al.* 1986; Cruise 1991; Hunt & Eisner 1991).

Information on the internal organization of peninsular Bronze Age settlements remains limited. The well-known rock-cut houses of Luni sul Mignone now seem unlikely to be Bronze Age, and certainly they are anomalous: Apennine Bronze Age sites invariably consist of collections of pits and stakeholes suggesting simple encampments. A series of family households has been inferred at the Torre Spaccata site near Rome (Anzidei *et al.* 1985). The Biferno valley sites divided into two categories, small collections of surface pottery in areas measuring less than 50 x 50 metres, and much larger assemblages in areas between about 50 and 100 metres in diameter. Geophysical investigations and test excavations of a series of these sites suggested that the former represented single huts for individual families and the latter small clusters of huts perhaps for three to five family groups. It is only really in Etruria that by the Late Bronze Age we can begin to discern a significant settlement hierarchy dominated by local centres (Di Gennaro 1991–2; Fig. 8.6), the network in many respects presaging the development of Villanovan Iron Age and Etruscan cities. The best investigated settlement, Sorgenti della Nova, was characterized by substantial oval cabins on its summit and smaller rock-cut dwellings downslope, which the excavator suggests were used respectively by higher and lower social groups (Negroni Catacchio 1989).

Throughout the peninsula, Bronze Age communities grew a range of cereals and legumes – the botanical remains commonly include emmer, barley, club wheat, spelt, millet, bean, vetch and pea – and managed their stock for both meat and secondary products (Agostini *et al.* 1991–2; Barker 1995; Grossi Mazzorin 1995; Wilkens 1991–92). Within Etruria, the emergence of regional settlement hierarchies around the Tuscan copper ores in the Late Bronze Age coincided with significant changes in subsistence and economy: an expansion in arable cultivation is registered in several pollen diagrams, catchment studies emphasize the increasing importance of access to good arable land (Pacciarelli 1982), the appearance of new crops implies intensification in the agricultural system (Follieri 1981), and within the pastoral sector there may have been a degree of diversification and specialization – sheep are the most frequent stock at Narce and Torrionaccio, cattle at Luni and Monte Rovello, pig at Sorgenti della Nova. Outside Etruria, however, the indications are of an agricultural society with few social divisions within individual communities or within regional groups, with a predominantly lithic technology, and production at the household level (Barker 1995). The dominant rituals known consist of food offerings by springs in caves (Whitehouse 1992), implying a secretive ritual strikingly different from the conspicuous destruction or discard of material wealth, the elaborate funerary rituals, and the ceremonial monuments of many contemporary societies in Europe. Occasional burials of humans accompanied by complete skeletons or part-articulated limbs of sheep, dog, or cattle provide hints at the pastoral ideology of these Apennine Bronze Age societies (Wilkens 1995),

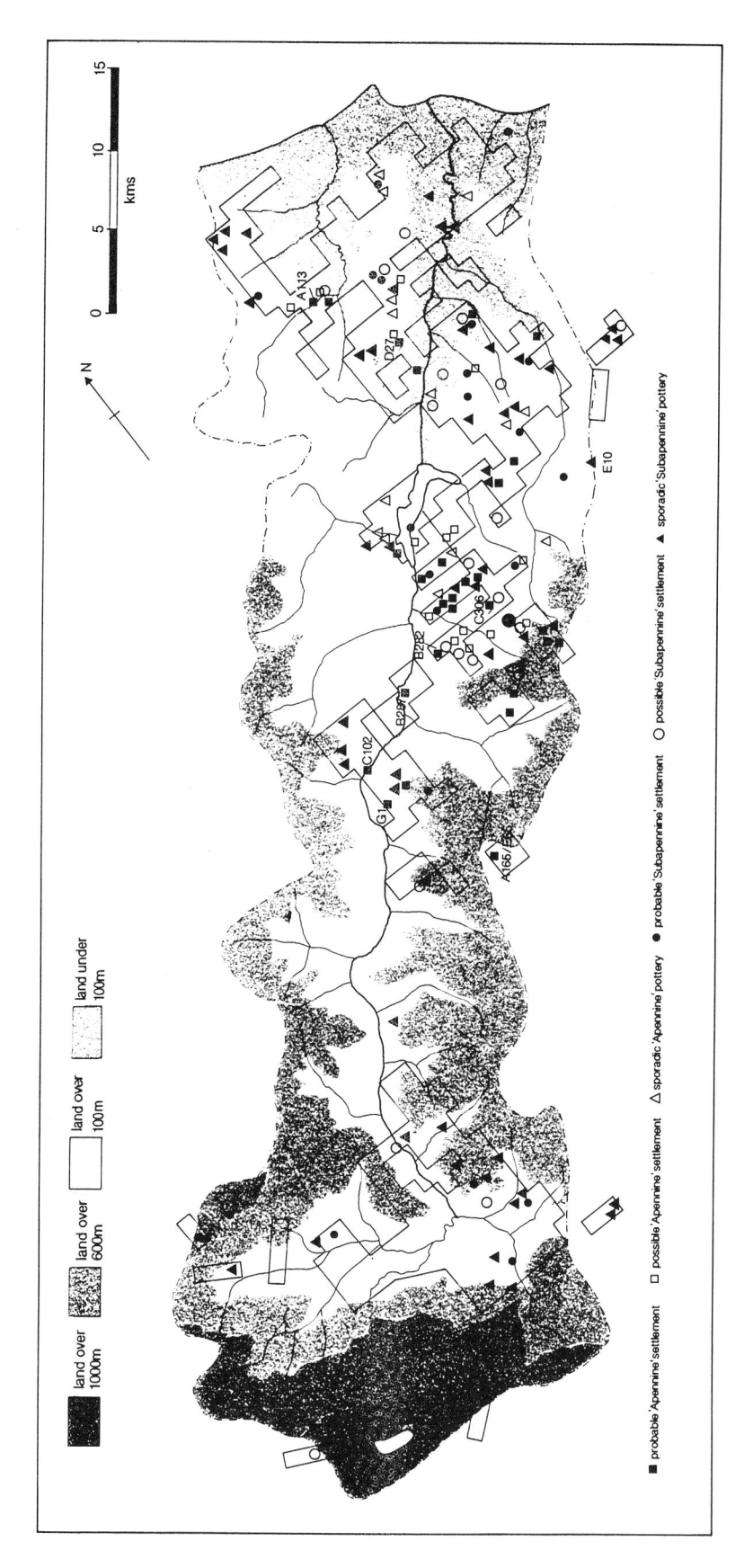

Fig. 8.5. Bronze Age settlement in the Biferno valley, central-southern Italy. After Barker 1995.

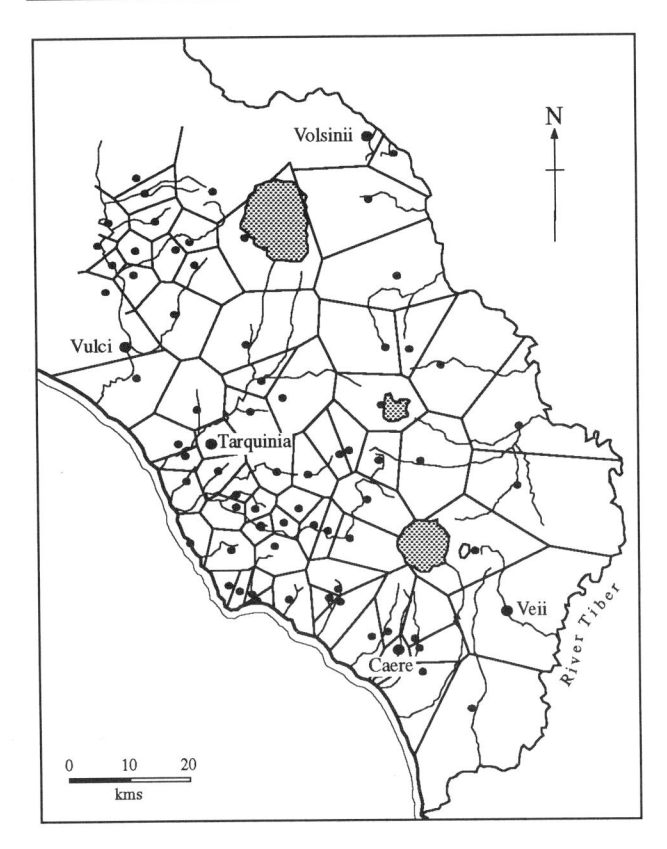

Fig. 8.6. Idealized (Thiessen polygon) territories of Late Bronze Age centres in Etruria. After Barker & Rasmussen 1998, adapted from Di Gennaro 1991–2.

an ideology that Robb (1994) argues was just as male-orientated as that of the Alpine communities around Monte Bégo and Val Camonica.

Bronze Age sites have been found in the Apennine mountains not just between 1000 and 1200 metres, where marginal farming is possible, but right up to 2000 metres, where such farming is obviously impossible. The second millennium BC clearly marked the first systematic use of high Apennine pastures, presumably for short-distance transhumant grazing from communities living in the immediately adjacent valleys and basins. The use of these high plateaux by shepherds and herders must have been a factor in the uniformity of Apennine Bronze Age pottery styles – the mountains were now surely a means of communication and interchange for the communities living on either side rather than a barrier.

On the other side of the Adriatic, the Neothermal Dalmatia Project, an integrated survey and excavation programme in the broken limestone country of the Croatian coast, has provided some of most detailed insights into regional settlement trends on the eastern side of the Adriatic (Chapman *et al.* 1996). The survey revealed a dramatic increase in settlement in the region during the third and second millennia BC: whereas the primary settlement zone was previously the main arable basins, the Bronze Age was characterized by the colonization of stony soils and bare limestone karst, and the use of dry-stone walls not just for settlements and enclosures but for field systems and terrace walls (Fig. 8.7). Trial excavations did not find enough faunal material to provide much information on livestock management, and it is also uncertain whether olive stones are from wild or domestic stock, but it seems most likely that polyculture based on terrace technology underpinned the settlement expansion. Clearance cairns were built on the newly-colonised land, their use for burials assumed to be an affirmation of ancestral rights to the land. As in Italy and the western Mediterranean, the settlement transformations of the second millennium in Dalmatia were in the context of new power relations involving the accumulation and exchange of prestige goods, and here too they impacted significantly on the landscape: every Bronze Age site on the karst excavated by the project produced evidence for a deeper soil profile at the time of the occupation, and for its erosion beginning during the occupation and continuing afterwards. The implication seems clear that Bronze Age farmers played a significant role in the creation of the Dalmatian karst.

The Eastern Mediterranean

The same seems true of Greece, on the evidence of a series of regional landscape projects integrating intensive programmes of field-walking with geomorphological studies. On Melos, for example, the Bronze Age witnessed not only a dramatic expansion of rural settlement within the territory of the emerging centre of Phylakopi (Renfrew & Wagstaff 1982) but also the beginnings of significant erosion (Wagstaff 1981). In the southern Argolid, debris flows indicate widespread sheet erosion in the Bronze Age, thought to be the result of the expansion of the arable farming to steeper slopes and the reduction of fallow land (van Andel & Runnels 1987; Pope & van Andel 1984; Fig. 8.8). Erosion and alluviation caused the sea to recede from formerly-coastal sites such as Dhimini and Tiryns (Zangger 1991), and there is mounting evidence for major hydraulic engineering at coastal Aegean centres such as Pylos and Troy to improve harbour facilities in an attempt to control silting (Zangger *et al.* 1997; in press) (Fig. 8.10).

The 25 years or so since the publication of Renfrew's *Emergence of Civilisation* have not significantly altered his arguments concerning the fundamental characteristics of the Aegean 'palace economies', though later research has provided further nuances, in particular indicating how these were integrated into the agricultural landscape as a whole. Palaces such as Knossos and Pylos owned huge estates in their territories and extracted surplus foodstuffs and other agricultural products such as wool from their subservient populations, giving food rations back in return – mainly bread and oil, the traditional poverty diet of the Mediterranean peasant. One of the more striking features

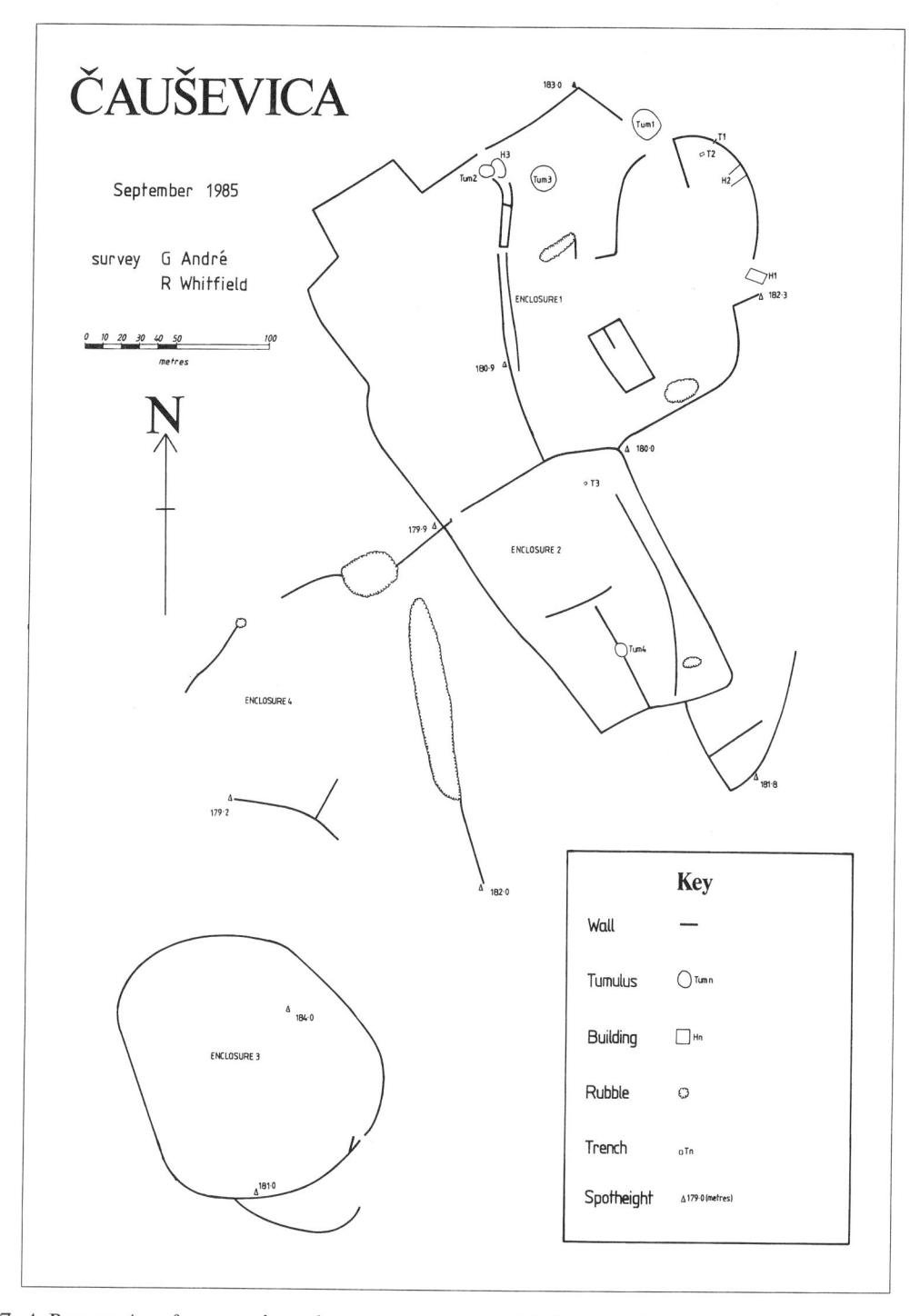

Fig. 8.7. A Bronze Age farmstead, enclosures and terraced fields in Dalmatia. After Chapman et al. 1996.

of the Linear B tablets is that a palace such as Pylos owned flocks of sheep in the tens of thousands, but probably only a dozen plough oxen – they are named individually in fact, emphazing the critical role they played in arable production. On Melos, too, the emergence of Phylakopi coincided with a rise in cattle in the faunal sample from Phase II, assumed to mark the greater importance of plough cattle as the arable sector was intensified to feed the growing urban population (Gamble 1982; Fig. 8.9). Halstead (1992a, 1994) suggests that the palace elites farmed their estates extensively and in a specialized way, the land being cultivated for cereals and oil and large flocks of sheep and goats being maintained, probably in systems of transhumance, though pollen analysis suggest that summer grazing in the mountains was still only of modest extent.

One note of caution about the role of polyculture has been sounded by Hamilakis (1996a), who emphasizes that

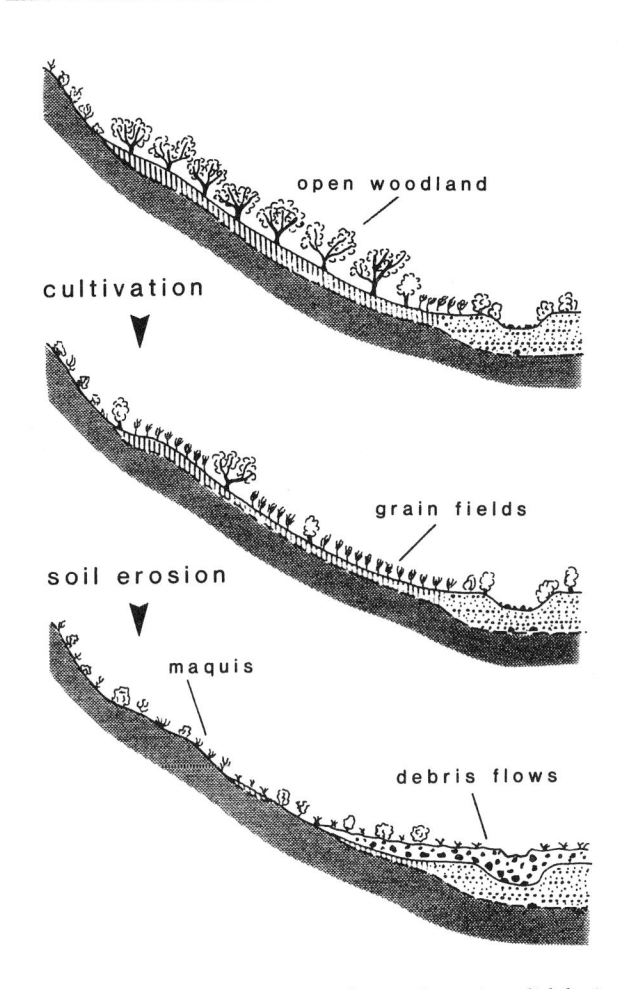

Fig. 8.8. Debris flow erosion in the southern Argolid during the Bronze Age, ascribed to agricultural expansion and intensification. After van Andel & Runnels 1987.

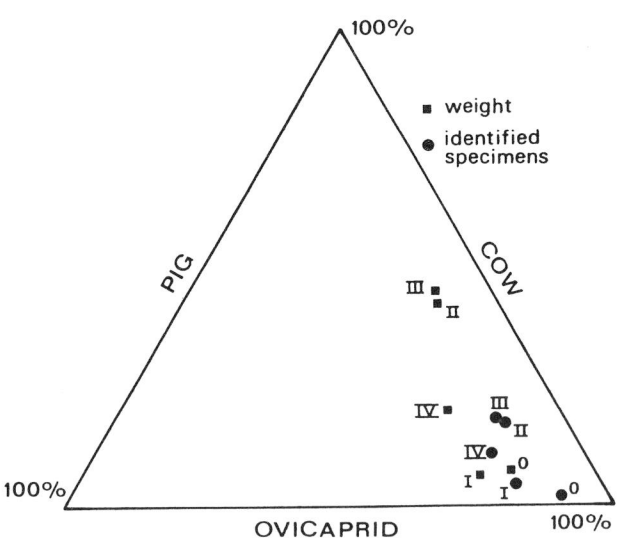

Fig. 8.9. Changing frequencies in both weight and number of specimens for the main domestic animals for each phase from Phylakopi. After Gamble 1982.

we need to understand the separate histories of products such as wine and oil: on Crete, for example, systematic wine production seems to have begun in the first palatial period and reached a peak in the second palatial period, whereas oil production started in the second palatial period and intensified in the post-palatial period. He argues that the primary importance of wine and oil was in support of elite social interactions such as feasting and drinking ceremonies, and gift exchange. Hunting played a similarly important role for the palace elites, its social and ideological role emphasized by both iconographic evidence and by dog bones buried in a number of Mycenaean tombs (Hamilakis 1996b).

The specialized palace system can be constrasted with a highly diversified 'black economy' outside the palatial sector, as revealed by archaeobotanical and archaeozoological studies of material from excavated farms: "small-scale horticulture may have remained the norm throughout the Bronze Age, with extensive agriculture largely a feature of land worked under palatial control" (Halstead 1994, 202). Diversification in both arable and pastoral husbandry can be observed at the level of individual settlements as well as regionally. Crops included a wide range of cereals (emmer, bread wheat, hulled and naked barley, millet), legumes (pea, bean, lentil, vetch), and oil-, fruit- and nut-bearing plants (olive, grape, flax, fig, pear, strawberry), as well as other plants grown as spices, dyes and perfumes. Sheep and goats were invariably the main stock, managed especially for meat production, though secondary products were also important. The entire system was meshed together in flows of goods and services to and from the palaces, a form of surplus banking that Halstead has termed 'social storage' (Halstead & O'Shea 1982). The system was a development of earlier Neolithic systems of exchange in foodstuffs and livestock which, whilst probably developed primarily to buffer neighbouring communities against risk of harvest failure (Halstead 1987, 1989; Halstead & Jones 1989), were in themselves an important element in the process of wealth differentiation and social ranking that culminated in the Aegean palace systems (Halstead 1992b).

Conclusion

Although this survey has been necessarily brief and selective, one striking feature of the data is the extent to which the major models that were being constructed in the early 1970s about the Mediterranean landscape in the Bronze Age – the development of floodwater as a way of coping with aridity in south-east Spain, the role of pastoralism in opening up many upland regions in the western and central Mediterranean and integrating them with the lowlands, the role of polyculture in the expansion of the arable zone and supporting the 'palace economies' of the Aegean – still remain valid in their essential characteristics. At the same time, of course, land use models have been

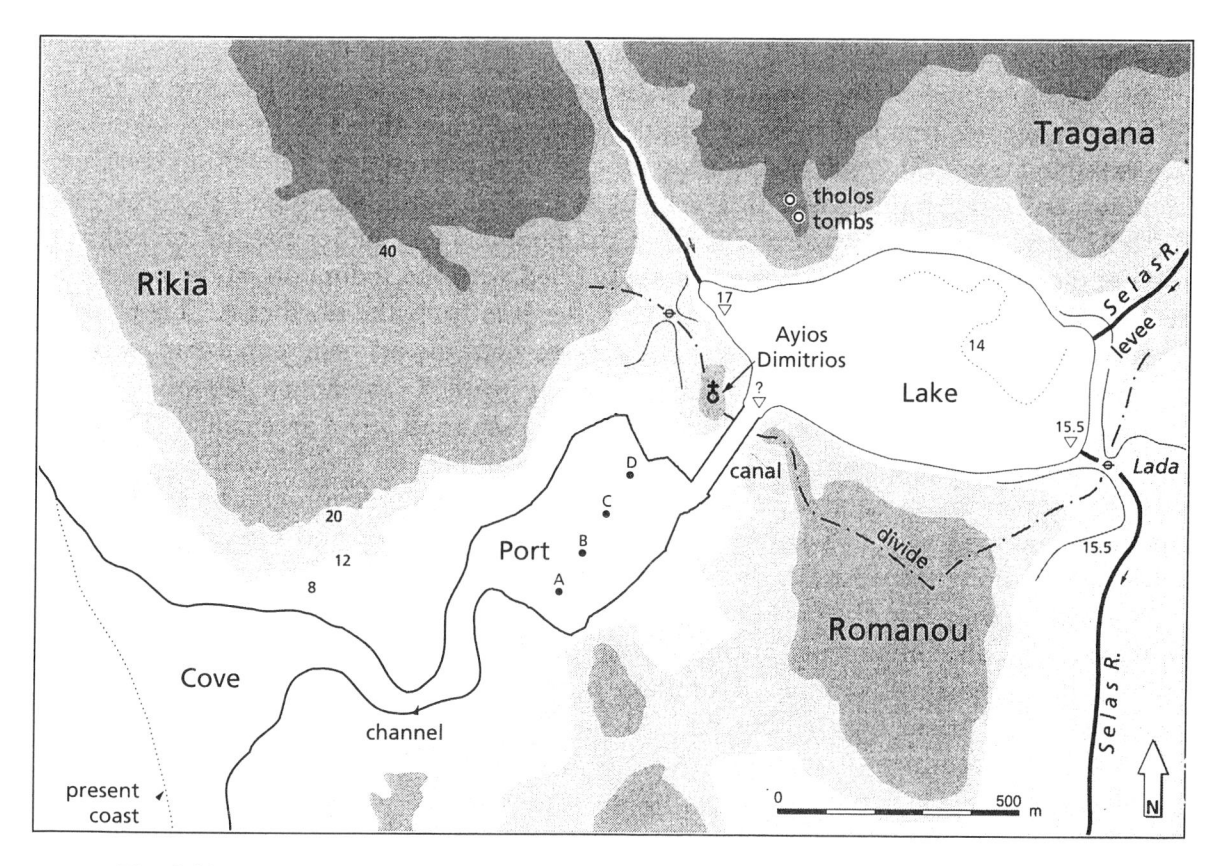

Fig. 8.10. Reconstruction of the Late Bronze Age port of Pylos. After Zangger et al. 1997.

greatly qualified and amended as survey and excavation data sets have allowed us to model regional systems of environment, settlement and land use with increasing detail. Significant developments in understanding include: the role of animal secondary products for many societies; the integration of horticulture, arboriculture amd small-scale pastoralism in south-east Spain; the density of lowland settlement in regions such as the Po plain; the common evidence for substantial settlement expansion in both lowlands and mountainous interiors; the development of specialized, permanently occupied, settlements in many upland areas alongside seasonal sites; and, in the Aegean, the importance of diversified peasant economies alongside the specialized palace economies documented in the Linear B archives, and the social as well as economic role of polyculture. Contrasting with this emphasis on regional diversity is the striking frequency of geomorphological and palaeoecological evidence for the accelerating scale of human impact on the Mediterranean landscape in terms of deforestation, colluviation, and alluviation.

Whilst the new regional data sets invariably emphasize spatial and temporal variability in Bronze Age land use, they also demonstrate how such variability can now be understood in terms of the integration of subsistence activities into regional economic and social structures. Foodstuffs, animal products and live animals were critical components of local and regional exchange systems, often alongside the prestige items that have always been easier for archaeologists to trace. It is increasingly clear that different systems of production and exchange operated side by side, not just regionally but in terms of individual communities and households. And in turn, these systems were embedded in systems of social reproduction in which ideologies played a profound role. Thirty years after hearing those lectures by John about how we had to try to understand Bronze Age landscapes through settlement excavations, subsistence data, material culture studies, and rock art studies, it is salutary to see how the lectures still hold true, though perhaps we have learned that what is most important is not what those different components contribute individually, but how they inter-relate.

Bibliography

Agostini, S., De Grossi Mazzorin, J. & D'Ercole, V. 1991–92. Economia e territoria in Abruzzo durante la media età del Bronzo, *Rassegna di Archeologia* 10, 419–26.

Alessio, M., Allegri, L., Bella, F., Calderoni, G., Cortesi, C., Dai Pra, G., De Rita, D., Esu, D., Follieri, M., Improta, S., Magri, D., Narcisi, B., Petrone, V. & Sadori, L. 1986. 14C dating, geochemical features, faunistic and pollen analyses of the uppermost 10 m core from Valle di Castiglione (Rome, Italy), *Geologica Romana* 25, 287–308.

Andel, Tj. van, & Runnels, C. 1987. *Beyond the Acropolis: the Archaeology of the Greek Countryside*. Stanford: Stanford University Press.

Anzidei, A.P., Bietti-Sestieri, A.M. & De Santis, A. 1985. *Roma e il Lazio dall'Età della Pietra alla Formazione della Città.* Rome: Quasar.

Asole, M., Foschi Nieddu, A. & Nieddu, F. 1995. Attività agricole delle comunità nuragiche del centro Sardegna: alcune annotazioni riguardo ai dati archeologici e agli aspetti socio-economici. In N. Christie (ed), *Settlement and Economy in Italy 1500 BC to AD 1500*, 179–81. Oxford: Oxbow.

Arteaga, O., Hoffman, G., Schubart, H. & Schulz, H.D. 1986. Investigaciones geológicas y archeológicas sobre los cambios de la l'nea costera en el litoral de la Andalucía mediterránea. Informe preliminar (1985), *Anuario Arqueológico de Andalucía II. Actividades Sistematicas*, 117–22. Sevilla: Junta de Andalucía.

Bailloud, G. 1966. La civilisation du Rhône et le Bronze ancien du Midi de la France, *Revue Archéologique de l'Est et du Centre-Est* 17, 131–164.

Balista, C., Carancini, G.L. & Guerzoni, R.P. 1991–92. Insediamenti nell'area della conca velina (Province di Terni e Rieti), *Rassegna di Archeologia* 10, 403–10.

Barfield, L.H. 1971. *Northern Italy Before Rome*. London: Thames and Hudson.

Barfield, L.H. & Chippindale, C. 1997. Meaning in the later prehistoric rock engravings of Monte Bégo, Alpes-Maritimes, France, *Proc. Prehist. Soc.* 63, 103–28.

Barker, G. 1972. The conditions of cultural and economic growth in the Bronze Age of central Italy, *Proc. Prehist. Soc.* 38, 170–208.

Barker, G. 1975. Prehistoric territories and economies in central Italy. In E.S. Higgs (ed.) *Palaeoeconomy*, 111–175. Cambridge: Cambridge University Press.

Barker, G. 1995. *A Mediterranean Valley. Landscape Archaeology and Annales History in the Biferno Valley*. London: Leicester University Press.

Barker, G. & Rasmussen, T. 1998. *The Etruscans*. Oxford: Blackwell.

Barker, G., Coccia, S., Jones, D.A. & Sitzia, J. 1986. The Montarrenti survey, 1985: problems of integrating archaeological, environmental and historical data, *Archeologia Medievale* 13, 291–320.

Bernabò Brea, M., Cardarelli, A. & Cremaschi, M. (eds) 1997. *Le Terramare. La Più Antica Civiltà Padana*. Milan: Electa.

Cardarelli, A. 1989. L'età del bronzo: organizzazione del territorio, forme economiche, strutture sociale. In *Modena dalle Origine all'Anno Mille. Studi di Archeologia e Storia I*, 86–127. Bologna: Panini.

Chapman, J., Shiel, R. & Batović, Š. 1996. *The Changing Face of Dalmatia: Archaeological and Ecological Studies in a Mediterranean landscape*. London: Leicester University Press and Society of Antiquaries of London.

Chapman, R.W. 1990. *Emerging Complexity. The Later Prehistory of South-East Spain, Iberia and the West Mediterranean*. Cambridge: Cambridge University Press.

Chapman, R.W. 1996. Problems of scale in the emergence of complexity. In J. Arnold (ed), *Emergent Complexity. The Evolution of Intermediate Societies*, 35–49. Ann Arbor: International Monographs in Prehistory.

Clark, G. 1986. Economy and environment in northeastern Italy in the second millennium BC, *Papers of the British School at Rome* 54, 1–28.

Cremaschi, M. 1997. Terramare e paesaggio padano. In M. Bernabò Brea, A. Cardarelli, & M. Cremaschi (eds), *Le Terramare. La Più Antica Civiltà Padana*, 107–25. Milan: Electa.

Cruise, G.M. 1991. Environmental change and human impact in the upper mountain zone of the Ligurian Appennines: the last 5000 years. In R. Maggi, R. Nisbet & G. Barker (eds), *Archeologia del Pastorizia nell'Europa Meridionale II*, 175–94. Bordighera: Istituto Internazionale di Studi Liguri.

Di Gennaro, F. 1991–2. Insediamento e territorio, *Rassegna di Archeologia* 10, 197–205.

Driesch, A. von, Boessneck, J., Kokabi, M. & Schäffer, J. 1985. Tierknochenfunde aus der bronzezeitlichen Höhensiedlung Fuente Alamo, Provinz Almería. Munich, *Studien über frühe Tierknochenfunde von der Iberischen Halbinsel* 9, 1–75.

Fédéroff, N. & Courty, M.-A. 1995. Le rôle respectif des facteurs anthropiques et naturels dans la dynamique actuelle et passée des paysages méditerranéens. Cas du bassin de Vera, sud-est de l'Espagne. In S. van der Leeuw (ed), *L'Homme et la Dégradation de l'Environnement*, 115–141. Sophia Antipolis: APDCA.

Follieri, M. 1981. Significato dei resti vegetali macroscopici. In N. Negroni Catacchio (ed.) *Sorgenti della Nova: una Comunità Protostorica e il suo Territorio nell'Etruria Meridionale*, 261–68. Rome: Consiglio Nazionale delle Ricerche.

Gamble, C.S. 1982. Animal husbandry, population and urbanisation. In C. Renfrew and M. Wagstaff (eds) *An Island Polity: the Archaeology of Exploitation in Melos*, 161–71. Cambridge: Cambridge University Press.

Gasco, J. 1988. L'Age du bronze final en Languedoc occidental, état de la question, *Mémoires du Musée de Préhistoire d'Ile de France* 1, 465–580.

Gasco, J. 1994. Development and decline in the Bronze Age of southern Fance: Languedoc and Provence. In C. Mathers & S. Stoddart (eds) *Development and Decline in the Mediterranean Bronze Age*, 99–128. Sheffield Archaeological Monographs 8. Sheffield: University of Sheffield.

Gilman, A. 1976. Bronze age dynamics in southeast Spain, *Dialectical Anthropology* 1, 307–19.

Gilman, A. & Thornes, J.B. 1985. *Land Use and Prehistory in South-East Spain*. London: Allen & Unwin.

Gimbutas, M. 1965. *Bronze Age Cultures in Central and Eastern Europe*. The Hague: Mouton.

Grossi Mazzorin, J. 1995. Economie di allevamento in Italia centrale della media età del bronzo alla fine dell'età del ferro. In N. Christie (ed), *Settlement and Economy in Italy 1500 BC to AD 1500*, 167–77. Oxford: Oxbow.

Guilaine, J., Rancoule, G., & Vaquer, J. 1986. *Carsac, une Agglomeration Protohistorique en Languedoc*. Toulouse: Centre d'Anthropologie des Sociétés Rurales.

Halstead, P. 1987. Traditional and ancient rural economy in Mediterranean Europe: plus ça change? *J. Hellenic Studies* 107, 77–87.

Halstead, P. 1989. The economy has a normal surplus: economic stability and social change among early farming communities of Thessaly, Greece. In P. Halstead and J. O'Shea (eds), *Bad Year Economics: Cultural Responses to Risk and Uncertainty*, 68–80. Cambridge: Cambridge University Press.

Halstead, P. 1992a. Agriculture in the Bronze Age Aegean. In B. Wells (ed.) *Agriculture in Ancient Greece*, 105–17. Stockholm: Skrifter Utgivna av Svenska Institutet i Athen 4, 42.

Halstead, P. 1992b. Dimini and the 'DMP': faunal remains and animal exploitation in late neolithic Thessaly, *Annual British School Athens* 87, 29–59.

Halstead, P. 1994. The North-South divide: regional paths to complexity in prehistoric Greece. In C. Mathers & S. Stoddart (eds) *Development and Decline in the Mediterranean Bronze Age*, 195–219. Sheffield Archaeological Monographs 8. Sheffield: University of Sheffield.

Halstead, P., and Jones, G. 1989. Agrarian ecology in the Greek islands: time stress, scale and risk, *J. Hellenic Studies* 109, 41–55.

Halstead, P. and O'Shea, J. 1982. A friend in need is a friend indeed: social storage and the rise of the Minoan palace. In C. Renfrew and S.J. Shennan (eds) *Ranking, Resource and Exchange*, 92–99. Cambridge: Cambridge University Press.

Hamilakis, Y. 1996a. Wine, oil and the dialectics of power in Bronze

Age Crete: a review of the evidence, *Oxford J. Archaeology* 15 (1), 1–32.
Hamilakis, Y. 1996b. A footnote on the archaeology of power: animal bones from a Mycenaean chamber tomb at Galatas, NE Peloponnese, *Annual British School Athens* 91, 153–66.
Harrison, R.J. 1985. The 'Policultivo Ganadero' or the Secondary Products Revolution in Spanish agriculture, 5000–1000 bc, *Proc. Prehist. Soc.* 51, 75–102.
Harrison, R J. 1994. The Bronze Age in northern and north-eastern Spain. In C. Mathers & S. Stoddart (eds) *Development and Decline in the Mediterranean Bronze Age*, 73–97. Sheffield Archaeological Monographs 8. Sheffield: University of Sheffield.
Higgs, E.S. 1976. The history of European agriculture – the uplands, *Philosophical Trans. Royal Soc. London* B, 272, 159–73.
Higham, C.W. 1967. Stock-rearing as a cultural factor in prehistoric Europe, *Proc. Prehist. Soc.* 33, 84–106.
Hunt, C.O. and Eisner, W.R. 1991. Palynology of the Mezzaluna core. In A. Voorrips, S.H. Loving, & H. Kamermans (eds) *The Agro Pontino Survey Project*: 49–59. Amsterdam: Studies in Prae- en Protohistorie 6.
Jones, G.A. & Rowley-Conwy, P. 1985. Agricultural diversity and sub-Alpine colonisation: spatial analysis of plant remains from Fiavé. In C. Malone & S. Stoddart (eds), *Papers in Italian Archaeology* IV Part ii, 282–95. Oxford: British Archaeological Reports, International Series 244.
Junghans, S., Sangmeister, E. & Schröder, M. 1960. *Metallanalysen kupferzeitlicher und frühbronzezeitlicher Bodenfunde aus Europa*. Studien zu den Anfängen der Metallurgie 1. Berlin: Mann.
Junghans, S., Sangmeister, E., & Schröder, M. 1968. *Kupfer und Bronze in der frühen Metallzeit Europas*. Studien zu den Anfängen der Metallurgie 2. Berlin: Mann.
Laval, H., & and Médus, J. 1994. Une séquence pollinique subboréal-subatlantique dans la vallée des Baux: changements de végétation climatiques et anthropiques de l'Age du Bronze à celui du Fer en Provence, *Arcs. Sciences Genève* 47, 83–93.
Lewthwaite, J. 1985. Social factors and economic change in Balearic prehistory, 3000–1000 bc. In G. Barker & C.S. Gamble (eds) *Beyond Domestication in Prehistoric Europe: Investigations in Subsistence Archaeology and Social Complexity*, 205–231. London: Academic Press.
López, G. 1988. Estudio polínico de seis yacimientos del sureste español, *Trabajos de Prehistoria* 45, 335–45.
Lowe, J.J. 1991. The chronology and correlation of evidence for prehistoric pastoralism in southern Europe. In R. Maggi, R. Nisbet & G. Barker (eds), *Archeologia del Pastorizia nell'Europa Meridionale II*, 151–73. Bordighera: Istituto Internazionale di Studi Liguri.
Maggi, R. (ed) 1990. *Archeologia dell'Appennino Ligure. Gli Scavi del Castellaro di Uscio*. Bordighera: Istituto Internazionale di Studi Liguri.
Maggi, R. & Nisbet, R. 1991. Prehistoric pastoralism in Liguria. In R. Maggi, R. Nisbet & G. Barker (eds), *Archeologia del Pastorizia nell'Europa Meridionale I*, 265–96. Bordighera: Istituto Internazionale di Studi Liguri.
Malone, C. & Stoddart, S. 1994. *Territory, Time and State: the Archaeological Development of the Gubbio Basin*. Cambridge: Cambridge University Press.
Mathers, C. 1994. Goodbye to all that? Contrasting patterns of change in the south-east Iberian Bronze Age c.24/2200–600 BC. In C. Mathers & S. Stoddart (eds) *Development and Decline in the Mediterranean Bronze Age*, 21–71. Sheffield Archaeological Monographs 8. Sheffield: University of Sheffield.
Miari, M. 1987. La documentazione dei siti archeologici dei bacini del Fiora e dell'Albegna: criteri di classificazione e analisi dei modelli di insediamento dell'età del bronzo, *Padusa* 23, 113–45.
Negroni Catacchio, N. 1989. L'abitato del Bronzo Finale di Sorgenti della Nova (VT). Possibilità di confronti con i modelli abitativi dei centri villanoviani. In *Atti del Secondo Convegno Internazionale Etrusco*, 271–83. Florence: Istituto di Studi Etruschi.
Östenberg, C.E. 1965. *Luni sul Mignone e Problemi della Preistoria d'Italia*. Rome: Acta Instituti Romani Regni Sueciae 4, 75.
Pacciarelli, M. 1982. Economia e organizzazione del territorio in Etruria Meridionale nell'età del Bronzo media e recente, *Dialoghi di Archeologia* 2, 69–79.
Perini, R. 1987. The typology of the structures on Bronze Age wetland settlements at Fiavé and Lavagnone. In J.M. Coles & A.J. Lawson (eds) *European Wetlands in Prehistory*, 75–93. Oxford: Oxbow.
Pope, K.O. and van Andel, Tj.H. 1984. Late Quaternary alluviation and soil formation in the southern Argolid: its history, causes and archaeological implications, *J. Archaeol. Science* 11, 281–306.
Provensal, M. 1995. Holocene sedimentation sequences in the Arc river delta and the Etang de Berre in Provence, southern France. In J. Lewin, M.G. Macklin, & J.C. Woodward (eds) *Mediterranean Quaternary River Environments*, 159–65. Rotterdam: Balkema.
Puglisi, S. 1959. *La Civiltà Appenninica. Origine delle Communità Pastorali in Italia*. Florence: Sansoni.
Renfrew, C. 1972. *The Emergence of Civlisation*. London: Methuen.
Renfrew, C. and Wagstaff., M. 1982. *An Island Polity: the Archaeology of Exploitation in Melos*. Cambridge: Cambridge University Press.
Rivera Núñez, D. & Walker, M.J. 1989. A review of palaeobotanical findings of early *Vitis* in the Mediterranean and of the origins of cultivated grape-vines, with special reference to new pointers to prehistoric exploitation in the western Mediterranean, *Review of Palaeobotany and Palynology* 61, 205–37.
Robb, J. 1994. Gender contradictions, moral coalitions, and inequality in prehistoric Italy, *J. European Archaeology* 2.1, 20–49.
Rodríguez, Ariza M. & Vernet, J.L. 1987. Etude paléoécologique du gisement Chalcolithique de Los Millares. In W.H. Waldren & R.C. Kenward (eds) *Oxford International Western Mediterranean Bell Beaker Conference*, 1–7. Oxford: British Archaeological reoports, International Series 331.
Rodríguez, Ariza M. & Vernet, J.L. 1991. Primiers resultats paléoécologiques de l'établissement Chalcolithique de Los Millares. In W.H. Waldren, J.A. Ensenyat & R.C. Kenward (eds) *IInd Deya Conference of Prehistory. Recent Developments in Western Mediterranean Prehistory: Archaeological Techniques, Technology and Theory* 1, 1–16. Oxford: British Archaeological Reports, International Series 574.
Rowley-Conwy, P. 1991. Arene Candide: a small part of a larger pastoral system? In R. Maggi, R. Nisbet & G. Barker (eds), *Archeologia del Pastorizia nell'Europa Meridionale II*, 95–116. Bordighera: Istituto Internazionale di Studi Liguri.
Rowley-Conwy, P. 1997. The animal bones from Arene Candide: final report, *Memorie dell'Istituto Italiano di Paleontologia Umana* 5, 153–277.
Ruíz, M., Risch, R., González Marcén, P., Castro, P., Lull, V. & Chapman, R.W. 1992. Environmental exploutation and social structrure in prehistoric south-east Spain, *J. Mediterranean Archaeology* 5 (1), 3–38.
Scaife, R. 1991. Pastoralism and the upper montane tree limit of the Italian Alps. In R. Maggi, R. Nisbet & G. Barker (eds), *Archeologia del Pastorizia nell'Europa Meridionale II*, 195–211. Bordighera: Istituto Internazionale di Studi Liguri.
Sherratt, A.S. 1981. Plough and pastoralism: aspects of the Secondary Products Revolution. In I. Hodder, G. Isaac & N. Hammond (eds) *Pattern of the Past: Studies in Memory of David Clarke*, 261–305. London: Duckworth.

Stevenson, A.C. & Harrison, R.J. 1992. Ancient forests of Spain. A model for land-use and dry forest management in south-west Spain, *Proc. Prehist. Soc.* 58, 227–47.

Trément, F. 1994. *Histoire de l'Occupation du Sol et Évolution des Paysages dans le Secteur des Étangs de Sainte-Blaise (Bouche-du-Rhône). Essai d'Archéologie du Paysage.* Aix-en-Provence: Université de Provence, Thèse de Doctorat Nouveau Regime.

Vernet, J.-L. 1991. L'histoire du milieu méditerranéen humanisée révélée par les charbons de bois. In J. Guilaine (ed) *Pour une Archéologie Agraire*, 369–408. Paris: Colin.

Vernet, J.-L. 1995. Anthracologie, biostratigraphie et relations homme-milieu en région méditerranéenne. In S. van der Leeuw (ed.) *L'Homme et la Dégradation de l'Environnement*, 175–84. Sophia Antipolis: APDCA.

Wagstaff, J.M. 1981. Buried assumptions: some problems in the interpretation of the 'Younger Fill' raised by recent data from Greece, *J. Archaeol. Science* 8, 247–64.

Walker, M.J. 1973. *Aspects of the Neolithic and Copper Ages in the River Basins of the Segura and Vinalopó, Southeast Spain.* Oxford: unpublished D.Phil. thesis.

Waterbolk, H.T. 1964. The Bronze Age settlement of Elp, *Helinium* 4, 97–131.

Whitehouse, R. 1992. *Underground Religion: Cult and Culture in Prehistoric Italy.* London: University of London, Accordia Research Centre.

Wilkens, B. 1991–92. I resti faunistici di alcuni insediamenti dell'età del Bronzo nell'Italia centro-meridionale, *Rassegna di Archeologia* 10, 463–69.

Wilkens, B. 1995. Animali di contesti rituali nella preistoria d'Italia centro-meridionale, *Atti della I Convegno Nazionale di Archeozoologia*, 201–207. Rovigo: Centro Polesano di Studi Storici Archeologici ed Etnografici.

Zangger, E. 1991. Prehistoric coastal environments in Greece: the vanished landscapes of Dimini Bay and Lake Lerna, *J. Field Archaeology* 18, 1–16.

Zangger, E., Timpson, M.E., Yavzenko, S.B., Kuhnke, F. & Knauss, J. 1997. The Pylos regional archaeological project, Part II. Landscape evolution and site preservation, *Hesperia* 66:4, 549–641.

Zangger, E., Timpson, M., Yazvenko, S. & Leiermann, H. in press. Searching for the ports of Troy. In P. Leveau, K. Walsh, F. Trément & G. Barker (eds) *Mediterranean Landscape Archaeology 2: Environmental Reconstruction.* Oxford: Oxbow Books.

9. From Skåne to Scotstown: some notes on amber in Bronze Age Ireland

George Eogan

Abstract: Amber was used in Ireland during the two main periods of the Bronze Age, the Earlier and Later periods, beads being the objects used. As it has not been unequivocally established that natural material occurs in adequate quantities to meet demand it appears that it had to be imported, from Britain and ultimately from the Danish area. During the Earlier Bronze Age the British source appears to have been Wessex; for the Later Bronze Age possibly the Covesea Group of eastern Scotland. The earlier group, small in number, came from graves and, therefore, had a ritual function; the later group had an abundance of beads and in contrast came from more varied find places – habitation sites, but especially in hoards and unassociated necklaces. Like contemporary gold ornaments amber was worn as a personal ornament but it probably had a wider significance, serving as an item of prestige and thereby indicating that its owners were persons of power and wealth.

Introduction

Like gold, amber has been prized and valued throughout the ages and consequently objects fashioned from it would have been attractive to wear as ornaments but could also have had a special significance. As amber does not occur naturally in Ireland, it would have been a rare material and that would add to its value both materially and intrinsically. Apart from a small number of Early Bronze Age objects – cups, spacer-plates for necklaces, gold-bound discs – which were confined to the south of England (Gerloff 1975, 198–200; 257–58), no special objects were made from it in either Britain or Ireland. Therefore, the bulk of the amber that was used during the Bronze Age consisted of beads which could have constituted necklaces.

Over the past two hundred years amber has become an aspect of Irish archaeological studies. An early find, possibly from a burial, at Castlemartyr, Co. Cork, was discovered in 1805 and was published by Crofton-Croker some years later (1824, 253). Since then numerous finds of amber have come to light and a number have been published (Coffey 1912; Gogan 1932; Prendergast 1960). In 1945 Eoin MacWhite reviewed the material as a whole, while subsequently in 1976 Catherine Feeney carried out a comprehensive study, but this has not been published. The extensive study of amber in prehistoric Britain by Beck and Shennan (1991) is most relevant. Amber can be a poor survivor; when subjected to air its surface can corrode so that many examples may have disintegrated, but the bog finds are generally well preserved. Apart from some finds from habitation sites, mainly discovered within recent years and dating from the end of the Bronze Age, and a small number of graves dating to the Earlier Bronze Age, practically all the finds form either parts of hoards or consist of single finds of necklaces. There are also some finds of single beads. The finds from the habitation sites and most of the burials are the result of controlled excavation. Apart from Rathtinaun, discovered during excavations at a lake habitation site, the other hoards and individual necklace finds have turned up by chance mainly due to turf-cutting. Taking that set of evidence, which only covers the final (Dowris) phase of the Bronze Age, there are 37 finds. Of these the find-places of 21 are known. Fifteen came from bogs, three from arable land, two from stony land and one from the lake-side settlement of Rathtinaun. Therefore, the finds are predominantly "wet finds", more specifically bog finds (Table 9.1).

Author's Address: George Eogan, 59 Brighton Road, Rathgar, Dublin 6.

County	Townland	Collection and Registration No.	Nature	Find place and year	No. of beads	Publication
Antrim	Craigbilly/Connor	Some in U.M.	Necklace	Bog "A few years before 1879"	about 40, possibly two necklaces	Sotheby, *Sale Catalogue of the Knowles Collection* 1929, 49, lot 709.
Antrim	----------	212	Necklace (some beads "ancient")	----------	32	MacWhite 1944, 127.
Antrim	----------	----------	Necklace	----------	about 120	Gogan 1932, 66.
Cavan	Callanagh	----------	Hoard	Bog, about 1885	-------	Eogan 1983, 62.
Cavan	Kilmore	----------	Necklace (also bronze(?) spacer rings)	----------	25	MacWhite 1944, 123.
Cavan	Skeagh	N.M.I. 1927: 2633–42	Necklace	Bog, 1921	19	MacWhite 1944, 127.
Cavan	----------	N.M.I. 1897:23	Necklace	Bog	278	MacWhite 1944, 127.
Cork	Mountrivers	N.M.I. 1908:8–13	Hoard	Agricultural land, 1907	13	Eogan 1983, 77.
Cork	Murrahin North	Cork Pub. Mus. G159	Necklace	Bog, about 1920	80+	O'Kelly *J.C.H.A.S.* 55(1950), 96–7.
Derry	nr. Bellaghy	----------	Necklace	Bog, about 1770	----------	Sotheby *Sale Catalogue*, 13.7.70.
Derry	Kurin	U.M. 1962:260 U.M. 1966:A342 Cork Pub. Mus.	Necklace	Bog	about 556	Flanagan *U.J.A.*, 27(1964), 92. Flanagan *U.J.A.*, 31(1968), 52.. O'Kelly *J.C.H.A.S.*, 55(1956), 96–7.
Donegal	Meennalabban	----------	Necklace	Bog, 1932	108	MacWhite 1944, 122–7.
Fermanagh	Killycreen West	Co. Museum Armagh 50–52:1938	Hoard	Bog, shortly before 1939	6	Eogan 1983, 85–6, no. 79.
Galway	Derrybrien	N.M.I. 1954:11	Necklace, gold fragment	Bog, 1954	about 500	Prendergast 1960.
Kilkenny	Croghtenclough	N.M.I. WG. 34–47	Necklace (inc. gold beads)	----------	about 13	MacWhite 1944, 123.
Laois	Portlaoise	U.M. Arch. Eth. Camb. MC/99/249.1–159	Hoard	?Agricultural land, 1872	109+	Eogan 1983, 101, no. 97.
Limerick	Tooradoo	N.M.I. SA. 1927:2	Hoard	Bog, 1926	105	Eogan 1983, 104–5, no. 103.
Mayo	Ballycurrin	N.M.I. 1862:581–84, R611–13 whereabouts of others not known	Hoard	Bog, 1861–64 (found at different times and locations)	at least 249	Eogan 1983, 107–108, no. 107. Briggs, 1997.
Meath	Whitegates	N.M.I. 1897:23	Necklace	Bog	278	MacWhite 1944, 127.
Monaghan	Mullaghmacanteer	N.M.I. 1956:312	Necklace	Bog, c.1866	"many"	----------
Monaghan	Scotstown	N.M.I. 1879:6–18a	Hoard	Agricultural land, 1870s	----------	Eogan 1983, 114–15, no. 116.
Monaghan	Sheeaghan	----------	Necklace	Bog, 1848	38	Moore, *Arch. Jour.*, 9(1852), 303–04.
Offaly	Ballylin	N.M.I. 1982:75 a–j	Necklace	Bog, 1908	10	Kelly 1983–4
Offaly	Meenawaun (Banagher)	N.M.I. 1918:349–53 N.M.I. 1971:206–08	Hoard	Field, rock, early 20th century	128	Eogan 1983, 115–16, no. 117.
Offaly	Cogran	N.M.I. 1890:46 B.M. 1854.7-14.298	Hoard	Stony field, 1847	about 160	Eogan 1983, 116–17, no. 118.
Sligo	Rathtinaun	N.M.I. E21:553–612	Hoard	On edge of crannog, 1954	31	Eogan 1983, 151–52, no. 24–54.
Ireland	----------	N.M.I. 1863:2084	Necklace	----------	9	----------
Ireland	----------	N.M.I. 1864:1841	Necklace	----------	58	----------
Ireland	----------	N.M.I. 1882:103–137	Necklace	----------	35	----------
Ireland	----------	N.M.I. 1882:138–148	Necklace	----------	11	----------
Ireland	----------	N.M.I. 1907:53	Necklace	----------	80	----------
Ireland	----------	N.M.I. 1907:54	Necklace	----------	48	----------
Ireland	----------	N.M.I. 1907:55	Necklace	----------	11	----------
Ireland	----------	N.M.I. 1907:56	Necklace	----------	58	----------
Ireland	----------	N.M.I. C 841	Necklace	----------	75	----------
Ireland	----------	N.M.I. C 849	Necklace	----------	21	----------
Ireland	----------	N.M.I. C 839	Necklace	----------	101	----------
Ireland	----------	B.M. 1854:12-27.59	Necklace	----------	58	----------

Table 9.1. Provisional list of amber from hoards and individual necklaces from Late Bronze Age (Dowris Phase), Ireland

Over the past forty years or so there has been a marked decrease in the number of amber finds that have come to light. As mentioned, nearly all of these finds come from bogs; the last bog find of a hoard/necklace was in 1954, the Derrybrien necklace. This decrease coincides with the increased mechanisation involved in turf-cutting. Previously when turf was cut by hand it was much easier to detect amber finds (indeed other finds also), but as a result of the use of machines, many of which are enormous in size, the possibility of noticing amber objects is virtually non-existent.

Due to its nature, a resin exuded from trees, the working of amber is not difficult. In nature there are, however, different forms which are difficult to define and whose origin is hard to determine. For Ireland Stephen Briggs (1983–4; 1997), largely as a result of various mentions of amber or amber-like substances in earlier accounts or inference from geographical conditions, postulated that it should be possible to collect specimens of natural amber. But there are no visible deposits, nor are beach or other viable scatters known. It is, however, possible that lignite deposits, for instance, could contain amber but extraction from such a source would involve major quarrying operations. On the evidence to hand it appears that natural pieces that have been collected are small and scrappy, whereas it is common to have beads over 2 cm in diameter, and as these are well-formed they had to be shaped from larger pieces. For the Late Bronze Age the large number of beads known – and these must only be a fraction of the total number in use – indicate that amber was used in quantity. But on the evidence available there was hardly significant native amber available to meet demand.

Native amber is, of course, known from Norfolk and other parts of eastern England. Infra-red spectroscopy has shown that such amber is "Baltic" and its presence on the western side of the North Sea is the result of natural relocation from Jutland or adjoining areas. It has not been established on scientific grounds that even the amber used in Bronze Age England was "native". It is, however, the opinion of Beck and Shennan (1991, 37) that only a small amount of natural amber would have been available, which need not have been sufficient to meet the needs of English users. If that was the case, there would hardly have been sufficient quantities also to serve the Irish demand. Accordingly it seems more likely that the amber used in Ireland was imported from the north of Europe, Jutland or the West Baltic region. Due to the variety in size and to some extent in shape, it was probably raw material that was imported; bead manufacture would have taken place locally.

The present paper is a limited review of the use of amber in Ireland during the Bronze Age. It is based on published accounts of hoards, unassociated necklaces, habitation sites and grave finds. That amounts to 48 finds and about 3,500 beads. In addition there are finds of individual amber beads. Such unassociated finds are difficult to date but on form some, for instance the bead from Marahill, Co. Cavan (*JRSAI* 94 (1964), 103), could date from the Bronze Age, more likely the latter part. It may be noted that amber was not used in Ireland in pre-Bronze Age times, while in post-Bronze Age times it only had a limited use and the beads in use during those periods tend to be of different forms to those used during the Bronze Age (cf Hencken 1950, 150–1). Even if individual finds that date from the Bronze Age are not particularly common, by not including them the overall interpretation is restricted, not only numerically but spatially as well.

In view of John Coles's special interest in Baltic and Scandinavian Bronze Age problems, as well as British and Irish developments and interrelationships, it may be appropriate to offer this small contribution which I hope he will consider relevant to the overall theme of the conference, part of which is concerned with Scandinavian connections during the Bronze Age. The fact that it is possible to put forward in this paper some interpretations owes much to the fruits of his wide-ranging research. They have been heavily drawn upon.

The Material

Earlier Bronze Age Amber

This was a time of extensive use of amber in different parts of Europe, including England where up to one hundred find places are known (Fig. 9.1). The great concentration was in Wessex, especially in Wiltshire where it was frequently associated with rich burials, one of which, the "Golden Barrow" at Upton Lovell, had amongst its grave goods a spacer-plate necklace that consisted of at least a thousand beads (Beck and Shennan 1991, 175).

There is no clear evidence that amber was used in Ireland during the Beaker period; it was only during the Earlier Bronze Age that amber came into use and then only to a limited extent (Fig. 9.2). Due to its rectangular shape it is possible that the chevron-decorated sheet gold plate from Castlemartyr, already mentioned, might have been in use during the initial stage of the Bronze Age, the Killaha-Ballyvalley Stage. This stage is approximately equivalent to Wessex I. At least three Wessex graves, Bush Barrow (2 examples), Upton Lovell (1 example), Clandon (2 examples) and also the contemporary Norfolk grave at Little Cressingham had sheet gold decorated plates, either rectangular or lozenge in shape (Taylor 1980, 188, pls. 23b; 25 a, b, c; 26 a, b). The finds from the inhumation burial of a young male in the Mound of the Hostages, Tara, Co. Meath, and also those from graves at Kiltierney, Co. Fermanagh and Dromara, Co. Down, should in view of their associations date form the Derryniggin-Omagh stage, which is equivalent to Wessex II. The Castlemartyr bead is somewhat irregular in shape and is well-preserved. The Dromara bead is missing. The beads from Tara and Kiltierney are not so well preserved and in form they tend to be flat. The Tara burial is the richest: it contained a necklace consisting of five beads of amber, and also beads

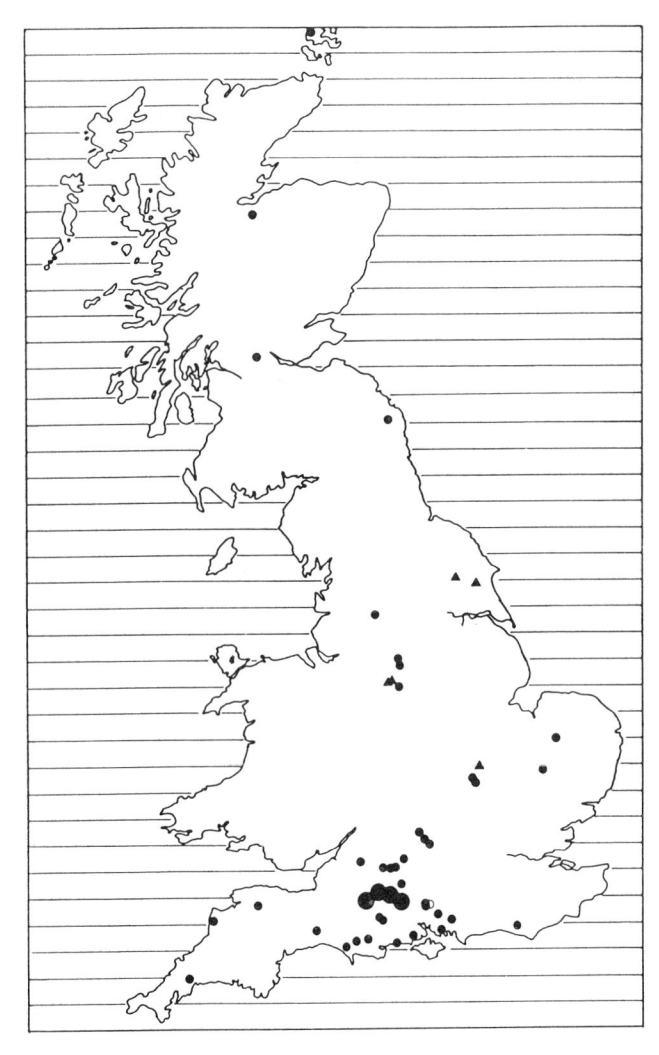

Fig. 9.1. Distribution of Earlier Bronze Age amber finds in Britain. From Beck and Shennan 1991, Fig.6.1.

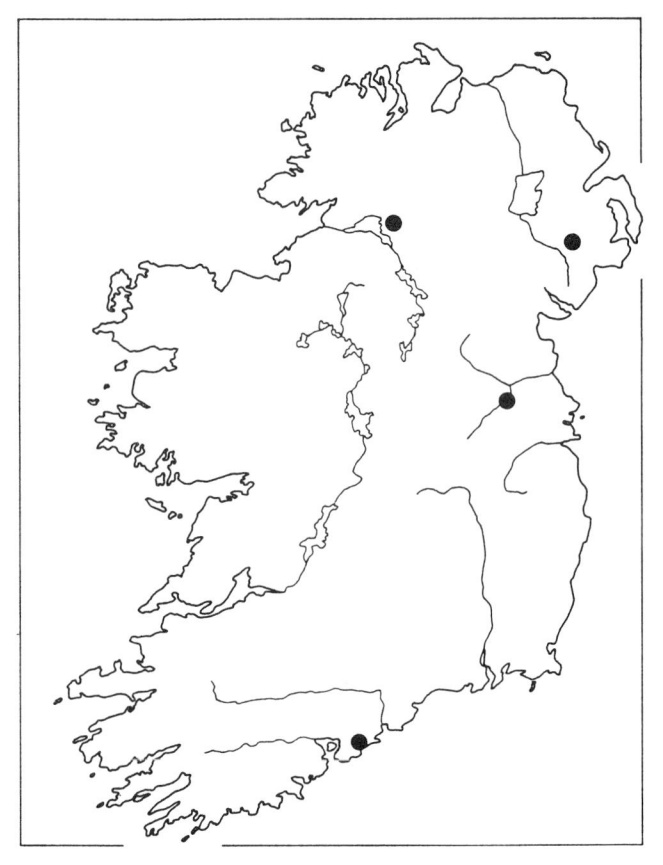

Fig. 9.2. Distribution of Earlier Bronze Age amber finds in Ireland.

of faience, shale and tubular bronze. Near the feet there was a bronze razor and a piece of a bronze awl (Ó Ríordáin 1955). Burial 7, from the stone circle at Kiltierney, was a cremation in a pit. The grave-goods consisted of four amber beads, three of which were spherical, the fourth being lozenge-shaped (Daniells and Williams 1977, 37, 39, fig. 7: 4–9). The Dromara, Co. Down, burial (?cremation) contained a biconical pigmy cup placed inside an urn, now lost. An amber bead may also have been present (Kavanagh 1977, 82). These amber beads probably functioned as necklaces, the composite example from Tara being the most elaborate. The young man who wore it must have been a person of high social status.

Apart from a possible association of a bead and palstave from Colchester, Essex (Beck & Shennan 1991, 152), amber does not appear to have been used in Britain and Ireland during the succeeding centuries (Acton Park-Killymaddy Stages). A slight revival took place during the Taunton-Bishopsland stage, but only in Britain. It is recorded that amber was associated in a burial with a gold "cape" at Mold, Flintshire (Powell 1953) and amber beads were also present in the hoards from Wedmore, Somerset and Glentrool, Kircudbrightshire (Beck & Shennan 1991, 176, 188; Coles 1959–60, 113–14). No amber has been recorded from Ireland during the equivalent Bishopsland stage or the succeeding Roscommon stage. But the pattern changed during the final stage of the Later Bronze Age.

Later Bronze Age Amber (Dowris Phase)

At an equivalent time in Britain (Ewart Park stage) there are nine hoards containing amber constituting in all about 63 beads. The greatest number is in Scotland with five hoards producing about 40 beads, 25 of which came from one hoard, Balmashanner (Table 9.2). In England amber has been found in two hoards, both in the east of the country: Feltwell, Norfolk (*Inventaria Archaeologia*, GB55, 13) and Heathery Burn, Co. Durham (*Inventaria Archaeologia*, GB35, 16), but each had only one bead. Both Welsh hoards are on the other side of the Irish Sea from Dublin, in Anglesey, from Ty Mawr and Llangwyllog (Lynch 1970, 210–13, 206–10). Between them these contained 21 beads. For the whole of Britain this makes a total of about 63 beads from the nine associated finds. There are also finds from some habitation sites, such as Runnymede, Surrey (Spence in Needham & Spence 1996, 188–9). It is difficult to be certain about the date of some other finds such as the seven beads from the Covesea cave,

Object	Balmashanner Angus (Coles 1959–60, 98–9)	Orrock, Fife (Coles 1959–60, 109–10)	St. Andrews, Fife (Cowie et al. 1991)	Adabrock, Lewis, Ross (Coles 1959–60, 127)	Glentanar, Aberdeen (Pearce 1971; 1979)	Ty Mawr (Lynch 1970, 210–13)	Llangwyllog (Lynch 1970, 206–10)
Sword (Ewart Park)			1				
Carps Tongue-shaped sword			1				
Plain leaf-shaped spearhead			9	1		1	
Socketed axehead	1			2	4	2	
Straight blade socketed knife			6			1	
Curved blade socketed knife			1				
Tanged knife			1				
Tanged chisel				1		1	
Gouge			1	1			
Hammer				1			
Amber beads	25	1	7+	2	5	4	16
Jet/shale beads	5						3
Gold beads				1			
Glass beads				1			
'Hair' rings	3						
Lock rings	4		4				
Penannular bracelet with outwardly expanded solid terminals			22+		2		
Penannular bracelet with evenly expanded solid terminals	11	3					
Double and hooked bracelets			1				1
Swans' neck disc-headed pins		1	16+				
Bifid razor			1	2			1
Tweezers			2				1
Bugle-shaped object			1				
Peaked object			1				
Solid annular rings	11	1	22		1	4	11
Shale ring		1			21		
Hollow ring (semi-tubular)		2					
Boar's tusk			1				
Disc			6				
Bronze bowl with straight handle	1						
Bronze bowl with cross handle	1						
Bronze cup with cross handle					2		
Whetstone				2			
Pottery sherds	x						
Fragments of wood			x				
Fragments of textile			x				
Fragments of leather			x				
Fragments of bone/antler			x				
Fragments of thread/cloth			x				
Spiral rings			3				
Small penannular rings			6				
Ribbed ornament with ring			1				
Jet/shale armlets			3				
Ringed harness studs							5
"Mount"							1
Double ring							1
Ring with lateral perforation							3

Table 9.2. Provisional list of amber from Late Bronze Age hoards in Scotland and Wales.

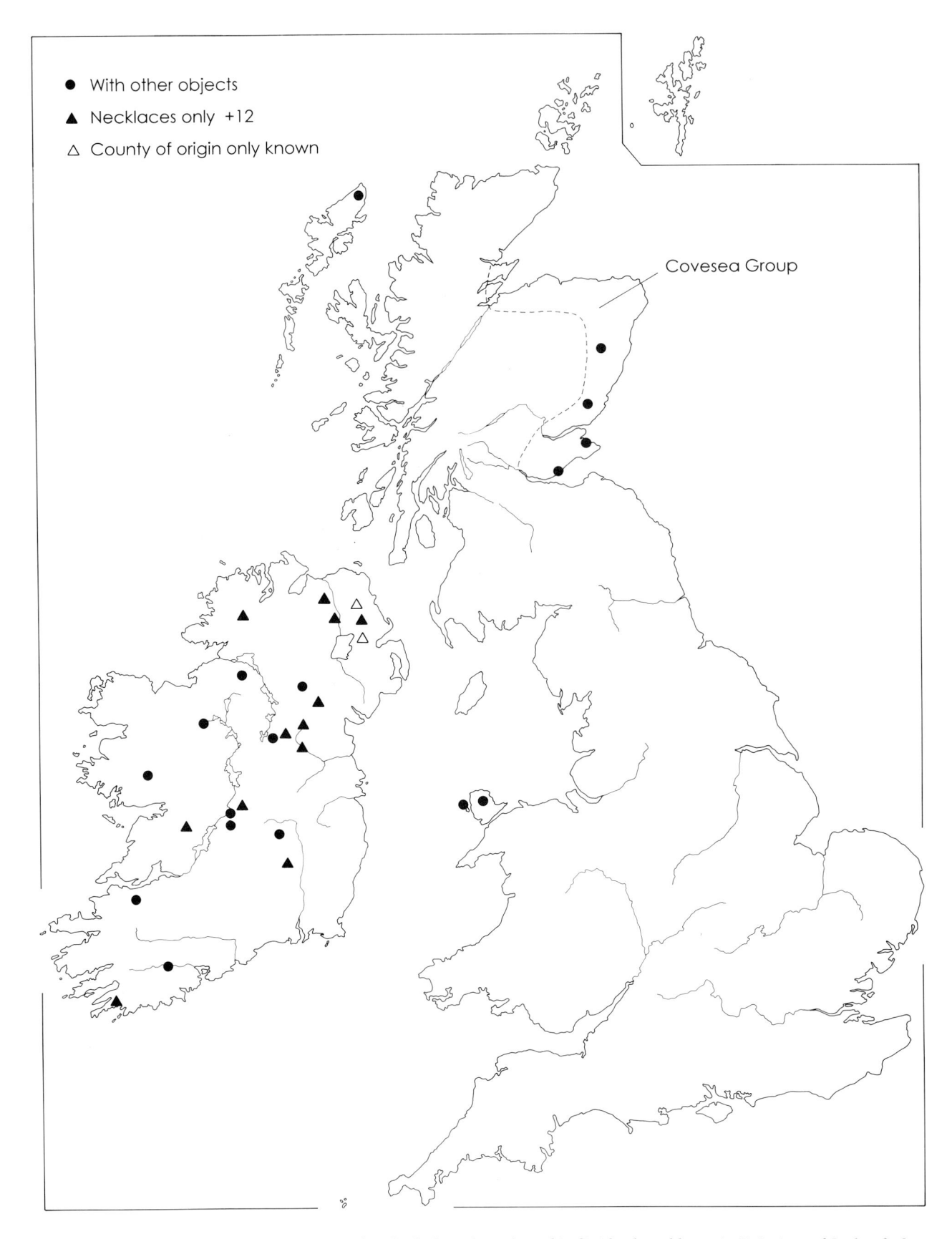

Fig. 9.3. *Distribution of Late Bronze Age amber finds from hoards and individual necklaces in Britain and Ireland. Open symbols indicate that only county of origin is known.*

Morayshire, which did contain Late Bronze Age but also later material (Benton 1931, 198–9). Britain also has finds of individual beads which may date from the Bronze Age.

The precise function of the British beads is difficult to determine. The graded beads from Llangwyllog and those from Balmashanner could have formed necklaces. A find of beads from Sustead, Bessingham, Norfolk might constitute an unassociated necklace but there may be some doubts about the authenticity of this find (Beck and Shennan 1991, 173). As a result it is not included on the distribution map.

It was at this time that there was a major increase in the amount of amber in use in Ireland (Fig. 9.3). Amber beads have been found in ten hoards with other objects, and there are also 28 finds of unassociated necklaces (Table 9.1). In combination these consist of up to 3,500 beads but this is a minimal number since due to loss or damage many beads are unaccounted for. It has been stated that the Cullinagh hoard contained "hundreds" of beads, but precise figures are not available. The Mullaghmacanteer necklace consisted of "many beads". Neither is the number of amber beads that constituted the necklaces from Bellaghy and Scotstown known. Twenty-one bead groups contain less than one hundred beads. Twelve finds contained over one hundred beads each. Of these, seven finds consisted of between 100 and 190 beads ("Cavan", Meenalabban, Portlaoise, Tooradoo, Meenawaun, Cogran and "Ireland"), three between 200 and 299 beads ("Cavan", Ballycurrin and Whitegates), and then there are two huge necklaces, Derrybrien and seemingly Kurin, each of which had over 500 beads. Weights are not available, but from the large number of beads known it is clear that Ireland was at this time a main area of amber use. The bulk of the finds constitute parts of hoards and unassociated necklaces, but amber beads have also been found on occupation sites. In Co. Offaly the settlement sites of Ballinderry II and Clonfinlough produced beads (Hencken 1942, 13; Moloney 1993, 129) as did Knocknalappa, Co. Clare (J. Raftery 1942, 53), Dún Aonghasa, Co. Galway (Cotter 1993, 9) and Moynagh, Co. Meath (Bradley 1997, 54). A bead was also found in the area of a workshop that was part of a habitation complex at Rathgall, Co. Wicklow (B. Raftery 1976, 346).

As was the case during the earlier stages of the Bronze Age, the use of amber was confined to beads but a much greater number was now in use and these varied in shape and size. The largest examples can be up to 5 cm in diameter but there are many small examples that are only a centimetre or so in diameter. In shape specimens can be spherical, biconical or disc-shaped, the latter being the most common form. The colour can also vary from light to dark. In the main the beads would have been used to form necklaces, but as no necklace has been found intact it is only possible to surmise the nature of their stringing. It does appear that the single stranded variety was the most common. In these it was normal for the beads to diminish in size from the centre to the ends. Their content may vary from a few beads as from Killycreen West, Co. Fermanagh, to many hundreds as from Kurin, Co. Derry, or Derrybrien, Co. Galway. At Kurin the largest bead is 45 mm in diameter and 34 mm thick. This would have been centrally placed with the beads on each side regularly diminishing in size to 7 mm in diameter and 3 mm thick. The only clear evidence for a multi-stranded necklace comes from Derrybrien (Prendergast 1960); this is also the most elaborate necklace. It has six strands and the beads vary in size from 30 mm to 6 mm in diameter. The larger beads are rounded in shape but as they decrease in size they become ovoid or disc-shaped. Each has a central perforation; this is cylindrical and varies in diameter from 3 to 5mm. In addition, as is the case with some bronze rings of Dowris Phase date, a small number of beads have a transverse perforation; this is smaller than the central perforation. Such beads could have served as spacers. In the outer row the largest beads are in the centre of the strand; from there to the ends they graduate downwards in size. A somewhat similar arrangement exists in the five inner strands (Fig. 9.4).

Fig. 9.4. Multi-stranded amber necklace, Derrybrien, Co. Galway. Photo: National Museum of Ireland.

Discussion

The available evidence suggests that it was during the Earlier Bronze Age that amber was first used in Ireland, all finds coming from graves. The background must have been Wessex in view of the widespread use of amber in that region, an area that had contacts with continental Bronze Age complexes. If native supplies were inadequate to meet the demand, this might have directly involved the Danish area, or there could have been a westward offshoot from the central European route. From Wessex a north-westward expansion is indicated by the presence of six amber beads as part of grave goods that accompanied the burial of an adult male (Pot H) at Bedd Branwen, Anglesey (Lynch 1971, 24, 30–1, 67–8). Amber may not have been the only material that reached Ireland from Wessex; faience beads (Stone and Thomas 1956, 58–61) may have been another. If the gold plate from Castlemartyr, Co. Cork, is contemporary with the Wessex plates, then it is possible that amber came into use during the earliest stage of the Bronze Age, the Frankford-Killaha stage. During the succeeding Derryniggin stage amber had a wider geographical circulation but use was limited, only three finds being known (Fig. 9.2). The most elaborate of these is the composite necklace which accompanied a burial of a male youth in the Mound of the Hostages, Tara (Ó'Ríordáin 1955). That would have been the burial of a prominent individual. At an approximately equivalent time in the Wessex region amber was extensively used; about one hundred find-places, chronologically spread over Wessex I and II, are known. These mainly concentrate in the Wiltshire region but finds are known from other areas, notably Norfolk and the Peak District (Fig. 9.1). Northwards there is only a scatter but this includes the rich Knowes of Trotty burial (Orkney), with four gold discs in addition to portions of an amber spacer-plate necklace (*Inventaria Archaeologia*, GB33). These and other amber finds are mainly associated with females. For the north of Britain the jet-spacer plate necklaces (Craw 1928–29) may also indicate the presence of significant females in that region. The scarcity of amber finds from Ireland is in marked contrast to Britain. There, they are usually found with other types of objects and with objects made from diverse materials. Many of the graves can be described as rich. Despite the limited number of finds from Ireland and the scarcity of amber in the graves, nevertheless not only Tara, but the other finds also, may indicate that those graves contained the remains of important persons. There can hardly be any doubt that prominent persons existed at this time and that their distribution was widespread. The best evidence for this is provided by the gold ornaments, especially the lunulae (Taylor 1980, 25–41; Eogan 1994, 30–8). These are not known from graves so they were governed by different depositional rules than those containing amber. Perhaps amber ornaments represented the trappings of individuals whereas gold ornaments represented the community as a whole.

For the centuries between the Derryniggin stage and the Dowris stage, at the end of the Bronze Age, there is no evidence that amber was used in Ireland and that was virtually the case in Britain too (Beck & Shennan 1991, 99–101). But the picture utterly changes during the Dowris phase. Comparing it to Britain, the situation is the reverse to that pertaining during the Earlier Bronze Age. Ireland was now the principal area of use. Finds mainly come from the middle of the country and are scarce in the eastern and western coastal counties (Fig. 9.3). However, unlike Earlier Bronze Age Britain there are no regional concentrations. Of course, for distributional studies the fact that twelve necklaces are unprovenanced is a disadvantage. There are more finds in south-east Cavan and adjoining counties than elsewhere, but nevertheless the overall distribution does not coincide with any particular geographical region. But further work may change that picture. In this connection it is relevant to note that the recent programme of excavations on the habitation sites at Dún Aonghusa, Aran Islands, and Clonfinlough, Co. Offaly, have produced amber beads. Accordingly amber may have a wider distribution than is known at present. As already mentioned, the source of amber used in Ireland has not been conclusively established but neither, on present evidence, can it be

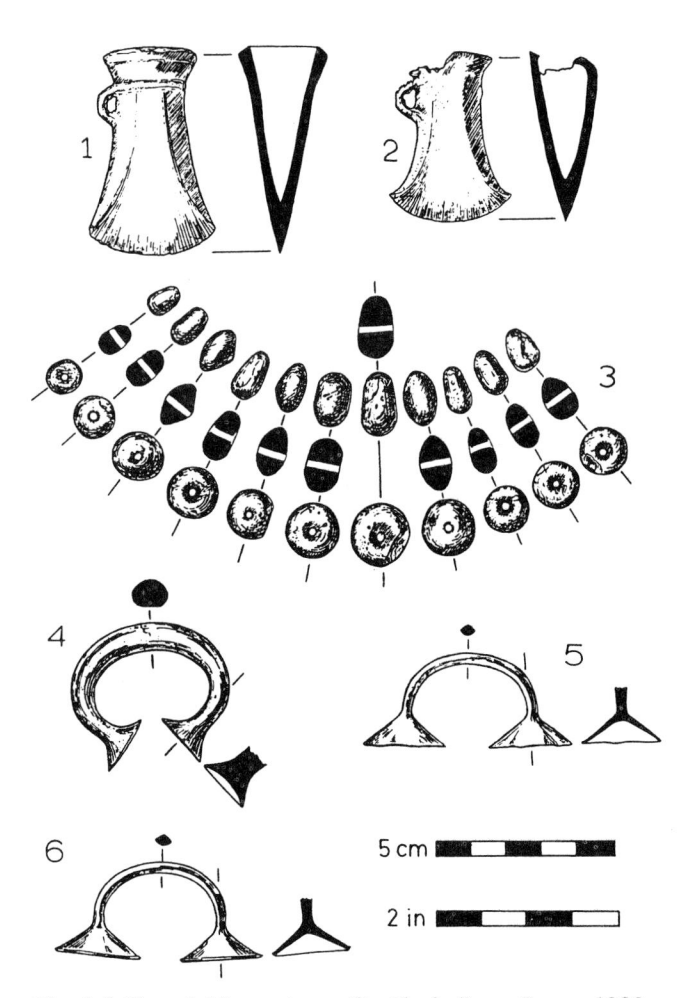

Fig. 9.5. Hoard, Mountrivers, Co. Cork. From Eogan 1983, Fig.38. Single-stranded necklace is No.3.

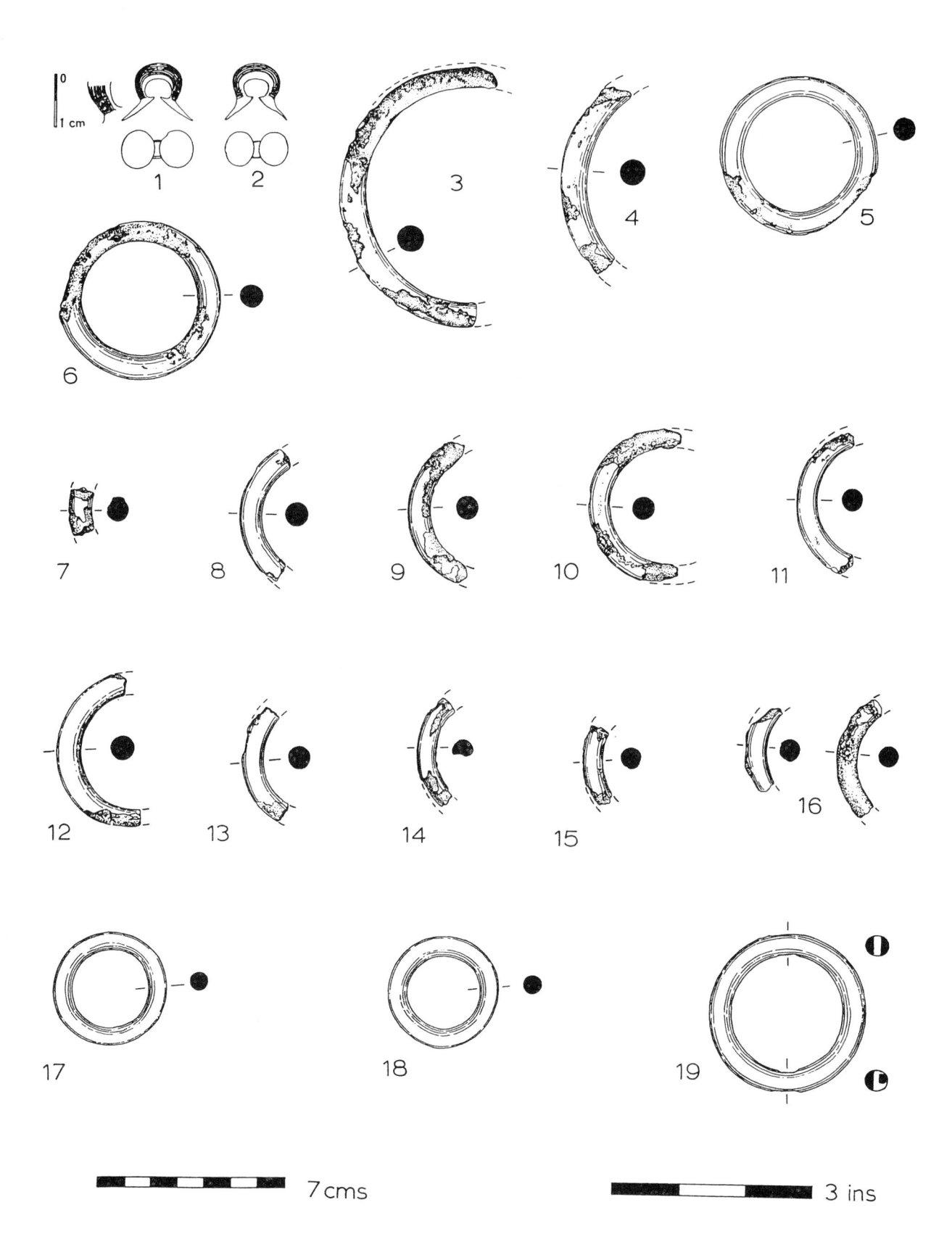

Fig. 9.6. Hoard, Scotstown, Co. Monaghan. From Eogan 1983, Fig.62. Only fragments of amber beads were found.

established that sufficient quantities could have been produced locally. As a consequence, importation from either England or the western Baltic remains a strong possibility. Analysis of a selected number of beads from the Newtown, Co. Antrim, necklace indicated that they were made from "Baltic" amber (Beck & Shennan 1991, 36–7, 104). If England is excluded then one has to consider areas further afield, as has already been done (cf MacWhite 1945). On geographical grounds the sources that are closest at hand occur in Jutland. The final (Dowris) Phase of the Late Bronze Age was a time when influences, even possibly types, from Denmark and adjoining areas were reaching Ireland (Hawkes, in Hawkes & Clarke 1963, 219–20). John Coles's study of one of these types, the horn (1963), has confirmed evidence for such Nordic connections which in addition seem to have been the source or inspiration of other types that became current, including disc-headed pins (Eogan 1974), "dress-fasteners", toggle, annular bracelet with ring, "bowls", boxes, U-notched shields, and possibly "sleeve-fasteners" (cf Eogan 1994, 96). As was suggested by Hawkes, perhaps there was a complementary trading or exchange network which allowed Irish material, such as copper or gold, to go northwards (Hawkes, in Hawkes & Clarke 1963, 217–20; 236–39). But there may have been more than objects or materials: aesthetics could have been part of the newly introduced assemblage. The new Irish art forms, especially concentric circles, may have had a Nordic background. The horns were musical instruments, so music must also have been part of the novelties.

If a route of contact existed it may be assumed that it went across Britain as that would have been the shortest way. Christopher Hawkes (*op. cit.*, 237–8) considered a route from Ireland to Lower Saxony via East Anglia. In this connection it may be noted that a variety of penannular bracelet, with flat body and solid terminals that are usually evenly expanded, tends to exhibit linear distributions in Britain. One is southern and extends between the Lower Thames and the Bristol Channel/Cornwall; the other is north-western and extends from the Norfolk coast to Anglesey (Eogan 1994, fig. 69:7; bronze example from Ty Mawr hoard, Anglesey to add). On the other hand, some Irish types of gold ornaments have been found in north Britain (Eogan 1994, figs. 39, 40). In that area another gold ornament, the "lock-ring", has a linear distribution which extends from Anglesey to Angus (Eogan *op. cit.*, fig. 41). The latter region is within an area that has distinctive metal types first defined by Coles (1959–60, 39–44) and termed by him the Covesea Group. This group is mainly found in the good agricultural lands of eastern Scotland between the mountains to the west, the sea to the east, and the Firths of Forth and Dornoch respectively to the south and north. Some elements of the Covesea Group can be found to the south in the Carp's Tongue Sword and contemporary complexes, but other elements of it, such as the necklets and the swan's neck sunflower pins, may have their background across the North Sea (Coles 1958–59; 1959–60, 40–3).

What is also relevant is the fact that it is four hoards of the Group that provide the overwhelming associated evidence for amber in Scotland (Table 9.2). In the region of the Covesea Group, most of the hoards with amber, and also the swan's-neck sunflower pins, concentrate in the coastal lands of its southern portion, in the area between the Firths of Forth and Tay. If a trans-North Sea trade route existed, perhaps it was the southern Covesea region that was the centre of contact on the western side, while on the eastern side western Jutland, with its natural amber, could have been an equivalent area. It may also be recalled that it was in the latter area, at Abildholt, that a variety of the predominantly Irish type cauldron, the Tulnacross type, was found. Interestingly enough, another cauldron of the same type came from Hattenknowe in Peeblesshire, not too far south of the Firth of Forth (Gerloff 1986, 96–7, 110, no. 15; 108, no. 7). It may, therefore, have been the Covesea Group that played a significant role in international trade

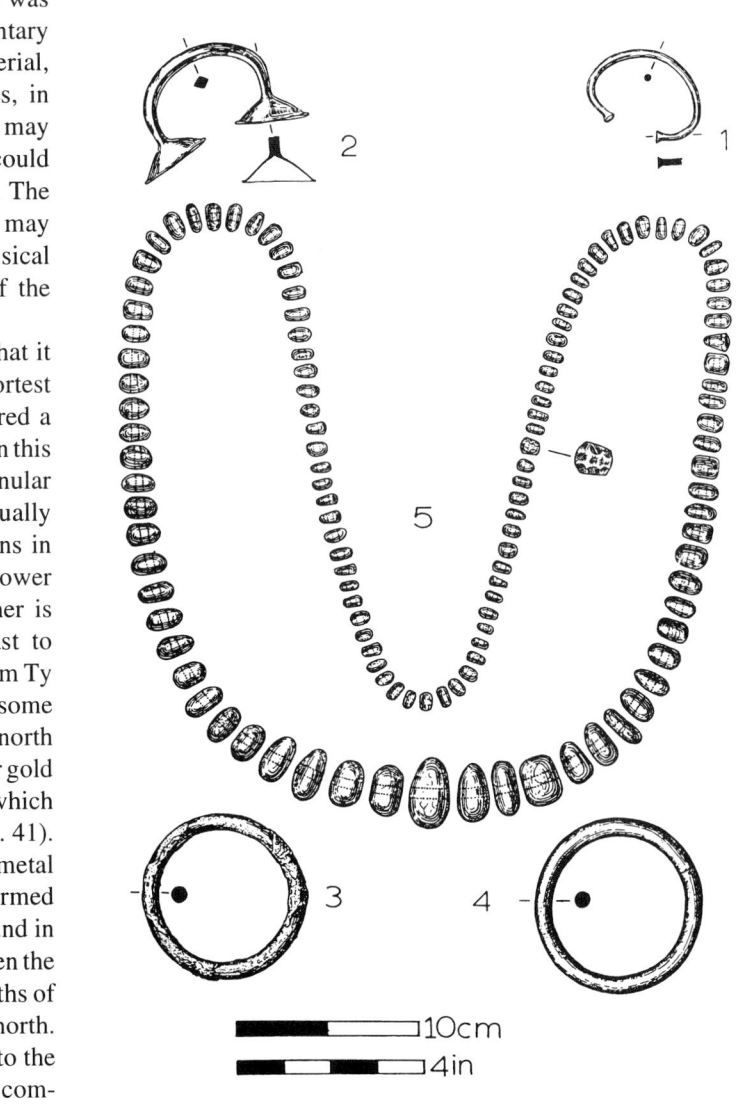

Fig. 9.7. Hoard, Meenawaun (Banagher), Co. Offaly. From Eogan 1983, Fig.63. Single stranded amber necklace is No.5.

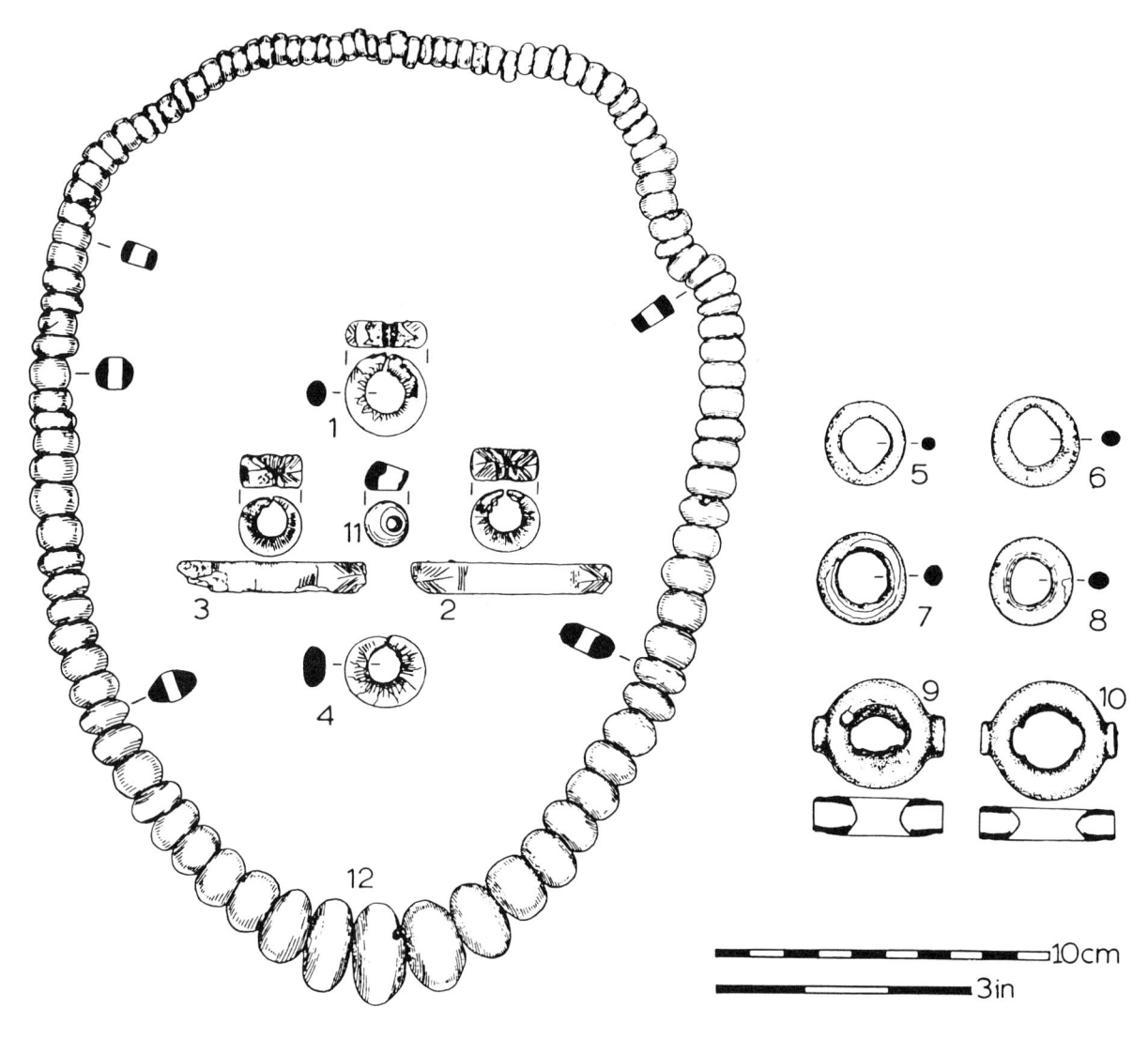

Fig. 9.8. Hoard, Tooradoo, Co. Limerick. From Eogan 1983, Fig.58. Single-stranded necklace is No.12.

as a recipient of influences emanating from the eastern side of the North Sea, in turn acting as an agent of diffusion of northern continental types to other areas in Britain and Ireland. As noted, the "lock-ring" distribution in northern Britain may suggest a land route; if so it might have been along that route that amber was transported and it is interesting that the Anglesey amber finds are at its "end" on the British side. Anglesey probably played a key role in wider Later Bronze Age contacts between Britain and Ireland. These were two-way, as Irish items (gold penannular bracelets with evenly expanded solid terminals) have turned up in Anglesey (Eogan 1994, fig. 39).

Visually, amber, like gold, must have been a striking material that was pleasing to the eye but also gave status to the wearers. Some of the associated finds such as Tooradoo, Co. Limerick, Meenawaun (Banagher), Co. Offaly, Scotstown, Co. Monaghan (Eogan 1983, nos. 103, 117, 116, Figs. 9.6–9.8) and possibly Port Laoghais, Co. Laois (no. 97), and also the unassociated necklaces, can be described as personal jewellery sets that were worn by people of note. There are also mixed hoards that contain tools in addition to ornaments: Mountrivers, Co. Cork (Fig. 9.5), and Killycreen, Co. Fermanagh (Eogan 1993, nos. 65 and 73). These could represent female-male combinations. It may be noted that away to the north-west of Scotland, at Adabrock in the Island of Lewis (Coles 1959–60, 127), there is another hoard with amber beads, in content resembling the Anglesey hoards. Taking this in conjunction with other evidence, such as the clay mould for casting an Irish type sunflower pin from Jarlshof, Shetland (Hamilton 1956, Fig. 14:1), perhaps there was also an Irish Sea – Atlantic area of secondary amber diffusion. The Dowris phase was a time of large-scale industrial and agricultural activities. As a result, a wealthy society with overseas connection emerged. Amber objects may then have been the property of such an upper class of society. This gives support to the view that elite households with people of wealth and power were a feature of Ireland at the end of the Bronze Age (Eogan 1997).

Acknowledgements

I wish to thank Róisín Barton and Niamh O'Broin for all their assistance. For help with material from the National Museum of Ireland I am indebted to Mary Cahill.

Bibliography

Beck, C. and Shennan, S. 1991. *Amber in Prehistoric Britain.* Oxford: Oxbow Monograph 8.
Benton, S. 1931. The excavation of the Sculptor's Cave, Morayshire, *Proc. Soc. Antiq. Scotland* 65, 177–216.
Bradley, J. 1997. Archaeological excavations at Moynagh Lough, Co. Meath 1995–96, *Ríocht na Midhe* 9 (no. 3), 50–61.
Briggs, C.S. 1983–84. Amber in Ireland: some geographical notes, *Éile* 2, 81–85.
Briggs, C.S. 1997. The discovery and origins of some Bronze Age amber beads from Ballycurrin Demesne, Co. Mayo, *J. Galway Archaeol. & Hist. Soc,* 49, 103–121.
Coffey, G. 1912. Recent prehistoric finds acquired by the Academy, *Proc. Royal Irish Academy* 30C, 85–7.
Coles, J.M. 1958–59 [1961]. Scottish swan's-neck sunflower pins, *Proc. Soc. Antiq. Scotland* 92, 1–9.
Coles, J.M. 1959–60 [1962]. Scottish Late Bronze Age metalwork, *Proc. Soc. Antiq. Scotland* 93, 16–134.
Coles, J.M. 1963. Irish Bronze Age horns and their relations with Northern Europe, *Proc. Prehist. Soc.* 29, 326–56.
Cotter, C. 1993. Western stone fort project. Interim report, *Discovery Programme Reports* 2, 1–11.
Craw, J.H. 1928–29. On a jet necklace from a cist at Poltalloch, Argyll, *Proc. Soc. Antiq. Scotland* 63, 154–89.
Croker, T.C. 1824. *Researches in the South of Ireland.* Dublin.
Cowie, T., O'Connor, B., & Proudfoot, E. 1991. A Late Bronze Age hoard from St. Andrews, Fife. In Chevillot, C. and Coffyn, A. (eds), *L'Age du Bronze Atlantique*, 49–58.
Daniells, M.J. & Williams, B.B. 1977. Excavations at Kiltierney Deerpark, Co. Fermanagh, *Ulster J. Archaeology* 40, 32–41.
Eogan, G. 1974. Pins of the Irish Late Bronze Age, *J. Royal Soc. Antiq. Ireland* 104, 74–119.
Eogan, G. 1994. *The Accomplished Art: Gold and Gold-working in Bronze Age Ireland.* Oxford: Oxbow Monograph 42.
Eogan, G. 1997. Hair-rings and Late Bronze Age society, *Antiquity* 71, 308–20.
Feeney, C.S.G. 1976. *Aspects of Irish Amber Finds.* Unpublished dissertation, University College, Dublin.
Gerloff, S. 1975. *The Early Bronze Daggers in Great Britain.* Prähistorische Bronzefunde, Abteilung VI, 2. München: Beck.
Gerloff, S. 1986. Bronze Age Class A cauldrons: typology, origins and chronology, *J. Royal Soc. Antiq. Ireland* 116, 84–115.
Gogan, L.S. 1932. A graduated amber necklace, gold-plated rings and other objects from Cnoc na bPoll, *J. Cork Hist. & Archaeol. Soc.* 37, 58–71.
Hamilton, J.R.C. 1956. *Excavations at Jarlshof, Shetland.* Edinburgh: Ministry of Works Archaeological Reports No. 1.
Hawkes, C.F.C. and Clarke, R.R. 1963. Gahlstorf and Caister-on-Sea: two finds of Late Bronze Age Irish gold. In J.L. Foster and L. Alcock (eds.), *Culture and Environment: Essays in Honour of Sir Cyril Fox*, 193–250. London: Routledge and Kegan Paul.
Hencken, H. 1942. Ballinderry Crannog No. 2, *Proc. Royal Irish Academy* 47C, 1–76.
Hencken, H. 1950. Lagore Crannog: an Irish royal residence of the 7th to 10th centuries AD, *Proc. Royal Irish Academy* 53C, 1–247.
Kavanagh, R.M. 1977. Pygmy cups in Ireland, *J. Royal Soc. Antiq. Ireland* 104, 74–119.
Kelly, E.P. 1983–84. A prehistoric amber find from Ballylin, Co. Offaly, *Éile. J. Roscrea Heritage Soc.* 2, 67–85.
Lynch, F. 1970. *Prehistoric Anglesey.* Llangefni: Anglesey Antiquarian Society.
Lynch, F. 1971. Report on the re-excavation of two Bronze Age cairns in Anglesey: Bedd Branwen and Treiorwerth, *Archaeologia Cambrensis* 120, 11–83.
MacWhite, E. 1944. Amber in the Irish Bronze Age, *J. Cork Hist. & Archaeol. Soc.* 49, 122–7.
Moloney, A. 1993. *Excavations at Clonfinlough, County Offaly.* Dublin: Irish Archaeological Wetland Unit.
Needham, S. & Spence, T. 1996. *Refuse and Disposal at Area 16 East Runnymede.* London: British Museum Press.
Ó'Ríordáin, S. 1955. A burial with faience beads at Tara, *Proc. Prehist. Soc.* 21, 163–73.
Pearce, S.M. 1971. A Late Bronze Age hoard from Glentanar, Aberdeenshire, *Proc. Soc. Antiq. Scotland* 103, 57–64.
Pearce, S.M. 1979. Amber beads from the Late Bronze Age hoard from Glentannar, Aberdeenshire, *Proc. Soc. Antiq. Scotland*, 108, 124–9.
Powell, T.G.E. 1953. The gold ornament from Mold, Flintshire, North Wales, *Proc. Prehist. Soc.* 19, 161–79.
Prendergast, E. 1960. Amber necklace from Co. Galway, *J. Royal Soc. Antiq. Ireland* 90, 61–66.
Raftery, B. 1976. Rathgall and Irish hillfort problems. In D.W. Harding (ed.), *Hillforts*, 339–57. London: Academic Press.
Raftery, J. 1942. Knocknalappa Crannog, Co. Clare, *North Munster Antiq. J.* 3, 53–72.
Stone, J.F.S. and Thomas, L.C. 1956. The use and distribution of faience in the Ancient East and prehistoric Europe, *Proc. Prehist. Soc.* 22, 37–84.
Taylor, J.J. 1980. *Bronze Age Goldwork of the British Isles.* Cambridge: University Press.

10. Swords, Shields and Scholars: Bronze Age Warfare, past and present

Anthony Harding

Abstract: This paper briefly reviews the artefactual evidence for Bronze Age warfare, pointing to the different interpretations which have been placed on swords, spearheads and body armour, and searching for common ground over the nature of warrior combat. The crucial role of John Coles' experiments with shields is recognised, and the method of use of swords and spears discussed. Recent approaches to Bronze Age warfare are also introduced.

One of John Coles' best-known and most influential papers, emanating from his 'early' period, is that published in the *Proceedings of the Prehistoric Society* for 1962: "European Bronze Age shields" (Coles 1962). Together with his massive presentation of Scottish Late Bronze Age metalwork published in the same year, and another influential paper on Irish Bronze Age horns the following year, this established the young(ish) Coles as a major voice in British archaeology, both as a Bronze Age scholar and as an experimental archaeologist. (Only two years later, he also published a major paper on the Mesolithic of south-west Scotland, establishing himself in another important, but quite different, academic niche.) In that 1962 paper, Coles discussed all the known shield finds and their typology, setting out a lineage for their development and discussing their dating (very much in traditional style), but also making a strikingly original contribution in examining the techniques of manufacture of the shields, and assessing their battle-worthiness. He did this, as is well-known, not just by examining the manufacturing traces on the preserved shields themselves, as scholars such as Hans Drescher or Herbert Coghlan had done for many years, but by making copies of both bronze and leather shields and testing them out for himself (Fig. 10.1). The conclusion, that leather would have been much more effective than bronze, was revolutionary, and has influenced all thinking about sheet-bronze armour ever since.

Shields were only one aspect of Bronze Age warfare; they were part of a panoply of defensive items that may have served to protect the Bronze Age warrior from the worst of the effects of hand-to-hand combat, the main other items being the corslet, the greaves and the helmet. Offensive weapons, including the swords of my title and also the spear, were the other aspect. Studying the artefacts alone is not likely to be a reliable guide to Bronze Age warfare, however, at least as far as obtaining an understanding of its social context is concerned. For this, we need to look at other material – without, however, forgetting the material culture, its varying forms, its distribution through time and space, and the technology of its manufacture.

Appearances to the contrary, the title of this paper is not intended as a direct incitement to experimental archaeology, bringing the first item directly to bear on the third. Rather, it is meant to indicate how the study of Bronze Age warfare has developed through the decades, and to incorporate a reference to the different aspects of John Coles's study of the topic. In other words, the sources available for study are threefold: artefactual studies; artistic depictions, notably on the rock art of Scandinavia and the southern Alps; and experimental archaeology, which in this case typically takes the form of the testing of materials and forms for strength, effectiveness, and durability – though perhaps it could also test out warfare

Author's Address: Anthony Harding, Department of Archaeology, University of Durham, South Road, Durham, DH1 3LE

techniques, for instance those used in individual combat.

Using these methods, the study of Bronze Age warfare has been an ongoing source of fascination for decades, and many of the ideas and preoccupations of today's generation of Bronze Age scholars are much the same as those of archaeologists studying the problem fifty or more years ago. On the other hand, this should not disguise the fact that a number of striking new approaches have been developed in the last few years. This paper will review these modes of study, indicating which have resulted in the most notable advances in understanding, and in which direction such studies might reckon to proceed in the future.

Sources of evidence

Warfare, or to be more accurate combat, was intimately bound up with other aspects of Bronze Age life, notably social relations and social organisation, settlement and territoriality, technology of weaponry and transport, and other matters. In seeking to understand how the armour and weapons, the forts and defensive earthworks functioned, we are inevitably drawn to the accounts of ancient warfare that seem nearest in time and space to the area and period under review: the descriptions of battle and fighting in the Iliad. This is not the place to review the date and historical context of the Homeric poems; while a date well into the first millennium BC is usually accepted for the main phase of creation of the poems, it is commonly believed that much of what is described emanates from a period that was rather earlier, and potentially much earlier, in other words the Bronze Age. This does, however, raise the question of the appropriateness of the Homeric mode of warfare as a model for that in the European continent as a whole.

Some of the characteristic features of this warfare mode are:– individual combat between warriors, with the personal prowess of individuals being paramount; transport to the scene of battle in a chariot (*pace* Drews 1993); a system of retainers serving the important warriors; and a set of social values lying behind the willingness, indeed keenness, to engage in combat, along with the sense of honour that accompanied this willingness to fight. Concomitant features of Homeric warfare were the long time-scale of the fighting, for wars if not battles or individual fights; the inconclusiveness of most encounters; the difficulty of siege warfare; and what seems to us the relatively trivial nature of the *casus belli*, at least in geopolitical terms. While some of these aspects cannot realistically be recovered from the material culture remains that survive to us, others can.

In archaeological terms, the Bronze Age was characterized by the emergence of a series of new inventions intended for combat, real or simulated. Whether or not they were intended to be truly effective in the field, the fact that they did emerge must speak for their importance in the sphere of socio-political relations, and the value of the threat of war, if not of warfare itself. First, while weaponry was not a new aspect of human production in the Bronze Age, the period did nonetheless see a series of changes in both offensive and defensive implements: the sword (in its various manifestations), the spear, and body-armour. Previously the main weapon was the bow and arrow, intended for long-distance contact, and there is little or no sign – at least until the Copper Age – that fighting at close quarters was practised, though we must be careful to recognise that there may have been a 'prehistory' of metal weapons in non-metal materials (bone, antler, wood). In the Bronze Age, by contrast, there is a preponderance of weapons for hand-to-hand fighting. The other big change is the creation of fortified sites – not merely enclosed, as had occurred from time to time in many areas and periods previously, but equipped with large and effective defensive works, of earth, wood and stone. The implications of this change are again potentially far-reaching.

Swords

Bronze Age swords have been an object of special study for over 100 years. In the last century, Greenwell and Naue devoted studies to them, and in this century Sprockhoff and Cowen were particularly important. Since 1970, however, the rise and progress of the *Prähistorische Bronzefunde* series and related works has meant that through the extension of the systematic lists of Sprockhoff there is now a corpus of material extending over the greater part of Europe available for study. Here we are not concerned with typological minutiae, but with the way in which swords were used – literally and metaphorically. In other words, what was their mode of use in battle? And from what social and personal context did they emanate?

Over the years, an orthodoxy has sprung up concerning the different uses of offensive blade weapons. Daggers, with blades shorter than 20 cm, were obviously for fighting at close quarters and for the delivery of stabbing blows. 'Dirks' (if the term has any scientific meaning) are somewhat longer, but presumably used in a similar way. Rapiers and swords, by contrast, seem initially to have been used for thrusting blows, but then to have developed into a stouter weapon capable of delivering cutting blows. Both blade and hilt developed accordingly: the blade of rapiers is relatively long and narrow, while swords were by definition always broader-bladed and probably acquired the leaf-shaped blade in order to give more weight to the weapon and therefore the cutting blow it could strike. The hilt, originally of organic material and therefore rarely surviving, was to begin with slight and poorly balanced, only achieving what we would consider comfortable balance and proportions towards the end of the Bronze Age. Anyone who has handled these swords will know that the grips often seem too small for effective manipulation of the weapon; even if Bronze Age hands were generally smaller than ours, the balance of many swords would make

Fig. 10.1. John Coles and Don Allan engaged in hand-to-hand combat using reconstructed Bronze Age swords and shields. Photo: L.P. Morley, University Museum of Archaeology and Anthropology, Cambridge.

it difficult to wield the weapons. On the other hand Bridgford (1997) has estimated the effectiveness of some 70 Irish swords in terms of their balance, as well as the degree of edge damage to them, finding that they were generally easy to handle and usually showed extensive signs of having been used (shown by edge damage). These measures should now be applied to other areas and other classes of sword. It would be particularly interesting to know if solid-hilted swords followed the same pattern, since it is especially on these pieces that the worst balance seems to occur.

Osgood (1998) sees a marked change in the earlier part of the Late Bronze Age with the development of the leaf-shaped sword, suitable for mobile combat associated with raiding. This suggests that the preceding rapiers may have been used for duelling and display, whereas developments at the very end of the Bronze Age and the beginning of the Iron Age may have been related to the start of cavalry fighting. On this analysis, there might be expected to be a correlation between the presence of leaf-shaped sword blades and the rise of defended sites, both bespeaking a mode of warfare in which raids were the favoured method of attack, and against which defensive measures had to be taken. We shall return to this question below.

Bridgford's demonstration that edge damage was frequent can be supplemented by the observation that it is much more frequent on some types of sword than others. For instance, my impression is that grip-tongue (flange-hilted) swords are usually damaged; solid-hilted swords much less frequently so; this impression needs confirmation through inspection of the weapons. The amount of damage, and therefore resharpening, presumably correlates with the amount of use. Kristiansen's (1984) work on the resharpening of Danish swords can be used to support either or both of two hypotheses: the weapons were used more, i.e. there was more fighting; or the weapons were used over a longer period, i.e. metal was not available to replace them sooner. Whether we can seriously believe that some swords were used so heavily for striking opponents that they became worn down with resharpening is a question perhaps best left open. Most blows presumably hit not human flesh and bone, but other swords, or defensive weaponry and armour. In practice, it is likely that warriors will have struck blows on dummy targets, for instance of wood; so it is possible that heavily worn swords do not actually mean there was a prevalence of fighting.

On the other hand, we would be foolish to ignore the possibility that swords really were extensively used – even if not in combat as we understand it from Cecil B de Mille films. The depictions of warriors with swords on rock art (Fig. 10.2), or on the statue stelae of Filitosa (Fig. 10.3), show us that swords were very much a part of Bronze Age life (as the large number of surviving weapons corroborates). However, the practice of depositing swords in graves was very far from frequent. It is certainly possible to identify some graves with swords that seem on other grounds to have been 'rich', in the sense that they also contained many other objects. The well-known graves from Velatice or Seddin are cases in point. The latter example, however, as studied by Wüstemann (1974, 1978), introduces another aspect: there is structure to the way weaponry is deposited in graves. In the Seddin area, Wüstemann identified a series of grave combinations ('sword graves', 'knife graves', 'spear graves' etc). While graves containing swords were generally the least frequent and thus presumably the most prestigious, it is striking that swords and spears do not generally appear in the same graves (Fig. 10.4). For Wüstemann this was an indicator of a hierarchical social structure; one might equally speculate that the structuring of the grave-goods reflected a deliberate mechanism for reflecting the warrior's function in battle, possibly even to the extent of suggesting that some warriors fought with swords, or swords and other weapons, others only with spears.

Of course the appearance or non-appearance of swords in graves may not be related to their actual 'possession' and use by Bronze Age people, and the situation certainly differed from area to area. If we look at the finds of swords in Bronze Age Britain (Colquhoun & Burgess 1988), there are no certain grave finds at all, and just a few cases where it is possible that the sword was in a grave (e.g. found in a cist, or with human bones: nos. 134 Wetheringsett, 462 Dalton-in-Furness, 770 Strathblane). In Germany there are a certain number of grave finds, for instance the well-known Erbenheim and Wollmesheim graves (Schauer 1971, 168 f., pl. 76), but a tiny number in relation to the whole. In the former Jugoslavia, the only swords that are known to have emanated from graves are early (Early or Middle Bronze Age), late (late Urnfield or early Hallstatt), or emanating from the southern and more remote parts of the country (Macedonia, Kosovo-Metohija, parts of Bosnia) where they appear to have had a different social role from that obtaining in the Danube-Sava lowlands (Harding 1995). On the other hand, in the Nordic area large numbers occur in graves, as the pages of Aner and Kersten's catalogue (1973–95) show clearly. In other words, the precise way in which swords were used varied from area to area. The same must be true from a consideration of sword finds from wet places (mainly rivers or bogs) or votive deposits, such as the Flies' Cave at Škocjan in Slovenia. The sword from Blatna Brezovica in the same country was found standing upright in the river bed (Harding 1995, 23); in other parts of the former Jugoslavia, as elsewhere, significant numbers of swords were found in rivers. Well-known groups of material falling into this category are those from the Elbe at Velké Žernoseky (Porta Bohemica) (Plesl 1961, 155 pl. 54), or

Fig. 10.2. Warrior on rock art panel from Hede, Bohuslän, showing sword (with the chape at the foot of the scabbard clearly visible) and shield. Photo: J.M. Coles.

Fig. 10.3. Filitosa, Corsica: statue-stela showing sword and scabbard hanging from the belt. Photo: A.F. Harding.

	Sword	Spear	Knife	Axe	Bridle	Vessel	Razor	Tweezer	Pin	Neckring	Armring
1	■					■					■
2	■			■							
3	■			■					■	■	
4	■		■						■		
5 *	■		■		■	■	■		■		■
6	■		■			■	■				
7	■		■				■				
8	■										
9	■					■	■	■			
10	■				■						
11		■				■	■				
12		■									
13		■									
14		■									

*Fig. 10.4. Diagram showing grave contents of fourteen Late Bronze Age graves containing weapons in the Seddin area of Brandenburg (source: Wüstemann 1978). Nos. 1–10: 'Sword graves'; nos. 11–14: 'spear graves'. * No. 5: Seddin, 'Königsgrab'.*

from the Danube in Hungary (Mozsolics 1975). Numerous swords come from the Thames and other southern English rivers. Swords were only one part of the material that was accorded this treatment, but they seem to have been a special part.

All these lines of argument lead to a presumption that swords were very important in Bronze Age life, whether or not they were an indicator of real fighting. Even though the indications that they were a regular part of the warrior's equipment are equivocal, it is evident that they served a special role in graves, whether or not they were the personal possessions of those buried. It is a reasonable assumption that relatively few Bronze Age farmers ever actually saw, let alone used, a sword, but in some parts there clearly were people for whom possession and display of a sword were crucial aspects of what it meant to be a warrior in the Bronze Age.

Spears

The spear was an item of warrior equipment from the Early Bronze Age onwards. In spite of this (and Randsborg has suggested that they may have been commoner than appears to be the case because when mounted on shafts they were too long to be put into graves) little is known about how exactly they were used. Were they thrown like javelins, held firm to make the opponent risk impaling himself while charging, or were they thrust at the opponent at close quarters? Could they have been used by or against mounted warriors?

The difference between thrown and held spears has been debated many times, though a conclusion is as hard to achieve as it ever was. Most authorities have thought that small spears were thrown and large ones held, but in fact this argument is far from watertight. Throwing a spear would have been a risky business. The chances of hitting an opponent must have been slight – unless we are to imagine that the rules of engagement meant one had to stand still while one's opponent took a potshot. The distance that a javelin could be hurled could not in any case have been very great – even with a modern high-precision aluminium sports javelin weighing 800 g in total the world record stands at only a little over 100 m, for which the flight time is several seconds. One would think therefore that avoidance of a Bronze Age spear, even hurled over as little as 20 or 30 m, would have been quite easy, though admittedly the wearing of heavy armour would have hindered movement. Furthermore, by hurling one's spear, one would leave oneself without a significant part of one's armoury, and place a weapon in the hands of the opponent. Either strict reciprocation must have occurred, or the weapons are unlikely to have been hurled.

Nevertheless, some spears did strike their targets since it has been pointed out that shields sometimes have holes in them that can only have come from a rapier thrust or a spear (see below). The trauma on skeletons from Dorchester and Tormarton also suggests damage from spear thrusts (Osgood 1998, 19).

What is of most interest is the fact that spears regularly accompanied warriors, either present in graves or shown in depictions. The Litsleby warrior (Fig. 10.5) indicates that spears could be accoutrements of major figures, and the commonness of the form in metalwork assemblages also speaks for its importance. As discussed above, Late Bronze Age grave assemblages in the area around the

Fig. 10.5. The Litsleby warrior. Photo: A.F. Harding.

Seddin grave in eastern Germany were sometimes dominated by spears. While far from universal, spears recur in enough different contexts to indicate their continuing importance in time and space.

Shields

It has generally been believed that the earliest defensive armour appeared in Europe at the start of the Urnfield period, and is to be connected with changes in fighting techniques that accompanied that change. Most of what survives to us is in metal, but this obviously disguises a potential 'prehistory' in organic materials, notably leather and wood. Nothing is known about corslets or cuirasses in leather; only with the appearance of metal pieces, such as that from Čaka in Slovakia, do we have any information, but it seems inconceivable that pieces in organic materials were not present. Helmets, too, must have been made in leather or possibly wood, and some objects may be interpreted as fittings for such cap-like pieces. With shields, however, we are on somewhat firmer ground since leather examples survive, and there are the numerous depictions on the art of Bohuslän, Valcamonica and the Iberian grave stelae which show shields accompanying warriors – though *in corpore* examples have never been found in those areas. John Coles' demonstration that leather shields were functionally superior to metal ones was a notable landmark in studies of armour, raising the possibility that much sheet metal armour was primarily for display, for striking fear into the hearts of enemies, perhaps during the preliminary stages to single combat when taunts and insults were exchanged. Homer's account of the arming and appearance of Achilles suggests much the same procedure.

Yet, as mentioned above, metal shields were used too: Needham noted the damage to the Long Wittenham shield, and the famous Plzeň-Jíkalka shield also has a perforation that might result from a spearhead blow. Shields were in general made by being beaten out, though it is stated in the literature that the Plzeň example was cast. A cast shield would be much more resistant to thrusting and cutting blows than a beaten one, so one might expect that more would have been found if they really were intended to be functional.

It is indeed likely that shields have a rather greater antiquity than John Coles and other scholars have supposed. In 1962, much turned on the date of the Plzeň shield, which might or might not have been found with a hoard of metal objects of Br D date. On typological grounds Coles favoured a much later date, right at the end of the Bronze Age, using the late notched shields of the Mediterranean as the main argument. More recently Kytlicová (1986) has shown clearly that there are two groups of finds at Jíkalka, one early and one late, and the shield could belong to either. In 1968 Patay published shield fragments from Hungarian hoards which clearly dated to the early Urnfield period, so there should be no objection in principle to accepting an early date for Plzeň. Now we have a radiocarbon date of 3445 ± 70 BP (1950–1540 cal BC) (Hedges *et al.* 1991, 128 f.) for the Kilmahamogue (Co. Antrim) wooden shield mould, confirming suspicions that defensive armour started much earlier than metal finds alone would lead one to suspect.[1] Late Bronze Age metal shields were thus merely the culmination of centuries of experimentation and use in organic materials.

Though most shield finds are from wet places and therefore presumed to be votive in nature (cf the magnificent group of sixteen shields from Fröslunda on the southern edge of Lake Vänern: Hagberg 1988), the Iberian stelae and the rock art give good grounds for thinking that in those areas at least they were the regular accompaniment of the warrior. Yet, as suggested above, ideas have changed on how the warrior would deploy his weapons and armour and thus what their significance to him would have been. Other recent publications have highlighted these changes (see below).

Bronze Age warfare: new perceptions of an old problem

From such studies of artefacts, some progress has been made in identifying the context and mode of use of particular weapon types. Of course, no overall picture of Bronze Age warfare can be obtained without also bringing into consideration the locales in which fighting took place. For practical purposes, this means the study of forts and fortifications, though the detail of these lies beyond my present scope. What is important about the rise of fortified sites is the clear perception that they must be connected with forms of warfare that involved mobile bands of fighters, in other words raiders, perhaps on horseback. This suggestion, long considered to be likely, has recently been reiterated by Osgood (1998, 89). At the same time, a suggestion by Rynne (1992) that some of the Irish forts, notably the extraordinary coastal sites such as Dun Aonghasa, were ritual in nature should be borne in mind: sites, like artefacts, cannot be judged merely on the basis of what we, as observers from a different social and technological milieu, consider likely.

If Bridgford (1997) is correct that swords really were used in battle, we should be wary of going too far down the road of attributing merely designer status to them and objects like them. At the same time, it is possible to go too far in supposing that the structure of Bronze Age warfare can be reconstructed from the details of hoard finds, as Randsborg (1995, 44 ff.) has recently done with Early Bronze Age Danish hoards, and by supposing that the Hjortspring Iron Age boat provides an analogy for Bronze Age warfare. At the same time, Randsborg is surely right in his aim of analysing how the introduction of new weapon types for new methods of fighting impacted on other areas of Bronze Age deposition.

A further important concern is to understand the social context in which fighting, and the concept of the warrior, emerged. Paul Treherne (1995) has introduced the idea of 'warrior companionage', or the *Männerbund*, as known from various periods of ancient and medieval European history (Homer; Germanic Europe; etc), and discussed how the warrior's body represented the values important to Bronze Age society (honour, valour, beauty), hence the prevalence of ornaments in Bronze Age graves, and the idea that weapons are an extension of the body and the self. In this view, the life-style of the emergent warrior elite is represented by razors, weapons and so on. These interesting ideas, when fully published, will stimulate intense debate about the aptness of the historical analogues proposed.

Scholars have taken a largely practical view of how Bronze Age warfare was conducted, much influenced by received notions of individual combat as expressed by Homer, and massed troop actions as depicted in the cinema. In the gradual move towards a more realistic view of what was involved, the work of John Coles has played a seminal part. The results and conclusions he presented to the world in 1962, along with those of other scholars whose ideas have been presented here, mean that the Bronze Age world is no mere shadowy no-man's land, but a vibrant and exciting world where old and new ideas can mix to produce advances on a wide variety of fronts.

Notes

1 One recalls here Colt Hoare's belief that Bush Barrow contained the remains of a wooden shield with bronze studs, though Coles (1962, 172) found no way the surviving pieces, and the description of what was found, could be reconstructed to make a shield.

Bibliography

Aner, E. and Kersten, K. 1973–95. *Die Funde der älteren Bronzezeit des nordischen Kreises in Dänemark, Schleswig-Holstein und Niedersachsen, I–X, XVII–XVIII.* Copenhagen/Neumünster: Karl Wachholtz.

Bridgford, S. 1997. Mightier than the pen? An edgewise look at Irish Bronze Age swords. In *Material Harm. Archaeological Studies of War and Violence*, ed. J. Carman, 95–115. Glasgow: Cruithne Press.

Coles, J.M.1962. European Bronze Age shields, *Proc. Prehist. Soc.* 28, 156–90.

Colquhoun, I. and Burgess, C. 1988. *The Swords of Britain*. Prähistorische Bronzefunde, Abt. IV, 5. Munich: Beck.

Drews, R. 1993. *The End of the Bronze Age. Changes in warfare and the catastrophe ca. 1200 BC*. Princeton NJ: Princeton University Press.

Hagberg, U.E. 1988. The bronze shields from Fröslunda near Lake Vänern, West Sweden. In *Trade and Exchange in Prehistory. Studies in Honour of Berta Stjernquist*, eds. B. Hardh, L. Larsson, D. Olausson and R. Petré, 119–26. Acta Archaeologica Lundensia, series in 8°, 16. Lund: Historiska Museum.

Harding, A.F. 1995. *Die Schwerter im ehemaligen Jugoslawien*. Prähistorische Bronzefunde, Abt. IV, 14. Stuttgart: Franz Steiner.

Hedges, R.E.M., Housley, R.A., Bronk, C.R. and van Klinken, G.J. 1991. Radiocarbon dates from the Oxford AMS system, *Archaeometry* 33, 121–34.

Kristiansen, K. 1984. Krieger und Häuptlinge in der Bronzezeit Dänemarks. Ein Beitrag zur Geschichte des bronzezeitlichen Schwertes, *Jahrbuch des Römisch-Germanischen Zentralmuseums* 31, 187–208.

Kytlicová, O. 1986. Der Schild und der Depotfund aus Plzeň-Jíkalka, *Památky Archeologické* 77, 413–54.

Mozsolics, A. 1975. Bronzkori kardok folyókból, *Archaeologiai Értesitő* 102, 3–24.

Osgood, R. 1998. *Warfare in the Late Bronze Age of North Europe*. BAR International Series 694. Oxford: Archaeopress.

Patay, P. 1968. Urnenfelderzeitliche Bronzeschilde im Karpatenbecken, *Germania* 46, 241–48.

Plesl, E. 1961. *Lužická kultura v severozápadních Čechách*. Prague: Czech Academy of Sciences.

Randsborg, K. 1995. *Hjortspring. Warfare and Sacrifice in Early Europe*. Aarhus: University Press.

Rynne, E. 1992. Dún Aengus and some similar ceremonial centres. In *Decantations. A Tribute to Maurice Craig*, ed. A. Bernelle, 196–207. Dublin: Lilliput.

Schauer, P. 1971. *Die Schwerter in Süddeutschland, Österreich und der Schweiz I (Griffplatten-, Griffangel- und Griffzungenschwerter)*. Prähistorische Bronzefunde Abt. IV, 2. Munich: Beck.

Treherne, P. 1995. The warrior's beauty: the masculine body and self-identity in Bronze Age Europe, *J. European Archaeology* 3.1, 105–44.

Wüstemann, H. 1974. Zur Sozialstruktur im Seddiner Kulturgebiet, *Zeitschrift für Archäologie* 8, 67–107.

Wüstemann, H. 1978. Zur Sozialentwicklung während der Bronzezeit im Norden der DDR. In *Mitteleuropäische Bronzezeit. Beiträge zur Archäologie und Geschichte*, eds W. Coblenz and F. Horst, 195–209. Berlin: Akademie-Verlag.

11. The Bronze Age Hoards of Hampshire

Andrew J. Lawson

Abstract: The aim of this paper is to draw attention to the scale and diversity of bronzework in Hampshire, not least because recent discoveries further enrich the wealth of this material. A number of observations can be made from this preliminary assessment which should provide a stimulus for the future detailed examination of individual bronzes, the types represented or their metal compositions, which the finds merit.

Introduction

The study of metal types has traditionally played a critical role in our understanding of Bronze Age societies. This paper is concerned with metalwork from Hampshire, which is normally spread amongst the display cases or safely guarded stores of a number of institutions. As with similar studies elsewhere, it "is an attempt to bring the mass of material... into some order, to divide it regionally and chronologically" (Coles 1959–60, 16), so using it as a tool to distinguish different communities and to identify contact or isolation between them.

Although brief overviews of the evidence for the Bronze Age in Hampshire have been compiled (Fasham & Schadla-Hall 1981; Tomalin 1996), they make little mention of the scope or value of typological analysis. Various notes on individual bronzes or hoards have been published but there has been no recent overview dealing specifically with Hampshire. While acknowledging that "it is the evidence for settlement, for economic practices and for social division that probably encapsulates, more than any number of metal finds, the essence of Bronze Age life" (Coles & Harding 1979, 16), we cannot ignore the growing number of discoveries and the contribution they make both to the archaeological record and the broader understanding of the period.

When considering the composition of hoards, it is essential to have confidence in the validity of association of the objects and in the total recovery of the original contents. This is not a problem for discoveries which are made under controlled archaeological excavation but such occurrences are very rare. Unfortunately, we are frequently reliant on incomplete or inaccurate records of the events surrounding discoveries, especially in the case of old finds. In this account, which is primarily concerned with new discoveries, little has been done to verify old records and no attempt has been made to re-designate the finds as 'area finds', 'undocumented groups' etc (Needham *et al.* 1985).

In some instances such doubts exist that the finds have been deliberately excluded. For example, three palstaves have been reported from Brambridge. Clark and Godwin (1940, 63) postulated that they might be from a hoard and by 1955 Ordnance Survey recorders had associated a flat axe and a flanged axe from the area with it. Because there is currently no evidence that these objects were originally associated, they are not listed here. Over a period of time a number of bronzes have accumulated from the Silkstead area (indeed, four further bronzes have come to light since the publication of the earlier reports: Dr G. Denford pers. comm.) but there is no conclusive evidence that they were purposefully deposited together (Denford 1993, 39) and, hence, they are also not listed here. Similarly, bronzes of different types or dates have come from restricted areas, for example, from Ashley Camp (inf. Winchester Museum), Kingsclere (David Allen pers. comm.) or Sandel Heath,

Fordingbridge (Wrey 1954), but none has evidence of association.

In other instances, it seems probable that not all the objects which were once associated have been recovered. For example, it is thought that the collection of palstaves from Nursling (Table 11.1) comprised more than 60 axes which were dispersed amongst workmen, and that the gravel in which they occurred had been imported from elsewhere (Frank Green pers. comm.). Doubts are naturally reduced where search and recovery have been thorough, as is now frequently the case when metal-detectors are used. All but one of the new discoveries reported here have been made in this way. Those responsible for the discoveries have usually been conscientious in reporting the finds to archaeologists so that investigative fieldwork could follow. Nonetheless, there remains a nagging concern that other discoveries may have been made which are not yet reported. New discoveries can not only make a valuable contribution to our knowledge and significantly alter the complexion of Hampshire's Bronze Age assemblage, but offer the exciting prospect of yet more material in the future if new codes for reporting are honoured (Department of National Heritage 1996).

Middle Bronze Age Metalwork

Although the practice of depositing a number of metal objects together as a hoard had commenced in the middle of the third millennium BC (Needham 1996, 124), the earliest Hampshire hoards belong to the Middle Bronze Age.

In his seminal research, Rowlands (1976) catalogued both isolated finds and associated assemblages of the Middle Bronze Age (MBA) including 13 hoards from Hampshire. Amongst these, the hoards from Colden Common, Twyford and Owlesbury contain Late Bronze Age (LBA) objects alongside the earlier pieces. For the purposes of this paper, all the hoards are considered chronologically by the date of the latest bronze in each assemblage, and therefore these two hoards are listed with LBA finds (below). Since Rowlands' research, there have been eight further discoveries of MBA hoards in the county, bringing the total to 19 (Table 11.1). The finds from Nursling, South Wonston and Anderwood Enclosure have already been published (Hughes & Champion 1982; Needham & Denford 1985), but the others are described here.

Clay Hill, Minstead

Around the end of April 1978, Mr M A Zillwood of Chandlers Ford made a chance find of palstaves 'while playing around with a metal detector'. All the objects were apparently found within an area about 1m across, '3–6 inches deep in clay soil' (7–15 cm), on the side of a track in an area badly disturbed by vehicles. In December 1978, the details of discovery and descriptions of eleven palstaves were recorded by the British Museum. In February 1980, Hampshire County Museums Service (HCMS) bought eight of these palstaves and two further fragments at Christie's. The whereabouts of the other three bronzes are not known.

All the palstaves are broad-bladed and the majority have weakly defined stop ridges, a characteristic of the Werrar type, the distribution of which is centred on the north-east corner of the Isle of Wight (Rowlands 1976,33). Five were originally looped, although the loops of four are broken. The palstaves are decorated with a variety of different devices including shield patterns and midribs (Figs. 11.1A and 1B).

Gouldings Farm, Blashford

During 1979, Mr Mark Vincent, then 15 years old, conducted a methodical metal-detector search of his family's farm. In one wet field close to the River Avon, which he surmised had formerly been a marsh, and at a depth of '15 inches' (38 cm), he found part of the blade of a palstave and 'half an inch' below it, a complete looped palstave. The find was made on 18 May and on the following day two further blade fragments were found 'in exactly the same spot' (information from the British Museum).

The objects were retained by the finder and have not been examined, but his simple sketches show that all the palstaves appear to be broad-bladed.

Hayling Beach

Dr Stuart Needham (British Museum) has recorded that six palstaves were found by Mr Brian Kilshaw and Mr Daniel Clahane on three separate occasions in November 1985 between one pair of groynes and between high and low water marks. The finds (Fig. 11.2) were made just after the importation of large quantities of dredged gravel for the formation of a flood-relief barrier at the beach head. It was Mr Kilshaw's belief that the finds derived from the gravel which probably came originally from Owrs Bank, off Selsey Bill. Although not proven, it seems most likely that the bronzes are from the seabed and form part of a lost Bronze Age cargo.

One palstave has a splayed cutting edge and is decorated with a trident motif. The other five have narrow blades with curved stop ridges, gently flared and concave-sided blades, and low flange profiles. O'Connor (1980) and Needham (1980, 40) have discussed palstave discoveries of this form and have identified their origin in the *Bronze Moyen 3*, the equivalent of the Taunton phase in Normandy, although a slightly later date is also possible.

Kents Copse, Vernham Dean

In 1988, Mr K Whatley found on two different occasions a total of seven largely complete palstaves and fragments of three others whilst using a metal-detector on the corner of Kents Copse on Horns Farm. Previously, one complete

	Location	Museum	NGR	Date	Armring	Q-h pin	Pin	Torc	Palstaves	Un-id	Source
1	Broad Oak Pit, Burley	BM	SU213016	c. 1927					12		Rowlands No 57, Pl. 5
2	Lower Swanwick	Winchester; 1 lost	SU5009	1927					4		Rowlands No 63, Pl. 7
3	Pear Tree Green, Southampton	BM; Winchester	SU4310	1898					41		Rowlands No 66, Pl. 6, 54
4	Near Southampton	Ashmolean	SU4214	c. 1803					3		Rowlands No 70, Pl. 30
5	Near Titchfield	Southampton	SU5406	1897					9		Rowlands No 72, Pl. 5
6	Clay Hill, Minstead	Lyndhurst; Chilcomb; Private	SU287118	1978					13		BM ; this paper
7	Gouldings Farm, Blashford	Private	SU153069	1979					4		BM
8	Nursling ?	Chilcomb; Private?	SU368152	1984					c. 60		Rees 1993, Fig 6
9	Hayling Beach / Owrs Bank?	BM	SZ747979	1985					6		BM: this paper
10	Kents Copse, Vernham Dean	Andover	SU333598	1920–88					14		HCMS: this paper
11	Hayling II	Havant	SU7101	1995					20		HCMS: this paper
12	Liss	BM	SU7727	a. 1881	2						Rowlands No 62, Pl. 14
13	Bowers Farm, Plaitford	Winchester	SU2718	1928			1	2			Rowlands No 67
14	South Wonston	Private	SU455371	1979	3			4			Hughes &Champion 1982
15	HMS Sulton, Gosport	Southsea Castle	SZ620 993	1968	1				18		Rowlands No 59, Fig 3
16	Gable Head, Hayling Island	Southsea Castle	SZ7199	1960	2	1			27		Rowlands No 60, Pl. 55–6
17	Milton, Portsea Island	Lost	SZ6799	a. 1921	4				1		Rowlands No 68
18	Woolmer Forest	BM	SU800320	1840	4			2	1		Rowlands No 74, Pl. 13
19	Anderwood Enclosure, Burley	Private	SU243063	1961+1984	2		1		6	9	Needham & Denford 1985

Table 11.1. Contents of Middle Bronze Age hoards in Hampshire (objects and fragments combined) with locations of collections.

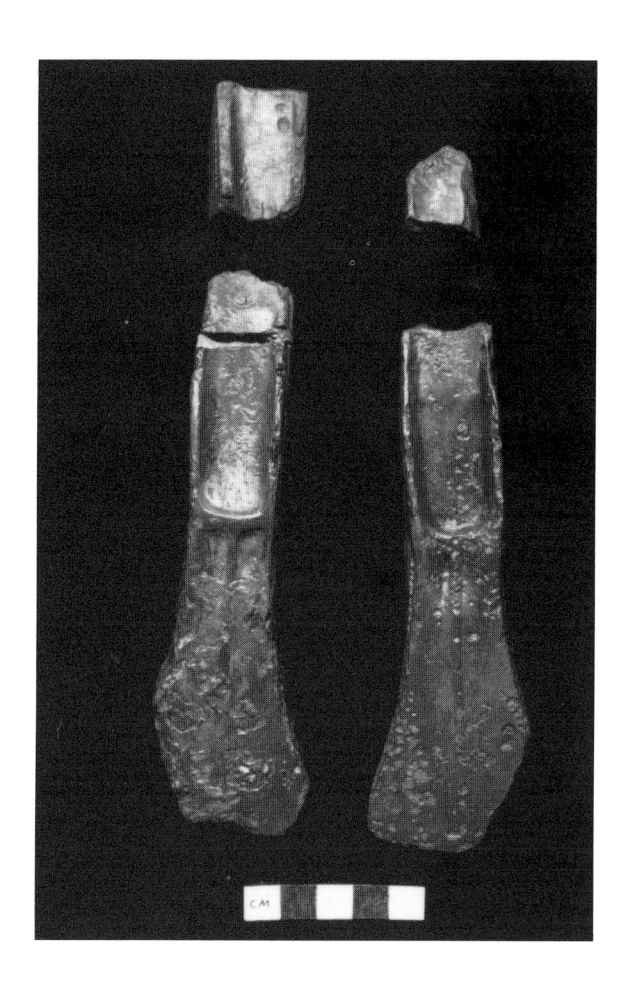

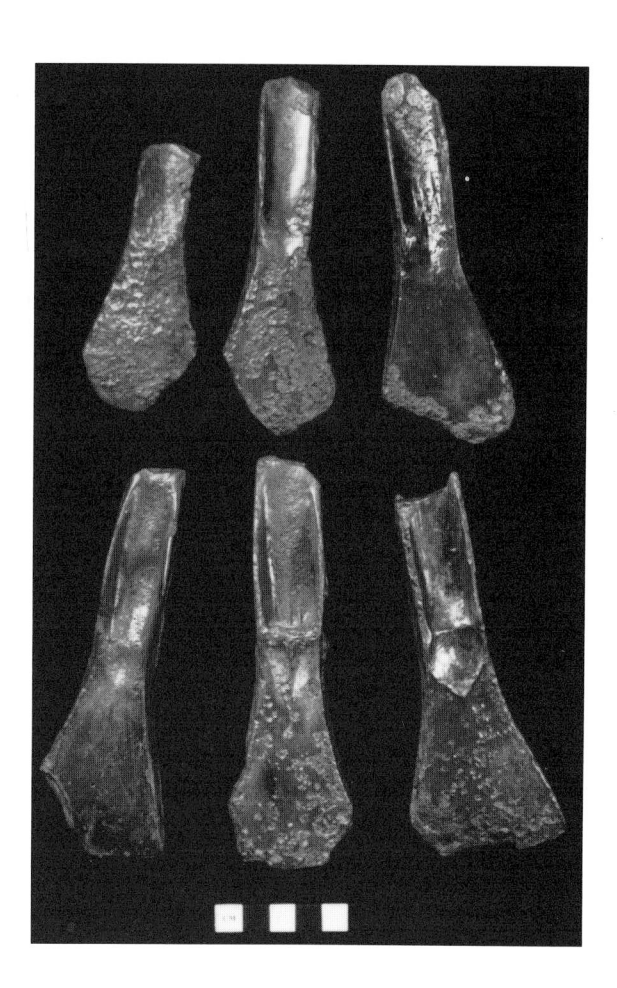

Fig. 11.1. The Minstead Hoard: A (left) palstaves in Lyndhurst Mueum, B (right) in Chilcomb House, Winchester

Fig. 11.2. The Hayling Beach assemblage

and one fragmentary palstave had been reported from the same area by the then farmer, Mr R Herriot of Upper Vernham Row (Crawford 1920, 92; Roskill 1938, 19–20). Apparently, fragments from both discoveries fit together (Dave Allen pers. comm) so it seems likely (*pace* Rowlands 1976, 308) that all the objects once constituted a single hoard. A small excavation of the site by Dave Allen and Frank Green demonstrated that the bronzes had been deposited in a carinated and partly burnished pottery vessel, now highly fragmentary. The vessel has a fine flint filler and may bear a single finger-tip impression.

No two of the palstaves are alike (Fig. 11.3). Most have moderately broad triangular blades and low, curved flanges. Two have been heavily reworked to create widely splayed cutting edges and two have loops. One example is somewhat narrower and has lower, straight flanges. Despite this variation, the palstaves can be accommodated within the range of forms of the Taunton metalworking tradition of southern Britain.

Hayling Island II (Near Fleet?)

The find, comprising 20 palstaves (Fig. 11.4) was detected by Mr Walbridge on the edge of a garden in January 1995 (information from Dave Allen, Andover Museum). He had earlier discovered another hoard (below) not far to the south.

The majority of the palstaves are unlooped, but at least four, probably five, originally had loops. The flanges are low and the stop-ridges are either rounded or straight. All have triangular blades of moderate width but two are somewhat broader than the others. The sides of the blades are mainly straight, although several have a slightly crinoline outline, while one has a concave outline. Three palstaves are plain, twelve have a median rib and three have side-flanges. Nine have a double hollow beneath the stop, rather like a bovine footprint, while trident designs occur on three and shield designs on a further two. Whereas the broader examples and those decorated with shield and trident motifs can be accommodated in the axes of the Taunton phase, many of the other examples are similar to those from Hayling Beach ascribed to the traditions of Northern France.

Discussion

The range of types represented in the hoards helps to define preferences amongst those who accumulated the objects, while comparison with the overall assemblage of isolated

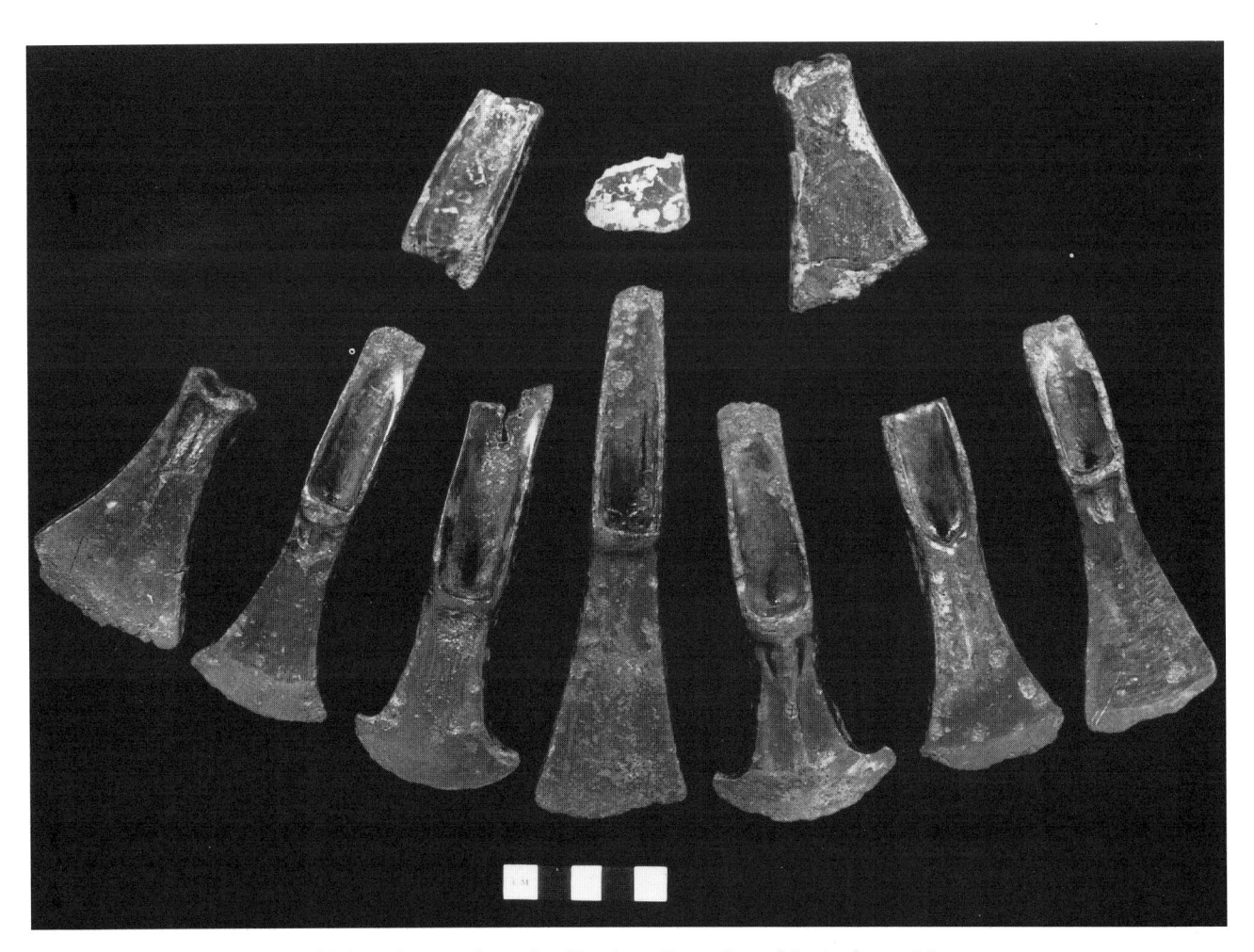

Fig. 11.3. Palstaves from the Vernham Dean hoard in Andover Museum

finds from the county helps to determine selectivity in the composition of the hoards.

A simple analysis of the contents shows that the hoards can be divided between those with palstaves only, those with ornaments only, and mixed hoards (Table 11.1), these compositions obviously resulting from deliberate selection. The number of types represented is extremely restricted, even in the the mixed hoards, but the composition is dominated overall by palstaves of a variety of forms. Although broad classifications already existed, Rowlands created his own typology for palstaves and clearly demonstrated that they can be used to define the products of different 'industries' or regional traditions operating within limited geographical areas, and to recognise cultural links between different areas. In quantifying bronzes from each county, Rowlands also showed the contribution which palstaves make to the character of local 'industries': the number of palstaves from Hampshire (then 160) and neighbouring Sussex (166) far exceeding its nearest rivals (Cambridgeshire 117; Somerset 82 etc). His observations are augmented by the new hoards.

As noted above, the distribution of examples of the Werrar type of palstave (Rowlands 1976, Class 4 group 1; map 6) is very largely restricted to the Isle of Wight and the New Forest. The type is a good example of a distinctive local product and its distribution an indication of the geographical limits of its market (Hodder 1974, 176–7). The Minstead find reinforces this picture.

The Vernham Dean hoard contains palstaves of widely different forms. Such diversity is characteristic of a cluster of hoards in southern Britain (Rowlands 1976, 105). By contrast, the two collections from Hayling Island are markedly different in character, comprising mainly narrow-bladed forms. These are distinct from the indigenous 'transitional' type (Smith 1959a, 184) but have been recognised for some time as related to the series in Northern France (Burgess 1968; Rowlands 1976, 149–52; Needham 1980; O'Connor 1980, 45–9). Although not exclusively, hoards of palstaves containing such axes are sometimes large and are concentrated near the coast from West Sussex to Dorset (Lawson & Farwell 1990) and reflect the larger size of hoards in Northern France, especially Upper Normandy. O'Connor (1980, 45–9) examined contacts between Britain and France closely and identified amongst the hoards of Hampshire Breton palstaves (at Gosport), Norman palstaves (Gosport, Gable Head, Pear Tree Green, Swanwick) and a Centre-Ouest form (Gable Head). The occurrence of such types on both

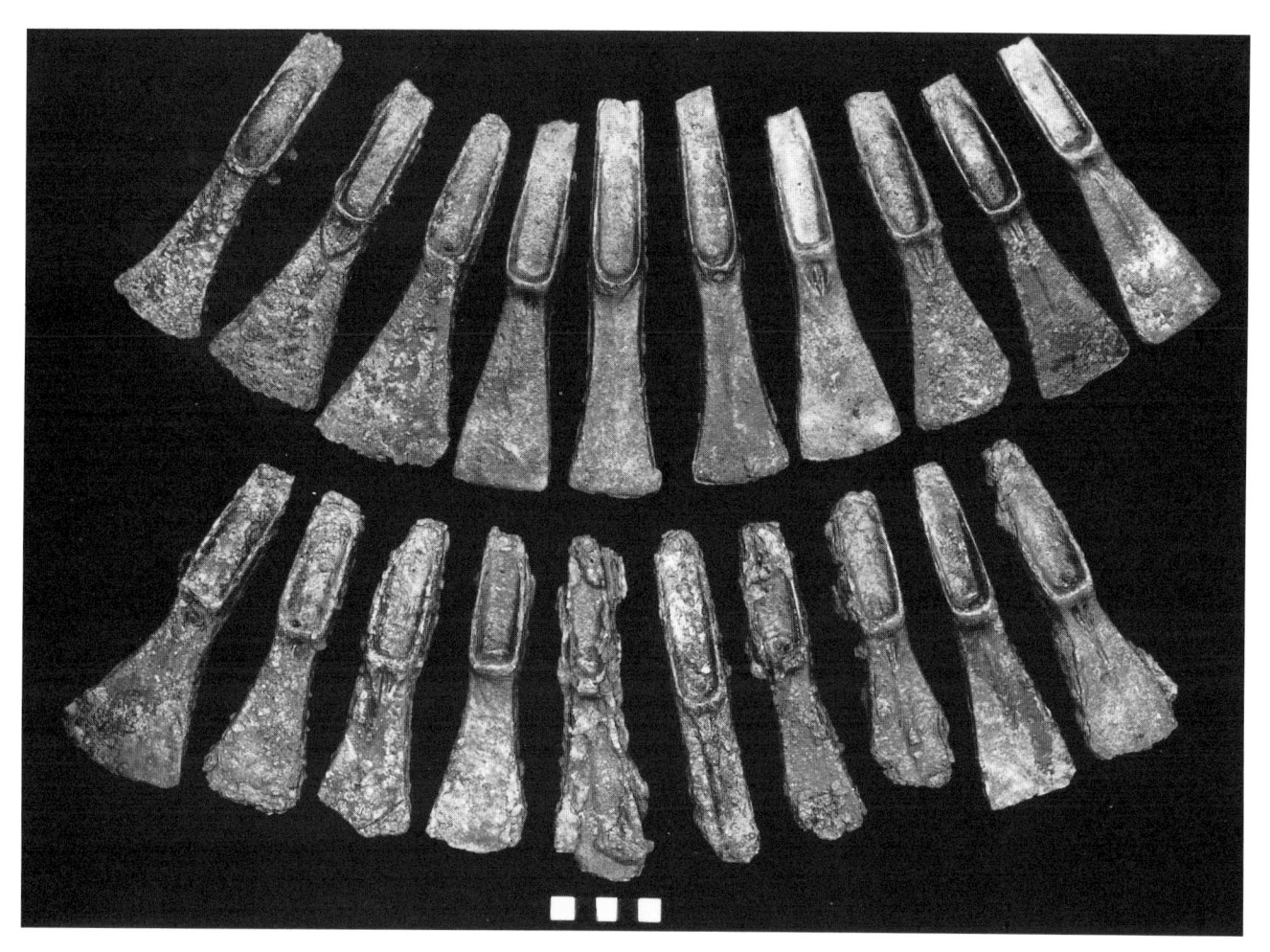

Fig. 11.4. The Hayling Island II hoard in Havant Museum

sides of the Channel and the proximity of the hoards to the coast strongly suggest regular waterborne trade, both coastal and cross-channel. The flow of palstaves seems mainly to have been in one direction and they were presumably exchanged for less durable exports such as animals or cereals.

It may be no coincidence that substantial, plank-built boats (such as North Ferriby, Dover or Goldcliff) appear in the archaeological record at much the same time as these hoards, and in Scandinavia there is a flourish of art depicting large boats (Coles 1990; Coles *et al.* 1993). The absence of any evidence for substantial craft in earlier periods may indicate that it was not until the Middle Bronze Age that boats of a more durable nature were constructed, sophisticated wooden designs supplementing skin-covered craft. The recovery of lost cargoes from the seabed, such as those from Langdon Bay, Dover (Coombs 1975a, 9) and Moors Sand, Devon (Muckleroy & Baker 1979), which include weapons attributable to the slightly later North French *Bronze Final 1,* the equivalent to our Penard tradition, offers proof for such connections. Concentrations of hoards of a variety of later Bronze Age dates in coastal locations (for example, the Isle of Thanet and Thames Estuary; Coombs & Bradshaw 1979, 181) imply a continuing connection between waterborne transport and the stockpiling of metalwork. We know nothing of the form of ports at this time, but natural, sheltered harbours and estuaries where shallow-draught craft could be beached safely must have been favoured. Those that have subsequently been inundated, such as Langstone Harbour, beside Hayling Island, must offer great potential for major discoveries in the future.

The infrequency of continental forms in the general repertoire of individual bronzes from southern Britain makes a strong contrast with the evidence from the coastal caches. It seems that in their continental forms the imported objects did not always satisfy the needs of the local community and may have been transformed through recasting into acceptable alternatives even before they were used (as some of the examples from Hayling Island clearly show). The symbolic value with which each bronze type was specifically imbued and the social or ceremonial role it may have played is an intriguing subject but one we cannot explore here.

The total number of objects found in the Hampshire hoards can be divided between palstaves (86%), ornaments (10%) and fragments (4%). For comparative purposes, Rowlands' catalogue can be used as a reasonable basis for an assessment of unassociated finds. Amongst these, palstaves also dominate (82%), but whereas ornaments form a significant proportion of the hoarded metalwork, they are less frequent (2%) as isolated finds, being replaced instead by weapons (16%). The latter do not feature at all in the MBA hoards of Hampshire (but see below). Leaving to one side the fact that the ornaments themselves offer further evidence of continental contacts (Hawkes 1942; Smith 1959a; O'Connor 1980, 94) and probably played a different role in the customs of use and disposal of metalwork than palstaves, the hoards demonstrate a clear discrimination against the inclusion of weapons. While weapons undoubtedly had a potential military function, they also served ceremonial purposes and were sometimes deposited ritualistically (Needham 1990). It does not seem unreasonable to imply that the exclusion of weapons from the MBA hoards of Hampshire is indicative of belief systems which were different from other parts of the country, such as the Thames Valley or East Anglia.

The overall distribution of the hoards serves to indicate local differences in disposal customs. The geology of the county, which must have been a determinant in past land-use, can be divided into four zones (Fig. 11.5): the central chalk downland, the sands and clays of the Hampshire basin in the south, the greensand of the western end of the Weald in the east, and the clays of the London Basin in the north. Although ornaments are represented throughout the southern zones, there is a marked concentration of hoards with palstaves in the Hampshire basin and, with the exception of the Vernham Dean find, an absence from the chalk. There might be a totally practical explanation for this (access to imported metal, woodland management had a greater need for axes

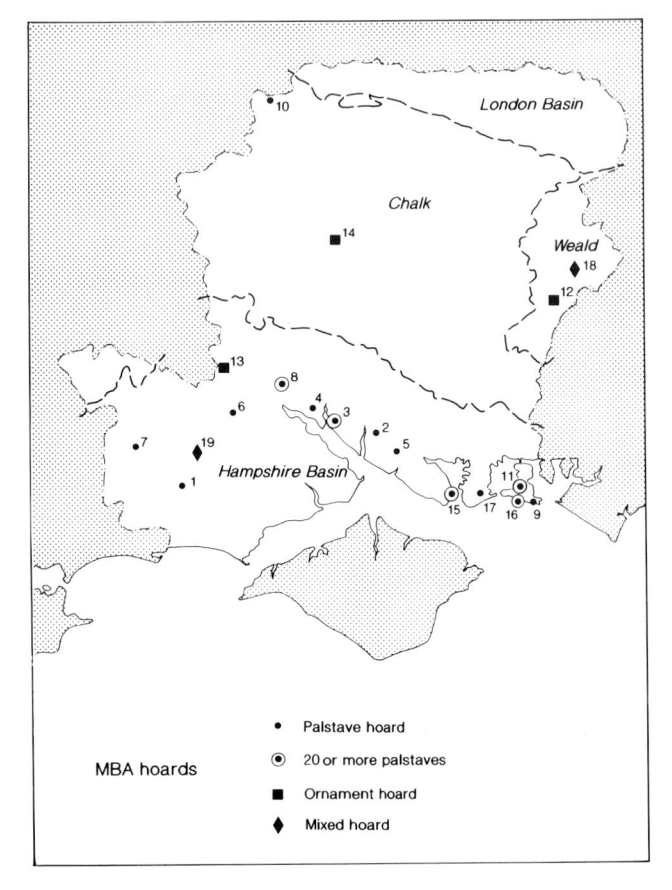

Fig. 11.5. Distribution of MBA hoards in Hampshire. Numbers refer to Table 11.1.

on the heaths of the Basin etc) but it may also serve to identify groups of people amongst whom hoarding was not a custom.

A full analysis of the date of each metal form and the relationship between metalwork and other strands of cultural evidence should be conducted. Nonetheless, Needham (1996) has usefully done this in general terms for the British Bronze Age. Having assessed the many newly available radiocarbon dates previously longed for (e.g. Coles 1963–64, 130), he has suggested a new periodisation of the Bronze Age based on 'prevailing cultural characteristics'. His scheme, which abandons the conventional tripartite division of the Bronze Age, enables us to correlate the MBA metalwork of Hampshire described above with the other cultural elements of his Period 5, dated between 1500 and 1150 BC (*op. cit.*133–4).

Late Bronze Age Metalwork

The boundary between the Middle and the Late Bronze Ages is not easily drawn. Burgess (1969, 3) selected several distinctive types, locally manufactured but whose design originated in the Urnfield tradition of Continental Europe, to characterise his transitional Penard phase. This embraced both developed MBA types as well as the novel forms. Nonetheless, it is generally accepted that the Wilburton tradition is most usefully taken to represent the earliest Late Bronze Age in Southern Britain (Burgess 1969, 9). Two large, new hoards from Hampshire include MBA types but these are associated with a few objects which would normally be attributed to the very beginning of the LBA. These hoards are:

Hayling Island I (near Newtown?)

The hoard was reported to the Hampshire County Museums Service in 1993. It was detected by Mr Walbridge on the edge of a paddock.

The 131 copper alloy items from the hoard (Fig. 11.6) include:

– 2 complete broad-bladed palstaves, one of which is looped, and 11 fragments, one of which has a spearhead fragment adhering, and two of which have amorphous fragments attached;
– 14 separate spearhead fragments, the pronounced mid-rib and narrow blades of the majority suggesting they are from basal looped forms, although two further fragments are certainly from side-looped varieties;
– A large lump of metal comprising at least four spear-

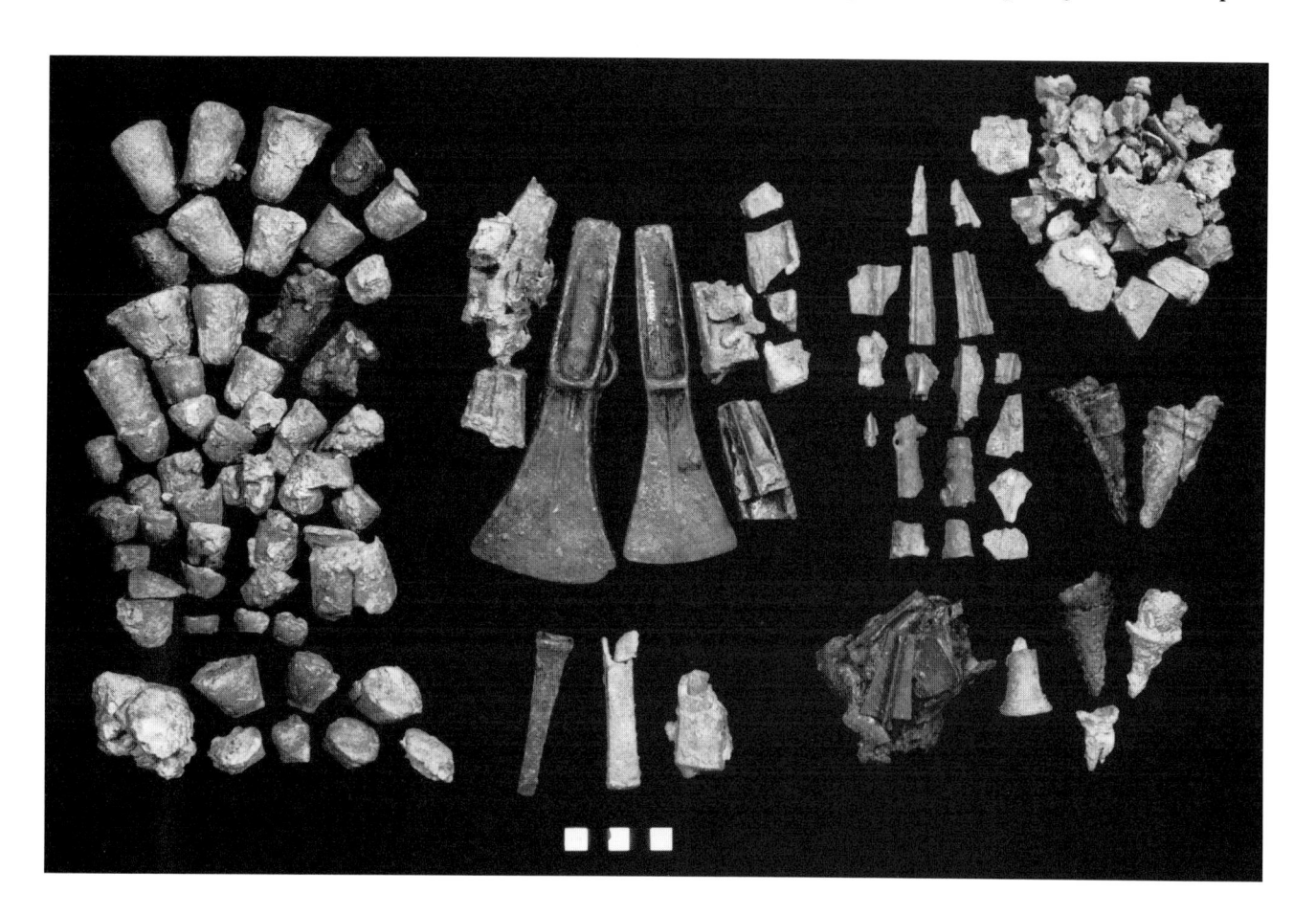

Fig. 11.6. The Hayling Island I hoard in Havant Museum

head fragments and three ingots (see below) fused together;
- 3 thin plate-like fragments with ribs on both faces probably from a sickle (or possibly the blades of spearheads);
- 36 small ingots, flat on one face and half-conical on the other, rather like shoe-lasts or small hooves;
- 7 conical jets and 4 fragments;
- 5 large lumps of metal comprising 'hoof-shaped ingots' fused together so that in total at least 64 ingots are present;
- a rough cast conical object with triple mouth moulding in three fragments, probably a mould. Possibly unrelated to the purpose of the mould but fused to the inner wall of the largest fragment is a conical socketed punch with heavy rectilinear mouth moulding;
- 4 socketed tools comprising a chisel, 2 fragmentary hammers and a narrow, fragmentary hammer (and a detached fragment);
- 2 clusters of flared conical objects (*tutuli* or *Hütchen*?), probably cast but later fused in groups of three and two;
- a small pointed object that may be a jet, conical rivet or small fragments fused together;
- a tubular object (ferrule?) with moulded disc foot;
- 34 further fragments of molten scrap, some of which are extremely small.

Some 30 flint-gritted sherds, probably representing a single Deverel-Rimbury vessel, were also recovered. The sherds appear to form part of a small bucket urn, *ca*.12 cm in diameter with straight, near-vertical walls, decorated with a single row of slight finger impressions beneath a plain flat rim.

Bentley

The hoard was found by Mr J Campbell of Farnham whilst using a metal-detector in 1994.

Although the hoard was originally said to contain 149 objects, the collection was obtained by the Hampshire County Museums Service and contains the following 139 pieces (Fig. 11.7):

- 28 sword fragments, including two from the hilt of a Wilburton sword, 21 from blades with simple lenticular section or with a more pronounced midrib and edge bevels, one tip and three blade fragments with grooves flanking the midrib. Of the latter, one has a single faint groove either side of the midrib, one has one groove on one side and three on the other (and the blade has been reworked in antiquity), and the third has four grooves on one side and three on the other;
- 19 fragments from long, ribbed chapes, including four bases (two with cast buttons);

Fig. 11.7. The Bentley hoard in Chilcomb House, Winchester

- 4 spearhead fragments;
- 2 ends of tubular ferrules;
- 1 heavy rectilinear mount with multiple mouth mouldings on one face, probably a harness or belt loop;
- 5 more-or-less complete 'late' palstaves and 10 fragments;
- 1 winged axe;
- 1 small length of bar with a curved section and chevron decoration from an ornamental fitting;
- 1 fragmentary ring with heavy casting flashes on either side;
- 2 fragments from the mouths of simple socketed tools (probably gouges), one with a casting jet still attached;
- 1 blade from an indented socketed axe;
- 6 curved fragments possibly from cast objects;
- 38 fragments of flat plate scrap, eight with ribs;
- 11 casting jets, five with a single ingate, five with two ingates and one from a palstave;
- 9 lumps of amorphous casting waste including part of a bun ingot.

The hoard has not been analysed metallographically but differences in metal composition or casting conditions are suggested from the surface appearance. Most pieces have a dull powdery, mottled olive and lighter green surface, but a few (the spearhead fragments, the sword tip and one lump) have a lustrous bronze finish, and others (a chape fragment and a plate fragment) have 'tinned' surfaces.

Discussion

In the absence of a published study of Hampshire's Late Bronze Age metalwork comparable to Rowlands' study of the MBA, it is difficult to gauge the quantity of material from the county. A number of museums both within the county and further afield contain hoards and unassociated finds, but the county SMR is not comprehensive, recording only five hoards and five items of this date. However, at least fifteen hoards can be listed (Table 11.2).

The hoards can be divided between those dominated by axes and those dominated by weapons. Even a cursory overview of the axes demonstrates that a considerable range of forms, derived from different metalworking traditions, can be noted. The socketed axes include Stogursey (Colden Common and Bitterne Park; Needham 1981, 62; Darwin 1894), South Eastern (Owlesbury and Grateley) and Breton (Lymington, Nether Wallop) forms which collectively span the LBA. Whether these axe-dominated hoards represent a continuity of the MBA philosophy for the deposition of palstaves is debatable, but in marked contrast to MBA practices the new Hayling Island I hoard introduces a new aspect of later hoards, namely the burial of scrap and molten objects.

The Hayling Island I hoard comprises almost exclusively MBA types, but its character is completely different from hoards of that date and the demonstrably MBA types are mixed with a few apparently later objects (as with the Colden Common find). Spearheads do not normally occur in the MBA hoards of Hampshire (above) and the provenance of this new find is peripheral to the normal distributions of both side-looped and basal-looped forms (in the Thames Valley, South Wiltshire and Dorset: Rowlands 1976, Maps 15–17). It is possible that the inclusion of MBA spearhead fragments may be chronologically significant (in that they only appear in local hoards at this time) but certainly the fragments of scrap and molten metal are more a feature of the Wilburton tradition than any earlier hoards. The 'hoof-shaped ingots' are novel. They appear to have been deliberately cast, possibly for the circulation of stock metal. Northover (1982) has demonstrated from metallographic analysis significant changes in the composition of bronze alloys at the start of the LBA resulting from the importation and mixing of metal from different sources. The 'hoof-shaped ingots' present a tantalising subject for future analysis.

Socketed tools, such as those in the Hayling Island I hoard, begin to occur in the MBA Taunton tradition and Burgess (1969, 34) listed them in the contents of his Penard material. For example, two socketed punches occur in the Taunton Workhouse, Somerset, hoard, a socketed chisel in the Orsett Hall, Essex, hoard and a socketed hammer in the contemporary Bishopsland, Ireland, hoard (Rowlands 1976, 43–5). Similarly, the conical objects of the hoard find parallels in the Monkswood, Somerset, ornament hoard (Smith 1959b, nos 17–8) and the settlement debris of Plumpton Plain, Sussex (Holleymen & Curwen 1935, fig. 17). Another example occurs in the later Yattendon, Berkshire hoard (Coghlan 1970, Y55). O'Connor (1980, 90–1) points out that sheet metal cones may be dress ornaments by comparison with finds (*Hütchen*) in Northern Germany, but does not extend the comparison to cast examples. Bearing in mind the spearheads from the Hayling Island I hoard, one wonders if the cones might be related to the pointed ferrules of the Penard phase. The fragmentary disc-foot ferrule from the hoard appears to be the latest piece and suggests a link with the repertoire of Wilburton metalwork.

The weapon-dominated hoards from the county have attracted attention previously and all earlier finds have been published in some detail (Table 11.2). The swords found in these hoards have been useful in relating their date to continental developments (Burgess 1969), the spearheads have been used to identify insular affinities (Burgess *et al.* 1972), and the balance between the two types has been used to suggest regionalised social stratification (Coombs 1975b).

Colquhoun and Burgess (1988) have examined the swords in detail and on the basis of their classification a chronological sequence for the weapon-dominated hoards of Hampshire can be suggested. Andover is probably the earliest with its Wilburton Variant A swords (Varndell 1979), followed by Blackmoor (Wilburton Variant B and Ewart Part SE Step 1) which is considered to be 'at the head of Ewart Park development' (*op. cit.*, 69; Colquhoun

	Location	Museum	NGR	Date	P	SA	Sw	Ch	SH	Fer	Co	Oth	Sc	Source
1	Hinton	Lost	SZ2195	1750		15								Lort 1779, 115
2	New Forest, Nr Lymington	Lost	SZ3396	c. 1779		?								Lort 1779, 114: Pl8, Nos 9 &10
3	Owlesbury	Winchester	SU5123	1906	1	1								Rowlands No. 65
4	Nether Wallop	BM, Andover, Southampton	SU307376	c. 1920		13+								Moore and Lewis 1969
5	Grateley	Andover	SU2741	?	1	1								HCMS
6	Bitterne Park, Southampton	Southampton: 1 lost	SU439141	1894	4	4	1							Darwin 1894 - 9, 53–66
7	Colden Common, Twyford	Winchester	SU475215	?	10	1			1			1		Rowlands No. 58
8	Hayling Island	Havant	SU7100	1993	13				14	1	5	10	88	this paper
9	Nr Winchester	Winchester	SU4730	?	2	3	3		21	1				Burgess et al 1972, 236
10	Andover	Andover	SU359470	1913			10	11	11	3				Varndell 1979
11	Bossington, Houghton	Winchester	SU3330	?			1	1						Burgess and Colquhuon 1988, 69
12	Blackmoor	Chilcomb	SU7833	1870			32	3	37	2		21		Colquhoun 1979
13	Ashley Wood	Winchester	SU3930	?	1		6		21	1		3		Burgess et al 1972, 236
14	Bentley	Chilcomb	SU7944	1994	17	3	28	18	3	2		10	58	this paper
15	Danebury	Andover	SU324377	1974–7		4	1		1			6		Cunliffe and O'Connor 1979

Table 11.2. Late Bronze Age hoards in Hampshire (objects and fragments combined) with location of collections. Weapon dominated hoards (8–14) enclosed, axe dominated above and 'collector's hoard' (15) beneath. Abbreviations: P: palstaves; SA: socketed axes; Sw: swords; Ch: chapes; SH: spearheads; Fer: ferrules; Co: cone; Oth: other; Sc: scrap.

1979). The sword (Ewart Part SE Step 1) and chape from Houghton are of comparable age to Blackmoor, while Ashley Wood (Ewart Park SE Steps 1 and 2) and 'Winchester', with its non-classifiable sword fragments but spearheads of Broadward affinity are successively slightly later.

Many of the objects in the Bentley hoard are characteristic of the Wilburton tradition, such as the long chapes and the ribbed plate scrap (cf Syon Reach: Needham 1987, fig. 5.15), the socketed gouges, 'late' palstaves and tubular ferrules (cf. Guilsfield: Burgess 1969, fig.9) and the indented socketed axe (cf. Wilburton itself: Burgess 1969, fig. 9). However, the sword fragments allow us to relate it chronologically within the sequence above. Not only does it contain fragments of Wilburton sword but also elements of blades with grooves which are best compared with the St Nazaire series (Colquhoun & Burgess 1988, 53–4). Such imported French weapons are not common in England, but it is interesting to note that a hilt fragment is included in the Blackmoor hoard with which the Bentley find is likely to be coeval.

A more precise date can be given to the Blackmoor hoard as a result of three recent radiocarbon dates which are centred on the 10th century BC. On the basis of these, Needham (1996, 136; Needham *et al*. 1997) has added to earlier arguments for the separation of a Blackmoor 'assemblage' intermediate between the Wilburton and Ewart Park metalwork. With the placing of the Hayling Island I hoard at the transition from the MBA to the Wilburton tradition, the back-dating of the Wilburton metalwork, the chronological position of Bentley with the Blackmoor assemblage and the evidence for early Ewart Park swords, the Hampshire hoards with weapons seem to belong to the narrow period between 1150 and 950 BC (Needham's Period 6).

The Hampshire LBA hoards exhibit continuity of certain ideas from the MBA but also distinct changes. Ornaments no longer play a part and have been replaced by weapons. Continental contacts remain strong, not least through the ties between the Wilburton tradition and that of northern France (the St Brieuc-des-Iffs metalwork: Burgess 1969: Coombs 1988). Certain items, for example the winged axe from Bentley, are likely to be imports. The mechanism of contact between the two countries must have continued to be through frequent maritime traffic. However, the pattern of deposition of hoards in Hampshire shows a dramatic change and presumably with it the relocation of controlling influences in the network of metalwork production, dispersal and disposal.

The distribution of hoards no longer emphasises the coastal zone but the chalk uplands (Fig. 11.8). Indeed, if the 'celts' from Hinton were re-interpreted as palstaves rather than socketed axes (a descriptive problem also encountered elsewhere, e.g. Coles 1968–69, 2) and we preferred to interpret the Hayling Island I hoard as MBA, the shift would be even more marked.

This period also sees the development of defended sites and it has been noted that some of the classic Iron Age hillforts of the county may be sited at important earlier nodal positions (Cunliffe 1990). From the array of earthworks, we might conclude that pressure on available land led to a coercive system for the formalisation of land division and the strict control of agricultural products, exemplified by the regular fields systems and hillforts of the succeeding Iron Age. It seems probable that this formal division of the upland landscape was achieved by those who also sponsored the production of weapons. The composition and distribution of LBA hoards can thus contribute to a broader consideration of social change in southern England, even if here we are restricting our review to one modern county.

The Iron Age

The momentum for bronze production which is in evidence in Hampshire since the MBA waned before the end of the LBA. As noted above, most of the weapon-dominated hoards belong to the Wilburton or early Ewart Park traditions, but these were not succeeded by prodigious later Ewart Park or Carps Tongue hoards. Hampshire was clearly outside the sphere for the recycling of the French scrap associated with Carp's Tongue metalwork, as seen in neighbouring Surrey or the Thames Valley (Needham 1987, 128). Although

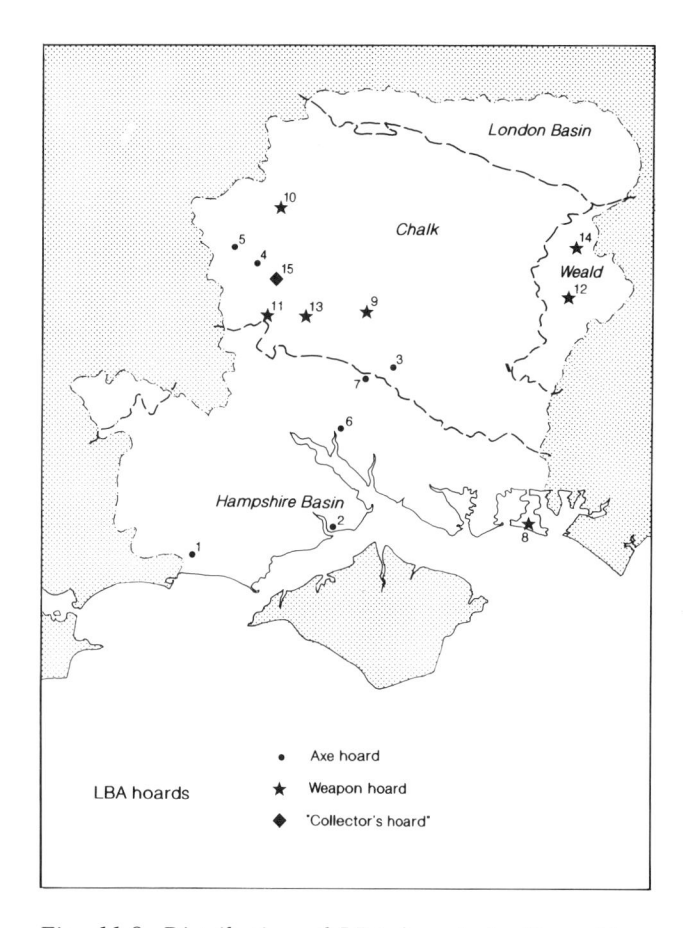

Fig. 11.8. Distribution of LBA hoards in Hampshire. Numbers refer to Table 11.2.

Breton style axes occur in the hoards from Lymington and Nether Wallop, Hampshire also seems to lie largely outside the distribution zone of the later Llyn Fawr metalwork (Moore & Lewis 1969; Thomas 1989, 270).

Nonetheless, a concept of hoarding continued into the Iron Age, although the purpose of the collector may have been different from that in earlier periods. The remarkable collection from Danebury includes objects from almost the entire breadth of the Bronze Age (Cunliffe & O'Connor 1979). This may be only one example of an Iron Age phenomenon of 'collector's hoards' in which an appreciation of typology, and possibly even antiquity, played an important part. The find from 'near Salisbury' in neighbouring Wiltshire (Stead 1991, 10–20) is clearly another example, and other find spots may be worthy of reconsideration. The investigation of the contexts of such finds must be a priority in the future if we are to understand the significance of the bronze collections. We may yet discover that an interest in ancient bronze implements and their creators is as deep seated as the Bronze Age itself!

Acknowledgements

I am grateful to the following staff of Hampshire museums for access to their collections, displays and records: Dave Allen, Andover; Kaye Ainsworth, Chilcomb House; Dr Geoff Denford, Winchester; Howard Gledhill, Lyndhurst; Chris Palmer, Havant; Karen Wardley, Southampton, also to Bruce Howard for information from the Hampshire County Council Sites and Monuments Record and Dr Dave Coombs for data from his own research. My thanks are extended to Elaine Wakefield and Liz James of Wessex Archaeology respectively for photography and illustration. Dr Stuart Needham, British Museum, has arranged access to the National Bronze Implements Index and for permission to reproduce Plate 2. As ever, he has been unstinting in his advice, for which I am most grateful.

My own interest in metalwork has been stimulated by the achievements of John Coles: his encouragement and trust throughout my career has always been greatly appreciated and I am, therefore, delighted to offer this modest paper in his honour.

Bibliography

Burgess, C.B. 1968. Breton palstaves from the British Isles, *Archaeol. J.* 126, 149–53.

Burgess, C.B. 1969. The later Bronze Age in the British Isles and north-western France, *Archaeol. J.* 125, 1–45.

Burgess, C., Coombs, D. and Davies, D.G. 1972. The Broadward complex and barbed spearheads. In F. Lynch and C. Burgess (eds), *Prehistoric Man in Wales and the West*, 211–83. Bath: Adams and Dart.

Clark, J.G.D. and Godwin, H. 1940. A Late Bronze Age find near Stuntney, Isle of Ely, *Antiq. J.* 20, 52–71.

Coghlan, H.H. 1970. *A Report upon the Bronze Age Tools and Weapons from Yattendon, Near Newbury, Berkshire*. Newbury: Borough of Newbury Museum.

Coles, J.M. 1959–60 [1962]. Scottish Late Bronze Age metalwork, *Proc. Soc. Antiq. Scotland* 93, 16–134.

Coles, J.M. 1963–64 [1966]. Scottish Middle Bronze Age metalwork, *Proc. Soc. Antiq. Scotland* 97, 82–156.

Coles, J.M. 1968–69 [1970]. Scottish Early Bronze Age metalwork, *Proc. Soc. Antiq. Scotland* 101, 1–110.

Coles, J.M. 1990. *Images of the Past: a guide to the rock carvings and other ancient monuments of Northern Bohuslän*. Hällristningsmuseet Vitlycke.

Coles, J.M. and Harding, A.F. 1979. *The Bronze Age in Europe*. London: Methuen.

Coles, J.M., Fenwick, V. and Hutchinson, G. (eds) 1993. *A spirit of enquiry: essays for Ted Wright*. Exeter: WARP Occasional Paper 7.

Colquhoun, I.A. 1979. The Late Bronze Age hoard from Blackmoor, Hampshire. In C. Burgess and D. Coombs (eds), *Bronze Age Hoards: some finds old and new*, 99–116. Oxford: British Archaeological Reports 67.

Colquhoun, I and Burgess, C 1988. *The Swords of Britain*. Prähistorische Bronzefunde, Abt. IV, 5. Munich: Beck.

Coombs, D. 1975a. The Dover Harbour bronze find - a Bronze Age wreck? *Archaeologia Atlantica* 1, 193–95.

Coombs, D. 1975b. Bronze Age weapon hoards in Britain, *Archaeologia Atlantica* 1, 49–81.

Coombs, D. 1988. The Wilburton Complex and Bronze Final II in Atlantic Europe. In P. Brun and C. Mordant (eds) *Le groupe Rhin-Suisse-France orientale et la notion de civilisation des Champs d'Urnes*, 575–81. Nemours: Mémoires du Musée de Préhistoire d'Ile-de-France, 1.

Coombs, D. and Bradshaw, J. 1979. A Carp's Tongue hoard from Stourmouth, Kent. In C. Burgess and D. Coombs (eds), *Bronze Age Hoards: some finds old and new*, 181–96. Oxford: British Archaeological Reports 67.

Crawford, O.G.S. 1920. Some Bronze Age and other antiquities, *Proc. Soc. Antiq. London* 2nd series 32, 85–96.

Cunliffe, B. 1990. Before hillforts, *Oxford J. Archaeology* 9, 323–36.

Cunliffe, B. and O'Connor, B. 1979. The Late Bronze Age hoard from Danebury, Hampshire. In C. Burgess and D. Coombs (eds), *Bronze Age Hoards: some finds old and new*, 235–44. Oxford: British Archaeological Reports 67.

Darwin, W.E. 1894 A hoard of bronze implements found at Bitterne, *Hampshire Field Club Papers* 3, 52–66.

Denford, G.T. 1993. Some exotic discoveries at Silkstead Sandpit, Otterbourne, and the possible site of an ancient temple, *Proc. Hampshire Field Club and Archaeol. Soc.* 48, 27–54.

Department of National Heritage 1996. *The Treasure Act 1996 Code of Practice*. London.

Fasham, P.J. and Schadla-Hall, R.T. 1981. The Neolithic and Bronze Age in Hampshire. In S.J. Shennan and R.T. Schadla-Hall (eds), *The Archaeology of Hampshire. From the Palaeolithic to the Industrial Revolution*, 26–36. Hampshire Field Club and Archaeological Society.

Hawkes, C.F.C. 1942. The Deverel urn and the Picardy pin, A phase of settlement in Kent, *Proc. Prehist. Soc.* 7, 26–47.

Hodder, I. 1974. Regression analysis of some trade and marketing patterns, *World Archaeology* 6, 172–89.

Holleyman, G.A. and Curwen, E.C. 1935. Late Bronze Age lynchet settlements on Plumpton Plain, Sussex, *Proc. Prehist. Soc.* 1, 16–38.

Hughes, M. and Champion, T. 1982. A Middle Bronze Age ornament hoard from South Wonston, Hampshire, *Proc. Prehist. Soc.* 48, 48–49.

Lawson, A.J. and Farwell, D. 1990. Archaeological investigation following the discovery of a hoard of palstaves near New Inn

Farmhouse, Marnhull, Dorset, *Proc. Dorset Natural History and Archaeol. Soc.* 112, 131–38.

Lort, The Rev. 1779. Observations on Celts, *Archaeologia* 5, 106–18.

Moore, C.N. and Lewis, E.R. 1969. A hoard of Breton socketed axes from Nether Wallop, *Proc. Hampshire Field Club and Archaeol. Soc.* 26, 19–20.

Muckleroy, K. and Baker, P. 1979. The Bronze Age site off Moor Sand, near Salcombe, Devon: an interim report of the 1978 season, *International J. Nautical Archaeology* 8, 129–210.

Needham, S. 1980. A bronze from Winterfold Heath, Wonersh, and its place in the British narrow-bladed palstave sequence, *Surrey Archaeol. Coll.* 72, 37–47.

Needham, S. 1981. *The Bulford-Helsbury Manufacturing Tradition. The production of Stogursey socketed axes during the later Bronze Age in Southern Britain*. London: British Museum Occasional Paper 13.

Needham, S. 1987. The Bronze Age. In J. Bird and D.G. Bird (eds), *The Archaeology of Surrey to 1540*, 97–138. Guildford: Surrey Archaeological Society.

Needham, S. 1990. Middle Bronze Age ceremonial weapons: new finds from Oxborough, Norfolk and Essex/Kent, *Antiq. J.* 70, 239–52.

Needham, S. 1996. Chronology and periodisation in the British Bronze Age. In K. Randsbourg (ed), *Absolute Chronology: Archaeological Europe 2500–500 BC*, 121–140. Acta Archaeologica 67. Copenhagen: Munksgaard.

Needham, S.P. and Denford, G.T. 1985. Middle Bronze Age metalwork from Anderwood Inclosure, New Forest. *Proc. Hampshire Field Club and Archaeol. Soc.* 41, 279–80.

Needham, S.P., Lawson A.J. and Green H.S. 1985. Context types for Bronze Age metalwork. *British Bronze Age Metalwork: A1–6 Early Bronze Age Hoards*, v–vii. London: British Museum.

Needham, S., Bronk Ramsey, C., Coombs, D., Cartwright, C., and Pettit, P. 1997. An independent chronology for British Bronze Age metalwork: the results of the Oxford radiocarbon accelerator programme, *Archaeol. J.* 154, 55–107.

Northover, P. 1982. The metallurgy of the Wilburton hoards, *Oxford J. Archaeology* 1, 56–109.

O'Connor, B. 1980 *Cross-channel Relations in the Later Bronze Age*. Oxford: British Archaeological Reports International Series 91.

Rees, H. 1993. Later Bronze Age and Early Iron Age settlement in the Lower Test valley. Evidence from excavations and finds, 1981–9, *Proc. Hampshire Field Club and Archaeol. Soc.* 49, 19–46.

Roskill, V. 1938. The bronze implements of the Newbury region, *Trans. Newbury District Field Club* 8, 10–41.

Rowlands, M.J. 1976. *The Production and Distribution of Metalwork in the Middle Bronze Age in Southern Britain*. Oxford: British Archaeological Reports 31.

Smith, M.A. 1959a. Some Somerset hoards and their place in the Bronze Age of Southern Britain, *Proc. Prehist. Soc.* 25, 144–87.

Smith, M.A. (ed) 1959b. The Monkswood Hoard. *Inventaria Archaeologica* GB 42.

Stead, I.M. 1991. Many more Iron Age shields from Britain, *Antiq. J.* 71, 1–35.

Tomalin, D. 1996. Towards a new strategy for curating the Bronze Age landscape of the Hampshire and Solent region. In D.A. Hinton and M. Hughes (eds), *Archaeology in Hampshire: a framework for the future*, 13–25. Winchester: Hampshire County Council.

Thomas, R. 1989. The Bronze-Iron transition in southern England. In M.L. Stig Sørensen and R. Thomas (eds), *The Bronze Age-Iron Age Transition in Europe*, 263–86. Oxford: British Archaeological Reports International Series 483.

Varndell, G.L. 1979. The Andover hoard - a Late Bronze Age of Wilburton tradition from Hampshire. In C.Burgess and D. Coombs (eds), *Bronze Age Hoards: some finds old and new*, 93–98. Oxford: British Archaeological Reports 67.

Wrey, E.C. 1954. Bronze Age axes near Fordingbridge, *Papers and Proc. Hampshire Field Club and Archaeol. Soc.* 18, 70.

12. Gold Reflections

Joan J. Taylor

Abstract: The purpose of this paper is to report preliminary research by the Prehistoric Gold Research Group seeking to link gold sources to prehistoric artefacts, in particular Early Bronze Age goldwork from Ireland and Britain, which updates the interpretation of prehistoric goldwork postulated by the author thirty years ago under the guidance of John Coles.

Introduction

The tracing of the actual gold sources represented in artefacts, particularly Early Bronze Age objects, may now be a feasible concept technologically (Taylor *et al.* 1997), while other metal artefact studies attempting to trace the ore sources and other raw materials that make up the constituent parts of an artefact, particularly where alloying is involved, are still in their experimental stages (Joel *et al.* 1997; Joel *et al.* forthcoming; Craddock 1995; Budd *et al.* in press). It has always been desirable to trace from ore to artefact (Taylor 1970; Taylor 1980), and it may now be becoming possible with substantial, recently available geological information, coupled with advanced trace element technology.

Analytical advances

The preliminary research of the Prehistoric Gold Research Group (PGRG) brings together a range of expertise to study all aspects of the problem (Taylor *et al.* 1997; Shell *et al.* 1998; Chapman *et al.* forthcoming) and uses a Laser Ablation-Inductively Coupled Plasma-Mass Spectrometer (LA-ICP-MS) to explore the gold sources and artefacts. The LA-ICP-MS has a detection sensitivity measurable in parts per billion (ppb) and parts per trillion (ppt) in some instances, as opposed to that of the emission spectrograph used in the 1960s and early 1970s by Axel Hartmann for the Arbeitsgemeinschaft für Metallurgie, Stuttgart. The latter's sensitivity was only in parts per million (ppm) (Hartmann 1970; 1982). LA-ICP-MS potentially provides the required detection limits on about fifty important elements, certainly useful in any attempt to link trace elements associated with sources through to the artefact. Electron-probe micro-analysis (EPMA) is used in the same research protocol for several reasons, giving the added advantage that the two methods produce complementary analyses. A check can thus be provided on the LA-ICP-MS results, which are interpreted in terms of ratios of measured counts, giving semi-quantitative analyses for the higher concentrations of elements present (Watling *et al.* 1994). Extensive work using the EPMA for sourcing at the British Geological Survey, and subsequently by our group at the University of Leeds, where they are also looking at the mineral inclusions found in gold sources, gave over 5000 analyses of gold grains from 150 source sites (Chapman *et al.* forthcoming); the Bracks Farm, Cambridgeshire, bar-flanged torc section, on which numerous LA-ICP-MS analyses had been made, was examined using the EPMA, and the correlations agree well with each other. Likewise both confirmed the principal element analyses for the same object which had been produced by A. Hartmann and Johnson Matthey (Taylor 1980; Taylor *et al.* 1997; Warner 1993).

Author's Address: Joan J. Taylor, Department of Archaeology, University of Liverpool, William Hartley Building, Brownlow Street, Liverpool L69 3BX

A. Hartmann agreed in the 1960s to analyse some of the ores supplied to him as reported in *Bronze Age Goldwork of the British Isles* (Taylor 1980), but he did not discuss these sources, since he took the view that a single source was likely for all the British Isles: that of Wicklow. Accordingly his statistical interpretation did not entertain the possibility of a different Irish source for some of the unique and geographically restricted artefacts such as the lunulae, for which he argued a continental origin for the metal, and by implication for the lunulae themselves (Hartmann 1970). He held a similar view for the Food Vessel hilt bands from Collessie, Fife; Skateraw, East Lothian; and Blackwaterfoot, Arran, with their diagnostically high tin trace (Taylor 1983).

Advantages of the new method

Why choose LA-ICP-MS, when the cost per sample has not appreciably decreased since mass spectroscopy was developed in the late 1960s? It is always desirable, if possible, to find a non-destructive quantitative method with high sensitivity and a large elemental range, when sampling artefacts of great antiquity and rarity. Although samples must still be removed from the object, each sample, when mounted in acrylic blocks, is conserved, apart from the points of laser ablation, for further analyses and may be returned to the museum for future study. The laser volatilizes the gold directly into the analytical chamber without dissolving it first in highly corrosive acids, which might cause solvent contamination and interaction from the machine components and containers used for the sample. Extremely sensitive, the wide-ranging analytical technique provides the opportunity for a significant step forward from former programmes, with its previously unobtainable much enhanced detection levels. The archaeologist now may re-assess and interpret more precisely the range of golds that may have been available during the period under study, and investigate the circumstances of their use by the prehistoric artisan and the significance of his or her choice.

The LA-ICP-MS analysis may detect a suite of up to 50 elements in a manner comparable to the range potentially detectable by emission spectroscopy, but with far greater sensitivity. Discrete element associations show an ability to distinguish between, for example, an initial set of alluvial gold samples form Ireland and from Scotland. The analysis may characterise these alluvial sources and there is the potential to define a unique signature for each. Confirmation of this, of course, requires a comprehensive programme of analyses for all known sources that may have been exploited in antiquity.

The multi-disciplinary approach

This research strategy provides an objective study of prehistoric gold incorporating not only J. Watling's analytical work but interpretation by archaeologists J. Taylor, M. Cahill, and R. Warner, metallurgists C. Shell and R. Chapman and geologists R. Leake and R. Chapman, all working together to reconstruct the progression from geological source to the finished product (Taylor *et al.* 1997). The ore geneticist, R. Leake, a process mining metallurgist, R. Chapman, an archaeometallurgist, C. Shell, and an archaeologist, R. Warner, all interact to see that any deviation from the premises postulated is quickly identified.

C. Shell conducts melting experiments on some of the ore source material to discern any changes caused by refining and manufacturing processes. The remelting of samples of alluvial gold shows a predictable slight loss of the more volatile elements, but fair stability in the great majority. It also provides a volume of source gold appropriate for use as internal standards for all analyses.

To allow a valid comparison, the geological data required must be sufficiently discrete, with characteristics that can be defined either microstructurally or chemically. The potential number of exploitable sources must be sufficiently small to be identified at least regionally or to a generic origin, if not to a specific identifiable source. The focus of the geological aspect of this research thus far has been to obtain samples from as full a range of alluvial sources as possible within Britain and Ireland, and also from the prehistorically exploitable hard rock ores capable of being exploited in antiquity (Chapman *et al.* forthcoming). The experience of the prospector as well as the ore geneticist provides insight into the types of matrix prehistoric collectors might exploit as well as what inclusions might be introduced from these sources. Working together, the metallurgist, the mining geologist/metallurgist and the ore geneticist allow us to predict what technological processes are likely to have been employed to obtain the finished product. For example, the possibility of matrix tin dissolving into the gold in the process of melting the alluvial gold seems unlikely, unless a reducing atmosphere is present: thus, when among the inclusions found in the Bracks Farm torc section there are a small number composed of calcium stannate, it is possible they derive from the fusion of cassiterite and calcite during melting, which points to an oxidising state during the melt (Chapman & Leake, pers. comm.). The reducing atmosphere is unlikely to have been present in earlier gold working, and in studies of West China early copper alloys, the angular grains of cassiterite show that additions of cassiterite must be made in a reducing atmospheres or they are ineffectual in forming an alloy (Mei *et al.* forthcoming).

The research premises

Certain assumptions have formed the premises of the work. The first is that gold associated with a specific mineralising event can inherit a trace or ultra element signature unique to that event or process. Secondly, it is assumed that this signature can be detected in early gold artefacts, in cases where it is believed they were simply formed by melting up and shaping the alluvial gold. Thirdly, we assume that re-cycling, which could mix sources in the final object, was minimal during the period we are studying and fourthly, that the defining characteristics are capable of surviving to be recognised in the artefact through the process of its manufacture, as well as through deposition and degradation as an ore, and through recovery and subsequent conservation (Taylor *et al.* 1997). This latter assumption may only safely be made with *gold* as the raw material: as stated before (Taylor 1980); the properties of gold, as a non-corroding metal with very little depth of surface enrichment, lend themselves to this study. It has a simple progression from its molten into its solid state. With these various assumptions made, the focus of our study is an attempt to investigate what are the best possible circumstances for linking a prehistoric metal artefact to a region for its raw material.

Gold as a prehistoric metal

During the Early Bronze Age in Britain and Ireland, gold did not require reduction of the ore by smelting, and there is no evidence that refining processes were used in the prehistoric period. Finds of small 'bullet' ingots, reputedly Bronze Age, suggest that gold was actually formed into cast rough blanks before being cold-worked into its final sheet form, for which an almost exclusive preference was shown in the Early Bronze Age. This early use of sizeable quantities of sheet gold for the manufacture of over one hundred collars or lunulae is limited geographically to the British Isles and the Coastal Atlantic region of Continental Europe, especially Brittany. It seems a fair assumption that the objects made when gold first became current in society in the Early Bronze Age will be the least adulterated. The social preference for sheet objects, which was certainly *not* forced upon them by limited technological achievement, enjoyed a more prolific use within the British Isles than elsewhere. Also, there is a survival here of the greatest range of artefact types, far exceeding that of the rest of Western Europe at this time.

The classic early example of the Irish goldwork is the lunula, a gold collar uniquely not committed to the grave. The lunulae apparently were not personal items, but must have performed within society as emblems, whether inherited, used in a 'political' way, or possibly not worn but used as religious items for the adornment of statuary. Remarkably little wear damage occurs on the relatively fragile sheet in lunulae as opposed to that found on, for example, solid bracelets, suggesting that little abrasive movement could have taken place. Lunulae found near prominent landmarks in the landscape, or deposited in wooden boxes in peat bogs, occur as single finds: very rarely they are incorporated into hoards and, when found in such contexts, are usually there with later items, simply as gold for re-cycling. The few associations of lunulae with barrows suggest that the barrows were simply used as obvious landmarks, and the lunulae were not in any funerary context (Taylor 1970; 1980). From art historical considerations, these collars can be related to the indigenous Beaker society. (The preliminary results of lunulae analyses are reconsidered below.)

Questions to be considered

The possibility of workshops, individual smiths, itinerant smiths, and elaborate trade networks, formerly identified by detailed measurements, art-historical decorative analysis and observed patterns of technological details in the artefacts' manufacture, can, we hope, be confirmed by trace element analyses, providing solid scientific evidence for their existence. Although A. Hartmann's results reflected both chronological and geographical groupings, they did not reach to the point of providing the more detailed interpretation that archaeologists required. We never expected to know whether it was the customer commissioning the item or the goldsmith who was the supplier of the gold, but, as argued below, it is now becoming possible to suggest what may have been happening between them. The fact that at least some of the artisans worked not only a range of metals but also other exotic materials, such as amber or shale, needs to be addressed. If possible, we are interested in knowing how much recycling of gold took place, and when it can first be detected in the archaeological record. Was gold traded or exchanged in its finished state, or were ingots traded, and if so, over what range? Were they traded internally or externally? Can a source be seen to have been exploited only for a limited time within the Bronze Age, or can it be identified as having also been used subsequently? Are we in error if we suggest that a particular group of gold ornaments must be from a particular period because that is when the source is predominantly visible in the archaeological record? Is the reasonably high copper trace in some Early Bronze Age artefacts simply indicative of a dirty crucible, originally used in bronze casting, now being used for gold casting, or is it reliably indicative of a particular source, or even of the extraction method employed by the miner? At present, it seems that the increasing number of sources of gold with distinctive high copper traces being discovered may preclude at least the dirty crucible argument.

Importance of geological factors

Almost as many pertinent new areas of interest arise from this research for the geologist as for the archaeologist. Some years ago, Hartmann and Taylor vigorously debated whether the presence of tin was an indicator of an alluvial source or whether the absence of tin always implied a mined source (Taylor 1980); it may be that they were both wrong. The presence of tin in alluvial sources could be identified in only a few instances, one of which is in the Mountains of Mourne. This is most interesting, when related to the traces of tin that are detected from the artefacts: the absence of tin is one of the reasons that we can now discount Mayo as a source for any of the artefacts so far analysed. Chapman has even suggested that there may have been little use made of the alluvial sources (Chapman *et al.* forthcoming). This is a preliminary hypothesis, to say the least, but certainly an idea for further investigation. The several recent discoveries of early copper mines in Britain and Ireland, with their associated mining techniques and ores, especially Ross Island with its associated Beaker artefacts and house dated to 2400 BC (O'Brien 1995), and the production mines of Parys Mountain and the Great Orme in North Wales (Ambers 1990; Dutton & Fasham 1994), suggest that technologically the winning of gold, be it from hard rock sources or from alluvial sources, was fully within the ability of the earliest miners. In many instances, alluvial gold occurs with cassiterite, so further sources may have come on stream throughout the Bronze Age as bronze became more widely used. Research continues into the ore sources, and a picture is already beginning to emerge of where prehistoric goldworking was or was not leading, but there is one more generic ore in the British Isles that we must examine in detail before we accept an invitation to work on the continental material.[1]

Some preliminary results from Wessex

It is pleasing to report here that the conclusions put forward by John Coles and the present author in 1971 (Coles & Taylor 1971) still apply, especially where gold is concerned. Three Wessex grave groups have been analysed in our preliminary study by LA-ICP-MS (Wilsford G.8, a cremation; Upton Lovell G.2(e), probably a secondary cremation; and Bush Barrow (Wilsford G.5), an inhumation containing a tall, elderly man). I can confirm the minimal view of twenty-seven years ago that an indigenously developed Wessex elite is suggested by the funerary offerings buried in each of those cases, and can further extend the evidence for such an argument through the PGRG's examination of the gold sheet work, although we are still in the preliminary stages of our research into identifying the sources of golds used in the manufacture of such artefacts. Only about twenty of the numerous exotic graves comprising the Wessex period burials ever contained gold, and even fewer had more than one gold object. These gold grave goods were in pristine condition, although beaten to a thinness of sheet comparable almost to today's household heavy duty aluminium foil (Taylor 1979). We now see, through our analyses, that small amounts of gold of different composition were employed in the manufacture of the funerary artefacts, suggesting that gold was a scarce commodity within the Wessex society despite the use of other luxury materials deposited in generously endowed grave assemblages. Although several natural sources remain to be characterised, and it is within the realms of possibility that some of the Wessex items could have been produced from such golds, it is also possible that these analytical groups represent the recycling of gold from various different sources. The question of who supplied the gold for any object, commissioner or goldsmith, therefore remains unanswered, as the commissioner could have been exchanging old regalia for re-designed, newly crafted pieces, and not have been entitled to any return, perhaps because the goldsmith's reward for the manufacture of the piece was allowed for in the exchange; alternatively, the smith may have supplied the materials and have been rewarded for his work in some other manner. As identified by Coles and Taylor in 1971, the concept of a single master-goldsmith in Wessex, who also worked in amber and shale, and whose work occurs in the two geographical areas of Britain and Brittany, is further strengthened by the recent analyses. Not all items within any grave group come from a single gold source, but internally within the three grave groups some objects share a single source: for example, the Bush Barrow back-plate and hook, which are two separate parts of the same belt-hook, are from the same source. Also, some items in each group share sources with objects from the other two grave assemblages.

The Bush Barrow (Wilsford G.5:168) belt large lozenge, which may be a template for the later re-building of Stonehenge (Shell and Robinson 1988; Thom *et al.* 1988), shares the same analytical source as one of the small cylindrical beads from Upton Lovell G.2(e), while the small lozenge plate from Bush Barrow (Wilsford G.5:177) and the pendant cover from Wilsford G.8 (182) share the same composition (Figs 12.1–12.2.). A third group includes (so far) the Upton Lovell G.2(e) button cover and one of the cones from the same funerary assemblage. There were sufficient art historical and technological grounds in 1971 to trace these three grave groups back to the master goldsmith, but the new evidence extends the known range of his work and confirms the association of the assemblages analytically and chronologically. As regards the stylistic evidence, the dotting of the seams of some objects, different from the dots within the grooves found on the gold-bound amber discs and the Clandon lozenge plate, links many pieces into the repertoire of the one craftsman. This suggests that the same craftsman was working with multiple gold sources, and that some of these gold groups may even derive from a single crucible of re-cycled gold containing sufficient volume to provide material for more than one item, which became dispersed among the three grave groups. To put the matter of quantities into perspective, the total volume of gold contained in all Wessex graves still remains no more than the amount required to make one, or possibly two, of the Irish lunulae. The close comparison afforded by the analytical results certainly strengthens the suggestion that only a very short time is represented by the gold fabricated by the master smith, and, incidentally, that

WESSEX, EARLY BRONZE AGE GOLD: dissimilarity matrix ((AVRAT-1)*100)	Wilsford 176(B)	Wilsford 176(A)	Wilsford 192	Wilsford 181	Wilsford 182	Wilsford 177	Upton Lovell 232	Wilsford 168	Upton Lovell 226	Upton Lovell 233	Upton Lovell 231B	Wilsford 169	Upton Lovell 231A	
Wilsford (G5) 176(B)		111	409	703	606	632	975	933	755	1408	2715	1618	6708	belt-hook
Wilsford (G5) 176(A)	111		246	378	317	352	497	445	394	777	1428	952	6924	belt-hook
Wilsford (G8) 192	409	246		425	**139**	194	223	269	198	502	618	439	9543	pendant-cover
Wilsford (G8) 181	703	378	425		219	257	429	474	580	585	613	983	1501	button-cover
Wilsford (G8) 182	606	317	**139**	219		**103**	116	152	165	240	321	314	4197	pendant-cover
Wilsford (G5) 177	632	352	194	257	**103**		**133**	183	250	328	451	328	5345	lozenge-plate
Upton Lovell (G2e) 232	975	497	223	429	116	**133**		**108**	162	136	165	191	8524	rect.-plate
Wilsford (G5) 168	933	445	269	474	152	183	**108**		**138**	139	187	160	17063	lozenge-plate
Upton Lovell (G2e) 226	755	394	198	580	165	250	162	**138**		214	302	342	26512	bead
Upton Lovell (G2e) 233	1408	777	502	585	240	328	136	139	214		**120**	202	14062	button-cover
Upton Lovell (G2e) 231B	2715	1428	618	613	321	451	165	187	302	**120**		278	10329	cone
Wilsford (G5) 169	1618	952	439	983	314	328	191	**160**	342	202	278		32478	dagger-stud
Upton Lovell (G2e) 231A	6708	6924	9543	1501	4197	5345	8524	17063	26512	14062	10329	32478		cone

Fig. 12.1. Dissimilarity matrix for Wessex goldwork, derived from the analyses described in the text. Lower numbers indicate closer similarity in metal content (bold numbers indicate closest links). Figure by R. Warner.

cremation and inhumation were contemporary and not consecutive rites.

With this evidence for contemporaneity of manufacture, but unfortunately lacking the assistance of dendrochronology to pin calendar events tightly on Wessex burials, the Wessex chronology cannot be fixed to a narrower timescale than a single generation, perhaps suggesting about thirty years for the deposition of all the gold objects. Therefore, the identification of a master craftsman's work deposited in several principal grave assemblages still implies that the golden age of Wessex was extremely brief and that all these graves were roughly contemporary within a period of about thirty years. Are we witnessing one specific short episode in funerary fashion? The Wessex graves certainly existed in other forms for over three hundred years.

Miniaturisation may also be a factor caused as much by the actual scarcity of gold as by social choice, and it certainly suggests that the power with which such objects were imbued was not compromised by their small size. Certainly, the quality of the pieces suffered little from the reduced volume of gold, as they are some of the most exquisitely executed goldwork in the whole European Bronze Age. Therefore, the quality of the goldsmith's work may have been at least as important as the overall volume of wealth represented in gold, shale and amber. Miniaturisation does not lessen the generously exotic nature of these grave assemblages.

Within the Wilsford G.8 grave group, there is good analytical correspondence between the gold cover of the bone pendant (182) and the small lozenge plate of Bush Barrow (Wilsford G.5:177), while moderately close correspondence also exists internally in Upton Lovell G.2(e) between the cylindrical bead and the sheet, often referred to as a manchette or bracer, from the same grave assemblage. At Bush Barrow, the analyses suggest that the belt hook and back plate definitely came from the same crucible melt. The hand of the same goldsmith had already been identified on technological and art-historical grounds for these items, but in the case of the two Wilsford G.8 pendants (182 & 192) and the Bush Barrow small lozenge (Wilsford G.5:177), there is no stylistic correlation, although the internal correspondence as well as external correspondence are now confirmed by trace element analysis. In cross-referencing between grave groups, the Bush Barrow items just mentioned, together with the large lozenge, are close to one of the cylindrical beads in Upton Lovell G.2(e) and significantly close to the button cover (see Fig 12.1). It may be assumed therefore that the small items not previously attributed to this goldsmith can now be assumed to be his or her work, that is, the cover for the bone pendant and the cylindrical bead. The small outlining dots on many of the pieces also appear to form a part of this individual's repertoire of characteristic finishing techniques, and in this instance can also be seen on the horned pendant from Wilsford G.8, as well as the cylindrical beads. As mentioned in passing above, there is a further important archaeological implication, namely that the location of Bush Barrow next to Wilsford G.8, and the shared gold objects between the two primary graves, shows that the funerary rite of inhumation (Bush Barrow) and cremation (Wilsford G.8) were contemporary. The Bush Barrow inhumation was definitely a tall elderly man, but can we be sure that the Wilsford G.8 cremation was a female?

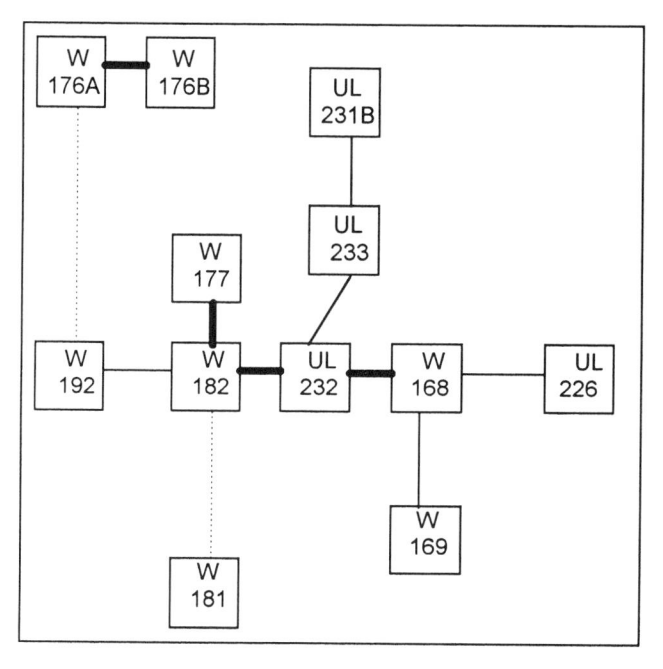

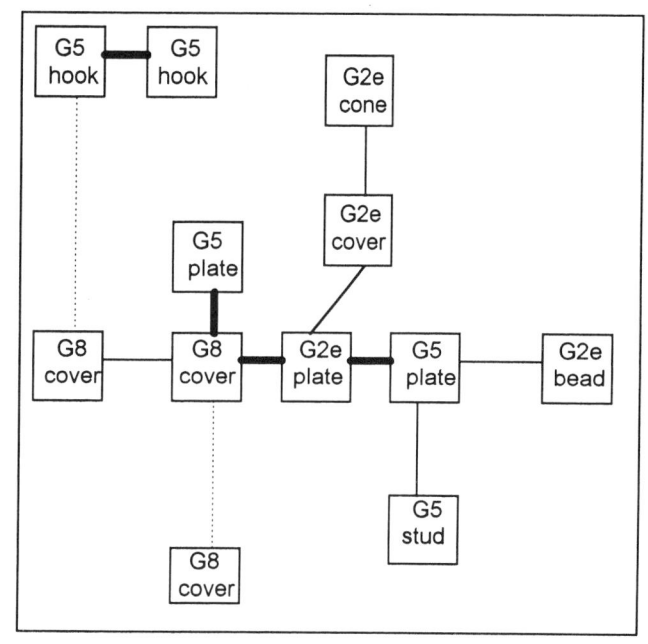

Fig. 12.2. Graphical representation of the similarity of gold compositions from Early Bronze Age Wessex, as shown in Fig. 12.1; the shorter the linkages the more similar the compositions. Left: Analysis numbers, with W (Wilsford) and UL (Upton Lovell); right: grave numbers with object descriptions. Figure by R. Warner.

Although still in its early stages, the research reported here strongly suggests that even with only three of the eight major grave assemblages examined, it is possible to reinforce previous art-historical conclusions with sound objective evidence. It should be stressed that this is merely the beginning of such evidence, and one hopes that more will shortly be forthcoming.

Beaker goldwork, including the lunulae

Questions about Beaker goldwork found in the British Isles concern the origin of the gold sources, whether certain 'symbols of power' formed discrete groups composed from a single source and whether the sources were also used for the production of other artefact types. Were some items imports or indigenous copies? The question of identifying workshops on stylistic grounds was considered in 1970 (Taylor 1970): does analytical evidence support this approach in the way it does the evidence for the Wessex gold grave groups, discussed above?

Thus far, our dissimilarity measures based on preliminary analytical results suggest that there are at least two gold groups, which together incorporate lunulae, Beaker discs and Beaker basket earrings, but that these groups do not correspond exclusively either to type or to provenance (Figs. 12.3–12.4). Two of three lunulae from Banemore, County Kerry, two lunulae of four from Dunfierth, Co. Kildare, and two strips from Bellville, Co. Cavan, are closely connected on the dissimilarity matrix, implying that both the analyses and the dissimilarity algorithm are meaningful; the other associated gold objects have not yet been analysed. The fact that the Beaker discs and the lunulae are analytically indistinguishable appears to confirm the claimed Beaker social context for the latter. This point had already been made on stylistic grounds of ornamentation (Taylor 1970) but, as lunulae were never used as grave goods, their social and chronological positions were always open to doubt. So far, this analytical group lacks tight geographical integrity, although all the objects are Irish, and the importance lies in the linkage between Beaker earrings, discs and lunulae lying together in this group.

The Deehommed gold find, similar to Iberian Beaker earrings, but possibly imitating a Central European racquet-headed pin in its prehistoric Irish use, can be described as closer to the *Blechstil* technique of sheet work in character, the imitation and technique both pointing back toward Central European origins (Taylor 1980), so it is not surprising that it has proved analytically quite different from any other British or Irish provenanced artefact. Nor does it, on the evidence of Hartmann's Iberian analyses, match the Iberian earring group, as one might perhaps have expected (Hartmann 1982). All we can say at present is that its source must lie elsewhere in Europe.

Conclusion

The analytical research described here is still at a preliminary stage; although substantial progress has been

IRELAND, EARLY BRONZE AGE: dissimilarity matrix ((AVRAT-1)*100)	Banemore 1756	Banemore 1757	Rappacastle	Ireland	Bellville W71	Bellville(W81	Dunfierth W4	Tremoge	Dunfierth W9	Cloyne	Cong	Rosgarron	West Mayo	Deehommed	
Banemore (Kerry) 1756		478	**155**	158	206	184	324	191	287	322	277	546	714	4036	lunula 1756
Banemore (Kerry) 1757	478		260	**164**	522	254	262	367	217	300	339	208	684	1363	lunula 1757
Rappacastle (Mayo)	155	260		**130**	271	174	356	282	355	265	211	332	906	2264	beaker disc
Ireland	158	164	**130**		291	152	247	245	277	253	187	229	430	1638	basket earring
Bellville (Cavan) W71	206	522	271	291		**130**	732	193	319	264	528	850	1865	7065	band W71
Bellville (Cavan) W81	184	254	174	152	**130**		403	140	173	213	522	561	998	3271	band W81
Dunfierth (Kildare) W4	324	262	356	247	732	403		232	**126**	244	159	282	293	1959	lunula W4
Tremoge (Tyrone)	191	367	282	245	193	140	232		**95**	113	331	526	510	4514	lunula
Dunfierth (Kildare) W9	287	217	355	277	319	173	126	**95**		102	221	326	538	2768	lunula W9
Cloyne (Cork)	322	300	265	253	264	213	244	113	**102**		290	398	1010	3677	beaker disc
Cong (Mayo)	277	339	211	187	528	522	159	331	221	290		**151**	394	1405	lunula
Rosgarron (Derry)	546	208	332	229	850	561	282	526	326	398	**151**		455	1100	lunula
West Mayo	714	684	906	430	1865	998	**293**	510	538	1010	394	455		1746	lunula
Deehommed (Down)	4036	1363	2264	1638	7065	3271	1959	4514	2768	3677	1405	1100	1746		object

Fig. 12.3. Dissimilarity matrix for Irish Early Bronze Age goldwork (cf Fig. 12.1). Lower numbers indicate closer similarity in metal content (bold numbers indicate closest links). Figure by R. Warner.

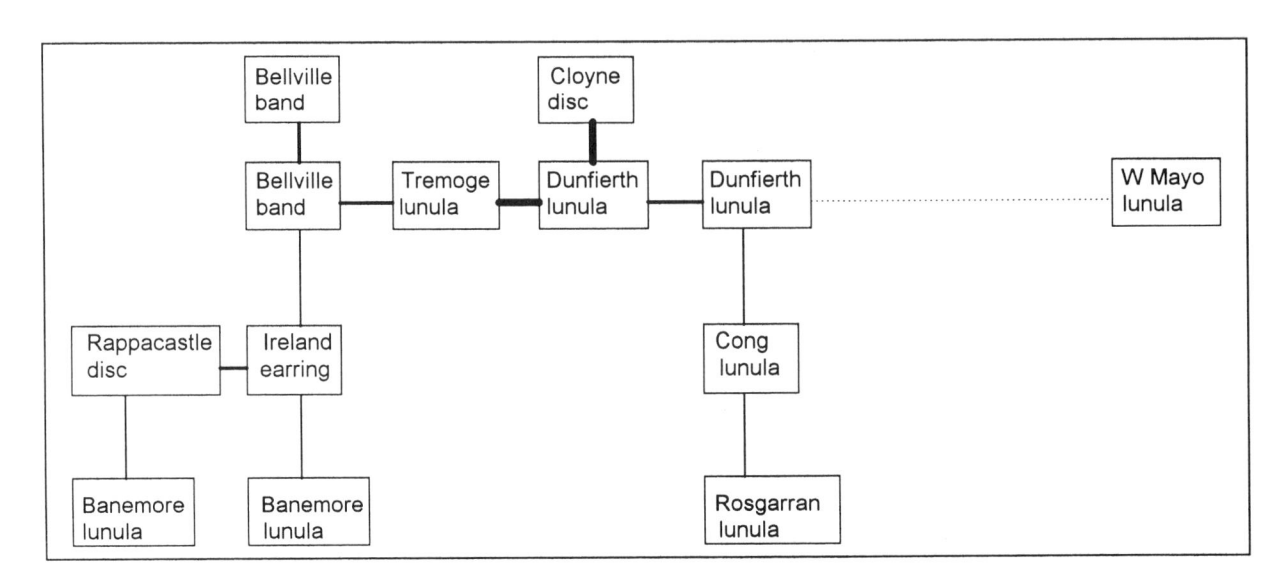

Fig. 12.4. Graphical representation of the similarity of gold compositions from Early Bronze Age Ireland, as shown in Fig. 12.3. Shorter linkages indicate more similar compositions. Figure by R. Warner.

made, much remains to be done. The approach has been shown to work and, from the technical point of view, the LA-ICP-MS, coupled with less sensitive techniques essential to the examination of the specimens for inclusions and broad composition, appears to be the route to follow. Although many new questions, both geological and archaeological, have been raised, there is little doubt that objectively valid answers can now be obtained, providing an insight into gold sources used, technologically processed from source to metal, and then transformed from metal into artefact. From there, we have a secure base from which to address the questions of social interchange between commissioner and specialist craftsman (or woman), trade and exchange patterns, and social alliances in prehistory. Many aspects of our earliest metal working society, that of the Beaker people, are still emerging, and this research seems capable of yielding important new facts that will bring to life for us individual members of long vanished populations. It is the encouragement that the writer received from John Coles in the past, and his repeated insistence that any sample must be specific to the problem being addressed, that have provided the essential inspiration for this research.

Acknowledgements

I wish to thank my team colleagues of the Prehistoric Gold Research Group (PGRG) and the institutions in which they are placed for their invaluable co-operation in this research: Ms M. Cahill (National Museum of Ireland), R. Chapman (University of Leeds), R. Leake, ore geneticist (retired), C.A. Shell (University of Cambridge), R.J. Watling (Curtin University, Australia), and R. Warner (Ulster Museum).

The Research Development Fund of the University of Liverpool has given several grants to aid the development of this research and assist its progress, and a number of Irish institutions have assisted by providing samples and travel moneys. Paul Robinson and the Wiltshire Archaeological and Natural History Society deserve special thanks for allowing Bush Barrow, Upton Lovell and Wilsford G.8 gold to be sampled in this preliminary study. Thanks are also due to the Museum of Archaeology and Anthropology at Cambridge for the loan of the Bracks Farm section. I am grateful to the British Academy for a generous grant in 1998 for the continuation of this project in the search for, and analysis of, a particular generic ore source.

Notes

1 We are grateful to the British Academy for their funding of this future work.

Bibliography

Ambers, J. 1990. Radiocarbon, calibration and early mining: some British Museum radiocarbon dates for Welsh copper mines. In P. & S. Crew (eds) *Early Mining in the British Isles*, 59–63. Proc. Early Mining Workshop, Plas Tan y Bwlch Occasional Paper 1.

Budd, P., Haggerty, R., Pollard, A.M., Scaife, R & Thomas, R.G. in press. New heavy isotope studies in archaeology, *Israel J. Chemistry*.

Chapman, R.J., Leake, R.C., Shell, C.A., Taylor, J.J., Warner, R.B., Watling, R.J. & Cahill, M. in press. The identification of exploitable gold ores of Britain and Ireland and their relationship to early prehistoric gold artefacts: recent advances with PMA and LA-ICP-MS. Proceedings of Metals in Antiquity conference, Harvard, 10–13 September 1997.

Coles, J. & Taylor, J. 1971. The Wessex Culture: a minimal view, *Antiquity* 45, 6–14 with plates III–VI.

Craddock, P. 1995. *Early Metal Mining and Production*. Edinburgh: University Press.

Dutton, A. & Fasham, P.J. 1994. Prehistoric copper mining on the Great Orme, Llandudno, Gwynedd, *Proc. Prehist. Soc.* 60, 245–86.

Hartmann, A. 1970. *Prähistorische Goldfunde aus Europa*. Berlin: Gebr. Mann Verlag, Studien zu den Anfängen der Metallurgie, Band 3.

Hartmann, A 1982. *Prähistorische Goldfunde aus Europa II*. Berlin: Gebr. Mann Verlag, Studien zu den Anfängen der Metallurgie, Band 5.

Joel, E., Taylor, J.J., Ixer, R.A., & Goodway, M. 1997. Lead isotope analysis and the Great Orme mine. In Sinclair, A, Slater, E, Gowlett, J. (eds.), *Archaeological Sciences 1995*. Oxford: Oxbow Monograph 64.

Joel, E., Taylor, J.J. & Vocke, R.D. in press. Geological implications of the lead isotope data on ores from the Great Orme mine, North Wales, U.K. Proceedings of the American Chemical Society San Francisco Spring Meeting 1997. *J. Archaeol. Science*.

Mei, J., Shell, C.A., Li, X. & Wang, B. in press. A metallurgical study of early copper and bronze artefacts from Xinjiang, China, *Bulletin of the Metals Museum*.

O'Brien, W 1995. Ross Island and the origins of Irish-British metallurgy. In J. Waddell and E. Shee Twohig (eds) *Ireland in the Bronze Age: Proceedings of the Dublin Conference, April 1995*, 38–48. Dublin: Stationery Office.

Shell, C. & Robinson, P. 1988. The recent reconstruction of the Bush Barrow lozenge plate, *Antiquity* 62, 248–60.

Shell, C.A., Taylor, J.J., Warner, R.B. & Watling, R.J. 1998. LA-ICP-MS and the study of the compositional integrity of the two gold hoards from Downpatrick, Northern Ireland. In C. Mordant & V. Rychner (eds.), *L'atelier de bronzier: élaboration, transformation et consommation du bronze en Europe de XXe au VIIIe siècle avant notre ère*, 237–248. Proceedings of the Council of Europe Bronze '96 Colloquium, Neuchâtel.

Taylor, J.J. 1970. Lunulae reconsidered, *Proc. Prehist. Soc.* 36, 38–81 with plates I–XII.

Taylor, J.J. 1979. Early Bronze Age technology and trade, *Expedition* 21:3, 23–32.

Taylor, J.J. 1980. *Bronze Age Goldwork of the British Isles*. Cambridge: University Press.

Taylor, J.J. 1983. An unlocated Scottish gold source or an experiment in alloying? In A. O'Connor & D.V. Clarke (eds) *From the Stone Age to the Forty-Five, Studies presented to R.B.K. Stevenson*, 57–64. Edinburgh: John Donald.

Taylor, J.J., Watling, R.J., Shell, C.A., Ixer, R.A., Chapman, R.J., Warner, R.B. & Cahill, M. 1997. From Gold Ores to Artifacts in the British Isles: a preliminary study of a new LA-ICP-MS analytical approach. In *Archaeological Sciences 1995*, 144–54. Oxford: Oxbow Monograph 64.

Thom, A.S., Ker, J.M.D. & Burrows, T.R. 1988. The Bush Barrow gold lozenge: is it a solar and lunar calendar for Stonehenge? *Antiquity* 62, 492–502.

Warner, R.B. 1993. Irish prehistoric goldwork: a provisional analysis, *Archaeomaterials* 7, 101–13.

Watling, R.J., Herbert, H.K., Delev, D. & Abell, I.D. 1994. Gold fingerprinting by laser ablation inductively coupled plasma mass spectrometry, *Spectrochimica Acta* 49B, 205–19.

13. Rise and fall: the deposition of Bronze Age weapons in the Thames Valley and the Fenland

Roger Thomas

Abstract: This paper analyses and compares the pattern of deposition of Bronze Age weaponry in two areas of south-east England: the Thames Valley and the Fenland. In addition, comparisons are made between the Upper and Lower Thames Valley. Distinct contrasts emerge, spatially and chronologically. In terms of weapon deposition, the Lower Thames Valley became increasingly dominant between the end of the Early Bronze Age and the end of the Late Bronze Age. Possible reasons for this are discussed.

At an early stage in my archaeological career, while I was an undergraduate or perhaps even while I was still at school, I acquired a copy of the *Festschrift* volume for Stuart Piggott, *Studies in Ancient Europe*. The volume was edited by J.M. Coles and D.D.A. Simpson (Coles & Simpson 1968). The paper in that volume which most aroused my interest was that by Bridget Trump on 'Fenland Rapiers' (Trump 1968) and my imagination was particularly caught by the suggestion that the many rapiers found in the Fens of East Anglia had been ritually deposited, cast as offerings "into the dark pools and sluggish rivers of the Fens to appease spirits ... believed to reside there", as Trump evocatively put it (*ibid.*, 222). I developed a strong interest in the problems of the deposition of Bronze Age metalwork, and was later privileged to study this subject under the supervision of John Coles at Cambridge.

Thus, both indirectly and directly, John Coles has had an important influence on the development of my academic interests, and this paper is intended as a tribute to that influence. The paper is concerned with a field (the study of Bronze Age metalwork) to which John made a major contribution in an early phase of his career, but it also touches on another area (the archaeology of the Fenland of East Anglia) which has been one of John's major interests of more recent years.

The study of Bronze Age bronze metalwork – chronology, deposition and social aspects

The abundant bronze metalwork of the British Isles has long been an object of archaeological study. Many studies from the late nineteenth century onwards have been concerned with typology and chronology. In recent years, however, there has been considerable interest in the wider social and economic aspects of this material. Attention has focused on two areas in particular: the reasons for the material entering the archaeological record, with emphasis being placed especially on the possibility that much of the material was deliberately deposited for 'ritual' or 'votive' reasons, and the place of metalwork in wider systems of social and economic reproduction (e.g. Bradley 1990).

Of particular relevance to the present essay are papers by Rowlands (1980), Kristiansen (1978) and Gardiner (1980). Rowlands presents a model for later Bronze Age societies in which social status depended on the ability to obtain prestigious artefacts (such as bronze weapons), which in turn relied on being able to produce agricultural surpluses for use in exchange. Kristiansen proposes a correlation between the productivity of agricultural land and the ability to acquire bronze weapons, as indicated by the varying lengths of time for which swords remained in circulation before deposition (measured by differing levels of wear on

---

Author's Address: Roger Thomas, English Heritage, 23 Savile Row, London W1X 1AB

the hilts of bronze-hilted swords). Gardiner analysed the distribution of Middle and Late Bronze Age metalwork in Lincolnshire, and concluded that the distribution of Middle Bronze Age metalwork is related to the distribution of good quality agricultural land, while the distribution of Late Bronze Age material is related to access to the river system. She suggests that this indicates a shift in the Late Bronze Age from control over land to control over exchange.

The present paper attempts to pursue similar themes through an analysis of the patterns of deposition of Middle and Late Bronze Age weapons in the Thames Valley and the Fenland.

Daggers, dirks, rapiers and swords from the Thames Valley and the Fenland

The Thames Valley and the East Anglian Fenland (of Cambridgeshire, Norfolk and Suffolk) have long been recognised as being the two areas in Britain which are most prolific in finds of Bronze Age metalwork, with both areas having major concentrations of this material. The location and extent of the areas studied is shown is Fig. 13.1. Both areas have, in particular, been noted for the very large number of weapons (many of them in very fine condition) which they have produced. However, there has been no detailed consideration of the actual numbers of finds involved, and of the possible significance of changes through time in these numbers. This paper will address this theme, concentrating on single finds of daggers, dirks, rapiers and swords. The data on which the paper is based is taken from three corpora in the *Prähistoriche Bronzefunde* series: those by Gerloff (1975) on Early Bronze Age daggers, Burgess and Gerloff (1981) on Middle Bronze Age dirks and rapiers, and Colquhoun and Burgess (1988) on Late Bronze Age swords. No attempt has been made here to take account of finds, such as those made in recent years, that are not included in these corpora.

There are three reasons for this focus. First, this series of weapons is considered to represent a broad sequence of stylistic development within a single category of artefact, in which daggers were replaced by dirks and rapiers, and dirks and rapiers were replaced by swords. The chronology of this sequence has been studied in detail and appears to be relatively well-understood. Second, it seems likely that these weapons had a symbolic importance in the Bronze Age, very probably as indicators of personal status or authority. It can be argued that there is a continuity in this symbolic role (paralleling the continuity in the typological development of the series) from the Early Bronze Age to the end of the Late Bronze Age (and, indeed, beyond: in historic times and even down to our own day, the sword has had symbolic and ceremonial connotations). This continuity is reflected in the range of depositional contexts in which these artefacts consistently occur, with a pattern of deposition in graves, as single finds (often in wet places) and

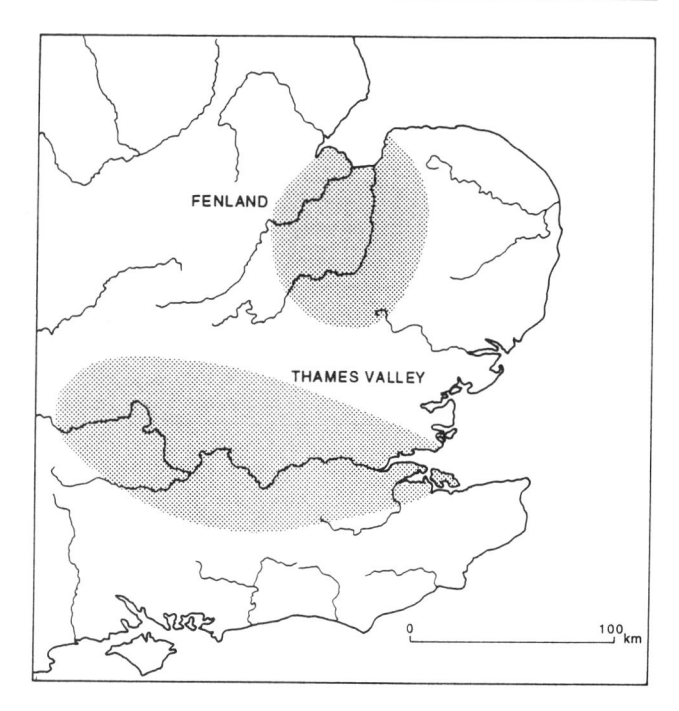

Fig. 13.1. South-east England showing the Thames Valley and Fenland (as defined in this study), where the greatest concentrations of Bronze Age weapons occur.

hoards (Bradley 1990). Third, three modern and authoritative corpora are available, covering the British material. This is essential for a study of the kind attempted here.

The focus on single finds also merits comment. There appears to have been a tradition in south-eastern Britain from the end of the Early Bronze Age onwards of depositing weapons (and other kinds of metal artefact) apparently singly and in isolation, and often in wet places of various kinds. This continuity of mode of deposition can, as suggested above, be taken to parallel the continuity of stylistic development and of symbolic role of this series of weapon types. Of course, these weapons are also found in other contexts. Daggers of the Early Bronze Age also occur in graves while rapiers are sometimes found in hoards, and swords (or parts of swords) occur frequently in hoards. Sword finds from the 'scrap' hoards of the Late Bronze Age are not considered in this analysis; although the reasons for the deposition of these hoards are not wholly clear (Bradley 1990, 144–47), they do seem to represent a different tradition from that of depositing weapons singly or as part of small groups of complete (rather than 'scrapped') objects.

Finally, some comment on recovery patterns and recovery bias is necessary. The majority of finds of Bronze Age metalwork have been made by chance, in the course of agriculture, quarrying, drainage, building and other activities. This means that differential patterns of recovery will almost certainly have affected the distribution of finds of this material. For instance, it seems highly likely that the intensity of dredging and other work in the lower reaches of the River Thames is at least partly responsible for the dense concentration of finds there. For this reason, using the absolute numbers of finds of a particular phase of the Bronze Age as an indicator of differing levels of activity in different areas would be questionable. However, the present paper considers how the relative proportions of finds of the same kind from different areas change through time. Such changes, if they exist, should not be affected by recovery bias, and the patterns observed should represent real changes through time in the relative levels of deposition of the same kinds of artefacts in different areas.

The pattern of deposition

The typology and chronology of British Bronze Age metalwork has been, and continues to be, much discussed (see, for example, Burgess 1974;1979; Needham 1996). The terminology and periodisation adopted for the present study is shown in Table 13.1. This scheme certainly oversimplifies the picture (notably by attributing all Group IV rapiers to the Taunton phase, whereas in fact this type continued into the Penard phase). However, this paper is concerned with broad, long-term trends within the sequence of weapon types, and the simplified scheme proposed is adequate for that purpose.

The sequence of types shown in Table 13.1 forms the basis for the analysis which follows. For the analysis, the numbers of examples of each type to have been found in the Thames Valley and the Fenland respectively were recorded. The proportion of each type to have come from each area was then calculated (as a percentage of the total number of finds from both areas). The finds from the Thames Valley were also subdivided, according to whether they come from the upper part of the valley or the lower part, and the proportion of the total to have come from each area was again calculated.

The Thames Valley and the Fenland

The absolute numbers and relative percentages of weapons of each metalworking phase to have been found in the two areas are discussed below. The figures are summarised, by metalworking phase, in Table 13.2. The picture which emerges is an interesting one.

Arreton phase: Fifteen weapons come from the Thames Valley and five from the Fenland. A number of these are grave finds from barrows. Overall, 25% of the total of these weapons comes from the Fens. This figure, however, masks significant differences between types: only 17% of Armorico-British C and 13% of Camerton-Snowshill daggers come from the Fenland, compared to 50% of Arreton daggers.

Acton Park phase: Eleven Group I weapons have come from the Thames Valley and five from the Fenland, while for Group II the figures are 31 and 22 respectively. Overall, 39% of the total number of these weapons come from the Fenland.

Period Division	Metalworking Phase	Weapon types
Early Bronze Age	Arreton	Armorico-British C daggers Camerton-Snowshill daggers Arreton daggers
Middle Bronze Age	Acton Park	Group I dirks and rapiers Group II dirks and rapiers
	Taunton	Group III dirks and rapiers Group IV dirks and rapiers
	Penard	Rod-tanged swords *Griffplattenschwerter* Solid cast hilt swords Type Coveney swords Type Ballintober swords Imported Early Urnfield Flange-hilted swords Type Clewer swords Type Limehouse swords Type Taplow swords Early Flange-hilted (unclassified) swords Type Mortlake swords Type Teddington swords
Late Bronze Age	Wilburton	Type Wilburton swords
	Ewart Park	Type Ewart Park swords Carp's Tongue swords
	Llyn Fawr	Western European Gündlingen Swords

Table 13.1. Terminology and periodisation of British Bronze Age metalworking phases and weapon types (based on Burgess 1974; 1979; Gerloff 1975; Burgess & Gerloff 1981; and Colquhoun & Burgess 1988)

Metalworking phase	Total number of finds	Number (and % of total) from Thames Valley	Number (and % of total) from Fenland
Arreton	20	15 (75%)	5 (25%)
Acton Park	69	42 (61%)	27 (39%)
Taunton	223	153 (69%)	70 (31%)
Penard	95	83 (87%)	12 (13%)
Wilburton	43	35 (81%)	8 (19%)
Ewart Park	82	68 (83%)	14 (17%)
Llyn Fawr	17	17 (100%)	–

Table 13.2. The changing proportions of weapon deposition in the Thames Valley and the Fenland

Taunton phase: Thirty-four Group III weapons have come from the Thames Valley and sixteen from the Fens; for Group IV the figures are 119 and 54 respectively. Overall, the Fenland accounts for 31% of the total number of weapons of this phase found in the two areas.

Penard phase: There is a marked contrast between the numbers of Penard phase weapons recovered from the Thames Valley and from the Fenland. One rod-tanged sword comes from Thames Valley, while none is known from the Fenland. Four *Griffplattenschwerter* are known from the Thames Valley and two from the Fenland. One Type Coveney weapon is known from the Fenland and none from the Thames. Twenty-three Ballintober swords come from the Thames Valley and two from the Fenland; eighteen Imported Early Urnfield swords (covering Types Reutlingen, Hemigkofen, Early Leaf-shaped Unclassified and Erbenheim) from the former area and only three from the latter; 37 of the local variants of Urnfield swords (covering Types Clewer, Limehouse, Taplow, Early Flange-hilted Unclassified, Mortlake and Teddington) from the Thames Valley and four from the Fenland.

Overall, then, 83 examples of these early swords come from the Thames Valley and 12 from the Fenland: the Fenland accounts for only 13% of the total number of finds.

Wilburton phase: Thirty-five Wilburton swords come from the Thames Valley and eight from the Fenland; the proportion of the total number of finds to have come from the Fenland is 19%.

Ewart Park phase: Sixty-four Ewart Park swords come from the Thames Valley and twelve from the Fenland; four Carp's Tongue swords come from the Thames Valley and two from the Fenland; overall, 17% of the total number of finds comes from the Fenland.

Llyn Fawr phase: In this phase, the contrast between the Thames Valley and the Fenland is absolute. Seventeen Gündlingen swords come from the Thames valley and none from the Fenland. This pattern continues into the succeeding phase of the Early Iron Age, with no iron daggers of Hallstatt D type known from the Fenland, as opposed to six from the Thames valley (Jope 1961).

The upper Thames Valley and the lower Thames Valley

In the previous section, the absolute and relative numbers of finds, from the Thames Valley and the Fenland, broken down by metalworking phase, were compared. Here, the total of finds from the Thames Valley as a whole is analysed in the same way, according to whether finds come from the upper or the lower part of the Thames Valley (the Goring Gap is taken as marking the divide between the two parts). The figures are summarised, by metalworking phase, in Table 13.3. Pieces with imprecise provenances (such as 'River Thames') are excluded from this analysis, so the totals of Thames finds considered here are different from those in the previous section and in Table 13.2. (In practice, many of the vaguely provenanced pieces are likely to have come from the lower part of the valley, in particular from the London area.)

Arreton phase: Out of fourteen daggers of this phase from the Thames Valley, eight are from the lower and six from the upper part of the valley. Thus, some 43% of the pieces are from the upper Thames; all of the Arreton daggers, however, are from the lower Thames.

Acton Park phase: Of ten Group I weapons from the Thames Valley, nine are from the lower and one from the upper part of the valley. For Group II weapons, the figures are 25 and none respectively. Overall, 3% of these early rapiers come from the upper part of the Thames Valley.

Taunton phase: Of 27 Group III weapons from the Thames Valley, 26 are from the lower and one from the upper Valley. Of 112 Group IV weapons, 105 come from the lower and 7 from the upper Valley. Overall, 6% of these pieces are from the upper part of the Valley.

Penard phase: Of 22 Ballintober swords from the Thames Valley, 20 are from the lower part and two from the upper. Of the remaining 54 swords of this phase from the Thames Valley, only one (of Type Limehouse) is from the upper Thames. Overall, 4% of the swords of this period from the Thames Valley come from the upper part of the valley.

Wilburton: Of 32 Wilburton swords from the Thames Valley, 29 are from the lower part of the valley and 3

Metalworking phase	Total number of finds	Number (and % of total) from lower Thames Valley	Number (and % of total) from upper Thames Valley
Arreton	14	8 (57%)	6 (43%)
Acton Park	35	34 (97%)	1 (3%)
Taunton	139	131 (94%)	8 (6%)
Penard	76	73 (96%)	3 (4%)
Wilburton	32	29 (91%)	3 (9%)
Ewart Park	56	55 (98%)	1 (2%)
Llyn Fawr	14	14 (100%)	–

Table 13.3. The changing proportions of weapon deposition in the lower and the upper Thames Valley. Imprecisely provenanced finds have been excluded, so the totals differ from those given for Thames Valley finds in Table 13.2.

from the upper part; this represents 9% of the total number of swords of this period from the Thames Valley.

Ewart Park phase: Of 56 Ewart Park swords from the Thames Valley, 55 are from the lower part of the valley. Only one Ewart Park sword has been found in the upper part of the Thames Valley; in other words, only 2% of the total number of swords of this period from the Thames Valley are from the upper part of the valley.

Llyn Fawr phase: No Gündlingen swords have come from the upper part of the Thames Valley, compared to 14 from the lower part of the valley. Similarly, no daggers of Hallstatt D type have come from the upper Thames Valley, compared to six from the lower part (Jope 1961).

Discussion

The analyses are summarised in Tables 13.2 and 13.3, which show (by metalworking phase) how the relative proportions of weapon type being deposited in the different areas change through time. An interesting pattern emerges. When compared to the Thames Valley, the number of weapons being deposited in the Fenland declined between the end of the Early Bronze Age and the end of the Late Bronze Age. The *floruit* of the Fenland, in terms of weapon deposition, really seems to have been the Middle Bronze Age. This conclusion is not fundamentally altered by the remarkable discoveries of Late Bronze Age metalwork at the Fengate Power Station site (Coombs 1992). In the Ewart Park phase, relatively few weapons were being deposited in the Fenland, and in the Llyn Fawr phase the contrast appears to be absolute. There was also a change, between the Middle and Late Bronze Age, in the quality, character and condition of the material being deposited. The Fenland has produced many very fine rapiers in good condition (Trump 1968). By contrast, some 45% of the sword finds of the Wilburton and Ewart Park phases are damaged or broken pieces, sometimes represented only by fragments of hilts or blades.

In terms of relative levels of deposition, it is possible that a somewhat similar pattern exists between the upper and lower parts of the Thames Valley, although the figures are less clear. The relative level of deposition in the lower Thames Valley was always much higher than in the upper Thames, but in the Ewart Park and Llyn Fawr phases the contrast seems to intensify, with very little Ewart Park weaponry and none of the Llyn Fawr phase being deposited in the upper Thames.

In summary, it seems that, in terms of the relative proportions of weapons being deposited in each area, the lower Thames valley became increasingly dominant, compared to the Fenland and to the upper Thames Valley, between the start of the Middle Bronze Age and the end of the Late Bronze Age. A similar picture emerged from Taylor's analysis of the degree of wear on objects deposited in Bronze Age hoards in southern Britain (Taylor 1993). As in the work by Kristiansen referred to above, Taylor takes the degree of wear to indicate the availability of metal supplies. He comments: "The supply of raw material from outside must have been quite limited in nearly all regions during LBA 3 [the Ewart Park phase]. The one exception was the Thames valley, where pieces with less wear were deposited, indicating the dominant position attained by this region in the overall system." (Taylor 1993, 78).

The kinds of model for later Bronze Age societies referred to above suggest that the ability to obtain or produce elaborate bronze weapons, and to consume these (through acts of deliberate 'ritual' deposition), depended on the ability to produce agricultural surpluses for use in exchange and to control exchange networks. Seen in this light, the changing geographical pattern of weapon deposition identified here may shed some light on the wider economic and social histories of the areas in question.

The pattern of weapon deposition can be located in a wider chronological and geographical context. Bradley and Barrett (1980, 247) have suggested that Wessex and the upper Thames Valley were 'core' areas in the Late Neolithic and Early Bronze Age. In the Early Bronze Age, finds of daggers are concentrated in graves in those two areas. From the end of the Early Bronze Age onwards, this pattern changes markedly, with the densest concentrations of daggers, dirks and rapiers being found as single finds in the lower Thames Valley and the Fenland. As the analysis above indicates, there appears to be a progressive relative concentration of weapon deposition in the lower Thames valley through the Bronze Age, with both the upper Thames Valley and the Fenland becoming relatively less prominent. By the Llyn Fawr phase at the end of the Bronze Age, the contrast had become almost absolute, with finds of the Hallstatt C Gündlingen swords occurring only in the lower Thames Valley. This pattern continues into the earliest Iron Age, with Hallstatt D iron daggers again being concentrated in the lower Thames Valley.

However, in the Llyn Fawr phase the overall pattern of metalwork deposition changed radically. In the Ewart Park phase, metalwork of all kinds was being deposited in abundance in the lower Thames Valley and the Thames Estuary. Hoards of this phase are common in this area in particular. However, metalwork of the succeeding Llyn Fawr phase is relatively scarce in the lower Thames Valley, with axes and axe hoards in particular being concentrated rather in Wessex, the upper Thames Valley and East Anglia (Thomas 1989). This period saw the widespread adoption of iron, and wider changes in settlement pattern (see below).

What factors might lie behind the long-term changes in the pattern of weapon deposition identified above? Two may be mentioned: the increasingly wet conditions that developed in the Fens in the later second and earlier first millennium BC, and the possibility that the inhabitants of the lower Thames valley were able progressively to develop control of the exchange networks through which prestige items of metalwork were obtained.

As to the first, the work of the Fenland Survey has considered the archaeology and topographical development of the Fenland in detail (Hall and Coles 1994). This work has shown how, in the later second and early first millennium BC, the Fenland was subjected to marine transgression, flooding and blanketing by peat. Hall and Coles state (1994, viii) that: "By the first millennium BC, much of the southern Fenland became a great peat fen and settlement was curtailed..." This circumstance may provide a context for the apparent decline in the quantity and quality of weapons being deposited in the area, and there is an echo here of Kristiansen's correlation of rates of sword deposition in Denmark with the agricultural productivity of land.

Turning to the second factor, we have already noted Gardiner's suggestion (1980, 113) that the control of exchange became more important in the Late Bronze Age than it had been in the Middle Bronze Age. The inhabitants of the lower Thames Valley were well-placed to exert such control, and the wide variety of metalwork types of exotic manufacture or inspiration found there attests to the range of the contacts which the people of this area had. However, the acquisition of prestige goods both required the production of surpluses (very possibly of agricultural produce) for exchange, and may also have provided a basis for continued economic success through cycles of production, exchange and consumption (Rowlands 1980). Thus, the relationship between patterns of metalwork deposition and patterns of settlement in the Thames Valley is potentially of some interest. While a detailed consideration of this point is well beyond the scope of this paper, some points may be noted.

There is now an increasing body of evidence for dense settlement and agricultural activity in the lower Thames Valley and its tributaries in the Middle and Late Bronze Ages. Excavations at such sites as Reading Business Park and survey work in the lower Kennet Valley suggest a high level of activity at this time. By contrast, evidence for Early Iron Age settlement in the area seems less abundant (Lambrick 1992). A rather different picture is found in the upper Thames Valley. While earlier suggestions that the upper Thames was only lightly populated in the later Bronze Age (Thomas 1989, 279) may need to be qualified to some extent in the light of more recent work (e.g. Mudd 1995; Lambrick 1992), evidence for Late Bronze Age settlement is much less abundant in the upper Thames than in the lower part of the valley. Barrett (1980, 308) notes that his post-Deverel-Rimbury 'plain-ware' ceramic tradition is hard to identify in the region, while Late Bronze Age metalwork of all types is relatively scarce from the area, compared to that from the lower Thames (Burgess 1968, Fig.14; Ehrenberg 1977, Fig. 28). In broad terms, therefore, there seems to be a correlation between levels of settlement evidence and levels of weapon and other metalwork deposition during the Middle and Late Bronze Age in the Thames Valley.

It is therefore possible that the control which the inhabitants of the lower Thames valley were able to exert over exchange networks served progressively to isolate the upper Thames from the cycles of production, exchange and consumption of the lower Thames. This may have led in turn to a cycle of decline in settlement, economic production and weapon deposition in the upper Thames. This interpretation reflects that of Gardiner, that the control of exchange routes became increasingly important in the Late Bronze Age.

Conclusions

It has long been recognised that the Thames Valley and the Fenland of East Anglia have produced the two largest concentrations of Bronze Age metalwork in Britain. The analysis presented here suggests that there was a progressive concentration of the deposition of weapons in the lower Thames valley, with a relative decline in such activity in the Fens and in the upper Thames valley, between the end of the Early Bronze Age and the end of the Late Bronze Age. It is argued that this pattern of changing relative intensity of weapon deposition relates to levels of activity of other kinds: notably the ability to produce the surpluses needed to obtain or to produce such artefacts, and the ability to lock into the networks of exchange by which such artefacts (or the raw materials for them) were obtained.

Ultimately, however, the system was not sustainable. During the Llyn Fawr phase, around the seventh century BC, the deposition of bronze metalwork seems to have lost much of its former significance, and settlement in the lower Thames valley may have declined. The direct control of agricultural land and production seems to have become much more important as a basis for social power (Thomas 1989). New foci of settlement emerged. Thomas (*ibid.*, 279) has drawn attention to the expansion of settlement in Wessex and the Upper Thames in the early Iron Age, while Evans has remarked on "the sheer number of earlier Iron Age sites given the relative paucity of later Bronze Age occupation" in the Fenland, and raises the question of whether this represents "major colonisation of the region during the later 1st millennium" (Evans 1992, 8). It may be that we are seeing a pattern in which areas peripheral to the lower Thames valley became relatively less populous during the course of the later Bronze Age, until the collapse of the system based on controlling the circulation of bronze metalwork. At that point, the earlier situation may have been reversed, with the lower Thames declining as an area of intensive settlement and the formerly peripheral regions of Wessex, the upper Thames valley and the Fenland apparently experiencing a marked renaissance. The long rise to pre-eminence of the lower Thames valley had been reversed.

Bibliography

Barrett, J. 1980. The pottery of the later Bronze Age in lowland England, *Proc. Prehist. Soc.* 46, 297–319.

Barrett, J. and Bradley, R. 1980. The later Bronze Age in the Thames Valley. In J. Barrett and R. Bradley (eds), *Settlement and Society in the British Later Bronze Age*, 247–69. Oxford: British Archaeological Reports 83.

Bradley, R. 1990. *The Passage of Arms. An Archaeological analysis of prehistoric hoards and votive deposits.* Cambridge: Cambridge University Press.

Burgess, C.B. 1968. The Later Bronze Age in the British Isles and North-Western France, *Archaeol. J.* 125, 1–45.

Burgess, C. 1974. The Bronze Age. In C. Renfrew (ed), *British Prehistory: A New Outline*, 165–232. London: Duckworth.

Burgess, C. 1979. A find from Boyton, Suffolk and the end of the Bronze Age in Britain and Ireland. In C. Burgess and D. Coombs (eds), *Bronze Age Hoards Some Finds Old and New*, 269–83. Oxford: British Archaeological Reports 67.

Burgess, C.B. and Gerloff, S. 1981. *The Dirks and Rapiers of Great Britain and Ireland.* Prähistorische Bronzefunde, IV, 7. Munich: C.H. Beck.

Coles, J.M. and Simpson, D.D.A. (eds) 1968. *Studies in Ancient Europe Essays presented to Stuart Piggott.* Leicester: Leicester University Press.

Colquhoun, I. and Burgess, C.B. 1988. *The Swords of Britain.* Prähistorische Bronzefunde IV, 5. Munich: C.H. Beck.

Coombs, D. 1992. Flag Fen platform and Fengate Power Station post-alignment the metalwork, *Antiquity* 66, 504–17.

Ehrenberg, M.R. 1977. *Bronze Age Spearheads from Berks, Bucks and Oxon.* Oxford: British Archaeological Reports 34.

Evans, C. 1992. Iron Age, *Fenland Research* 7, 8–10.

Gardiner, J.P. 1980. Land and Social Status a case study from Eastern England. In J. Barrett and R. Bradley (eds), *Settlement and Society in the British Later Bronze Age*, 101–14. Oxford: British Archaeological Reports 83.

Gerloff, S. 1975. *The Early Bronze Age Daggers in Great Britain and a Reconsideration of the Wessex Culture.* Prähistoriche Bronzefunde, VI, 2. Munich: C.H. Beck.

Hall, D. and Coles, J. 1994. *Fenland Survey. An Essay in Landscape and Persistence.* English Heritage Archaeological Report 1. London: English Heritage.

Jope, E.M. 1961. Daggers of the Early Iron Age in Britain, *Proc. Prehist. Soc.* 27, 307–43.

Kristiansen, K. 1978. The consumption of wealth in Bronze Age Denmark. A study in the dynamics of economic processes in tribal societies. In K. Kristiansen and C. Paludan-Müller (eds), *New Directions in Scandinavian Archaeology*, 158–90. Copenhagen: National Museum of Denmark.

Lambrick, G. 1992. The development of late prehistoric and Roman farming on the Thames gravels. In M. Fulford and E. Nichols (eds), *Developing Landscapes of Lowland Britain. The Archaeology of the British Gravels: A Review*, 78–105. Society of Antiquaries of London: Occasional Papers Volume 14.

Mudd, A. 1995. The excavation of a Late Bronze Age/Early Iron Age site at Eight Acre Field, Radley, *Oxoniensia* 60, 21–65.

Needham, S. 1996. Chronology and Periodisation in the British Bronze Age. In K. Randsborg (ed), *Absolute Chronology. Archaeological Europe 2500–500 BC*, 121–40. *Acta Archaeologia 67 (Acta Archaeologia Supplementa 1)*.

Rowlands, M. 1980. Kinship, alliance and exchange in the European Bronze Age. In J. Barrett and R. Bradley (eds), *Settlement and Society in the British Later Bronze Age*, 15–55. Oxford: British Archaeological Reports 83.

Taylor, R. 1993. *Hoards of the Bronze Age in Southern Britain. Analysis and Interpretation.* BAR British Series 228. Oxford: Tempus Reparatum.

Thomas, R. 1989. The bronze-iron transition in Southern England. In M.-L.S. Sørensen and R. Thomas (eds) *The Bronze Age-Iron Age Transition in Europe Aspects of continuity and change in European societies c. 1200 to 500 B.C.*, 263–286. Oxford: British Archaeological Reports International Series 483.

Trump, B.V. 1968. Fenland rapiers. In J.M. Coles and D.D.A. Simpson (eds), *Studies in Ancient Europe Essays presented to Stuart Piggott*, 213–225. Leicester: Leicester University Press.

14. Bronze Age Settlement in South Scandinavia – Territoriality and Organisation

Henrik Thrane

Abstract: A survey of recent developments in Nordic settlement archaeology of the Bronze Age, concentrated on the situation in Denmark, tries to outline the elements constituting the typical Bronze Age settlement. Emphasis has above all been focused on the longhouses, understandably enough as recent years have seen a veritable burst of recovery of house plans. Other elements of less obvious character for the function of a settlement should not be forgotten, however. Some may be recognised in the landscape, while others only appear fortuitously and some may elude us for ever. The paper tries to indicate problems rather than solve them.

I cannot present a single Scandinavian model of Bronze Age settlement because Central and Northern Scandinavia are so different from South Scandinavia that it is hardly possible to unite all three regions into a single model if we want to go beyond the level of banalities. The 'personality of Scandinavia' is not so simple if one tries to go into any detail (cf. Hyenstrand 1979; Regionindelning 1977) but at a large-scale level it suffices to give the old Danish realm of the Middle Ages (up to 1648) its own personality, namely that of a fairly fertile arable landscape. So I shall restrict myself to South Scandinavia (Fig. 14.1), meaning Denmark and the former Danish provinces of Scania and Schleswig, all of which exhibit the same level of environmental diversity within the North European lowland zone, a quite different environment from the Scottish one presented by Gordon Barclay and Graham Ritchie at this conference.

While we normally occupy ourselves with finds and sites which, one way or the other, are remarkable, we want to reach a level which expresses so many common features that it may be taken as 'normal'. This is easier said than done as so few settlements – if any – have been totally excavated and even fewer have been worked on beyond the discovery of one, or a few, in the main severely plough-damaged and therefore poorly preserved longhouses (Berglund 1981; Draiby 1985; Bertelsen *et al.* 1996 & others mentioned below, cf. Thrane 1996b). Accordingly, as usual, the definition of "normal" is difficult. Some of the more interesting cases come from marginal areas where windblown sand has covered the sites and preserved better information than on the heavily ploughed soils of eastern Jutland, Scania and the Danish isles. We have some reasonably well preserved structures from Thy and Mols (Kristiansen 1998; Bech 1993; Boas 1995) whereas east Denmark has been so intensively cultivated that preservation is sadly poor. In Scania it took a long time before longhouses were recognized (Tesch 1992). We have a stratigraphical sequence from Fragtrup (Draiby 1985), similar to the classical sequence from Pre-Roman Iron Age Grøntoft (Becker 1982), and we have some good landscape archaeology from the Ystad region of coastal Scania (Olausson 1992; Tesch 1992) supported by the now enormous contiguous excavation area at Fosie near Malmö (Björhem & Säfvestad 1993) and a smaller sample from southern Funen (Thrane 1989a). An average research situation is documented for north-west Jutland (Bertelsen *et al.* 1996) (Fig. 14.3).

These samples cover most of the Bronze Age and will be used here to present what I postulate to be an average settlement structure at the lower level, i.e. the primary settlement unit, be it farm or village.

Author's Address: Henrik Thrane, Institut for Forhistorisk Arkæologi ved Aarhus Universitet, Moesgård, DK-8270 Højbjerg, Denmark

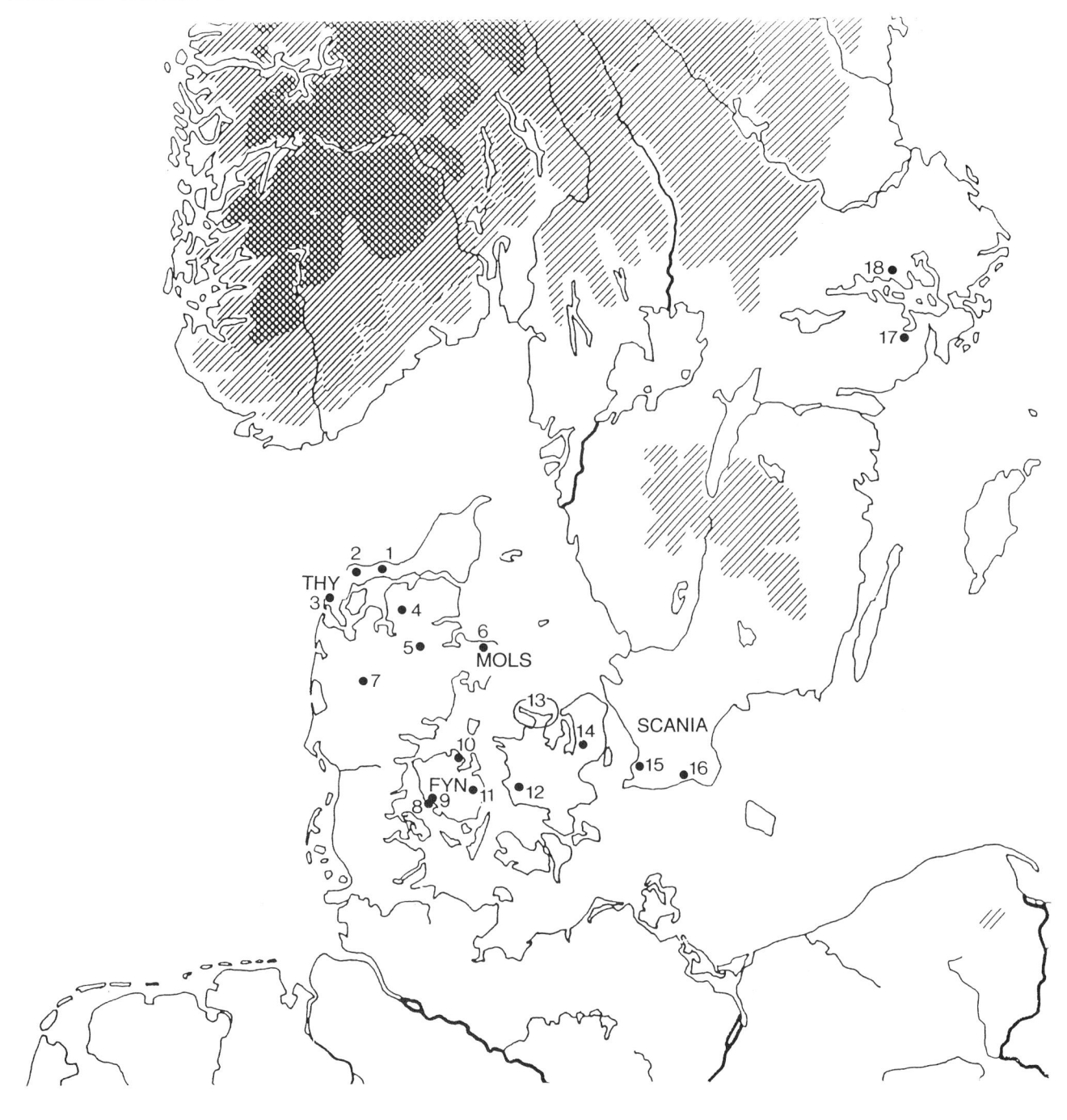

Fig. 14.1. South Scandinavia, showing sites and regions mentioned in the text. 1. Bulbjerg. 2. Bjerre. 3. Lodbjerg. 4. Fragtrup. 5. Kvorning. 6. Hemmed, Glæsborg & Egehøj. 7. Grøntoft & Spjald. 8. Brydegård. 9. Voldtofte, Kirkebjerg & Lusehøj. 10. Hasmark. 11. Rønninge Søgård. 12. Boeslunde & Borbjerg Banke. 13. Odsherred. 14. Brudevælte. 15. Malmö-Fosie. 16. Ystad. 17. Hallunda. 18. Apalle.

Village structure

First we have the problem of structure. It is still enigmatic whether we have villages in the Bronze Age. Settlements may be occupied long enough to leave stratified deposits like Apalle and Hallunda in Central Sweden (Ullén 1994) and Voldtofte on Fyn (Berglund 1981). They do, however, not have houses tied together in a contemporary layout.

There is no clearly delimited settlement like Early Iron Age Grøntoft or Hodde with their fenced-in village area (Becker 1982).

While it has been suggested by the excavator that Early Bronze Age Vadgård was a village, there is no proof of anything more than a few contemporary houses and they may not all have had the same function (Lomborg 1976; Rasmussen 1995). Se we have to accept that normally no more than one or two farms existed in a face to face situation as in a village. We have no hilltop forts or otherwise defensible sites from Scania or Denmark where open-air settlements seem to have been the rule. Fortified sites reach as far north as Mecklenburg (Schubart 1961) and occur, albeit rarely and not as the same phenomenon, in Central Sweden (Olausson 1995; Larsson 1994).

The basic element in the farm is the longhouse which developed from Late Neolithic (Reinecke A) right through to the Iron Age, as has been well elucidated in recent years from the whole area under review – and in fact much further north and west as well (Jensen 1988; Göthberg *et al.* 1995; Løken 1989).

From period II, the longhouse becomes three-aisled and is known in a wide variety of sizes, the largest reaching lengths up to *ca.* 50 m, with widths up to 8 m and living areas on average 200 m² in extent. The big houses are called halls, as an echo of Viking Age nomenclature, and are often immediately interpreted as chieftains' residences (e.g. Ethelberg 1995). Some longhouses have a hearth in each end room suggesting an occupation by two families. There is a group of smaller longhouses of *ca.* 50 m² area and a wide range of intermediate house sizes. Commonly, though not always, the longhouses are accompanied by a four-post structure which is interpreted as storage for hay (or similar) fodder (Zimmermann 1992). So a single farm would consist of a longhouse and four-poster plus additional structures, for instance the cattle or sheep corrals (?) from Bjerre (Bech 1993) (Fig. 14.2). (In Thy might the single smaller houses indicate the existence of another stratum of farm hands?).

The longhouse occasionally had partitions for the animals in the centre or in the east end – as became standard during the Iron Age – but why some houses had stables when most did not, we cannot tell. In supposedly treeless areas like Thy, where turves from heath bogs were used as additional fuel (Robinson 1996), might the stable have facilitated the gathering of cow-dung for fuel? It would have been sorely needed on the fields and there are indications that they really were manured. Incidentally, the rise in hulled barley during the Late Bronze Age is taken as an expression of the manuring of the fields (Berglund 1991). At present not enough is known to enable us to decide how soil and landscape development during the Bronze Age related to the variations of house construction and size.

Other elements in or at the settlement itself such as threshing floors or working areas have not been properly identified and need much better conditions of observation than are normally available during rescue excavations. Good grain finds may lead to an insight into the threshing procedure, and I think that there is a reservoir of information waiting to be observed in the prints of chaff and other threshing material preserved in daub.

Village and field

Fields have been observed in different contexts; some are still preserved in forests, others have been covered by sand dunes (Robinson *et al.* 1995; Boas 1995). Their only common features are their irregularity, their often oval shape and their small sizes (Bech 1993; Nielsen 1994) (Fig. 14.4), two to four hectares or even less at Bjerre (on Mols an ard-ploughed plot of 15 x 15 m was fenced in (pers. comm. N.A. Boas)), and the ard furrows (Thrane 1991b). Where remnants of fields are observed under barrows we rarely find more than the ard furrows, but occasionally a faint earth bank marks the edges of the field. This and the stone lines or terraces observed in other places indicate some permanence, although the ard furrows themselves do not indicate more than from one to three or four criss-cross ploughings. In view of the use in the Bronze Age of hurdles like the pretty ones from the Sweet Track excavated by John Coles (also documented in Lusehøj: Thrane 1984), it will be a fair assumption that coppices existed near the fields and that the cattle and sheep were kept out from the fields not only by herdsmen and their dogs, but also by easily renewable fences.

Pastures must have been very important especially for settlements like Voldtofte which specialized in cattle (Nyegaard 1997). We find the pastures reflected in the pollen diagrams and meet them in the barrows in fragmentary form, cut out for turves.

Cupmarks and hoards

In the fields, on grasslands or in the woods there were significant quantities of stone; only those stones bearing cupmarks are clearly defined as noted and used by Bronze Age people (Glob 1969). In my area these are nearly always just plain cupmarks on earth-fast boulders left by the ice and not subsequently removed by the Bronze Age or later farmers, in recognition of some quality which we now cannot recognize (radioactivity has been noted but the association must be accidental (Röschmann 1962)). While I think of these cupmarked stones as indispensable elements of any decent Bronze Age settlement, it is hard to decide whether this would also be true for other special, sacred sites such as bogs or lakes in which hoards were placed.

Recent work has shown that hoards may be quite closely connected with settlement, in some cases actually deposited in houses, viz. the axe hoard from Period II at Tyrrestrup, the amber hoard from Bjerre, the knife from a posthole at Kirkebjerg at Voldtofte, the socketed axe from Fosie IV in Scania etc. (Björhem & Säfvestad 1993; Thrane 1996a). Other hoards are found so close to contemporary settlements, e.g. the female ornaments from a dolmen chamber next to the settlement at the Bay of Helnæs (Madsen & Thrane 1983), or the hoard

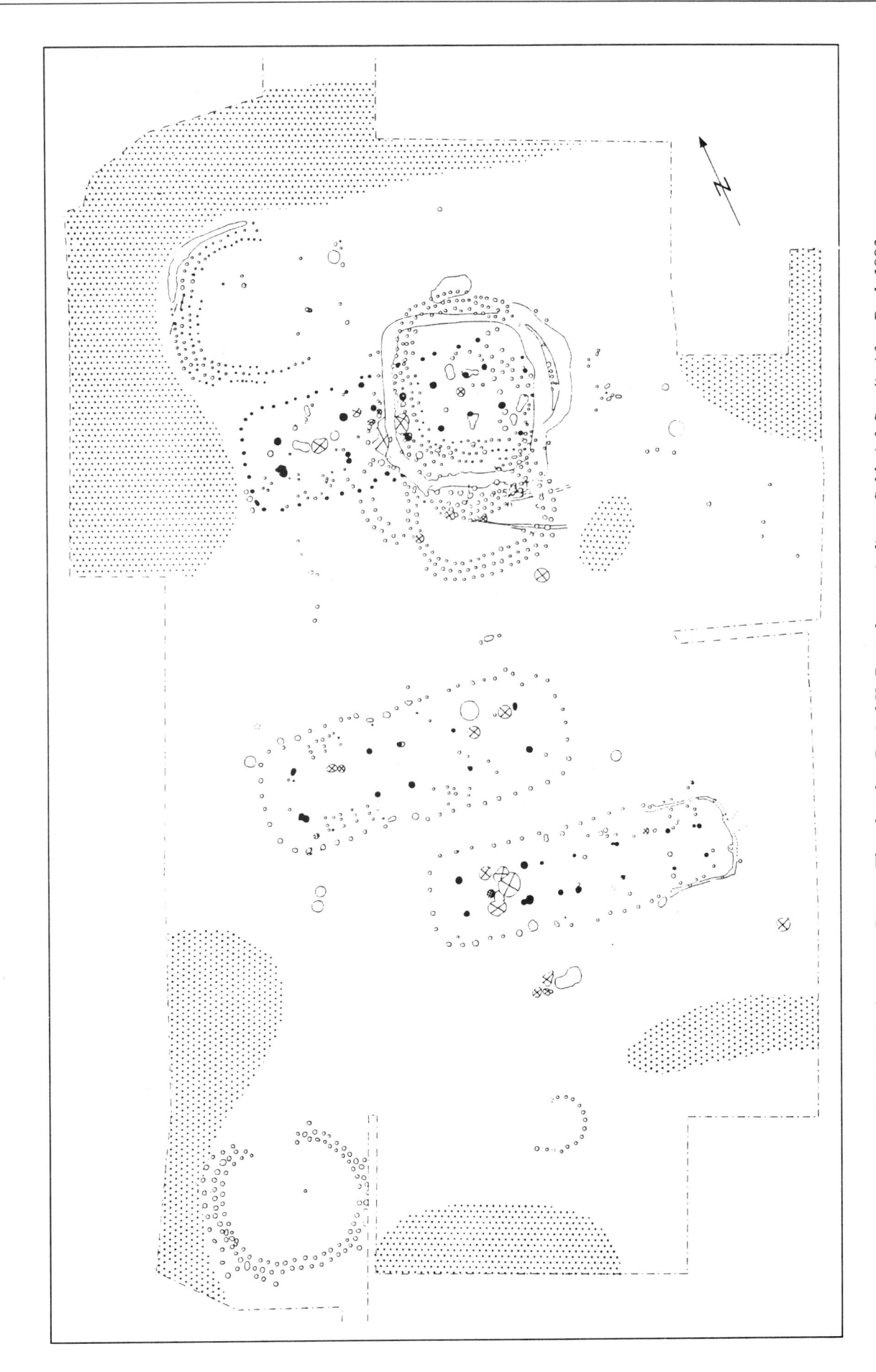

Fig. 14.2. Settlement at Bjerre, Thy, dated to Period II. Dotted areas indicate fields (cf. fig. 4). After Bech 1993.

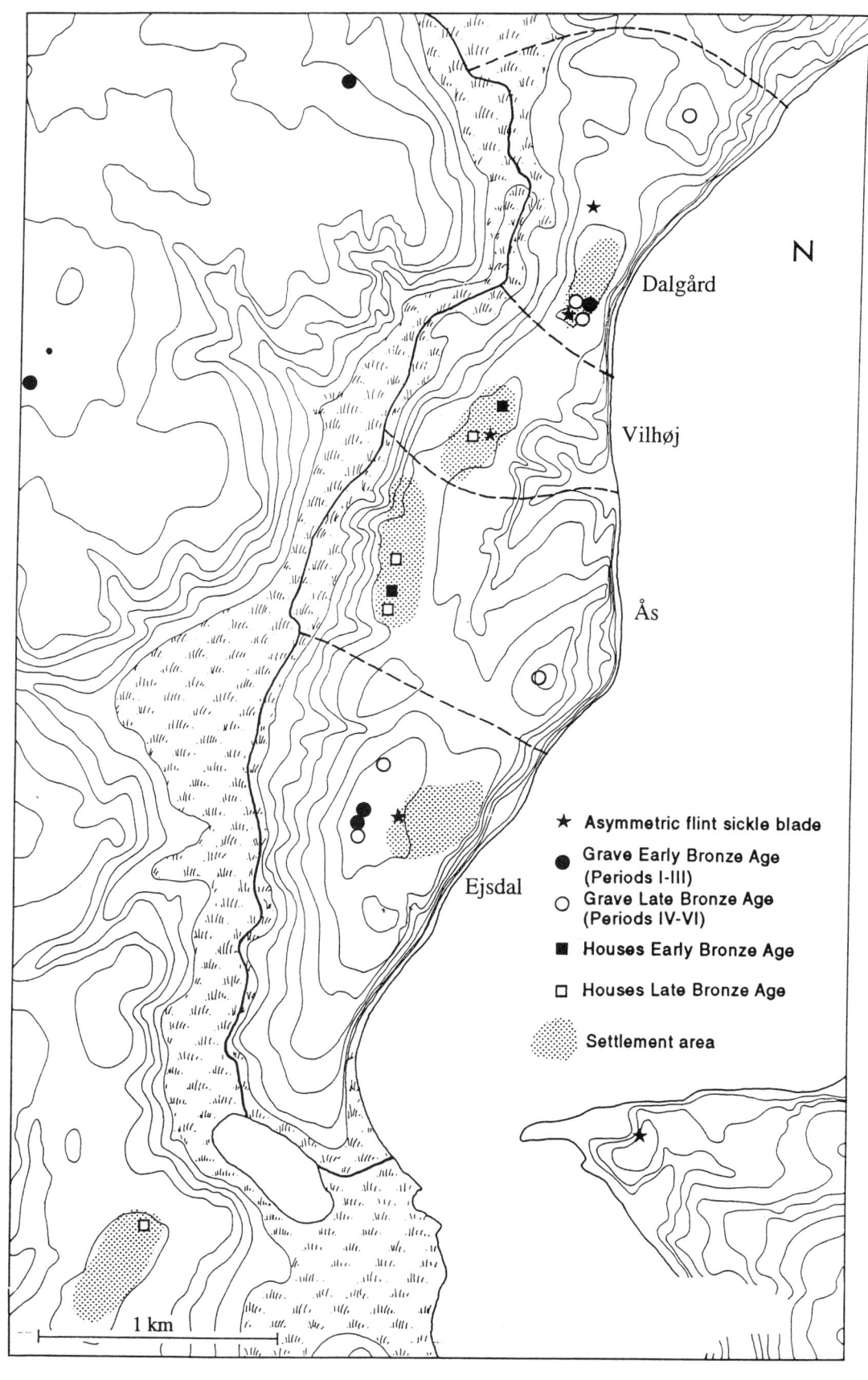

Fig. 14.3. Territory with Bronze Age settlements. Dotted lines indicate borders between individual settlements according to the excavator, but the whole ridge may be a case of a single settlement moving over it during a major part of the Bronze Age. After Mikkelsen in Bertelsen et al. 1996.

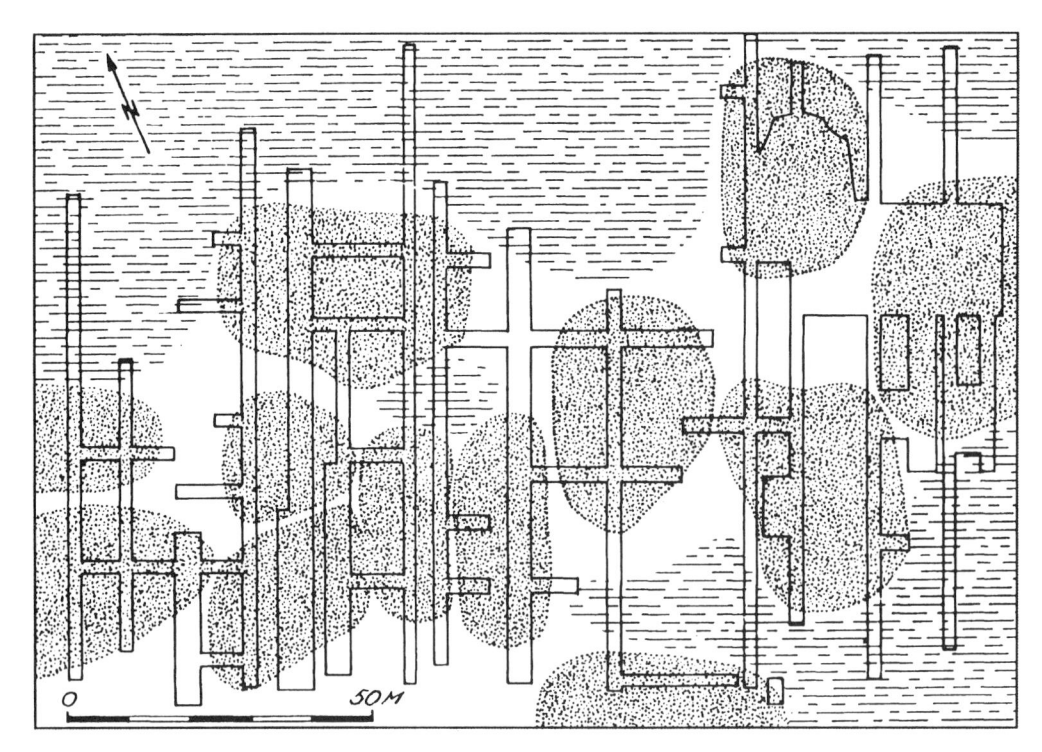

Fig. 14.4. Field system of the Late Bronze Age at Bjerre. After Bech 1993.

on the edge of a settlement on the island of Lindø (Fig. 14.5), that they must be regarded as integral elements of the settlement. Another group of hoards and single finds – typically socketed axes – does, however, come from peripheral areas, typically wet parts like lakes or bogs (Schmidt 1993). Whenever we are able to locate such finds in relation to contemporary settlements or graves, the deposition in wet areas seems to be part of the set-up (e.g. Thrane 1991a, fig.2) but there still remains lots of analysis to be done on this element of the social territory of the individual settlements.

These elements would all be combined in any ordinary settlement.

Other elements may have been maintained by individual settlements or, more likely, by settlements grouped together in larger units. One thinks of hoards that formed a cult assemblage (Levy 1982), or special site types. Away from the settlements we may find special sites (a neutral term for this enigmatic group), such as the Flag Fen-like Kvorning (Iversen 1996), the hundreds of cooking pits at Rønninge Søgård (Thrane 1989b), the Brudevælte bog with no less than three lur pairs (Broholm *et al.* 1949), or Borbjerg Banke with its two gold vessel hoards and with nearly 4 kg of gold from the immediate vicinity (Jensen 1994). These sites are all very different but have one feature in common: their size. There are too many cooking pits, too many lurs or too much gold just to represent a single settlement. These sites must have served regional groupings and thus a larger population.

Production sites

Away from the settlements we also have special production sites such as the seasonal coastal settlement sites where amber was sought, shells collected and seals hunted. These sites are rarely observed, but Bulbjerg (Müller 1919) and Lodbjerg (Liversage & Robinson 1995) on the north-west coast of Jutland may be taken as cases where the proper settlements were so far from the coast that a satellite summer camp had to be established. In other landscapes the permanent settlements were placed so that the coastal resources could be exploited along with the terrestrial ones, e.g. at Hasmark (Müller 1919; Nyegaard 1997) and Brydegård on Funen (Thrane 1989a, fig. 25).

Other special sites would be the flint seams in the cliffs of Stevns on the east coast of Zealand or other larger volumes of good flint. The demand for large flake implements of flint continued throughout the Bronze Age and is not likely to have been covered by the ice-transported blocks available on the surface locally. How this activity was organized is another problem.

Roads present a sadly under-represented group (Jørgensen 1993). We have wheel tracks under barrows (Aner & Kersten 1984, no. 3559); they were presumably made by four-wheelers of the Rappendam type (Schovsbo 1987).

While these sites can all be seen as elements in the subsistence production system – one way or the other – there is another element which has been so prominent in Bronze Age archaeology that for decades it dominated and prevented any other approach.

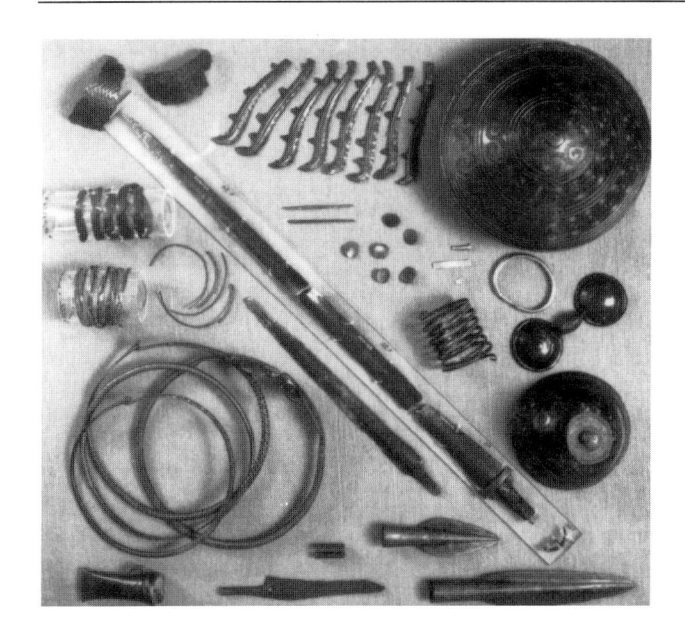

Fig. 14.5. This bronze hoard dating to Period V was buried in a storage jar at the edge of a contemporary settlement on the small island of Lindø in the Odense Fjord in north Funen; perhaps the reserve of the community? Photo: Fyns Oldtid, Hollufgård.

Barrows

Ever since Sophus Müller formulated his 'law' that a complete map of the Bronze Age barrows would also give a complete map of the Bronze Age settlement (1904), Bronze Age barrows have been the major source for the study of Bronze Age settlement – indeed the only one right up to 1955 when we got the first properly documented Late Bronze Age settlement site (Draiby 1985). The barrows are still the dominant group numerically and will long remain so. The hotly debated issue of the 1930s and 40s was whether the barrows had been placed so close to the settlements themselves that the distribution of barrows automatically gave us the distribution of the contemporary settlement. The total excavation of barrows as practiced from *ca.* 1950, and the large-scale excavations of settlements from *ca.* 1970 onwards, have shown the situation to be much more complicated than Sophus Müller suspected. We may find mounds placed on top of Bronze Age settlements and have other cases where the barrows had been placed well away from the contemporary settlements; some of the strongest evidence of Late Bronze Age settlements come from an area practically devoid of Bronze Age grave finds, not to mention barrows (Becker 1982). So no simple law is applicable and Müller's law is only useful in a very broad sense. Everyone should have this in mind when studying Brøndsted's (1939) or other nice maps of Bronze Age barrows.

The normal state would be to have a barrow serving a settlement, and, as time went by, barrow cemeteries developing, but we know settlements with practically no barrows or graves associated – of course mini-mounds would disappear easily in a heavily cultivated landscape. Mini-mounds (measuring <1 m by 5 m) could easily have been made by an elementary family (Thrane 1984). Grave data seem to support the notion of small primary social and production units (Strömberg 1974). The bigger mounds demanded a lot more manpower (Thrane 1984). The larger and wealthier settlements certainly invested considerable resources in the construction of the big mounds.

It has been repeatedly asked whether or not the whole population was interred in the barrows (Randsborg 1974). The answer must be negative. Even when we include the flat graves, the number of burials remains too small to make up a viable population. Incidentally the flat graves have remained rather elusive. They do not seem to bear any preferred relationship to settlements or barrows. Bronze Age reality again must have been more diverse than we often like to think.

Other features

I have now tried to list the elements constituting the ingredients of south Scandinavian Bronze Age settlements as we know them archaeologically. The list is of course incomplete. A number of sites or features we will not be able to identify because they have left no traces. I am thinking of sacred groves, sacred stones or trees, streams or lakes without archaeological deposits.

Rivers have not been as productive in Scandinavia as elsewehere but there is a handful of swords from rivers which should not be forgotten (Jensen 1973; 1997) and may be taken as indicating that rivers, or some of them – for instance the biggest Danish river, Gudenå (God's river) – played their part in the deposition pattern.

Links across the sea were vital, not only at the beginning of the Nordic Bronze Age but also for its continued maintenance, so we may safely infer that seafaring was necessary and frequent. The (still unknown) boats presumably did not require piers or harbours and the actual landing sites have escaped us so far. They may have shifted from year to year or from generation to generation depending upon the settlements to be served. This is a field where we have so far drawn a blank but may hope for future discoveries.

Territories

Finally we come to the application of the concept of territoriality to the elements which I have mentioned. Looking at the landscape surrounding the settlements that we now know by chance, there is little to take us further, since we have no dykes or linear earthworks as in Britain. Instead, my idea is that the settlements were separated from each other by water. I do not mean that they lay on

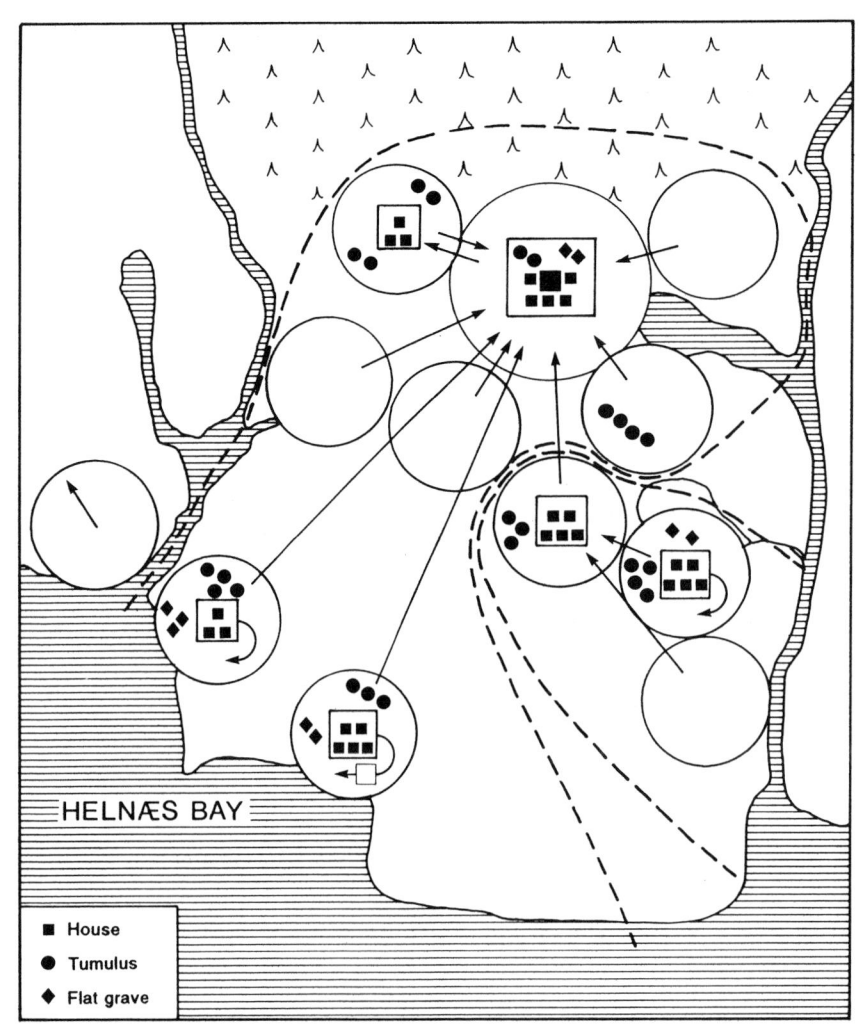

Fig. 14.6. Model for the settlement structure of the Late Bronze Age in south-west Fyn with the Kirkebjerg settlement in Voldtofte as the centre (large circle). Dashed lines: Hypothetical limits of political territories. Arrows: Direction of economic bonds.

islands or were lake villages like the Somerset ones, but rather that the more discrete elements of the south Scandinavian wetlands were used as borders. We are talking of small streams, there being no more than a handful of proper rivers like the Cam in Denmark and Scania, of small lakes or rather waterholes, of bogs and soggy areas. We know how widely the landscape was pockmarked by these wet features before draining became a mania during the last century. Every old map from 1785 onwards shows this (Nørlund 1942).

We can see from the distribution of the archaeological remains that large tracts of land were uninhabited. Even in the Late Bronze Age settlement did not penetrate uniformly into the depths of the bigger islands or Scania. Settlement seems mainly to have continued in the same areas that were occupied during the Neolithic, as best indicated by the dolmens, an earlier version of the barrow case (cf. Schmidt 1993 for variations).

The rivers were arteries leading from the coast into the inland settlement which was confined to a rather narrow zone. Beyond them must have been the surviving primeval forest.

Settlement was not evenly distributed over the landscape. I see each individual settlement as occupying a fixed territory marked by wetlands and wooded areas which separated it from its neighbours. Each territory would include the elements listed above – except the marginal and communal ones. The territory would be hereditary, i.e. containing tombs of a long row of ancestors, ancient sacred sites as well as those in current use. Within this social and subsistence territory the settlement(s) would move habitually each generation (?), which is why we may find several Early or Late Bronze Age settlements within each territory. Our inability to distinguish generations by archaeological means excludes us from the proof of this suggestion and is a major interpretational problem in this context.

It is probably too early to try to figure out mean territory size, as so few territories have been examined in any detail.

Fig. 14.7. The painted house urn from Stora Hammar, Scania - the Late Bronze Age idea of sweet home?

A study of the landscape at Odsherred in Zealand produced hypothetical territories ranging from *ca.* 9 km² to twice that size (Thrane 1991a). The reasons for this wide range may be multiple, in part probably the lack of sufficient intensive fieldwork, with a correspondingly poor volume of archaeological material. Of course my interpretation may be too simple, but I see the territory as the basic economic unit occupied by a single settlement composed of rather few individual farms in a spread-out pattern. Two or more such units could be united into larger territories, and indeed a whole hierarchy of settlement territories seems likely. I have suggested a model for the important Late Bronze Age area of Voldtofte (Thrane 1980) which may be special and more highly structured, as the rich finds indicate, with Kirkebjerg as the central settlement (Berglund 1982), and Lusehøj and other richly equipped mounds as the permanent symbols of power (Fig. 14.6). Although my model seems to have been accepted, it would be nice to see other case studies before we agree on it as a (or the) likely one. I hope that we may see such studies from different parts of south Scandinavia in the near future.

This interpretation as a hierarchical structure has been acclaimed as support for a chiefdom type of social organisation in the Scandinavian Bronze Age. I think that there are still grounds for continuing a cautious examination of this assumption. For a better definition of the level of political systems prevailing in the Nordic Bronze Age more carefully planned case studies are needed.

Bibliography

Aner, E. & Kersten, K. 1984. *Die Funde der älteren Bronzezeit in Dänemark, Schleswig-Holstein und Niedersachsen, VII Nordschleswig-Nord, Haderslev Amt.* Neumünster: Wachholtz.

Bech, J.-H. 1993. Settlements on raised sea-bed at Bjerre. In S. Hvass & B. Storgård (eds) *Digging into the Past*, 142–3. Herning: Aarhus Universitetsforlag.

Becker, C.J. 1982. Siedlungen der Bronzezeit und der vorrömischen Eisenzeit in Dänemark, *Offa* 39, 53–72.

Berglund, B.E. 1991. The late Bronze Age landscape. In B.E. Berglund (ed.) *The Cultural Landscape during 6000 years in Southern Sweden – the Ystad Project, Ecological Bulletins no. 41*, 73–77. Copenhagen: Munksgaard.

Berglund, J. 1982. Kirkebjerget – a Late Bronze Age settlement at Voldtofte, South-West Funen, *J. Danish Archaeology* 1, 51–63.

Bertelsen, J.B., Christensen, M., Mikkelsen, M., Nielsen, J. & Simonsen, J. 1996. *Bronzealderens bopladser i Midt- og Nordvestjylland*. Skive: De arkeologiske museer i Viborg amt.

Björhem, N & Säfvestad, U 1993. *Fosie IV. Bebyggelsen under brons- och järnålder*. Malmöfund 6. Malmö Museer.

Boas, N.A. 1995. Late Neolithic and Bronze Age settlements at Hemmed Church and Hemmed Plantation, East Jutland, *J. Danish Archaeology* 10, 136–155.

Broholm, H.C., W.P. Larsen & G. Skjerne 1949. *The Lurs of the Bronze Age*. Copenhagen: Gyldendal.

Brøndsted, J. 1939. *Danmarks Oldtid. 2, Bronzealderen*. København: Gyldendal (2nd ed. 1958).

Draiby, B. 1985. Fragtrup – en boplads fra yngre bronzealder, *Aarbøger for nordisk Oldkyndighed og Historie 1984*, 127–216.

Ethelberg, P. 1995. Two more house groups with three-aisled longhouses from the Early Bronze Age at Højgård, South Jutland, *J. Danish Archaeology* 10, 136–155.

Glob, P.V. 1969. *Helleristninger i Danmark*. Århus: Jysk Arkæologisk Selskab.

Göthberg, H., Kyhlberg, O. & Vinberg, A. (eds) 1995. *Hus och gård*. Riksantikvarieämbetet Undersökningar 13. Stockholm.

Hyenstrand, Å. 1979. *Arkeologisk regionindelning av Sverige*. Stockholm: Riksantikvarieämbetet.

Iversen, M. 1996. Fund fra Kvorning-vejen, *P.S.* 2 (Postscriptum til kulturhistorien på Viborg-egnen), 7–16.

Jensen, J. 1973. Ein neues Hallstattschwert aus Dänemark, *Acta Archaeologica* 43, 115–164.

Jensen, J. 1988. Bronze Age research in Denmark, *J. Danish Archaeology* 6, 155–174.

Jensen, J. 1994. Fem kilo bronzealderguld, *Fynske Minder 1994*, 41–52.

Jensen, J. 1997. *Fra Bronze- til jernalder*. København: Det kgl. nordiske Oldskriftselskab.

Jørgensen, M. Schou 1993. Land transport. In Hvass S. & B. Storgård (eds), *Digging into the Past, 25 Years of Archaeology in Denmark*, 228–230. Herning: Aarhus Universitetsforlag.

Kristiansen, K 1998. The construction of a Bronze Age landscape. Cosmology, economy and social organisation in Thy, northwestern Jutland. In B. Hänsel (ed) *Mensch und Umwelt in der Bronzezeit Europas*, 281–91. Kiel: Oetker-Voges Verlag.

Larsson, T.B. 1994. *Vistad, Kring en befäst gård i Östergötland och östersjökontakter under yngre bronsålder*. Umeå: Arkeologiska Institutionen, Umeå Universitet.

Levy, J. 1982. *Social and Religious Organization in Bronze Age Denmark*. Oxford: British Archaeological Reports Internat. Ser. 124.

Liversage, D. & Robinson, D. 1995. Prehistoric settlement and landscape development in the sandhill belt of southern Thy, *J. Danish Archaeology* 11, 39–56.

Lomborg, E 1976. Vadgård. Ein Dorf mit Häusern und einer Kultstätte aus der älteren nordischen Bronzezeit. In *Festschrift für Richard Pittioni zum siebzigsten Geburtstag. I. Urgeschichte*, eds H Mitscha-Märheim, H Friesinger and H Kerchler, 414–32. Wien: Deuticke.

Løken, T. 1989. Rogalands bronsealderboplasser sett i lys av områdets kulturelle kontakter. In J. Poulsen (ed.) *Regionale forhold i nordisk bronzealder*, 141–48. Højbjerg: Jysk Arkæologisk Selskab.

Madsen, C. & Thrane H. 1983. Sydvestfynske dysser og yngre stenalders bebyggelse, *Fynske Minder 1982*, 17–42.

Müller, S. 1904. Vej og bygd i Sten- og Bronzealderen, *Aarbøger for nordisk Oldkyndighed og Historie 1904*, 1–64.

Müller, S. 1919. Bopladsfund fra Bronzealderen, *Aarbøger for nordisk Oldkyndighed og Historie 1919*, 35–105.

Nielsen, V. 1994. Prehistoric field boundaries in Eastern Denmark, *J. Danish Archaeology* 3, 135–63.

Nyegaard, G. 1996. Faunalevn fra bronzealderen. En zooarkæologisk undersøgelse af sydskandinaviske bopladsfund. Unpubl. Ph.D. thesis Copenhagen.

Nørlund, P.E. 1942. *Danmarks Kortlægning*. København.

Olausson, D. 1992. The archaeology of the Bronze Age cultural landscape – research goals, methods and results. In Larsson, L., J. Callmer & B. Stjernquist (eds) *The Archaeology of the Cultural Landscape*, 251–82. Acta Archaeologica Lundensia ser. in 4° no.19. Lund: Almqvist & Wiksell.

Olausson, M. 1995. *Det inneslutna rummet – om kultiska hägnader, fornborgar och befästa gårdar i uppland från 1300 f. Kr. till Kristi födelse*. Stockholm: Riksantikvarieämbetet.

Randsborg, K. 1974. Social stratification in Early Bronze Age Denmark, *Prähistorische Zeitschrift* 49, 38–61.

Rasmussen, M. 1995. Settlement structure and economic variation in the Early Bronze Age, *J. Danish Archaeology* 11, 87–101.

Regionindelning 1977. *Naturgeografisk regionindelning av Norden*. Stockholm: Nordisk Ministerrad.

Robinson, D. 1996. Plantemakrofossilanalyse af materiale fra brandlaget i ligbrændingsgruben ved Damsgård, *Kuml 1993–94*, 191–2.

Robinson, D., Moltsen, A.& Harild, J. 1995. Arkæobotaniske analyser af bronzealder gårdsanlæg og marksystemer ved Bjerre Enge, Hanstholm, Thy. *NNU Rapport nr. 15*. København: Nationalmuseet.

Röschmann, J. 1962. Schalensteine, *Offa* 19, 133–38.

Schmidt, J.-P. 1993. *Studien zur jüngeren Bronzezeit in Schleswig-Holstein und dem nordelbischen Hamburg*. Bonn: Habelt.

Schovsbo, P.O. 1987. *Oldtidens vogne i Norden*. Frederikshavn: Baugsbomuseet.

Schubart, H. 1961. Jungbronzezeitliche Burgwälle in Mecklenburg, *Prähistorische Zeitschrift* 39, 145–75.

Strömberg, M. 1974. Untersuchungen zur Bronzezeit in Südostschonen. Probleme um die Besiedlung, *Meddelanden från Lunds Universitets historiska Museum 1973–74*, 101–168.

Tesch, S. 1992. The long-term development of a settlement region on the coastal plain – The Köpinge area. In Larsson, L., Callmer, J. & Stjernquist, B. (eds) *The Archaeology of the Cultural Landscape*, 161–250. Acta Archaeologica Lundensia ser. in 4° no. 19. Lund: Almqvist & Wiksell.

Thrane, H. 1984. *Lusehøj ved Voldtofte*. Fynske studier 13. Odense: Bys Museer.

Thrane, H. 1989a. Siedlungsarchäologische Untersuchungen in Dänemark, *Prähistorische Zeitschrift* 64, 5–47.

Thrane, H. 1989b. De 11 guldskåle fra Mariesminde, *Fynske Minder 1989*, 13–30.

Thrane, H. 1991a. Territoriality in a Bronze Age landscape. In Jennbert, K., Larsson, L., Petré, R. & B. Wyszomirska-Werbart (eds) *Regions and Reflections*, 119–128. Acta Archaeologica Lundensia ser. in 8° No. 20. Lund: Almqvist & Wiksell.

Thrane, H. 1991b. Danish plough-marks from the Neolithic and Bronze Age, *J. Danish Archaeology* 8, 111–25.

Thrane, H. 1996a. Von Kultischem in der Bronzezeit Dänemarks. Votivfunde und Kultplätze? In P. Schauer (ed.) *Archäologische Forschungen zum Kultgeschehen in der jüngeren Bronzezeit und frühen Eisenzeit Alteuropas*, 235–54. Regensburg: Habelt.

Thrane, H. 1996b. Bronze Age settlement in the Nordic region, *Colloquia 11 – The Bronze Age in Europe and the Mediterranean*, 191–199. UISPP Forli.

Ullén, I. 1994. The power of case studies. Investigation of a Late Bronze Age settlement in Central Sweden, *J. European Archaeology* 2, 249–262.

Zimmermann, H. 1992, The "helm" in England, Wales, Scandinavia and Northern America, *Vernacular Architecture* 23, 34–43.

15. Getting to Grips with Music's Prehistory: experimental approaches to function, design and operational wear in excavated musical instruments

Graeme Lawson

Abstract: Excavated remains of musical instruments provide us with an intriguing opportunity to examine evolution of design in a group of highly elaborate artefacts, and to consider the nature of the complex musical and communications systems which they were manufactured to serve. A practical, experimental approach is essential. Amongst many recent European discoveries are numerous small pipes of bone, whose finger-holes enable them to produce those series of musical pitches which make up the very frameworks of melody. Such tunings are direct consequences of finger-hole placement, shape and size; markers and adjustments suggest they were predetermined. Amongst the most remarkable finds are remains, many complete or almost complete, of flutes and reed-pipes of Anglo-Saxon, Roman and still earlier date. Continental finds include pipes of bird bone for which dates in excess of 30,000 bp are now emerging. Surface-wear replication is yielding new clues as to how they were played – and sounded.

Introduction: lyres

John Coles' well-known enthusiasm for experimental approaches to ancient music is a long-standing and stimulating feature of his work. Indeed, while it has undoubtedly been entertaining and thought-provoking, it has also been far more: in fact (although he would be too modest to admit it) it has exerted a vital influence, not just upon his students (such as, in the 1970s, Peter Holmes and myself) and younger colleagues working elsewhere in this field, but also on the whole modern renaissance and continuing evolution of the subject area. A first key statement came with the publication in 1963 of his influential study 'Irish Bronze Age horns and their relations with Northern Europe', a paper which still stands as a milestone in the archaeological treatment of organological research. In addition to lending timely impetus to the then slowly emerging sub-discipline of 'musical archaeology', this has since provided a starting-point for a wide range of new investigations, both amongst prehistoric horns and trumpets (for which see Lund 1986) and across a whole spectrum of other instrument types. Here John's essential emphasis on experiment has been especially valuable, for experience shows that some of the most crucial performance characteristics of excavated instruments – the acoustical properties and ergonomic components of their designs – cannot be determined theoretically but *only* by practical trials.

Back in the 1970s, while Peter Holmes was pursuing with John the technological implications of Bronze Age instruments, and while Cajsa Lund and Åke Egevad were independently setting out on their major practical exploration of Scandinavian musical prehistory (for some of the fruits of which see Lund 1985), I began my own research with John by looking at early stringed instruments, especially remains of early medieval lyres and harps. These are, from a technological point of view, extremely illuminating subjects to study. Like Chinese bells of the fifth century BC, the Bronze Age horns of Ireland and Scandinavia prove to be supreme examples of sophistication in the conception and practice of bronze-casting (Holmes 1986); and in the 6th century AD stringed instruments yield another remarkable pinnacle, in the elegant designs and skilful manufacture of a compact, six-stringed lyre of multi-timbered construction. Perhaps the best-known of these is the instrument from the royal ship-burial at Sutton Hoo (Bruce-Mitford 1983, 611–731) but a number of others have now been identified from more modest graves,

Author's Address: Graeme Lawson, McDonald Institute for Archaeological Research, Downing Street, Cambridge CB2 3ER

especially in East Anglia – and most recently at Snape (Lawson 1978, 1987a and forthcoming). Their fascination, from an experimental viewpoint, lies not only in the fine craftsmanship and skilful use of materials and structural principles which they exhibit, but especially in the subtleties of their acoustical and musical character, which can be fully appreciated only when reconstructed physically (for suggested examples see – or rather hear – Lawson 1985, tracks 1 and 6, and Lund 1985, track 30).

When you have built a working model or two and experimented with their elaborate string-tensioning mechanisms, such instruments quickly pose the question: how should we tune their strings? Were they high-pitched, like the banjo, or more mellow and harp-like in tone? Most important, within what *systems* of tonality – if any – would they have operated: diatonic, pentatonic – or something else entirely?

Traditional 'harmonic' instruments, such as horns and trumpets, jews' harps and simple whistle-pipes of willow-bark tubing, demonstrate how one fixed pattern of tuning occurs naturally in the behaviour of all such resonating systems. This is the so-called *harmonic series*, familiar as the basis of military bugle-calls, in which increased lip-pressure (in the case of flutes, over-blowing) induces in the column of air enclosed a rising sequence of discrete resonances conforming to the same immutable acoustical formula: first double the original frequency, then triple, then quadruple – and so on. Strings too may readily be made to behave in a closely analogous manner (as ancients like Pythagoras were well aware) by stopping them lightly at their mid-points, then at a point one-third the way along their length, then one-quarter and so to smaller divisions still: thus the individual strings of almost any stringed instrument can each generate such series, with their familiar-sounding intervals: octaves, fifths, fourths, major and minor thirds, tones and semitones. These are, quite literally, universal phenomena, natural properties of all such structures and air-columns – including many naturally occurring ones – which the enquiring mind of ancient humankind must quickly have discovered and which their successors would repeatedly have re-learned with each passing generation; they could therefore have exercised considerable influence upon the ways in which our ideas about pitch and its organization developed.

Unfortunately, this helps us in only general terms when we try to pitch the strings of the lyre relative to each other, for examination of tuning practices amongst modern world-musics warns that such pure, directly harmonic intervals are the exception rather than the rule; indeed they are largely limited to 'harmonic' instruments. In fact, it is a remarkable feature of popular traditions, away from the influence of modern Western tuning practices, that they seem persistently to exhibit regional, even local, tonal diversity. The tunings of the Javanese *gamelan*, of the Norwegian *Harding fele* and *langeleik* and of our own traditional Highland *piob mór* provide just three striking examples. Our Anglo-Saxon and still earlier musics, existing as they did in the same real world (albeit more than a thousand years ago), must surely have been subject to comparable variability: so the question is, quite simply, how – and where – might we begin to access information about such practices?

Bone flutes

One major opportunity may lie amongst finds from urban deposits in early medieval and later towns throughout Europe. The ubiquitous medieval animal-bone flute, although superficially unremarkable to look at, proves to be a very special kind of object. Made from the bone residues of the kitchen or cooking-hearth, these were for centuries a popular and widespread pastime – so today they are discovered quite often during excavations. A helpful feature of such pipes is that they can preserve the tunings to which they were originally set, or rather (because it would be damaging to attempt to play them directly) they embody the detailed information we need to determine experimentally the actual frequencies to which they were adjusted. And by an additional stroke of good fortune, microscopic examination and measurement of many of their surfaces reveals complicated and extensive traces of handling, perhaps related to the ways in which they were originally manipulated – and played (Fig. 15.1). Now, both tuning and performance have been to a large extent omitted (or side-stepped) in previous investigations, partly for want of technology, partly through inadequate sample size, and partly because they have been looked at in isolation from one another.

New directions: tuning and wear

Last year, however, a new initiative (the Ancient Musical Instrument Surfaces Project) was launched at Cambridge in order to investigate precisely these phenomena, and specifically to look at tuning and handling characteristics in tandem. There is very good reason to consider such

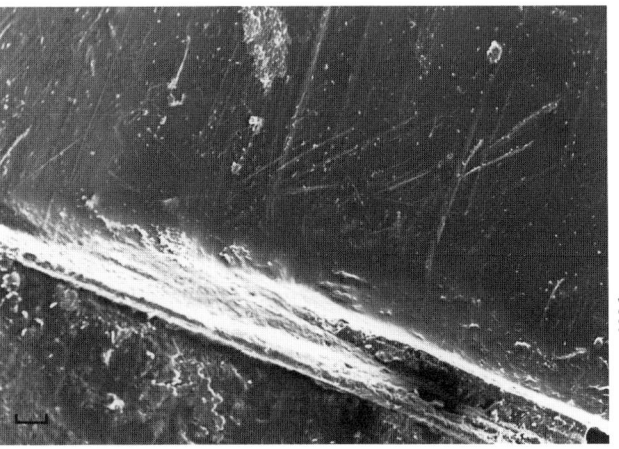

Fig. 15.1. Late Anglo-Saxon pipe of crane ulna from Wicken Bonhunt, Essex: scanning electron micrograph of surface textures around edge of finger-hole platform, showing tool striae obliterated by characteristic 'worn doorstep' polish. Scale: 100μ.

things together. One of the difficult and challenging features of finds from medieval excavations is that many if not most of them owe their presence in the ground to their having been thrown away. There are probably many *bona fide* reasons why a musical instrument might come to be thrown away. In most cases it is accidental damage which seems to have been the cause; but there is also one particularly interesting category, including many complete instruments, in which no such damage can be discerned. It is also a striking feature of many of these that their surfaces too are almost pristine. This may be vitally important. Whereas many of our other, damaged instruments show clear signs of having been cherished, much-handled possessions, microscopic studies show these undamaged pieces to bear little or no wear at all. Suspicion is hardening that such cases may represent failures in manufacture, even though to our eyes they appear to be in working order. Now, experiments with modern equivalent materials confirm that of the whole manufacture process the most tricky part is in gauging precisely where to drill the finger-holes in order to achieve a particular desired tuning. The naturally hollow bones have interiors which vary considerably from animal to animal, for example according to age and health, and their acoustical properties are consequently difficult to predict. Yet failure to achieve placement of just one of the three or four holes sufficiently precisely to permit adjustment to the pitch desired might well render the instrument musically unacceptable. It is only through studying the surfaces of each find that we can determine whether it has indeed successfully entered musical service. Many, evidently, did not, and so their 'tunings' cannot be regarded as reliable, or at least direct, evidence for actual musical practices. This, potentially, makes a great difference when we try to identify patterns of tuning amongst such instruments.

Wayward tunings

Work with accurate replicas is now revealing individual tunings from a wide range of recent finds. The instruments themselves cannot be used for fear of damaging the fragile

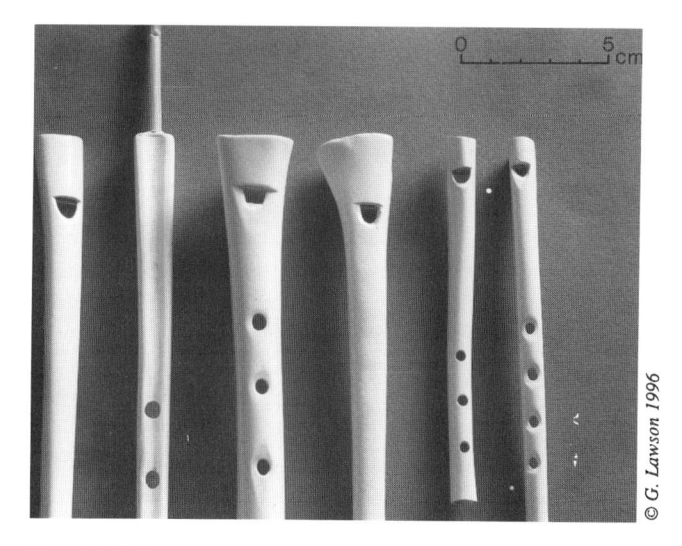

Fig. 15.2. Experimental non-contact hollow-mouldings in epoxy and polyester, of early medieval pipes of (from left) crane ulna, deer metatarsal, sheep tibia, swan ulna, goose ulna and goose ulna.

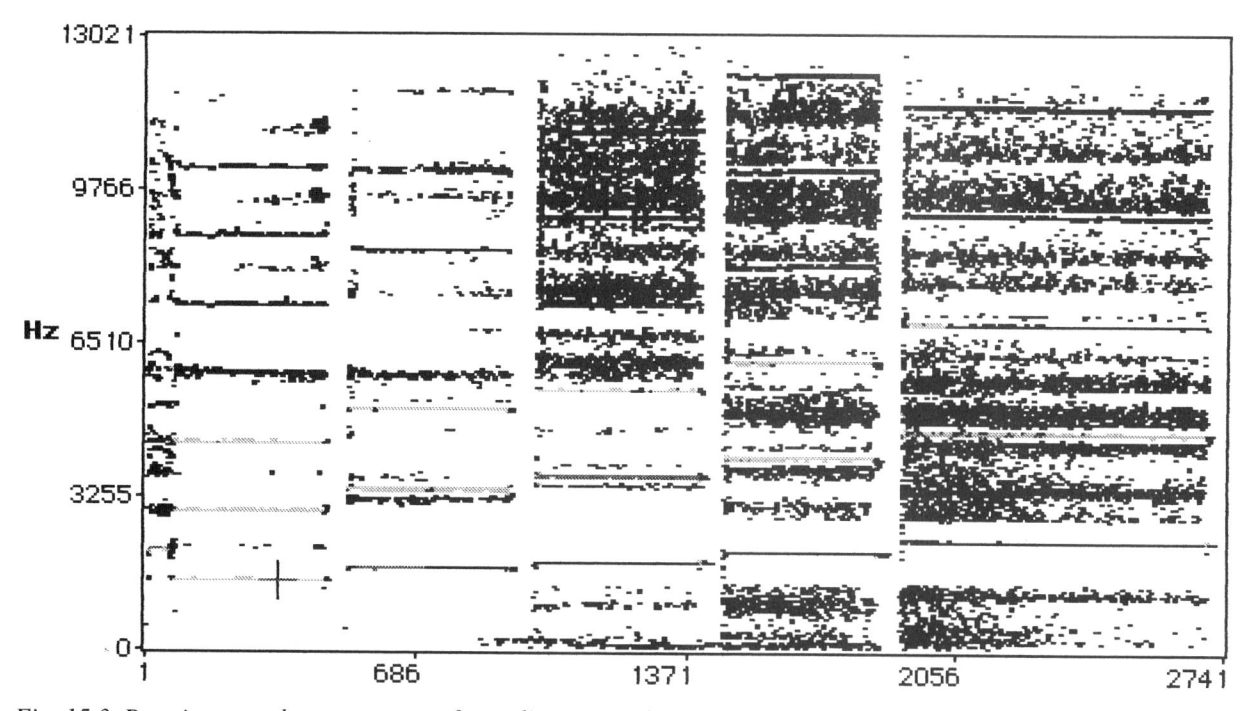

Fig. 15.3. Running sound-spectrogram of a replica swan-ulna flute from Norwich, circa AD 1200; analysis of ascending scale of five notes do-re-mi-fa-sol. The horizontal axis (time) is measured in frames (1 frame = 3 milliseconds) and the partials, which are harmonically related, show up as discrete horizontal lines. The clearest of these, the lowest (marked + in column 1) is the one most audible to the human ear. The intervals revealed are of 257, 134, 180 and 219 cents (cents are hundredths of a modern equally-tempered semitone) and the instrument itself is extensively polished through use. Source: Graeme Lawson and Ian Cross, using Lemur *(©CERL Sound Group, University of Illinois).*

originals, but great precision can be achieved in synthetic non-contact mouldings, laminated for example in epoxy resin, on pre-formed cores (Fig. 15.2). It is the shape of this core and the form it imparts directly to the bore of the replica which is so critical in defining the acoustical characteristics of these little instruments, rather than whether the replica is made of bone, epoxy or polyester. A further, decisive advantage of the technique over working in modern bone is its susceptibility to identical repetition for the purposes of repeat and control experiments which are so fundamental to proper experimental practice.

Procedures of this kind are now beginning to yield a useful range of experimental data, revealing individual tunings from many different instruments and regions. It is still too early to say, except with the ear of faith, that regional patterns of preference are beginning to emerge from them, though there are hints (for example in two goose ulna pipes from Thetford, Norfolk) that such may be the case. And as the pieces of the jig-saw puzzle begin to accumulate a correlation *is* already becoming evident between favoured, well-worn, instruments and what we might call 'melodically compatible' tunings – in the 'modern' European sense – despite the presence of what sound like 'bum' notes. Computer analysis of these sounds by means of specialized analytical software provides sound-spectrograms and precise measurements of the musical intervals involved. From them we can see that while many are made up roughly of tone- and semitone-like intervals, these may deviate considerably from their modern equally tempered values familiar from the piano. In the elegant four-hole pipe of swan ulna from twelfth-century Norwich analysed in Fig. 15.3, for example, the first interval, which we might innocently expect to approximate an equally tempered tone (*do-re*) of 200 cents, the value proves to be 257, giving the scale to our ears a curiously eastern character.[1]

It is nuances of musical pitch like this which provide the 'colour' that so distinguishes all these ancient folk-scales. Musical experimentation demonstrates how such eccentricities need by no means spoil instruments' effectiveness as vehicles for even familiar, traditional songs[2] as well as for melodies preserved within medieval manuscript sources (for which see Lawson 1985, tracks 3 and 4; 1987b, tracks 1 and 4).

Proving intention

Should we expect such odd tunings to have been deliberately selected? Could the makers of these pipes have had them precisely in mind? European ethno-organological studies suggest maybe we should, and that we should not be surprised to see emerging cultural, or at any rate geographical variation in their interval values. In many of the archaeological remains we can already detect signs at least of the prior determination of pitches. Contrary to some expectations, the distances between finger-holes are rarely uniform and may be quite irregular. In many cases scratched

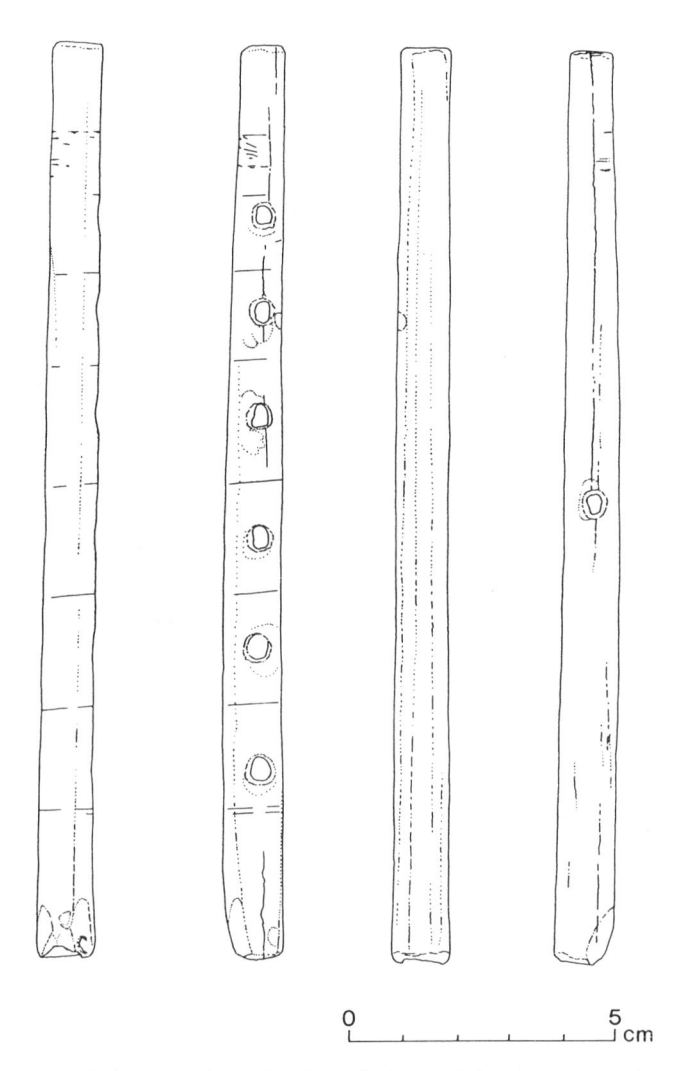

Fig. 15.4. One of a pair of reed-pipes of deer metatarsal from Middle Saxon Ipswich, Suffolk, showing finger-hole placements and finely scratched divisional markings invisible to the naked eye. Drawings: author.

or drilled markers suggest careful laying-out, based on calculation or the application of some rule-of-thumb (Fig. 15.4). A particularly informative group of finds from medieval Schleswig, Germany, currently the subject of new surface- and tonometric analysis by the present writer, includes amongst extensive residues of manufacture unfinished and marked-up examples illustrating the whole process (Reimers & Vogel 1989). Undercutting of finger-holes after drilling shows the importance attached to still finer adjustment. Clearly, simple though these instruments appear, they are embodiments of very special musical requirements and complex cultural systems.

Future research

The prospects which such finds hold for future research are considerable, especially for our appreciation of the evo-

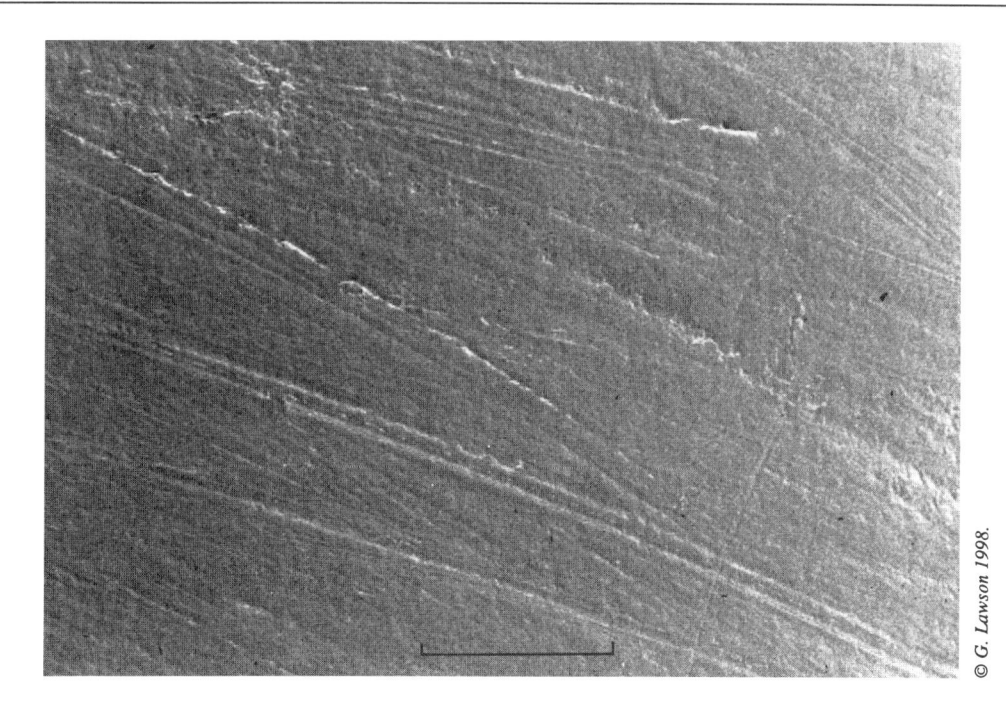

Fig. 15.5. High-resolution scanning electron micrograph image showing early effects of experimentally generated sliding-wear (horizontal texture) on a finger-hole margin (bird ulna, 970327.3; after 4 minutes). Scale: 20μ.

lution of human musical cognition. They may even, in turn, benefit our understanding of other important applications of pitch-perception, for instance in the genesis of speech-related behaviours. Amongst our most ancient musical relics are pipes of closely similar construction made, using stone tools, from ulnas of large birds (typically vulture) and found in Aurignacian and Gravettian contexts within Upper Palaeolithic caves in France. The recent announcement of a radiocarbon date of 36,000 bp for two well-preserved examples (and a possible whistle) from Geissenklösterle, southern Germany (Hahn 1996), by no means primitive in form, shows just how much farther back we may eventually expect such finds to go. It is one of the prime aims of the present programme to provide, by close scrutiny of our now very substantial medieval comparative sample, the necessary ground-work to enable these earliest finds to yield up their secrets. Looked at under the microscope during a recent preliminary evaluation,[3] many Palaeolithic pipes preserve extensive handling-wear closely comparable with the traces seen in scanning electron microscopy and profilometry of Roman and Anglo-Saxon finds. From these delicate traces experiments and statistical analysis are already yielding information about the fingering techniques which may have been employed during actual performance more than 20,000 years ago (Fig. 15.5). Some pipes possess arrays of up to four well-defined finger-holes, thus preserving in their forms and placements vital tuning data. When we look at – and listen – to the sounds produced by these remarkable little instruments, duly replicated, it is difficult not to feel a sense of awe: that we may be hearing through them an echo of one of the fundaments of the ancient human musical mind.

Notes

1 The writer is indebted to Dr Ian Cross, Faculty of Music, Cambridge, for his help in the preparation of this figure; the software used was Lemur, © the CERL Sound Group, University of Illinois, to whom especial thanks are also extended.
2 Amongst the examples played was *Down by the Sally Gardens*, performed on the replica swan ulna pipe from twelfth-century Norwich.
3 The material from the Grotte d'Isturitz, Pyrenées Atlantiques, now preserved in the Musée des Antiquités Nationales, Saint-Germain-en-Laye, Paris, by kind permission of Mme Marie-Hélène Thiault, Conservateur au Musée.

Bibliography

Bruce-Mitford, R.L.S. & M. 1983. *The Sutton Hoo Ship Burial Vol. III*. London: British Museum Publications.
Coles, J.M. 1963. Irish Bronze Age horns and their relations with Northern Europe, *Proc. Prehist. Soc.* 11, 326–56.
Hahn, J. 1996. Le Paléolithique Supérieur en Allemagne méridionale (1991–1995). In M. Otte (ed.) *Le Paléolithique Supérieur européen. Bilan quinquennal (1991–1996)*, 181–6. Forlì (ERAUL 76).
Holmes, P. 1986. The Scandinavian bronze lurs. In C.S. Lund (ed.) *The Bronze Lurs: Second Conference of the ICTM Study Group on Music Archaeology Vol. II*, 51–125. Stockholm: Kungl. Musikaliska Akademien.

Lawson, G. 1978. The lyre from Grave 22. In B. Green, A. Rogerson & S.G. White, *The Anglo-Saxon cemetery at Bergh Apton, Norfolk*, 87–97. East Anglian Archaeology 7.

Lawson, G. 1985. *Sounds of the Viking Age*. Music from Archaeology 1, Archaic APX851, Archaeologia Musica, Cambridge.

Lawson, G. 1987a. The lyre remains from Grave 97. In B. Green & A. Rogerson, *The Anglo-Saxon cemetery at Morning Thorpe, Norfolk*, 166–71. East Anglian Archaeology 36.

Lawson, G. 1987b. *Sounds from Norman Times*. Music from Archaeology 3, Archaic APX873, Archaeologia Musica, Cambridge.

Lawson, G. forthcoming. The lyre from Grave 2183. In T. Pestell & W. Filmer-Sankey, *The Anglo-Saxon Cemetery at Snape, Suffolk*. East Anglian Archaeology, forthcoming.

Lund, C.S. 1985. *Fornnordiska Klanger / The Sounds of Prehistoric Scandinavia*, Musica Sveciae series, His Masters Voice EMI 1361031, EMI Svenska, Stockholm. Re-issued on CD in 1991 by Kungl. Musikaliska Akademien, Stockholm, as MSCD101.

Lund, C.S. (ed.) 1986. *The Bronze Lurs: Second Conference of the ICTM Study Group on Music Archaeology II*, 51–125. Stockholm: Kungl. Musikaliska Akademien.

Reimers, C. and Vogel, V. 1989. Knochenpfeifen und Knochenflöten aus Schleswig. In V. Vogel (ed.) *Ausgrabungen in Schleswig: Berichte und Studien 7: das archäologische Fundmaterial I*, 19–42. Neumünster: Karl Wachholtz.

16. Experimental Ship Archaeology in Denmark

Ole Crumlin-Pedersen

Abstract: This paper considers the particular features of experimental archaeology that apply to ship reconstructions, with particular reference to those carried out at the Viking Ship Museum in Roskilde. Examples discussed include the Roar Ege, *which is considered in some detail.*

Experimental archaeology is one of the methods available to us in the process of studying the material remains of life in the past. Practical work with copies of ancient tools, weapons or built-up structures may serve the archaeologist as a good demonstration of the use of these elements, and it may lead him or her to become aware of important features that would otherwise remain hidden or unnoticed. The experiment may also be used to eliminate some of the desktop theories that lack support in reality. These simple statements are not new to us – they have been demonstrated on several occasions over the last century and John Coles should be given the credit for sucessfully introducing experimental archaeology to the international academic world (Coles 1973, 1979).

The examples given here will be drawn from the nautical world but they may be relevant for other fields as well. As regards the ships of the past, these hold great potential for the study of such general aspects of society as technology, communications, trade, warfare, fishing, and even cult, as well as the individual history of the ship. Ships are difficult to deal with, however, as they are highly sophisticated and complex structures.

In order to be able to exploit the full potential of a ship find, a multidisciplinary approach is needed, as well as a wide range of practical skills. To employ such an approach archaeologists have to supplement their own professional background with those of wood specialists, naval architects, boat-builders and sailors – not to mention the knowledge needed for the treatment of wood and iron according to proper ancient methods, for the manufacture of ropes and sail in unfamiliar materials, and for non-instrumental navigation and weather-forecasting.

Few, if any, maritime archaeologists have a sufficiently broad base of knowledge and skills to cover this full range of abilities. Consequently a range of specialists must cooperate with each other, using proper methodologies and under the guidance of the responsible excavator/investigator, in the analysis and publication of a ship find.

Methodology suggests several means by which we can achieve results that are informative and relevant, and which at best can provide new insights into the cultural context of which the find forms a part.

One of these is *experimental archaeology*. It provides the investigator of a ship find with an excellent opportunity to test the quality of the archaeological record and the relevance of the documentation in general. The challenge is to create a new vessel that will:–

- match the materials and techniques of the original in all preserved parts,
- have the missing parts recreated following the construction principles and lines of the preserved parts, possibly supplemented by evidence from other finds, iconography etc.,
- function as a seaworthy vessel in the right setting and

Author's Address: Ole Crumlin-Pedersen, Centre for Maritime Archaeology, Havnevej 7, Postboks 317, DK 4000 Roskilde

with a crew capable of handling this particular type of craft.

In carrying out such a project to a sober scholarly standard the investigator cannot avoid acquiring new insight into several aspects of the complex formed by a ship find, and the process opens up for a better-founded analysis and publication of the original find than would otherwise be possible. Thus the primary aim of the experimental process is to enable the investigator to present the evidence provided by the find in a way that is as competent as possible, after having had to cope with the variety of problems involved in constructing the ship and taking it through sea-trials as a fully functional unit. Normally such a project will have additional aims, exploiting the educational value of the new vessel etc., but these are not the subject of the present paper, which is focused on the scholarly value of experimental archaeology on the basis of the author's experience with various Danish projects.

Just as with other methods of analysing the evidence, there is a need to apply a strict methodology to the use of experimental archaeology. The concept applied here is in line with the explanation of the word *experiment* given in the Oxford Dictionary of Current English: *a scientific test done carefully in order to study what happens and to gain new knowledge*.

Recently, however, a total of ten British scholars presented their versions of some definitive principles of scientific enquiry within experimental ship-archaeology, based on the keywords *hypothesis, test* and *publication* (Coates et al. 1995). The background here is clearly the research principles applied in the natural sciences and physics: formulate a hypothesis, choose the material on which to test the hypothesis, run a rigid test procedure, and publish the results in relevant international journals.

The concept of a normal physical experiment is being challenged, however, once the archaeologist turns from simple, repeatable experiments, such as the grinding of flour or the felling of small trees, to complex contexts, such as Iron Age farming in general or the construction and trials of ships of the past on the basis of excavated evidence. A precondition for applying the experimental method is normally that only one single factor should be changed at a time, while all other features remain unchanged.

This definition of the word experiment, based on the natural science concept, is not in accordance with the present general use of the term experimental archaeology, as this is also applied to complex undertakings studying the interaction of several factors in context – in what might rather be called *full-scale working reconstructions*.

The construction and use of a ship is an extremely complex undertaking, characterized by factors that are mutually dependent and impossible to study and analyse one by one. Here the experiment must be organized according to a different standard – that of the functional unit (Crumlin-Pedersen 1995).

In general, ships are built to match the functions they are constructed for. In rare cases a ship may have been a constructional failure, for example the Swedish *Vasa*, but more often traces of wear are apparent which show that a vessel found as a wreck may have served its purpose for several years. Therefore the starting point for a full-scale reconstruction project should be taken in the fact that the ship would have been reasonably seaworthy in relation to its function and to the waters for which it was built. In contrast to land-based structures, a ship is a fully-functional unit, not dependent on other units, in short a self-contained vehicle for human needs.

A second precondition is that there existed an element of interdependence between the elements of the vessel: hull, propulsion and steering. Thus a ship with a hull with sophisticated sailing lines is likely to have had a rig of a similar standard, even if no parts of the rig have been found.

The main characteristics of a well-organized archaeological project involving the full-scale reconstruction and trials of a complex unit like a ship are:–

1. *An archaeological base* in substantial remains of an ancient structure, documented to a rigorous standard.
2. *A research strategy* for the analysis of the potential of the find.
3. Access to *materials* corresponding to those originally used.
4. A group of craftsmen and users with *relevant skills*.
5. *Documentation and publication* of the outcome of the experimental activity in relevant media.

With such a procedure the value of the work is not restricted to the recording of a few figures for, for example, tacking ability or speed of the vessel. The effort invested in the project is paid back in the form of a higher level of competence on the part of the excavator or investigator.

For several years, projects within ship-archaeology following the principles mentioned here have been carried out in Denmark. The centre for these activities has been in Roskilde at the Viking Ship Museum and the Maritime Archaeology Units of the National Museum, although people from several other parts of the country have been involved as well.

The main project has been the construction in 1982–84 and subsequent trials of *Roar Ege* (Fig. 16.1), built on the basis of comprehensive evidence from the 11th-century small coaster, the Skuldelev 3-ship, and rigged following extensive research in contemporary and later sources (Crumlin-Pedersen 1987; Andersen & Andersen 1989; Andersen et al. 1997).

A complete full-scale documentation of all parts recovered from the original ship forms the basis for the reconstruction of the structural lay-out as well as the lines of the hull, including the missing stern part (Fig. 16.2). In this case the uncertainty arising from the missing parts represents just a few percent of the original dimensions and features of the hull of the ship – unlike the normal

Fig. 16.1. The Roar Ege *full-scale reconstruction of the Skuldelev 3 ship under construction. Photo Viking Ship Museum, Roskilde.*

situation for the reconstruction of most other structures of the past, such as houses, defence structures etc., which often have to be based on the evidence of postholes and shadows in the ground alone.

The preparations for the construction of this ship provide a good illustration of the whole range of problems related to such vessels with respect to materials and techniques, and the implications of these factors for our understanding of past societies.

To give one example, the detailed preparations for the construction of *Roar Ege* prompted the author to study the Skuldelev 3 find and other vessels of the period in order to determine the original size of the planks (Crumlin-Pedersen 1986). This led to conclusions about the large size and high quality of the tree-trunks used. This again led to studies of the woodland background and to conclusions about possible preferential royal claims on the best shipbuilding oaks (Crumlin-Pedersen 1997, 183). By comparing the planks used in several wrecks, an increasing general shortage of good oak for planking between the 10th and the 13th centuries could be established, leading to an increase in the use of recycled wood in ships. With the growing size of sea-going ships, this situation created an impetus to changes in shipbuilding technology. Similar side-effects have resulted from other areas of investigation which the preparations for the construction of proper full-scale reconstructions have forced the investigator to look into.

Our search for copies of the right types of tools led us to a type of broad-axe, found in Viking-Age Hedeby, London and elsewhere, which turned out to be excellent for the purpose (Fig. 16.3). This is the type of axe that is shown on the Bayeux Tapestry as the trade-mark of the shipbuilder in the scene where orders are being given for the construction of the invasion fleet.

A pool of human resources in knowledge and skills relevant to the theme of the experiment is needed to provide the manpower and expertise to build and sail the new vessel to standards as close as possible to the original ones. No methodology of experimental archaeology should ignore this fact. In Denmark, such expertise has been built up over more than twenty years, and a considerable number of people share their talents with us, either professionally as craftsmen or students, or as amateurs. These people form the breeding ground for training newcomers in this field, and they are often the ones who can offer the most constructive criticism of reports and publications of the work.

Even if it is tempting to use modern boat-builders as specialists in building reconstructions of boats and ships of the past, this is a dangerous path to follow. During his years of apprenticeship, the modern professional craftsman is programmed to work according to certain principles, deeply grounded in recent and present-day technology. We have therefore trained our own boat-builders over the years to observe and work strictly from the archaeological evidence rather than from pre-conceived ideas and modern technologies.

The skills needed to work from an entirely axe-based technology with clove-boards include the selection of the right types of trees in the forest, which will provide elements of the size and shape needed for the job. This is a qualification modern boat-builders do not normally have. We have now come to the point where the Ship- and Boat-builders' Union in Denmark uses our boat-builders as instructors for their new apprentices in these skills.

The building process in itself incorporates a number of intricate problems, such as how to cut the complex stem- and stern-timbers without the use of drawings. This led to the analysis of the shape, showing that it was based on a system of lines and circles – indicating that this ship must have been one of a series of ships built from a sophisticated, non-paper-based set of rules (Fig. 16.4). With our present use of paper-based planning procedures for construction projects, this is hard to understand, and we tend to use the expression "rules-of-thumb" to indicate rela-

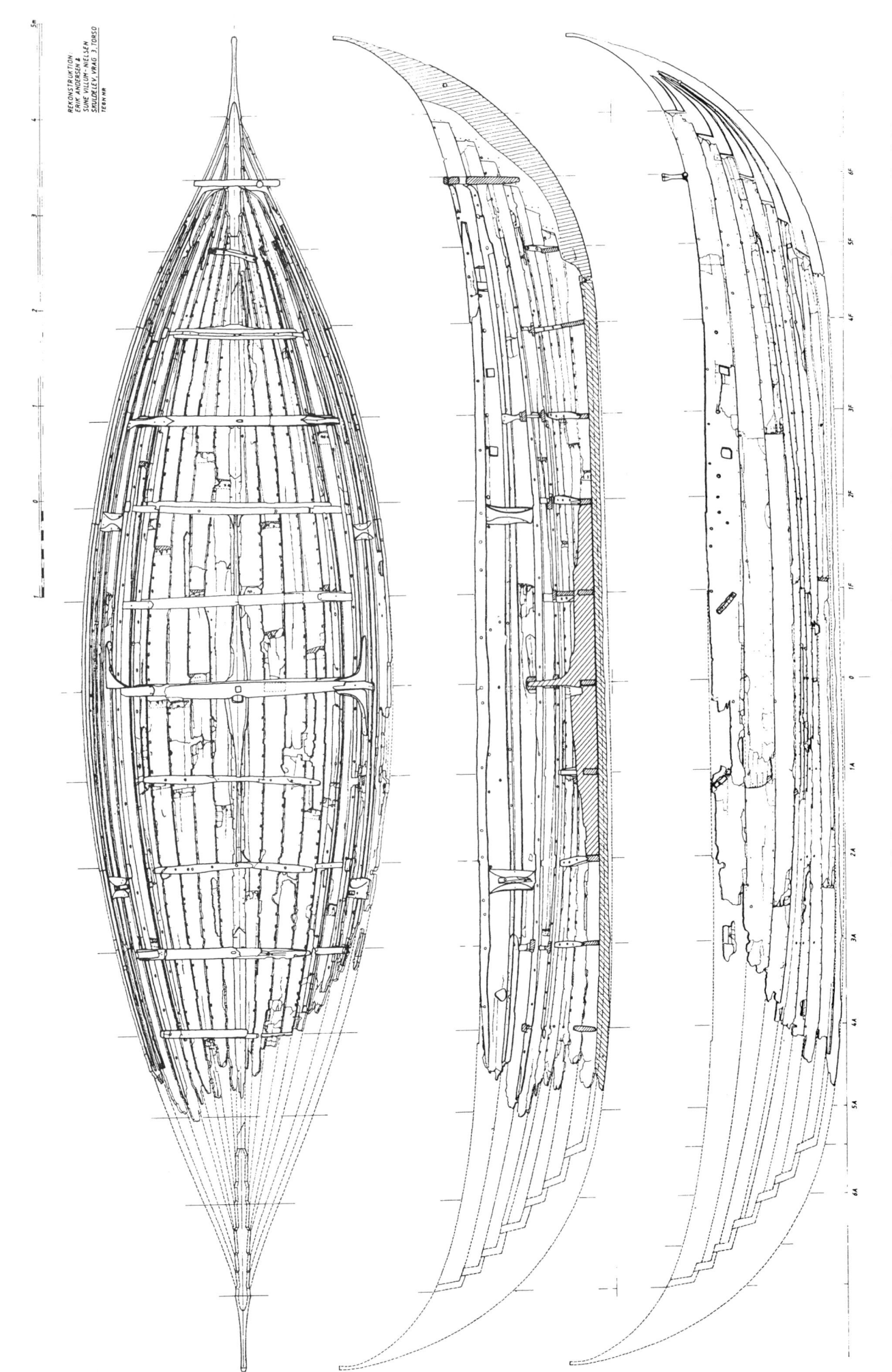

Fig. 16.2. All preserved parts of the Skuldelev 3 ship assembled in a "torso-drawing". Drawn by S. Villum Nielsen, Centre for Maritime Archaeology, Roskilde.

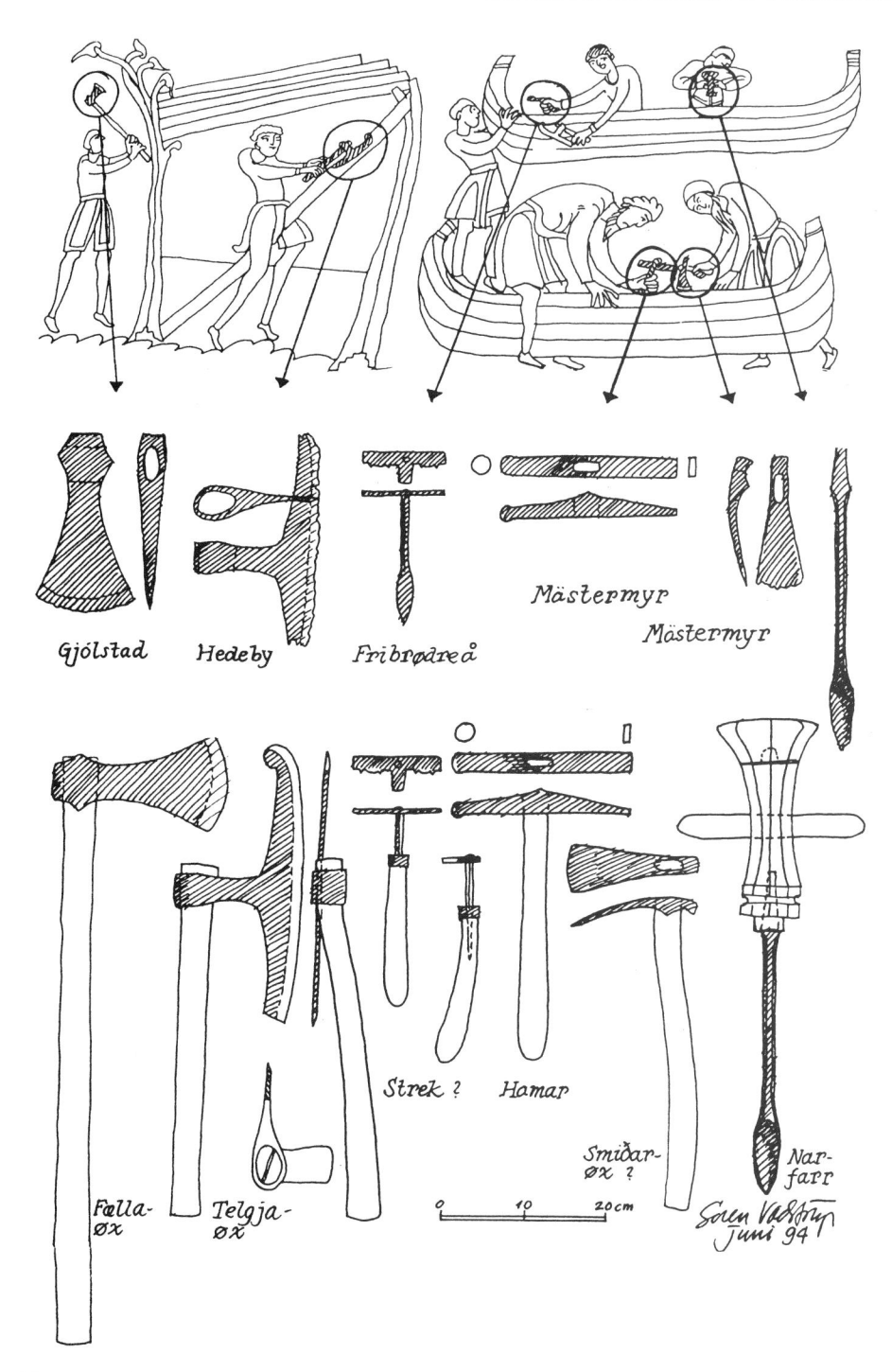

Fig. 16.3. Shipbuilding tools from the Bayeux Tapestry, from Viking-Age finds and as reconstructed for the Roar *project. Drawn by S. Vadstrup.*

tively simple and primitive procedures in those cases where no paper-work was involved. This is definitely not the case with the Viking-Age ships, which show themselves to be masterpieces of design and functionality.

In the ancient past, in northern Europe as well as in the Mediterranean, all plank-built ships were constructed by the shell-first procedure. Here the keel was laid and the planks cut to their individual shapes and interconnected to form the desired lines of the hull, which was then afterwards strengthened by the insertion of frames. This procedure was followed in the *Roar Ege* project as well, with the shape of the planking cut individually and the lines adjusted by means of the weight of stones from above and sticks from below. Once the bottom-planking was mounted, the floor-timbers could be cut to shape and the planking of the sides built up.

In order to build the ship without moulds or drawings, the control of the shape of the hull was achieved by taking

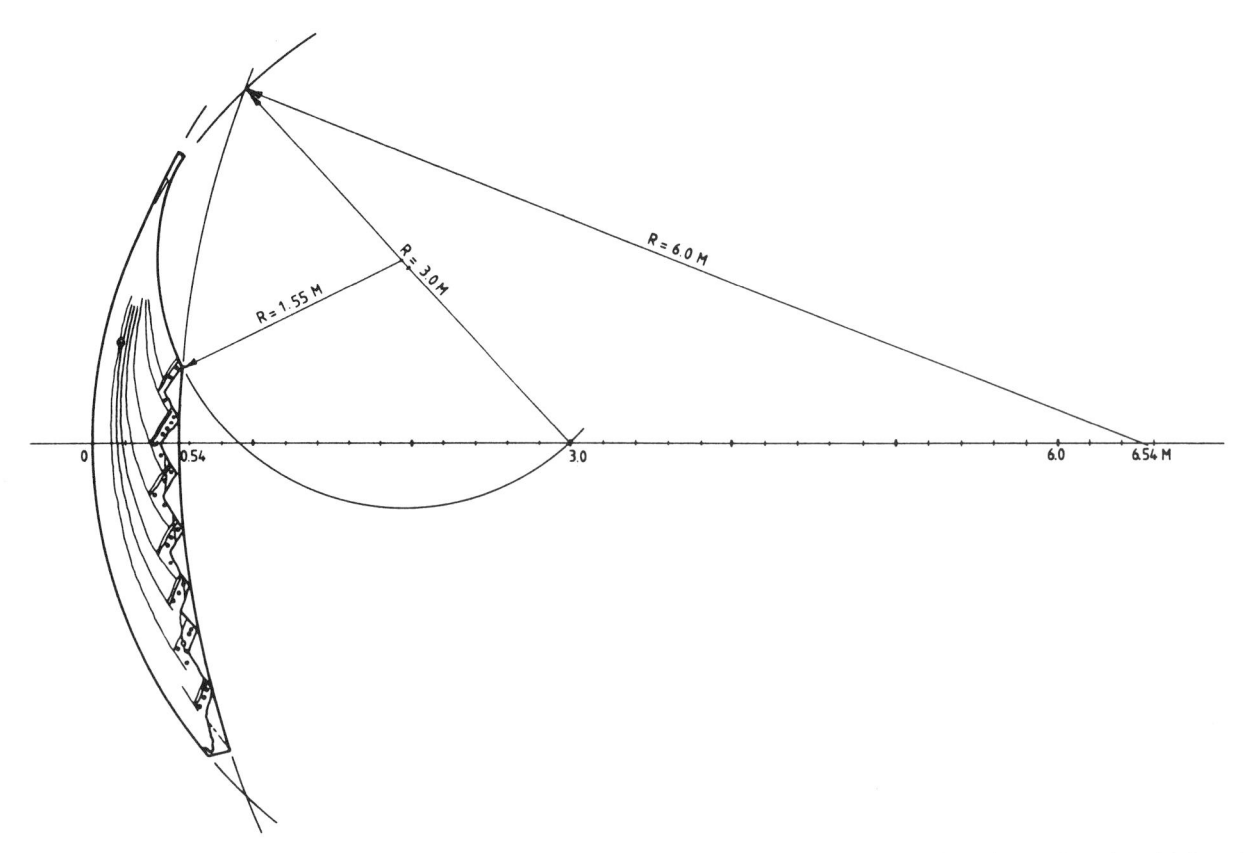

Fig. 16.4. The outline of the original Skuldelev 3 stem is defined within a simple system of circles with radii of 6.0 m, 3.0 m and 1.55 m with interrelated centres. The 0.05 m shift of the smallest circle away from the midpoint of the 3.0 m radius accounts for the elegant shape of the tip of the stem. From Crumlin-Pedersen 1986.

measurements from a model at 1:10, based on previous cardboard models in which the shape of the individual parts was taken from the detailed recordings of all elements of the ship. In this way one could be certain that the lines of the reconstructed ship matched those of the original closely, and any uncertainty remaining was within the margin of a few inches. Thus the *Roar Ege* is a true replica rather than a floating hypothesis of Skuldelev 3 as regards the hull.

The rigging was more uncertain, as the size and shape of the rig and sail had to be determined primarily on the basis of indirect evidence. There are indications in the ship, however, of the position of the mast and the points of fastening for the tack and sheet of the sail, giving good guidelines for the width of the lower leech of the sail. In this case the sail was clearly not a low, broad square-sail as shown on several early Viking-Age ship representations; here the archaeological evidence pointed to a sail of approximately the same width as height. In handling such a sail there were guidelines to be found in the ethnological evidence from western Norway, where the practice of sailing single-masted square-sail boats had remained in continuous use from the Viking-Age to the beginning of this century. The first set of sail for *Roar Ege* was made of linen, but later a sail was woven from the long-haired wool which was common in the Viking Age, and with sheets made of horsehair (Fig. 16.5). What still remains to be replaced are the hemp ropes for other functions in the ship, since ropes of lime-bast, and possibly walrus hide, were used originally.

The seamanship required to handle such a ship differs from that of modern yacht handling, as in the square-sail vessel there is a sophisticated balance between the centres of action of the sail, the hull and the rudder. This was clearly demonstrated on one occasion in *Roar Ege,* when the tiller broke as the ship was approaching the entrance of Hundested harbour in a strong wind. For other ships it could have been disastrous to loose control of the steering under such conditions, but *Roar Ege* could be steered without the use of the rudder by changing the longitudinal weight distribution so that the ship swiftly turned away from the harbour piers into open water, where the tiller could be repaired while the ship kept a steady new course.

An important element in the trials has been to study the speed of the ship under various weather conditions, as well as the tacking ability, the ability to make headway against the wind. For *Roar Ege*, extensive results of several weeks of trials are available, showing that this vessel may maintain speeds of up to 7–8 knots in strong winds and that it tacks at an angle of *ca.* 60° against the wind (Andersen *et al.* 1997).

Fig. 16.5. The Roar Ege *tacking, with its woollen sail double-reefed, on Roskilde Fjord in 1996. Photo Werner Karrasch, Viking Ship Museum, Roskilde.*

Since the launching of *Roar Ege* in 1984, the Roskilde centre has been involved in the construction of several other ship reconstructions, each adding new aspects to the study of medieval ship- and boat-building.

Saga Siglar, the reconstruction of the 11th-century Skuldelev 1 ship, was built in Norway in 1982–83, just as the original ship probably was before it ended its days in Roskilde Fjord in Denmark. Experts from Roskilde gave guidelines for the reconstruction of hull and rig, and took part in the initial trials of this ship, which included crossing the North Sea and the Atlantic under very severe weather conditions (Vinner 1995). This ship later circumnavigated the globe, the first undecked vessel ever to have been recorded to do so.

The warship type has been represented by the *Helge Ask*, a reconstruction of the 11th-century Skuldelev 5 ship, built in Roskilde in 1990–91, and offering the potential for studying the effect of combining rowing and sailing, as well as several other factors (Crumlin-Pedersen & Vinner 1993). This is a type of ship which is probably very close to the ships in which Danish Vikings raided the British Isles and France in the 9th century, as well as to the 11th-century Norman ships known from the Bayeux tapestry.

A small work-boat of the 12th century, found in the Isefjord/Lammefjord region at Gislinge, has been reconstructed at the Viking Ship Museum and tested by a group of archaeology students, while a barge of the same period, found at Egernsund, has been rebuilt at the Medieval Centre in Nykøbing. Here a replica of the Gedesby ship, the *Agnete* (Fig. 16.6), has also been built in close consultation with the Centre in Roskilde (Crumlin-Pedersen 1994; Bill & Vinner 1995). This is a late 13th-century cargo ship, constructed to carry live provisions to the Hanseatic towns on the Baltic from the farming areas of Lolland-Falster, as proved by the depositions of cattle dung found on board the wreck.

The examples given here have been medieval vessels,

Fig. 16.6. The full-size reconstruction of the late 13th-century Gedesby ship, the Agnete, *ready for launching in 1995. Photo Ole Malling, Medieval Centre, Nykøbing F.*

but the last example is an on-going project to build a full-scale reconstruction of the Early Iron Age Hjortspring boat, from 350–300 BC, which is as close as one can now come to the Danish Bronze Age vessels. The group building the replica in close contact with Roskilde started by constructing two separate sections of this long war-canoe to investigate various details of the construction before embarking on the 18 m-long boat itself (Valbjørn 1996). The very large lime trees needed for the full-length reconstruction could not be found in Denmark but had to be shipped in from Poland. At present construction is well under way, using copies of Iron Age tools. A good example of the volume of work involved is given by the bottom-plank of the boat, which has been carved out of a 2.3 tonne lime trunk to its final, very slender form, weighing just under 100 kg. This process is a striking example of the serious challenge it was for an Early Iron Age tribe to select and process the materials for the construction of such a vessel.

Against this background it may be fair to state that the experimental activity with the reconstruction of ancient ships directed from Roskilde is more than playing with floating hypotheses. The undertakings are not subjective; they represent successful working reconstructions, more solidly based on archaeological evidence than is the case for many other experimental archaeology projects. They therefore enable us to exploit the archaeological evidence to a degree that could not have been achieved without this methodology, and they help us to appreciate the authenticity of the ship finds.

Bibliography

Andersen, B. & Andersen, E. 1989. *Råsejlet – Dragens vinge.* Roskilde: Viking Ship Museum.

Andersen, E. et al. 1997. *Roar Ege – Skuldelev 3 skibet som arkæologisk eksperiment.* Roskilde: Viking Ship Museum.

Bill, J. & Vinner, M. 1995. The Gedesby ship under sail, *Maritime Archaeology Newsletter from Roskilde, Denmark* 5, 3–8.

Coates, J. et al. 1995. Experimental boat and ship archaeology: principles and methods, *Int. J. Nautical Archaeology* 24, 293–301.

Coles, J. 1973. *Archaeology by Experiment.* London: Hutchinson.

Coles, J. 1979. *Experimental Archaeology.* London: Academic Press.

Crumlin-Pedersen, O. 1986. Aspects of Wood Technology in Medieval Shipbuilding. In O. Crumlin-Pedersen & M. Vinner (eds), *Sailing into the Past,* 138–149. Proc. Int. Seminar on Replicas of Ancient and Medieval Vessels, Roskilde 1984. Roskilde: Viking Ship Museum.

Crumlin-Pedersen, O. 1987. Aspects of Viking-Age shipbuilding, *J. Danish Archaeology* 5, 1986, 209–228.

Crumlin-Pedersen, O. 1994. Original and replica, *Maritime Archaeology Newsletter from Roskilde, Denmark* 3, 4–7.

Crumlin-Pedersen, O. 1995. Experimental archaeology and ships – bridging the arts and the sciences, *Int. J. Nautical Archaeology* 24, 303–306.

Crumlin-Pedersen, O. 1997. *Viking-Age Ships and Shipbuilding in Hedeby/Haithabu and Schleswig.* Ships & Boats of the North 2. Roskilde: Viking Ship Museum.

Crumlin-Pedersen, O. & Vinner, M. 1993. Roar og Helge af Roskilde – om at bygge og sejle med vikingeskibe, *Nationalmuseets Arbejdsmark 1993,* 11–29.

Valbjørn, K. 1996. The Hjortspring boat under reconstruction, *Maritime Archaeology Newsletter from Roskilde, Denmark* 6, 17–18.

Vinner, M. 1995. A Viking-ship off Cape Farewell 1984. In O. Olsen, J. Skamby Madsen and F. Rieck (eds) *Ship-shape – Essays for Ole Crumlin-Pedersen on the Occasion of the 60th Anniversary,* 289–304. Roskilde: Viking Ship Museum.

17. Wood-tar and pitch experiments at Biskupin Museum

Wojciech Piotrowski

Abstract: This paper looks at a specific aspect of ancient technology that has been investigated through experimental reconstruction at Biskupin open-air Museum: tar and pitch. Pits for the production of birch bark tar and pine pitch were discovered at Biskupin in the 1950s and 1960s. In collaboration with colleagues from Berlin, successful reconstructions by various methods have been carried out, helping to enhance the tourist potential of Biskupin.

Excavations at Biskupin were initiated in 1934 and continued – with a short break during the Second World War – until 1974 when the excavation of the last, wide area trench was concluded. Since then greater attention has been devoted to preserving the wood of which the Lusatian culture fortified settlement is built. 25 per cent of the settlement area has been left uncovered and there is hope that archaeologists who will in future undertake excavation work at this wonderful site on the Biskupin peninsula will, being richer in knowledge and aware of both the good and bad experiences of their older colleagues, explain everything that conflicts or is incompatible with today's requirements, or is doubtful. Now however we may, with full conviction, say that the Biskupin excavations were an exceptional phase in the history of Polish archaeology, a phase which, for various reasons, cannot yet be considered as completely closed (Piotrowski 1998; Rajewski 1959).

When Professor J. Kostrzewski and his assistant Dr Z. Rajewski planned the wide scale interdisciplinary research to be carried out at Biskupin and the surrounding microregion, they did not forget about experimental archaeology. Experiments with making and firing pottery and with working wood, horn and bone were already being undertaken before the Second World War. After the war, the number and range of experiments grew considerably, especially in the 1950s when annual Archaeological Training Camps, in which most students of archaeology participated, took place at the site (Piotrowski 1998, 99–100; Piotrowski & Zajączkowski 1991; Rajewski 1952).

In the spring of 1949, Rajewski decided to cut a cross-shaped trench in a small hump near the base of the Biskupin peninsula, referred to as Biskupin site 6. Excavations were carried out by Dr W. Szafrańmski. After removing a layer of arable soil he noticed the outlines of a dozen or so pits. It soon emerged that most of them came from the early medieval period and that six had to do with the production and further preparation of pine pitch and birch bark tar (Szafrański 1949/1950, 455–63). Pit IIIa (Fig. 17.1) aroused particular interest because of its clearly defined shape and the presence of burned birch bark and birch bark tar mixed with sand in the filling. Basing his conclusions partly on ethnographic comparisons, Rajewski and Szafrański correctly interpreted the production process which had been used in this pit as the dry distillation of birch bark employing the two-vessel method (Fig. 17.2) (Szafrański 1949/1950, 464). This method had been used all over the Slavonic region till contemporary times (Moszyński 1929, 374–75).

Soon aflterwards, experiments with the dry distillation of birch bark were undertaken (Szafrański 1949/1950, 468–69). Two vessels were used: an upper, 1.5 litre vessel with holes in the bottom served as a container for the raw

---

Author's Address: Wojciech Piotrowski, Biskupin Museum / State Archaeological Museum, ul. Długa 52 – Arsenał, 00–950 Warsaw

material, and a lower, 0.5 litre one, was used to catch the final product (Fig. 17.3). The experiment was carried out several times, using both old, dried-out, and fresh birch bark. The length of time for which the fire was burned over the upper container was also varied; usually three to five hours. Szafrański reported that of the many experiments three were successful (Szafrański 1961, 69). One of these was carried out in laboratory conditions at the Biskupin site workshop (Fig. 17.4). The birch bark tar obtained during the experiments was examined by the chemist Dr K. Kapitańczyk who found that the new tar was closely compatible with the one discovered in the excavations (Szafrański 1949/1950, 469).

Work at Biskupin site 6 was continued until 1954, and one more birch bark tar pit was discovered. The group of birch bark tar and pine pitch pits and the remains of the other household features at the site helped to reconstruct its character. In the 10th–11th century it had been a service settlement (Fig. 17.5) for the inhabitants of the small stronghold standing on part of the Biskupin peninsula (Szafrański 1961; Piotrowski 1995). Fifty years after the pioneer birch bark tar experiments, Professor Szafrański recollected his experiences at Biskupin site 6 in his last article (Szafrański 1997). This distinguished scholar, who had made many significant contributions to Polish archaeology, died on April 15, 1998, in Warsaw, at the age of 78, and his ashes – in accordance with his last will – were strewn over the waters of Lake Biskupin.

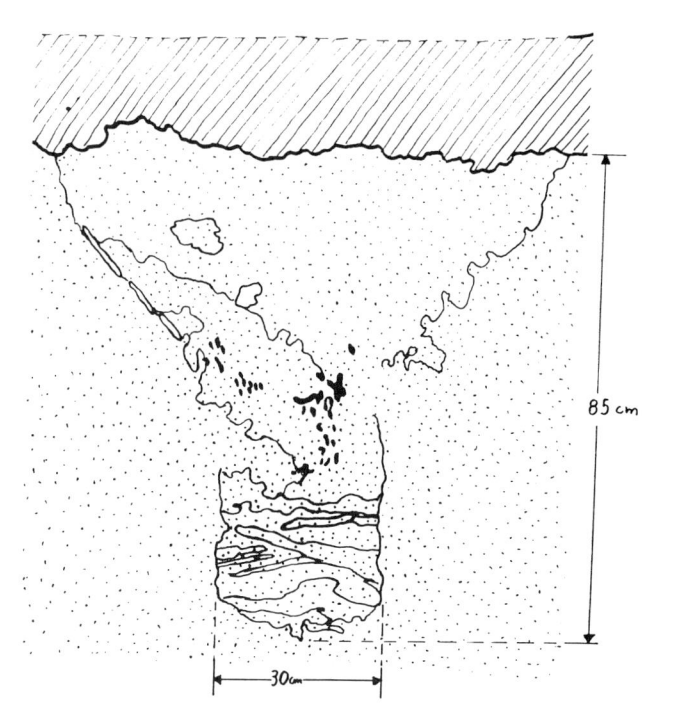

Fig. 17.1. Biskupin, site 6: pit IIIa, for birch bark tar production (after Szafrański 1949/1950, 457).

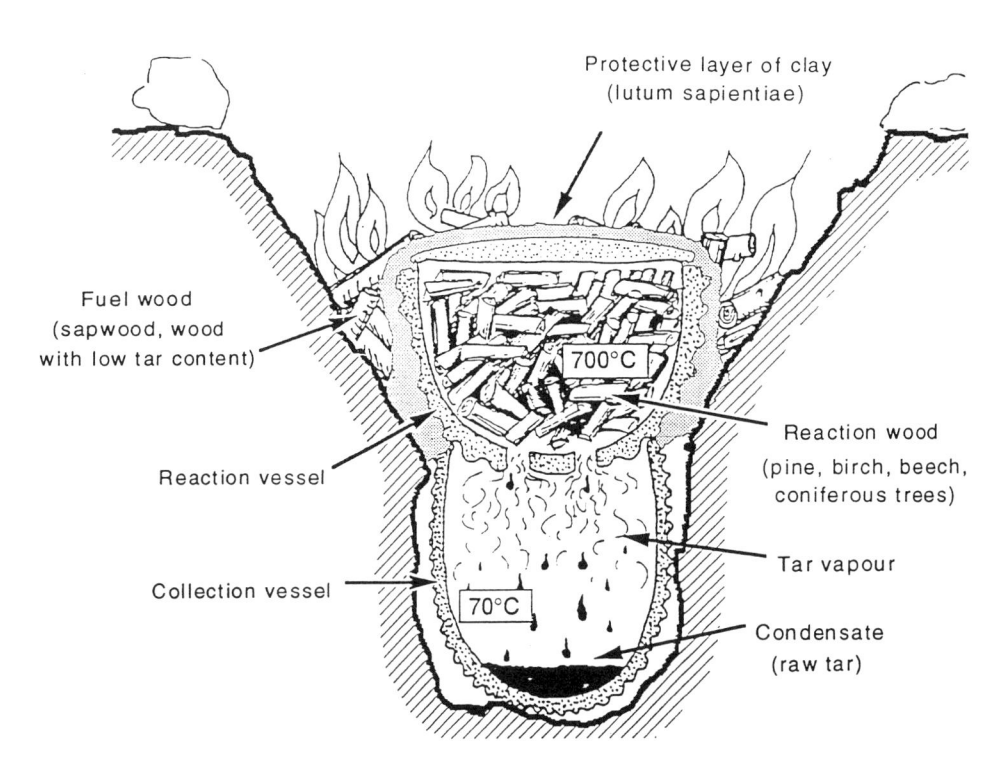

Fig. 17.2. The two-vessel method of dry distillation (after Kurzweil & Todtenhaupt 1991a, 400). The reaction principle is that of pyrolysis (the heating of wood in the absence of air); the technology involved is that of Destillatio descensum *and* Botus barbarus *(descending distillation and condensation process); the process lasts around 3 hours, and the yield is about 10% of the wood as tar, with charcoal as a by-product.*

Fig. 17.3. First attempt to distil birch bark tar at Biskupin, Biskupin, site 6, spring 1949. Photo J. Adamczewski (after Szafrański 1949/1950, 474).

In connection with the celebrations of the Thousand Years of the Polish State (the Millennium) which culminated in 1966, a wide range of archaeological works was carried out all over the country towards the end of the 1950s and in the 1960s. The Biskupin excavations comprised not only the on-going work on the peninsula but also the southern shore of Lake Biskupin where trial trenches and surface studies revealed several early medieval settlements from the 7th–12th centuries. At one of the settlements, Biskupin site 18, excavated from 1966 to 1970, a number of semi-subterranean dwellings and household pits were uncovered. Some of the pits had been used for smoking and for the production of wood tar and pitch (Głosik 1969, 214–16: Piotrowski 1995, 99–100). One of the wood tar and pitch pits resembled in shape pit IIIa from the Biskupin 6 site but was much bigger: about 180 cm deep and 150 cm wide at the top (Modrzewska 1966, 261). Since the feature was extremely important for further studies of early medieval wood tar and pitch production, a lacquer-profile (a thin band of the original section of the pit, preserved using lacquer on a linen base) was made and is now exhibited at the museum pavilion at Biskupin (Fig. 17.6). Together with Dr A. Kurzweil and D. Todtenhaupt, who conduct experiments with the dry distillation of wood at Museumsdorf Düppel in Berlin, we have often wondered how big the vessel for the raw material must have been when distillation was carried out in such a large pit. We knew so far about containers of

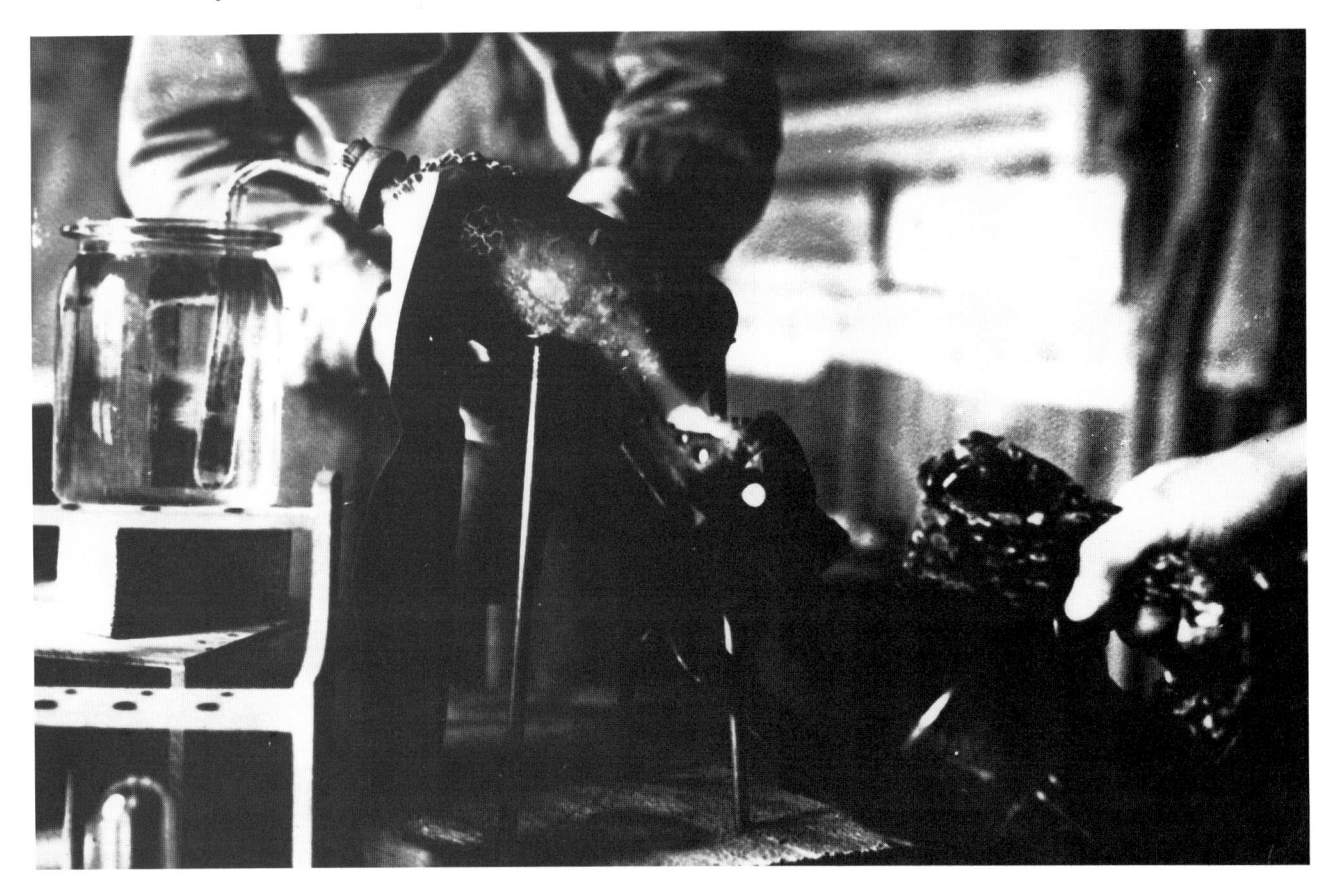

Fig. 17.4. The Biskupin laboratory. Heating a flask containing birch bark, spring 1949. Photo J. Adamczewski.

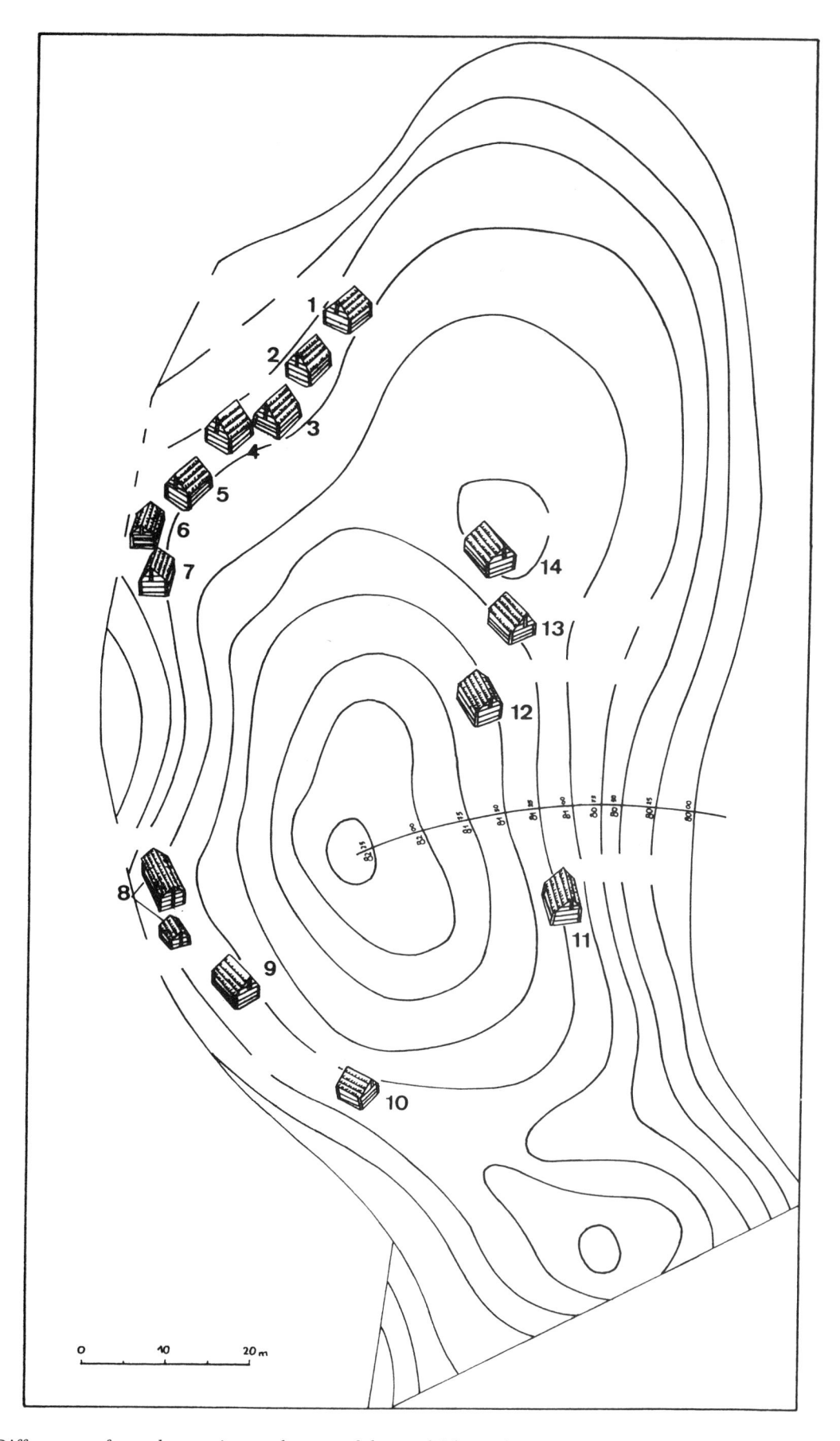

Fig. 17.5. Different crafts at the service settlement of the tenth/eleventh centuries AD (Biskupin, site 6). Buildings 1 and 8 are those of wood tar and pitch producers (after Szafrański 1997, 56).

Fig. 17.6. Section peel of the birch bark tar pit from Biskupin, site 18. Photo W. Piotrowski.

about 5 – 10 litres, but this one would have needed about 100 litres of finely cut resin pine wood. Our colleagues from Berlin may have found the solution to this problem. Analyzing some recent experiments with a pit similar in appearance to that from Biskupin site 18, they suggested that there was no ceramic vessel in the top part of the pit and the pine chips were placed directly into a funnel coated with clay (this is corroborated by ethnographic analogies) and covered with soil and turf (Fig. 17.7) (Todtenhaupt & Kurzweil 1996). The pine wood was set on fire in the same way as was done till recently in charcoal piles and large forest pitch distilling piles. This experiment will soon be repeated at Biskupin, in several pits of varying size.

The latest phase of experiments with tar and pitch production was initiated at Biskupin in 1986. Much is owing to our friendly and close contacts, in the field of popularization of science and experimental archaeology, with the Arbeitsgruppe Teerschwele at Museumsdorf Düppel, especially Dr A. Kurzweil. Every year, at the Biskupin reservation, we organize demonstrations of old methods of dry distillation of wood. Since 1995 we have included such demonstrations in the programme of the Archaeological Festival which takes place at Biskupin in the third week of September and is extremely popular, gathering as many as 70,000 visitors (Piotrowski 1996).

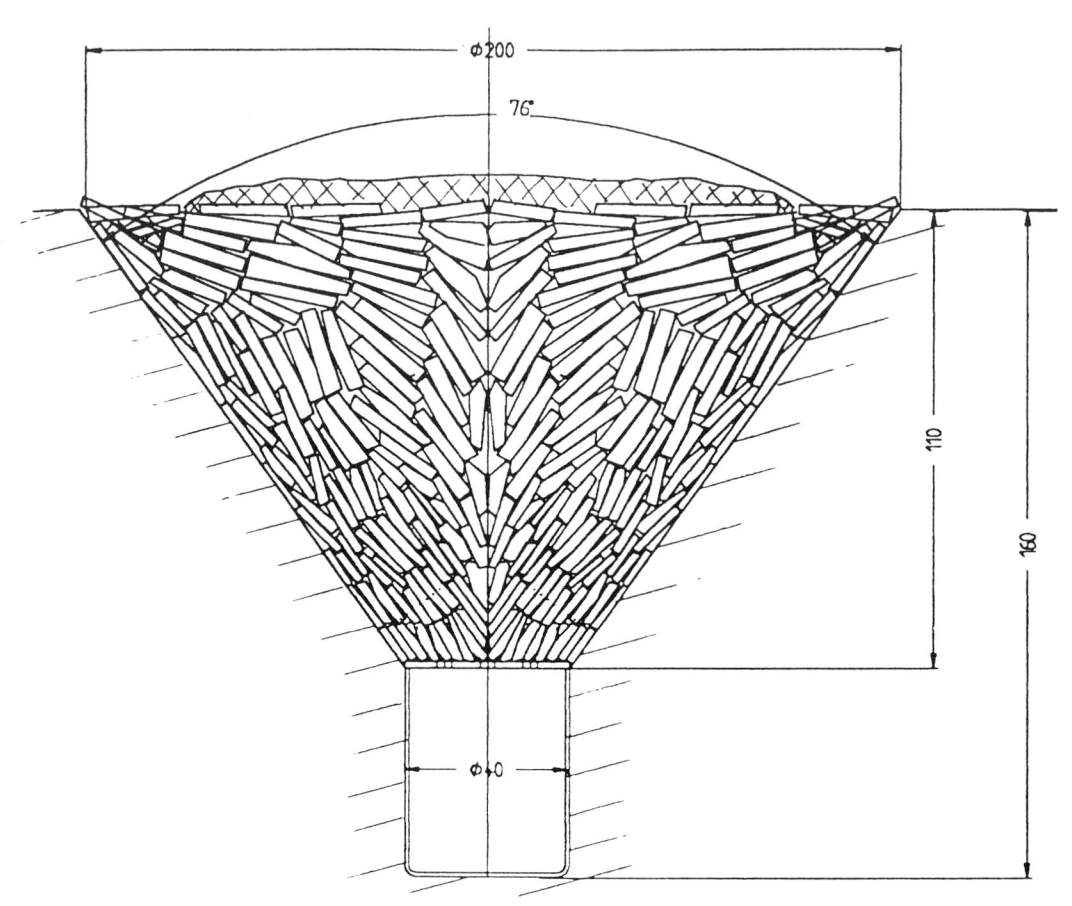

Fig. 17.7. Plan of pine pitch pit for the dry distillation process (after Todtenhaupt & Kurzweil 1996, 148).

Fig. 17.8. Biskupin 1993. Vessel containing birch bark within a second vessel for catching tar, placed in the ground. Photo W. Piotrowski.

Fig. 17.9. Biskupin 1993. Upper vessel covered with a lid and sealed with clay – including line where both vessels join. Photo W. Piotrowski.

We usually carry out experiments using the two-vessel method (Figs 17.8–17.10), since this seemingly simple technique still creates various problems. One of them is the durability of the clay vessels. In the nearly one hundred experiments carried out so far, the upper vessel, containing the raw material, usually cracked during the first, second or third firing. We are, therefore, cooperating with pottery makers, trying to obtain a mixture of clay which would resist repeated external firing. Another question is for how long the fire should be burned in the tar and pitch pit. It has been found that a small pile of chips burned for two hours is enough for the dry distilling of birch bark to obtain tar, taking care to avoid sudden changes in temperature. In the case of pine wood, for pitch the time should be extended to three to four hours. We always compare the amount of product obtained to the amount of raw material used. So far, the volume of the pitch or tar is about 10% of the birch bark or pine wood. We also experiment with the raw material, collecting bark from birches of varying age and distilling either fresh or naturally dried bark. The same procedures are used in the case of resin pine and we also intend to try distilling other coniferous trees – Douglas fir, larch and spruce. There are also plans to experiment with the dry distillation of juniper (*Juniperus communis*), a process known already in antiquity, especially along what is now the French shore of the Mediterranean (Acovitsioti *et al.* 1997), though in that climatic zone the raw material used was *Juniperus oxycedrus*.

Toward the end of the 1980s, together with Dr A. Kurzweil, we had the idea of organizing an international meeting devoted to the dry distillation of wood. We gradually acquired supporters and financial sponsors and in 1993, from the 1st to 4th July the First International Symposium on Wood Tar and Pitch took place at Biskupin, organized jointly by the Biskupin Museum and the

Fig. 17.10. Biskupin 1993. Fresh birch bark tar at a bottom of lower vessel. Photo W. Piotrowski.

Museumsdorf Düppel in Berlin. We felt that this would be a unique occasion to gather an interdisciplinary group of scholars – archaeologists, chemists, historians and philologists – from all over the world. The very interesting symposium bore fruit in the shape of a publication which is an attempt to sum up our present knowledge on the subject of dry distillation of wood and its products in the material, and to some degree spiritual, culture of Europe from the Stone Age until contemporary times (Brzeziński & Piotrowski 1997). This would seem to be a narrow

Fig. 17.11. Biskupin, 1 – 4 July 1993. First International Symposium on Wood Tar and Pitch. Distilling of birch bark using the single-vessel method. Photo A. Ring & B. Tropiło.

topic, of interest only to a limited circle of specialists but, in fact, wood pitch and tar, because of their various qualities and uses – preserving, isolating, sealing, disinfecting – have been recently 'discovered' to have been an indispensible commodity for our ancestors. The virtues of birch bark tar as a medicament for various skin diseases has been long appreciated by homoeopathic and veterinary medicine (Kurzweil & Todtenhaupt 1991a; 1991b; 1992; Piotrowski 1993; Rajewski 1970).

Experiments with the dry distillation of wood were also carried out at the Symposium at Biskupin, mainly using the two-vessel method, presented by teams of researchers from the Biskupin Museum and the Museumsdorf Düppel in Berlin (Piotrowski 1994; Brzeziński & Piotrowski 1997, 315–50). There was also a very interesting presentation of the Neolithic single-vessel technique (Fig. 17.11) by Dr D. Neubauer-Saurer. Recent excavations and discoveries at Neolithic and Bronze Age sites have supplied ever more material showing that wood tar and pitch were produced by the first farming communities in Europe and there is even mention of possible attempts to distill wood in the Mesolithic (Brzeziński & Piotrowski 1997, 19–50).

Wood tar and pitch experiments at Biskupin continue. The best season of course is spring, summer and early autumn, when the weather is fine. Tar and pitch producers always chose places that were dry and sheltered from the wind, and such can easily be found near Biskupin. Twice a year, in March/April and September/October, we remove the bark from live birch trees, which does not harm them

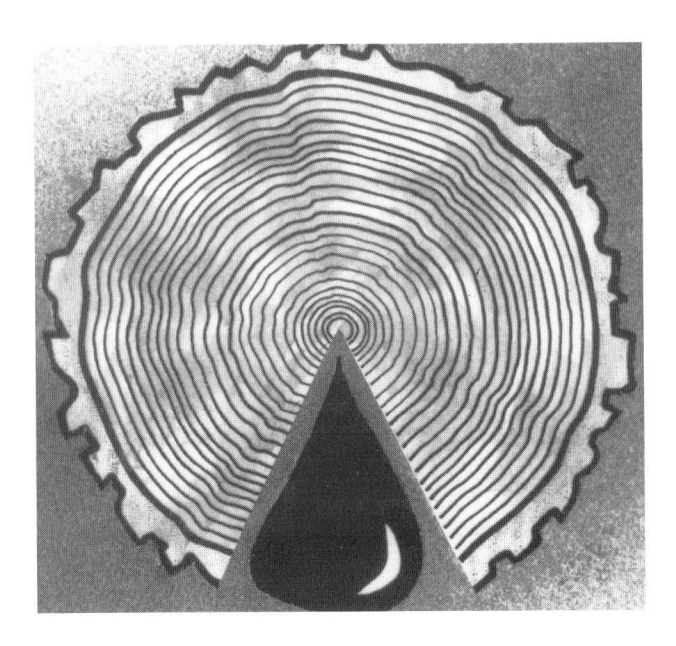

Fig. 17.12. Logo of the First International Symposium on Wood Tar and Pitch, which became the logo for groups experimenting with dry distillation of wood in Germany and Poland. Designed by A. Kurzweil & R. Splitter.

if done properly, and from cut trees. We also stock pine wood, preferably taken from tree stumps which have been left in the ground for several years. The material comes from the a nearby forest. We also remember to popularise our experiments – at Biskupin, which is visited by 250,000 – 300,000 people annually, it is an important aspect of our work. The occasion is exploited to increase the awareness of the young generation, brought up on television and computer games, showing them how wisely our forefathers coexisted with nature.

With each new tar and pitch experiment at Biskupin we recollect the instructions and advice of John Coles who, as no other scholar, perceived the advantages and disadvantages of experimental archaeology (Coles 1979, 243–50; 1997); and each time we appreciate how difficult it is to meet the necessary requirements. But only by trying to realise our objectives can we refer to our activities as experiments.

Translated by A. Petrus-Zagroba

Bibliography

Acovitsioti-Hameau, 'A., Hameau, P. & Rosso, T. 1997. Note on the destructive distillation of the wood of *Juniperus oxycedrus* L. In W. Brzeziński & W. Piotrowski (eds), *Proceedings of the First International Symposium on Wood Tar and Pitch*, 269–72. Warsaw: State Archaeological Museum.

Brzeziński, W. & Piotrowski, W. (eds). 1997. *Proceedings of the First International Symposium on Wood Tar and Pitch*. Warsaw: State Archaeological Museum.

Coles, J. 1979. *Experimental Archaeology*. London: Academic Press.

Coles, J. 1997. Experimental Archaeology. In W. Brzeziński & W. Piotrowski (eds), *Proceedings of the First International Symposium on Wood Tar and Pitch*, 307–12. Warsaw: State Archaeological Museum.

Głosik, J. 1969. Biskupin, pow. Żnin. Stanowisko 18, *Informator Archeologiczny Badania 1968*, 214–16.

Kurzweil, A. & Todtenhaupt, D. 1991a. Chemische Technik im Mittelalter. In *Experimentelle Archäologie Bilanz 1991. Archäologische Mitteilungen aus Nordwestdeutschland* 6, 399–402.

Kurzweil, A. & Todtenhaupt, D. 1991b. Technologie der Holzteergewinnung, *Acta Praehistorica et Archaeologica* 23, 69–91.

Kurzweil, A. & Todtenhaupt, D. 1992. "Destillatio per descensum", *Archeologia Polski* 37 (1–2), 241–64.

Modrzewska, H. 1966. Kronika, *Wiadomości Archeologiczne* 32 (1–2), 255–62.

Moszyński, K. 1929. *Kultura ludowa Słowian, T. I: Kultura materialna*. Kraków: Polska Akademia Umiejętności.

Piotrowski, W. 1993. Łyżka dziegciu w beczce miodu, *Żnińskie Zeszyty Historyczne* 8, 53–61.

Piotrowski, W. 1994. First international symposium on wood tar and pitch, Biskupin, 1 – 4 lipca 1993, *Archeologia Polski* 39 (1–2), 182–86.

Piotrowski, W. 1995. Biskupiński mikroregion osadniczy we wczesnym średniowieczu. In W. Niewiarowski (ed.), *Zarys zmian środowiska geograficznego okolic Biskupina pod wpływem czynników naturalnych i antropogenicznych w późnym glacjale i holocenie*, 97–113. Toruń: Turpress.

Piotrowski, W. 1996. The Archaeological Festival, Biskupin '95. In *Experimentelle Archäologie in Deutschland Bilanz 1996. Archäologische Mitteilungen aus Nordwestdeutschland* 18, 117–29.

Piotrowski, W. 1998. The importance of the Biskupin wet site for twentieth-century Polish archaeology. In K. Bernick (ed.), *Hidden Dimensions: the Cultural Significance of Wetland Archaeology*, 89–106. Vancouver: UBC Press.

Piotrowski, W. & Zajączkowski, W. 1991. Biskupin archaeology by experiment. In *Experimentelle Archäologie Bilanz 1991. Archäologische Mitteilungen aus Nordwestdeutschland* 6, 131–38.

Rajewski, Z. 1952. Archeologiczny obóz szkoleniowy w Biskupinie, *Z Otchłani Wieków* 21 (4), 141–46.

Rajewski, Z. 1959. Settlements of a primitive and early feudal epoch in Biskupin and its surroundings, *Archaeologia Polona* 2 (1), 85–124.

Rajewski, Z. 1970. Pech und Teer bei den Slaven, *Zeitschrift für Archäologie* 4, 46–53.

Szafrański, W. and Z. 1949/1950. Wczesnohistoryczna smolarnia z Biskupina w pow. żnińskim, *Slavia Antiqua* 2 (2), 453–85.

Szafrański, W. 1961. *Z badań nad wczesnośredniowiecznym osadnictwem wiejskim w Biskupinie*. Wrocław – Warszawa – Kraków: Polskie Badania Archeologiczne 6.

Szafrański, W. 1997. Die frühmittelalterliche Teerschwele in Biskupin. In W. Brzeziński & W. Piotrowski (eds), *Proceedings of the First International Symposium on Wood Tar and Pitch*, 53–62. Warsaw: State Archaeological Museum.

Todtenhaupt, D. & Kurzweil, A. 1996. Teergrube oder Teermeiler? In *Experimentelle Archäologie in Deutschland Bilanz 1996. Archäologische Mitteilungen aus Nordwestdeutschland* 18, 141–51.

18. The Nature of Experiment in Archaeology

Peter J. Reynolds

The object of the paper is to explore the nature of experiment in archaeology today and to assess its potential role insofar as it may confirm or deny interpretations of data from excavations. In addition, there is an urgent need to define the meaning of experiment and to dissociate archaeological experiments from both education and experience in archaeology.

In 1972, The Butser Ancient Farm was set up under the aegis of the Council for British Archaeology and the British Association for the Advancement of Science. It was designed as a programme for research and education, to focus on the Iron Age and Roman periods. It was, and continues to be, an open-air research laboratory devoted to testing, at a 1:1 scale, the theories and hypotheses arising from archaeological excavations. In the following year, *Archaeology by Experiment* by John Coles was published (Coles 1973). This significant book discusses the nature of experiment and reports on a wide range of archaeological experiments. It was my privilege then to lend some small assistance to John in my capacity as the appointed Director of the Ancient Farm. Since that time, I have been a regular beneficiary of John's unfailing support, gentle but acerbic criticism and ongoing friendship. This paper is intended to supplement and amplify his introduction to *Archaeology by Experiment* after some twenty-five years devoted to empiricism as a research and educational tool.

At the outset, it is a fundamental tenet that experiment has absolutely nothing to do with the exercises of 'living in the past', 'dressing in period costume', 're-enactment of past events' or, indeed, the teaching of well understood techniques – which may well have been originally established by the experimental process – like, for example, lithic technology, pottery manufacture or laying mosaics. The former are at best theatre, at worst the satisfaction of character deficiencies; the latter are simple skills which, should they need to be acquired, require learning. It is extremely unfortunate that these activities have become generally subsumed under the overall title of experimental archaeology since their inclusion militates against the real value of experiment and its acceptance professionally. Labelling an activity like shaving with a flint flake or even a Roman bronze razor an experiment rather than exploration is clearly absurd. It advances our knowledge not one iota and serves generally to increase our prejudices about history and prehistory.

The misunderstanding of experiment in archaeology has been brought about by the confusion of three separate issues: experiment, experience and education. Experiment will be dealt with at length below. Experience is a completely different issue and invariably involves people doing things and discovering for themselves the nature and application of a range of technologies. To manufacture a flint arrowhead, for example, is to experience, learn, and/ or execute a technology. Similarly, to coppice a hazel woodland, to till a field, to mix daub, or to manufacture a pot is on the one hand to come to terms with material, and on the other to appreciate the nature of hard physical work. That all of these and a myriad other activities are of value is undeniable. Indeed they are all the more laudable in that understanding of the requirements of these activities is gained, and thus an increased sympathy if not empathy

Author's Address: Peter J. Reynolds, Butser Ancient Farm, Nexus House, Gravel Hill, Waterlooville, Hants PO8 0QE

with the past is occasioned. There is nevertheless a great gulf between the experimental and the experiential.

Education is necessarily integral to both experiment and experience. The original remit of Butser Ancient Farm was a programme for research and education. Essentially, unless its results are communicated and are therefore educative, research is relatively valueless. Further, the methodology of research itself is a core element of education. Experience is perhaps the greatest and best teacher of all. Ancient technologies are a fundamental building block of the human state. However, experiment is the ultimate arbiter in that it supplies the confirmed material of and for both education and experience.

An experiment is by definition a method of establishing a reasoned conclusion, against an initial hypothesis, by trial or test (Margenau 1950). There is no doubt that experiment is a scientific term and, therefore, it engenders in the lay mind an almost pathological fear of non-comprehension. Experiment is seen to be from the complex worlds of physics, chemistry, mathematics and biology and is, therefore, arcane and, without lengthy training, incomprehensible. Sadly, this is the result of inadequate and uninspired education in most people's formative years. Consequently it is much easier to abandon such complexities to specialists and to rely upon their reports. These reports and findings may or may not influence politics, which is invariably driven by expediency, or the humanities which are similarly driven by fashion and/or religious conviction. Yet the methodology of experiment is extremely simple to understand. Its execution, on the other hand, is often likely to be detailed and demanding.

Archaeology has traditionally been an 'arts' subject and it is only relatively recently that science has begun to have a significant role. The normal pattern of archaeological activity has been, especially in the field of prehistory which is largely uncluttered by documentary evidence, to excavate a site and, within the perceptive knowledge and experience of the excavator, to interpret and publish the findings. It was O.G.S. Crawford who described this process as the 'disciplined use of the imagination'. Inevitably it has become more complex as the data-base has increased and as other subjects like ethnography, ethnology and the physical and biological sciences have made their contributions. Consequently interpretations have become more soundly based but, nevertheless, remain no more than interpretations. Their limitations are necessarily defined by the data, the excavated evidence, its quality and frequency and, not least, the manner of its recovery. The current practice of avoiding total excavation of a site and leaving a sector for future excavation, against a time when techniques are further refined, is a very real recognition of present day technological inadequacy, which in turn is superior to the methodology of even the recent past. It is against this background that any way of examining an interpretation has to be an improvement upon its blind or unquestioning acceptance. Consequently the experimental process actually enhances interpretation.

Its application can be readily appreciated by the following formula. A site is excavated and its product, described as the prime data, is subjected to analysis and interpretation. Rather than use the term 'interpretation' which implies full comprehension, the term 'hypothesis' is substituted. Hypothesis implies a deduced or reasoned conclusion which can and should be further subjected to test or trial to confirm or deny that conclusion. The method of testing is called an experiment. This is built to the specification of the reasoned conclusion using the prime data as the given evidence.

The experiment, therefore, is not an exercise imagined or concocted on an unconstrained basis by the experimenter. It is quite specific to a particular hypothesis and data resource. Partiality, therefore, is removed in principle. However, bias many still enter especially where sampling contains an element of human choice or estimation. Notwithstanding, the ambition of the experiment is not only to explore the hypothesis to its extremities but even to its destruction.

The requirements of an experiment are also specific. The experiment must satisfy the tenets of the academic or technological discipline within whose remit it falls. For example, an agricultural experiment must be acceptable within the disciplines of agriculture and agronomy. An experiment must be replicable and replicated. An experiment should be designed so that the results may be assessed statistically, otherwise the outcome is again little more than subjective or partial.

Once the experiment has been conducted within the above parameters, the outcome is compared directly with the prime data upon which the hypothesis was postulated. If the comparison is positive, the hypothesis can be accepted as valid. If negative, the hypothesis is to be rejected as disproved and, therefore, wrong. Given the focus upon the prime data during the construction and execution of the experiment, in the case of the hypothesis being dismissed as in error, it is often the case that an alternative hypothesis can be formed and subsequently tested. In this context, during the execution of an experiment it is occasionally realised that the experiment will be a failure unless it is altered. However, to do so in the midst of the trial would be to deny the point of the experiment itself. It is necessary to conclude the experiment and thus disprove the hypothesis before embarking upon a changed and, therefore, new experiment which is, in fact, testing a changed and new hypothesis. This new hypothesis is naturally enough the result of an enhanced perception of the prime data, taking account of the new information derived within the experiment.

Thus the formal experimental approach can be seen to be cyclical in form. However, in common with many formulae there is an important corollary. It is perfectly possible, especially given the limited nature of archaeological evidence, to derive more than a single hypothesis from a set of prime data. Nor is it unlikely that a number of such hypotheses could be reasonably validated. This factor itself underlines the significant difference between validity and truth or reliability.

There are further caveats to be aware of in the conduct of experiments, the most important of which is to dismiss the human element. It may seem rather odd to emphasise this point since archaeology is essentially the study of man in the landscape through or at a given time, but it is critical that an experiment is inanimate. No experiment can be designed to enhance our understanding of human motive or emotion in the recent or remote past.

It is also signally valueless to record the time taken to achieve an end product. Time taken may be of mild interest, even wonder, on the part of the experimenter, but that interest, that wonder, is entirely the result of the temporal state of the experimenter. It may have nothing to do with the actuality of the past. This, however, does not deny the significance of the time needed for a natural physical process to be completed. In the simple case of firing pottery, the time taken to achieve the ceramic change from clay to pottery within the context of the variables of kiln type, fuel type and clay fabric is of undoubted interest in that it is independent of human motive and emotion. Almost by definition, experimenters who record human input are recording their own prejudices, efficiency or inefficiency and are, therefore, not conducting experiments on those factors. Similarly those who record their feelings or emotions are recording modern and minor irrelevancies.

Once an experiment has been satisfactorily conducted within all the above limitations and the hypothesis has been validated, the result becomes an accepted 'given'. In the case of disproof there is clearly need for further analysis and experimentation. Thus experiment is locked into the interpretational process. It is a direct check against absurdity and wild flights of fancy, and removes the sometimes ludicrous claims of fashion. However, experiment is significantly associated with the basic hardware of archaeology in that it tests the understanding of the products of excavation. For example, an experiment can only be focused upon the nature of the primary evidence in so far as that represents structure, process and function. It is restricted to the building blocks of interpretation and can only have an influence upon the broad generalisation and period overview. That it can significantly affect these is without doubt. A peculiarity of Roman Britain, for example, has been the so-called Romano-British grain dryer (Morris 1979), which experiment proved conclusively would not dry grain efficiently or economically (Reynolds & Langley 1979). A second hypothesis, that such structures could have been malting floors for the production of beer, was tested and validated. The primary experiment denying the original hypothesis immediately removes these structures from the agricultural process because on the one hand it is a straightforward negative conclusion, on the other it is an important positive component in the consideration of the Romano-British agricultural economy overall. In the coin of interpretation, if the obverse is the hypothesis then the reverse is experiment.

The types of experiment are as naturally diverse as the material evidence they seek to examine. It is as well to realise and underline the fact that the data recovered by excavation, despite it being representative of less than one percent of the original material, is indicative of human activity in all its forms. Therefore, experiment will necessarily draw upon virtually all the sciences in its exploration of hypotheses. In order to simplify the complexity thus implied, it is possible to group experiments into broad categories provided it is clearly understood that these categories are complementary and inter-dependent rather than exclusive. In general terms experiments can be grouped into five categories: the construct, process and function, simulation, eventuality and technical innovation.

The construct is perhaps the easiest of these categories to understand. It is defined as the exploration, at a 1:1 scale, of the third dimension of foundation evidence of buildings and structures. It is exemplified by the examination of prehistoric, Roman and proto-historic houses and structures for which the evidence is only patterns of postholes or simple foundations identified by the excavator as buildings. At this point, however, it is critical to focus upon the purpose of the experiment. If the experiment is to explore a hypothesised structure, then by definition it uses a specific set of data from a specific site. The experiment is thus totally restricted to those data and cannot import further convenient data from other sites. The experiment in its execution explores the adequacy and inadequacy of the prime data and ultimately has the potential to feed back into the prime data features, necessary for the construct, which may have been unrecognised as associated with the hypothesised structure, or wrongly attributed – or even unseen but photographically recorded, and subsequently recognised as critical elements. This site-specific aspect of exploring a construct cannot be over-stressed.

It is ironic that over the last thirty years the building of pre- and proto-historic structures throughout Europe has become a growth industry. By the same token it is extremely regrettable that the motivation for a large number of these buildings has not been a genuine desire to explore the archaeological data from a specific site but rather to erect a generic museological and/or educational resource. It seems rather illogical, if not irresponsible, on the one hand to display and teach a fashionable image, on the other to lose the opportunity of testing a specific hypothesis.

The plethora of European long houses are generally identified by their overall similarity, by their having no specific ground plan as excavated, by their being thatched with river reed, whether the plant is available locally or not, and by their use of secreted 150 mm nails (fulfilling perceived health and safety requirements and the lack of faith of the builder). They are distinguished one from another by their level of internal decoration, by whether their attendants are in costume and playing a role or not, and by whether members of the public are voyeurs or potential participants. It is, no doubt, a reflection of modern society that the primary purpose is not the quest for enhanced understanding of the past but rather an enhanced bank balance. The real tragedy lies in the fact that with greater forethought and planning the causes of both specific experiment and museological resource could be equally served for similar expenditure. In recent years it has become the turn of the Romans to be exploited. It is now possible to bathe Roman-style in Holland and Germany, albeit in bath-houses built of modern materials. Had the Romans had access to modern building materials they would doubtless have used them. Since they did not, it is somewhat perverse to gull the public when it would have been perfectly possible at little increased cost to replicate the original materials and provide a research/academic model as well as a museological theme park. The supporting argument of 'n' thousand visitors and 'x' ecus is fallacious and deceptive.

In this context of experiment, the term 'construct' has been intentionally used throughout. Normally in any discussion or description of pre- and proto-historic or even Roman buildings, the word employed is 'reconstruction' which, in itself, implies for the lay reader if not the professional a spurious degree of certainty. From famous reconstruction drawings wherein wisps of smoke, elemental rainfall and convenient clouds shroud uncertainties (Sorrell 1981), to the certainty of reconstructed roundhouses which inconveniently collapse, the word is misapplied. Ideally its use should be associated with buildings or objects for which sufficient material evidence survives for accurate reconstruction to be possible. In effect, the building of a reconstruction is generally restricted to those open-air museums throughout Europe which seek to rescue exemplary period structures and subsequently present them to the public as specific time-capsules. Sixteenth century farmhouses like the Bayleaf Farmhouse at the Weald and Downland Open Air Museum at Singleton in England, or nineteenth century farm complexes at Szentendre Museum in Hungary are cases in point. When only a ground plan survives, any structure based upon it can only be conjectured and is, therefore, best described as a construct. Similarly such a construct should be quite specifically designed to explore the nature of the ground plan and any adjacent evidence which may not initially be recognised as being part of the ground plan.

However, the above does not deny a role for reconstruction within the experimental process. Indeed reconstruction is a quite vital element. For example, many wooden objects, particularly agricultural implements like prehistoric ards, have been recovered from waterlogged deposits (Glob 1951). To build accurate new replicas or reconstructions of such implements allows functional experiments to be conducted into the efficacy and efficiency of these tools. In fact the results of such trials with such ards have led to a complete re-appraisal of prehistoric agriculture. But this type of experiment falls into the second category, that of process and function. Since by definition this kind of experiment involves a passage of time, it is less susceptible to museological or thematic perversity. Ironically although the term 'process and function' clearly indicates the passage of time, as observed above, one of the least valuable results is that which measures human input. How long it takes to thatch a roof, plough a field, or make a joint, are questions dependent upon human motivation and skill with the tool to hand. Clearly the time taken to achieve an outcome is also subject to the perception of time within a historical context. Modern perception of time is undoubtedly different, embracing as it does a range of contemporary economic and political connotations and denotations contrasting strongly to that of even a century ago.

Process and function experiments seek to examine how things were achieved. One particular example involved the proposition that large pits found on many Iron Age sites in Britain and Europe were used for the long term storage of grain. A long and complex series of experiments were carried out by the author to explore this hypothesis. The experiments were particularly significant since the unsubstantiated interpretation proposed had been used as a major pillar in an argument to compute population estimates, based upon grain consumption per capita and against pit capacity, assuming that a pit had a functional life span. The experiments not only established the methodology of storing grain in underground silos and its efficiency or otherwise, depending upon a range of variables, they also proved that it is possible to store seed grain – that is, after storage in a pit the average germinability of the grain was in excess of ninety percent – and that the pit had an unlimited life. Thus the pit proved to be no more than an innocent container, and storage failure was due not to it becoming contaminated in any way but either to acceleration of the life-cycle of micro-organisms endemic to the grain being stored, or to water penetration, or a combination of both. Thus the experimental sequence, which spanned a period of fifteen consecutive years, validated the hypothesis (interpretation) that certain types of pits could have been used for the bulk storage of (seed) grain but invalidated any argument which sought to establish population estimates. In effect, the results of the experiments broadened considerably the understanding of the potential agricultural economy of the Iron Age (Reynolds 1988).

There is a continuing need for further process and function experiments, especially with regard to implements which currently attract definitive interpretations, as well as with structures which are customarily designated as buildings or features having only a single purpose. In this latter case one only has to consider the standard four-post structure found ubiquitously on prehistoric sites. To ascribe the standard or traditionally accepted interpretation to such structures, that they are overhead granaries, is not only to seize upon a convenient label and thus deliberately avoid potential concomitant data, but also denies the fact that virtually any structure from watch-tower to multi-functional shed can be based upon a rectilinear arrangement of four post-holes. In essence, unless there is a wealth of accompanying evidence of function, experimental studies could validate a whole range of hypotheses whilst confirming none of them.

Indeed, the third category of experiment is specifically designed to address problems of this nature. The overall category is called simulation. In simple terms, the objective is to understand elements of archaeological evidence by projecting backwards from the excavated state to the original or new state and then monitoring the deterioration through time until the archaeological state is reached. While such experiments are necessarily long-term, they are unlikely to require the passage of millennia. A construct has locked within it a simulation trial, should the construct be used and its deterioration observed and monitored. However, the best example perhaps is the experimental earthwork. Several experimental earthworks have been built in Europe this century but undoubtedly the most celebrated are the Overton and Wareham Down earthworks in Britain (Bell 1996). These were designed as linear earthworks with a bank and box-section ditch. Different materials like leather, bone and pottery were located in the bank in order to study their movement, degradation and potential survival. The overall purpose was to observe the erosion of both bank and ditch, through time, with an excavation programme scheduled on a binomial progression of years passed. The thirty-two year excavation of both earthworks has recently been completed. Subsequent to these monumental earthworks, a new series of earthwork experiments was implemented in the early 1980s (Reynolds in Bell 1996). These experiments were designed specifically to examine the nature of the typical domestic enclosure ditch of the Iron Age period. In detail, the nature of the ditch is a V-shaped section 1.50 m deep and 1.50 m across the top. The bank, of dump construction, contains variations of turf retaining walls and turf cores, with and without a berm. The standardised plan of the earthwork is octagonal with a twenty metre length of ditch and bank opposed to each main and intermediate point of the compass. The design purpose is far less complex than the Overton and Wareham Down earthworks, seeking only to monitor erosion and revegetation. The life span will be determined once revegetation is complete and, therefore, erosion has ceased; currently this is estimated at between ten and twenty years. At this point, a full history of the revegetation will have been recorded against a daily meteorological record. Sections will then be cut across each treatment variable, which will provide a working example, where the full history, including extremes, is known, for the field archaeologist to use to interpret excavated ditches.

The pilot scheme to the octagonal earthwork programme was designed only to study erosion episodes, and layer depositions unexpectedly reversed the accepted method of interpretation of ditch sections, in that the skewed layers are most affected by the open (non-bank) side of the ditch.

Because enclosures are found on a range of soil and rock types, experimental octagonal earthworks have been set up on, respectively, upper and lower chalk and the aeolian drift of the coastal plain of central southern England. One further such earthwork has been created in Catalonia, Spain, examining the same questions but against a hugely different climatic pattern and on *marga* rock (a sedimentary limestone) and its derivative soil.

The simulation experiment thus seeks to unravel the problems of how material evidence arrived at the state in which it was found. In practice it provides a paradigm which can be compared with the actual data and, if correlation is found, can elucidate the physical processes involved in creating the data. In addition, in the case of the experimental earthworks, there is an abundance of vegetational and meteorological data which are directly and fundamentally involved in, if not actually the cause of, the physical processes.

Present-day archaeologists are largely oblivious to the above processes and the natural world from which they derive. Thus it is essential to appreciate the need to study the nature of plant communities and their interdependence. For example, the results from the experimental earthworks demonstrate the following plant succession: the early plant colonisers, like the mosses, which cling to bare rock and initiate exploitable niches for other opportunist plants by trapping soil particles; the mid-term colonisers like nettles and thistles; the long-term occupiers, the grasses which, in their turn, will be dominated by brambles and thorns and ultimately provide the habitat for tree seedlings to take root and flourish. The impact of man in using any of these as raw materials must be separately tested.

The vegetation sequence above argues for interference management especially when an enclosure is used for living and working. Brambles, for example, recreate bare earth conditions which will initiate a new phase of erosion, which in turn might be observable in the layers deposited in the ditch. Similarly the snail populations vary against the nature and abundance of the vegetation cover. These and many other questions should have been addressed within the context of the earthwork programme but it is the very nature of this type of experiment which enhances and broadens the perception and indicates future programmes which need to be implemented, in order to understand the archaeological data more fully.

Such observations beg many supplementary questions. Is it possible to extract further working paradigms which will prove eventually what is seen to be happening? To take another example, incident pollen rain unfortunately depends for its survival upon soil acidity levels which are hostile to agricultural exploitation, but nonetheless a search for pollen is worth consideration.

The fourth category of experiment is virtually the combination of the first three categories. Described as an eventuality trial, it seeks to explore the potential product. For example, one of the greatest problems in understanding a prehistoric, classical or historical society is to be able to assess the underlying agricultural economy. Public buildings, fine cities, and complex societies all depend upon successful exploitation of the landscape. It is a truism to record that climate drives landscape drives man. Until recently, man's activities in exploiting landscape were circumscribed by the nature of the local climate and its variability, the underlying geology and the soil itself. Beyond the probably misunderstood technology of decreasing soil alkalinity by the application of animal dung, the farmer of the past was entirely constrained by his landscape and the flora it would bear. Against this background, given that climate has changed remarkably little in the last three millennia, with the exception of minor and relatively short-lived episodes, and that the soil types are also exactly similar, the best example of an eventuality trial is that which seeks to explore the agricultural potential of the past.

Our knowledge of ard/plough technology is considerable and capable of replication. Similarly, from carbonised seed evidence the crops grown, including some of the weeds of those crops, are also known. The landscape exploited is necessarily adjacent to the settlements and is to a very large extent unaltered by the passage of time or even the treatments of modern agriculture. Virtually all the cereals exploited in the remote past have survived to this day and are available, even if difficult to obtain.

For the past twenty years, a series of eventuality trials has been carried out at Butser Ancient Farm seeking to examine the potential of the late Iron Age agricultural economy (Reynolds 1988). The archaeological evidence indicates a full agricultural facility in terms of implements, embracing as it does the rip ard for cultivating virgin or fallow land, the tilth ard which is remarkably successful, even in comparison with modern ploughs, and the seed drill ard which argues for sophisticated plant management. Almost by definition this includes maximising the seed germinability, reducing input and, thus, creating an increased return as expressed by input:output ratio. The presence of hand tools like hoes and the scale of Iron Age fields imply regular plant maintenance within the context of artificial time-reward management, in that most agricultural requirements can be met within one working day. Similarly there is evidence for manuring and, by implication, non-manuring practice, autumn and spring sowing, and even crop rotation of nitrogen-fixing and nitrogen-using plants.

However, in setting up an eventuality trial there is still insufficient evidence for a precise research programme of specific replication. The deficiencies lie particularly in quantity choices – how much manure is applied and what weight of seed is planted per hectare. In consequence, the construction of the eventuality trial requires the establishment of a series of limits against which the variables can be examined. The output variable comprises simply the product, the yield per hectare. The weather pattern from planting to harvest is an input not under direct control. Other input variables are respectively the inputs and treatments, seed and manure, fallowing and rotation, planting times, and soil type.

Of all the variables the weather is doubtless the most significant. Infinitely variable in itself, despite the statistical comfort of averages, the weather has always been and continues to be the primary factor between agricultural success and failure. The farmer's perennial pre-occupation with the weather is entirely justified.

This type of experiment is extremely complex, because of the number of variables involved, and so needs to be repeated over a considerable number of years, a suggested minimum being a decade, not only to achieve statistical validity but also to ensure that all or as many as possible variations of the weather have been experienced within the trial period. Such a trial, for example, would be essentially valueless if run over one or two years. One further important consideration is sheer scale. The field areas involved must be sufficiently large to allow for typicality to be experienced. A field edge, for example, is subject to other important variables than the bulk of the field area, in that greater rooting facilities and inward nutrients may or may not be available. A research plot of a square metre, therefore, can have no validity whatsoever in assessment of yield.

The results of such an eventuality trial need to be treated with the greatest care simply because they are the product of specific combinations of variables. While averaging results through time, especially against climatic variability, may give an overall figure, the average is still specific only to the selected treatments, the weather and most particularly to the soil type. While it might reasonably represent the potential product of prehistory and history, it can only reflect the potential of a specific soil type and landscape. It is perfectly possible to manipulate the figures against different soils and landscapes but not at all sensible to transfer the figures indiscriminately.

In fact, this particular type of trial has been a core research programme of the Ancient Farm since its inception in 1972. To date, two soil types in different landscapes, on one underlying geology, have been examined for eighteen years. A further soil type on a different geology in a different landscape has been under examination for five years. In addition, research outstations in Catalonia, Spain (Reynolds 1997), and Hungary have been in operation for respectively seven and two years. Ultimately comparisons will be possible with appropriate adjustments. In reality none of the soil types, with the exception of Hungary, would be regarded as of the highest quality for cereal growing. Ironically, for the longest trial period, the reverse is the case with the trials operated under the worst possible option. Nonetheless if one averages the results for the worst option over all treatment variables the product or yield is some 2.5 tonnes per hectare, a figure which, remarkably, equates to the national average yield in Britain in AD 1950 (Reynolds 1992). If the experimental results are uprated to incorporate better soil types in less hostile landscapes, the expected yield must surely be larger still.

However, the experimental programme underlined the nature of prehistoric agricultural practice, as perceived, in that it was more comparable to market gardening than the cultivation of 'broad acres'. Input time would have been far in excess of that two millennia later. This does not deny, of course, that the countryside was far more densely populated in the Iron Age, and Caesar's reference to the export of grain in the first century BC is amply substantiated by the experimental results. Perhaps the most significant intermediate result of this ongoing research programme is the complete rebuttal of the proposition that agricultural production in the prehistoric period was at subsistence level and that it was not until the arrival of the Roman influence that commercial viability was achieved. Why this proposition gained credibility is difficult to understand, since the prehistoric agricultural technology of north-west Europe was the same as, if not actually superior to, Roman technology but with the added great advantage of a far better climate.

The fifth category of experiment, entitled technological innovation, is quite obvious if generally unrecognized and unappreciated as an experimental procedure. This kind of experiment describes the testing of new scientific equipment, though not necessarily new within its own designated area, to improve archaeological data acquisition. It also embraces the evaluation of equipment specifically designed for archaeological purposes. In the former case, the classic example is the assessment of the resistivity meter for use in prospection surveys. The initial application, with a device called the Mega Earth Tester, was an experiment. An example of the latter is the magnetic susceptibility meter which was specifically developed to examine the topsoil for traces of human activity. Similarly, recent experiments have been carried out with ground radar, X-rays, thermal sensing and many other techniques which may or may not prove to be of value practically or economically to archaeology. The whole thrust of this type of experiment is inspired by increased awareness of the potential within archaeological data. Especially is this so with the application of methodology from the physical sciences, not least of which is soil chemistry (Clark 1990).

The recognition that the topsoil is an archaeological resource has heralded a new range of approaches, all of which are initially, by definition, experimental. Indeed, an extremely simple experiment in this category was set up to monitor the manner and extent of movement of artificial artefacts comprising standardised pieces of plastic, containing a tiny magnet, placed systematically at 50 mm depth in the topsoil and subjected to modern and prehistoric cultivation practices. Far from the accepted hypothesis that artefacts were infinitely separated from their point of deposition, it was discovered that virtually ninety percent of the material remained within two metres of its start point.

From the above brief descriptions of the proposed categories of experiment, it can be readily appreciated that each and every category is not exclusive of all the others. It may well be simpler and clearer to divide them out for explanatory reasons but it would be quite wrong to regard each category as a stand-alone exercise.

The purpose of this paper has been to define experiment in archaeology and to argue that experiment is an inescapable element of interpretation. Where interpretation is capable of being tested, it should be tested. The testing process itself must be rigorous and should not admit the variables of human motivation. On completion, the test or experiment will provide a positive or negative result. A positive result will validate the interpretation or hypothesis. A negative result will disprove the interpretation, requiring another to be raised in its place. It should not be surprising that the contribution from experiment is most frequently negative. Experiment is necessarily restricted to those hypotheses which are capable of direct examination and have an adequate data-base, not only to allow the initial formulation of the hypothesis but also to formulate the experiment itself. In addition, an experiment must be repeatable, including repetition by others.

Bibliography

Bell, M., Fowler, P.J. and Hillson, S.W. (eds) 1997. *The Experimental Earthwork Project 1960–1992*. York: Council for British Archaeology, Research Report 100.

Coles, J.M. 1973. *Archaeology by Experiment*. London: Hutchinson.

Clark, A.J. 1990. *Seeing beneath the Soil*. London: Batsford.

Glob, P.V. 1951. *Ard og plov i Nordens Oldtid*. Jysk Arkaeologisk Selskabs Skrifter 1. Aarhus: Universitetsforlaget.

Margenau, H. 1950. *The Nature of Physical Reality: a philosophy of modern physics*. New York: McGraw-Hill.

Morris, P. 1979. *Agricultural Buildings in Roman Britain*. Oxford: British Archaeological Reports, 70.

Reynolds, P.J. 1988. Arqueologia experimental: una perspectiva de futur, *Eumo Editorial* (Vic), 85–135.

Reynolds, P.J. 1992. Crop yields of the prehistoric cereal types emmer and spelt: the worst option. In *Préhistoire de l'Agriculture: Nouvelles Approches Experimentales et Ethnographiques*, ed. P.C. Anderson, 384–93. Monographie du CRA no. 6. Paris: Editions du CNRS.

Reynolds, P.J. 1995. Rural life and farming. In *The Celtic World*, ed. M.J. Green, 176–209. London: Routledge.

Reynolds, P.J. 1997. Mediaeval cereal yields: an empirical challenge, *Acta Historica et Archaeologica Mediaevalia* (Barcelona) 18, 495–507.

Reynolds, P.J. in press. Butser Ancient Farm: history and development. Proceedings, World Archaeological Congress, Delhi, India, 1995.

Reynolds, P.J. & Langley, J.K. 1979. Romano-British corn drying oven: an experiment, *Archaeol. J.* 136, 27–43.

Sorrell, A. 1981. *Reconstructing the Past*. London: Batsford.

19. Somerset and the Sweet Conundrum

Bryony Coles

Abstract: This paper looks at the nature, construction method and date of the Sweet Track and considers its implications for the society that built it. For an apparently short-lived structure it encapsulates an enormous amount of work. But seen in relation to contemporary settlement sites in Germany, France and Switzerland where wood is preserved, especially those around the sub-Alpine lakes, the Sweet Track fits into a pattern where structures were not expected to last very long and had to be continually renewed.

Early in his Cambridge career, John Coles was introduced to the Somerset Levels by Grahame Clark, and guided in his early fieldwork by Harry Godwin. The combination of archaeology and palaeoenvironmental research, developed by Clark and Godwin in a series of joint projects since the 1930s, was vigorously applied by John to the particular wetland context of the Levels. In this he was helped by local amateur archaeologists such as Stephen Dewar, who had worked with Godwin, and by the rapid expansion of his own network of contacts amongst farmers and peat cutters. The work of the project that emerged from these beginnings in the mid-1960s is described elsewhere (Coles & Coles 1986). The present paper is concerned with a discovery made early in 1970 by one of the peat cutters, Ray Sweet, and reported to John in Cambridge.

The research which followed epitomises the way in which John's multi-disciplinary, enquiring, active approach to wetland archaeology and its publication ensured that a structure which could have entered the literature as a simple wooden pathway, little more than a footnote to the prehistory of the Levels, became instead known across the world. The Sweet Track, named after its discoverer, entered the Guinness Book of Records as the earliest built roadway, and it has become justly famous archaeologically for the range and detail of information which it holds concerning those who built it and their environment. The paragraphs which follow focus on one aspect, and in doing so may demonstrate one of John's tenets, that wetland archaeology is not a science apart but central to our study and understanding of the past.

From the time of its discovery in 1970, the Sweet Track was known to be early in the sequence of prehistoric structures from the Somerset Levels. It was sealed in the *Phragmites* and fenwood peats which accumulated immediately above blue-grey marine clays, well before any development of raised bog in the area. Godwin had already obtained radiocarbon dates for the peat sequence in the vicinity, in conjunction with the discovery of a stone axe blade; these put the peat/clay interface at 5510 ± 120 BP (Q-423), fenwood peats at 4540 ± 130 BP (Q-430) and raised bog peat at 3880 ± 115 BP (Q-645) and 3975 ± 115 BP (Godwin 1960). The Sweet Track therefore belonged somewhere in the period between *ca.* 5500 BP and *ca.* 4500 BP.

By 1973 eight radiocarbon dates had been obtained for samples of trackway wood and associated peat (Table 19.1), placing the structure in the later 6th millennium BP (or later 4th millennium bc to use the radiocarbon terminology of the 1970s). Associated artefacts such as a round-based pot, leaf-shaped flint arrowheads and a flaked flint axe-blade placed the trackway securely in the mainstream of British Earlier Neolithic material culture (Coles, Hibbert & Orme 1973).

Author's Address: Bryony Coles, Department of Archaeology, Queen's Building, University of Exeter, EX4 4QH

Sweet Track			
Q-963	hazel peg 325	5218 ± 75 BP	4048–3976 cal BC
Q-966	hazel slat 180	5159 ± 70 BP	4041–3936 cal BC
Q-962	hazel peg 303	5150 ± 65 BP	4008–3937 cal BC
Q-991	hazel and ash pegs	4887 ± 90 BP	3784–3621 cal BC
Q-1102	peat beneath rails	5140 ± 100 BP	4040–3900 cal BC
Q-1103	peat packing	5103 ± 100 BP	4000–3790 cal BC
Q-968	peat on plank	5224 ± 75 BP	4149–4058 cal BC
Q-967	peat on plank	5108 ± 65 BP	3993–3915 cal BC

Table 19.1. Radiocarbon dates from the Sweet Track.

The Sweet Track lent itself to a suite of archaeological and palaeoenvironmental analyses, in that the quality of preserved wood and other organic materials, coupled with the sealed context and secure dating, provided ideal research material at a time of rapid expansion in the archaeological sciences (Coles & Coles 1986). Oliver Rackham and Ruth Morgan both studied the Sweet Track wood, with Rackham (1979) suggesting Neolithic woodland management and Morgan rapidly expanding the application of tree-ring studies to species other than oak, and to wood of all ages, resulting in a comprehensive study of prehistoric woodlands and wood use in the Somerset Levels (Morgan 1988). It became clear that the Sweet Track had been built of wood drawn from mature and probably primary forest, from less mature and probably secondary forest, and from coppiced woodland that was probably deliberately managed to produce long, straight rods and poles of ash, hazel and oak.

Morgan's tree-ring analyses further indicated that the bulk of the Sweet Track wood had been felled in the same year. There was some earlier material, the presence of which is still not fully understood, and sporadic later material which was used to repair the trackways. The samples studied included an oak plank felled at least 3 years following the year of building, two ash planks felled at least 7 years later, and a number of hazel pegs cut 8–9 years later (Morgan 1988).

Wood from the trackway was examined to determine the extent of fungal and bacterial attack (Carruthers 1979; Boddy & Ainsworth 1984). Exposed wood is most likely to have suffered fungal attack, whereas track components covered by peat and waterlogged are more likely to have been attacked by bacteria. When first built, the upper components of the track did suffer fungal attack, but this ceased as the wood became increasingly waterlogged or overwhelmed by peat accumulation. It seems, particularly from Carruthers' work, that the period of track exposure was relatively brief, a few years at most. These results are congruent with those of the tree-ring analyses, suggesting that the Sweet Track was built in a single episode, then used and maintained for about a decade, whereupon it was engulfed by the rapidly accumulating peat.

Two further lines of enquiry support this interpretation. Experimental reconstruction of a stretch of trackway in 1983 (Fig. 19.1) (Coles & Orme 1984b) demonstrated that the structure could be built across a reed swamp very rapidly, once the components had been assembled. Revisiting the experimental structure a year later we found it covered and in places hidden from view by the vegetation which had died in the winter and collapsed over it, together with new growth alongside and between the experimental timbers that further obscured them. Morris (1984) and Brown (1986) both studied flints from the Sweet Track for use-wear and residues, and identified a series of flakes which had been used to slash reeds or similar vegetation. The experimental stretch of track showed both that there was a need for regular reed clearance to keep the walkway open, and that once such maintenance ceased the path would soon have disappeared from view.

The Sweet Track was built across 1.8 km of marshland, from the large lias island of Meare-Westhay, south to a much smaller, sandy island known as the Shapwick Burtle. Recent work (Brunning *et al.* forthcoming) has provided evidence for the probable continuation of the route from the Shapwick Burtle to the foot of the Polden Ridge, a further 300 m. The track walkway consisted of longitudinal planks (Fig. 19.2); measurement of plank lengths from excavations at intervals along the route indicates that at least twice as much planking survived as was required for the basic walkway. Pegs, including pegs made out of planking, were also in abundant supply. Tree-ring analyses confirm that almost all of the wood was cut in one episode. The extra wood cannot be explained away in terms of repairs. The over-generous supply occurred at all the sites excavated, from south to north, and the overall picture presented by the Sweet Track is one of profligate use of abundant supplies of wood, whether mature oak, ash and lime or young coppiced ash and hazel, or varied lesser forest species, with occasional supplements of locally-occurring willow, poplar and birch (Coles & Orme 1984a, 15–17).

In 1990, thanks to the combined efforts of the dendrochronology laboratories in Sheffield and Belfast, the floating oak chronology from the Sweet Track was matched to other sequences from southern Britain (Hillam *et al.* 1990). This gave a felling date for the track wood of 3807/6 BC, during the dormant season. For reasons outlined above, the period of use is estimated to have

Fig. 19.1. John Coles at work in the Somerset Levels - seen here with the author building an experimental reconstruction of the Sweet Track in 1983.

Fig. 19.2. Excavation of the Sweet Track, Turbary site, near the centre of the marsh. A longitudinal plank, which slipped from its supporting pegs in antiquity, is about to be lifted.

3806 BC

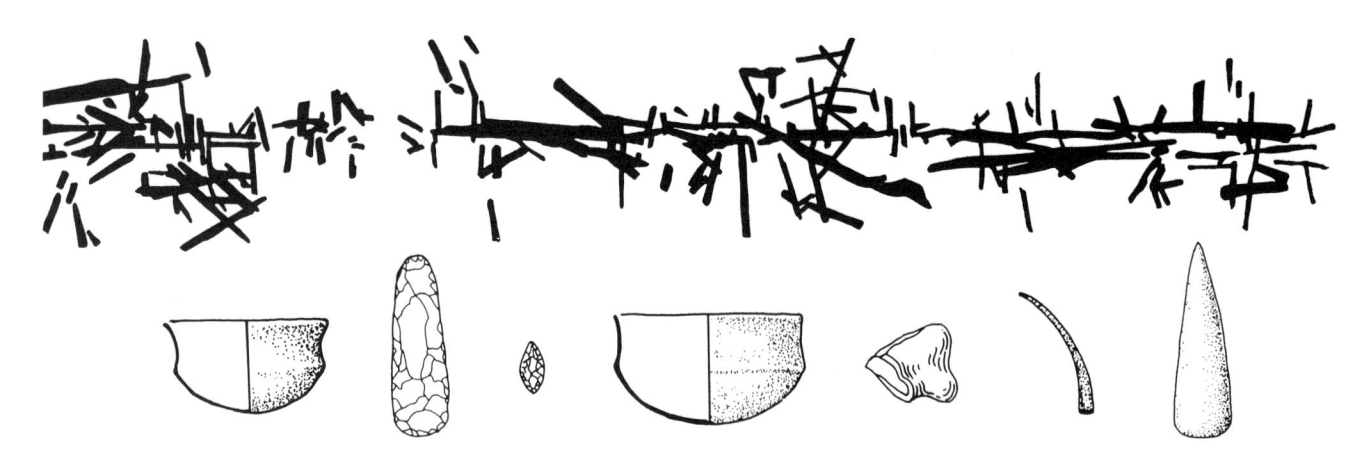

Fig. 19.3. The Sweet Track assemblage dated by dendrochronology.

been about 10 years, 15 at most to err on the side of caution. All the evidence contained in the trackway itself, and all the associated material, can be assigned to this short time-span: 3806–3790 BC (Fig. 19.3).

Why so much effort for a short-lived structure? Felling trees, cleaning the trunks, splitting out planks, amassing pegs and rails, shifting all this wood (twice as much as the basic requirement) from source to building site: was this task undertaken to create something special in the marshland landscape, with a function that was more than utilitarian? It has been suggested, from time to time, that the Sweet Track was a ritual structure with artefacts beside it placed as votive deposits. But to determine whether or not the Track's short life is indicative of a special function, we need to know what was the norm for the period. How long did Neolithic people expect their buildings and other structures to last? What expectation was embedded in their culture for the life-span of such things? Similarly, was the use of woodland resources, lavish to our eyes, no more than adequate as far as the people who actually built and used the trackway were concerned? And was the accumulation of artefacts incidental to the use of the track, or was the track's prime function the deliberate deposition of objects in marshland, from the black, burnished bowls to the pale green, polished jadeite axe blade revealed during the 1973 excavations? These questions are the essence of the Sweet conundrum: to what extent and in what ways is the track representative of its period?

At the time of writing, the Sweet Track is still the only Neolithic structure from Britain with a tree-ring date, although some of the Irish trackways are now dendrochronologically dated to the later Neolithic (Raftery 1990). Radiocarbon dating of British sites, however precise, still cannot match the definition of dendrochronology, and so it is contemporary wetland sites from Europe that provide the first comparisons for a discussion of the life expectancy of Neolithic wooden structures.

At Hauterive-Champréveyres, on the shores of Lake Neuchâtel in Switzerland, trees were felled in the spring of 3810 BC and used to build a house. Later that same year, a further five houses were built alongside. The resulting small hamlet was enclosed with an oak fence in 3801 BC, and in the same year one further house was put up. Several other buildings, a number of them quite small, were added at some stage, but they are not as yet dated. However, their context and the associated material culture indicate exact contemporaneity with the rest of the settlements. From 3810 to 3793 BC there were constant, small-scale repairs to the hamlet. Maintenance then ceased, suggesting that the inhabitants left either in 3793 BC or very soon after (Egloff 1989). The hamlet, exactly contemporary with the Sweet Track, had almost as short a life: probably seventeen years from foundation to abandonment (Fig. 19.4).

Other Neolithic settlements from the circum-Alpine region show a similar pattern of short occupation phases, with constant small-scale repairs. One of the most interesting and informative sites is that of Hornstaad-Hörnle 1A, a village on the shores of Lake Constance (the Bodensee) first built in 3913–3912 BC (Billamboz 1990; Dieckmann 1990; Billamboz *et al.* 1992). Stratigraphy and dendrochronology together indicate that the houses soon burnt down, probably in 3910 BC. They were immediately rebuilt. Maintenance and some new building continued to 3904 BC, soon after which the settlement was deserted. From foundation to abandonment, Hornstaad-Hörnle 1A lasted 8 – 10 years, maybe 15 years at the outside.

Late in the Neolithic, similar short-lived settlements can still be discerned, for example the small farming hamlet at Charavines-Les Baigneurs on Lake Paladru in eastern France (Bocquet 1994). Here, most building was in pine (sapin) which has provided a floating chronology for deciphering the sequence of building and repairs on the site. In addition, a single oak plank has been matched to an oak master chronology for France and Switzerland, enabling the first occupation phase to be placed between 2750 and 2730 BC. Starting with two houses and a few

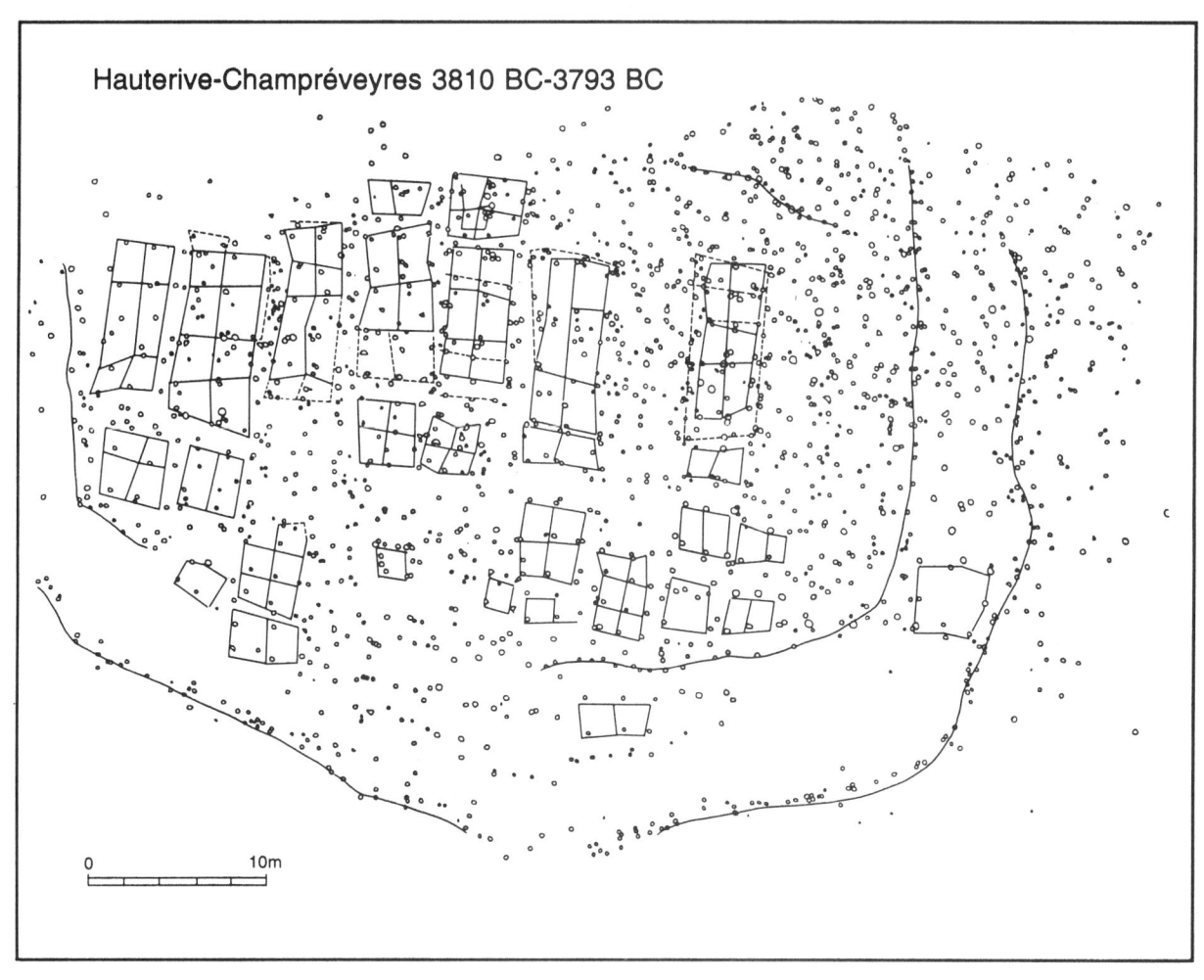

Fig. 19.4. Probable development of the Neolithic hamlet at Hauterive-Champréveyres, based on dendrochronological information.

minor buildings, by Year 4 the hamlet consisted of five houses. The following years saw the usual regular maintenance, rebuilding of one house in Year 9, and a more general re-organisation and rebuilding in Year 18. Maintenance ceased following Year 22, indicating probable abandonment. A sterile layer covering the occupation deposits, together with regeneration of forest cover, evident in the associated pollen diagram, confirms the dendrochronological indication of abandonment. Thirty-six years later, people returned and built a new group of houses on the same spot, the details of which are less clear than for the first hamlet, although occupation appears to have lasted for 21 years or so.

People who built in wood, whose blades for felling and whose wood-working tools were made from stone, built settlements that lasted for 10 to 20 years. Even within that short period, individual houses were re-built and sometimes the greater part of a village was re-modelled, only for the inhabitants to move away a year or so later. There was, it would seem, a generous supply of timber and labour, and an abundance of short-lived structures was

nothing out of the ordinary; in this respect the Sweet Track conformed to the norm.

It will be clear, however, that all the evidence discussed so far comes from wetland contexts, and it may not be representative of the full range of Neolithic building in wood. There is one structure from a dryland Neolithic settlement, built of oak wood, which has been dendrochronologically dated and which provides some insight into what may have been the normal lifespan for wooden structures away from wetlands, albeit still associated with water since the structure is a well.

The Linearbandkeramik (LBK) settlement of Erkelenz-Kückhoven was situated on a loess-covered plateau northwest of Cologne, about 2–3 km from a stream that flowed into the Rur, a tributary of the Maas. The archaeological evidence consists of the usual dryland postholes outlining houses, and typical LBK material culture (Weiner 1992a; 1992b; 1992c; 1994). Pottery typology and radiocarbon dating place the occupation of the village in the centuries from 5300 to 4900 cal BC. Lacking dendrochronology, the history of the village cannot be traced in detail, and it is not obvious whether occupation was continuous or episodic. However, the unexpected discovery of a massive oak-lined well shaft within the village has provided an insight into LBK building practices (and also well-preserved organic artefacts such as agricultural tools, but these are not of immediate concern here).

The dendrochronology of the Erkelenz-Kückhoven well dates the sinking of the first 15 m deep shaft to 5090 or 5089 BC. After a period of use, the well was abandoned and filled with rubbish until, in 5065 BC, it was cleared out and re-lined with new oak planks. In 5050 BC, a third shaft-lining was put in place, only 40 years after the first and a mere 15 years after the second. Although this sequence is not as yet correlated with any phasing of the associated settlements, it may be relevant that it can be divided into the same 10–20 year timespans as the wetland structures described above: 5090 BC construction, 10–12 years use to *ca.* 5078 BC, 10 – 12 years abandonment to 5065 BC, 15 years use to repair in 5050 BC, 10 years use and abandonment soon after 5040 BC.

Returning to the Bodensee, a further strand of evidence for the periodicity of Neolithic structures can be discerned in the pattern of regional settlement around Hornstaad-Hörnle (Fig. 19.5). The pattern includes both dryland and wetland villages, and the combination of dendrochronology, radiocarbon dating and typology on a regional basis enables the occupation phases of the dryland sites to be estimated in conjunction with the precise dating of the lake-shore settlements.

Billamboz has identified a phase of building activity in the Hornstaad-Hörnle 1A (HH1A) wood, which occurred *ca.* 3940 BC, 27 years before HH1A. The evidence is not re-used wood, but the fact that many of the oak posts had begun to grow in that year, their rapid straight growth indicative of shoots springing from the stump of a felled tree. The village site is as yet unidentified, but likely to have been within 1–2 km of the wood source (Coles & Coles 1996, 36–38), which itself would have been no more than 1–2 km from HH1A.

Also preceding HH1A in the region was a dryland village at Moos, where the typology of artefacts including pottery and beads suggests that occupation was very slightly earlier than that at HH1A. Moos should perhaps be placed *ca.* 10–15 years later than the village of 3940 BC, or 10–15 years earlier than HH1A, built *ca.* 3930 – 3925 BC.

Following HH1A, a village was built *ca.* 3900 BC at Hemmenhofen-Im Bohl westwards along the Bodensee shore. Another ten to fifteen years on, *ca.* 3890 ± 10 BC, the village at Gaienhofen-Untergarten was begun (the date is not precise, due to an absence of sapwood). Fifteen years or so later, in 3869 BC, people occupied a site adjacent to HH1A and built the village of Hornstaad-Hörnle II (HH1B, directly overlying HH1A, belongs three centuries later and does not concern us here).

The next lakeshore village in the vicinity and dated by dendrochronology is that of Wangen-Hinterhorn, built in 3825 BC. In the intervening forty-five years, if the emerging pattern is valid and has predictive value, there should have been a further two villages, one *ca.* 3855 BC and the second *ca.* 3840 BC. These could have been either lakeshore or inland sites.

The above reconstruction of settlement history, nine moves from 3940 to 3825 BC, rests on many assumptions, one being that no more than a single community occupied the area and left behind the material under discussion. However, the evidence is of unusually high quality for a prehistoric context, with the end as well as the beginning of several of the occupation episodes being well-dated. The

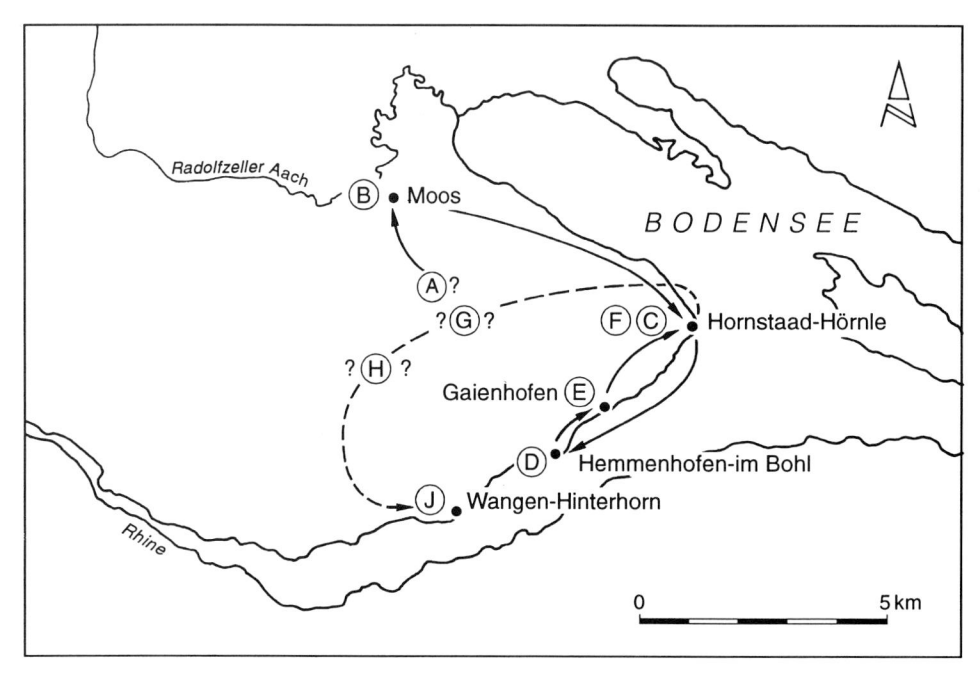

Fig. 19.5. Possible settlement pattern around the western Bodensee, derived from dendrochronological information.

one located dryland site, Moos, benefits from the close dating of ceramic and bead typologies achieved for the wetland sites of the region by a combination of stratigraphy and dendrochronology. Compared to a century of Neolithic settlement history in an intensively-studied but wholly dryland region, the area around Avebury in southern Britain for example, the picture for the western Bodensee and its hinterland is relatively clear, precise and detailed.

To return to the Sweet Track, seen in the light of European Neolithic settlements which are dated by dendrochronology, its ten to fifteen year span conforms closely to a likely set of expectations held by the community of builders: individual wooden structures lasted less than a human generation, and people might expect three or more shifts of settlement in a lifetime. The Sweet Track was not extra-ordinary in respect of the effort of felling and building put into a short-lived structure. It may have been extra-ordinary in other respects; we do not know.

The likelihood of frequent re-building of houses, and frequent new building of settlements, has implications for our understanding of Neolithic forest clearance, the development of woodland management, population size and settlement density, and land-use for crops. It seems possible, for example, that it was perceived shortages of building wood, rather than perceived shortages of arable land, that drove the cycle of settlement shift.

Equally, it seems probable that structures built in earth and stone had an extra-ordinary quality of endurance in the landscape, outlasting houses, villages and humans alike. These monuments perhaps belonged to another world, a world apart, a different sphere of activities, in more ways than the differences obvious to us, the excavators, between a house for the dead and a house for the living. Whittle, from his analyses both of the Wessex regional evidence (e.g. Whittle *et al.* 1993) and of that from the wider north-western European context (e.g. Whittle 1996, 231ff.) in essence makes a similar contrast between "a sparse population..... far from permanently settled" and "enduring built monuments". It is a contrast which may in part explain the frequent re-modelling, expanding, re-building and otherwise tinkering with stone and earth structures.

The very permanence of monuments may have elicited a desire for change amongst those who used them, whose own perceptions may have been that man-made things by their nature required renewal. To make something unchanging was to defy the natural order, a human characteristic of the modern world perhaps, but maybe not shared by our predecessors.

Bibliography

Billamboz, A. 1990 Das Holz der Pfahlbausiedlungen Südwestdeutschlands. In *Siedlungsarchäologische Untersuchungen im Alpenvorland*, 187–207. Mainz am Rhein: Verlag Philipp von Zabern.

Billamboz, A., Dieckmann, B., Maier, U. and Vogt, R. 1992. Exploitation du sol et de la forêt à Hornstaad-Hörnle 1 (RFA, Bodensee). In *Archéologie et environnement des milieux aquatiques: lacs, fleuves et tourbières du domaine alpin et de sa périphérie*, 119–48. Paris: Editions du Comité des Travaux historiques et scientifiques.

Bocquet, A. 1994. *Charavines il y a 5000 ans*. Dijon: Editions Faton.

Boddy, L. and Ainsworth, M. 1984. Decomposition of Neolithic wood from the Sweet Track, *Somerset Levels Papers* 10, 92–96.

Brown, A.G. 1986. Flint and chert small finds from the Somerset Levels. Part 1: the Brue Valley, *Somerset Levels Papers* 12, 12–27.

Brunning, R., Jones, J., Straker, V. and Weir, D. forthcoming. Investigation of a possible southern terminal of the Neolithic Sweet Track, Somerset, *Proc. Prehist. Soc.*

Carruthers, S.M. 1979. Examination of timbers from the Sweet Track for evidence of decay and microbial activity, *Somerset Levels Papers* 5, 94–97.

Coles, B. and Coles, J. 1986. *Sweet Track to Glastonbury*. London: Thames and Hudson.

Coles, J. and Coles, B. 1996. *Enlarging the Past*. Society of Antiquaries of Scotland Monograph Series No.11 / WARP Occasional Paper No.10.

Coles, J.M. and Orme, B.J. 1984a. Ten excavations along the Sweet Track (3200bc), *Somerset Levels Papers* 10, 5–45.

Coles, J.M. and Orme, B.J. 1984b. A reconstruction of the Sweet Track, *Somerset Levels Papers* 10, 107–109.

Coles, J.M., Hibbert, F.A. and Orme, B.J. 1973. Prehistoric roads and tracks in Somerset: 3. The Sweet Track, *Proc. Prehist. Soc.* 39, 256–293.

Dieckmann, B., 1990. Zum Stand der archäologischen Untersuchungen in Hornstaad. In *Siedlungsarchäologische Untersuchungen in Alpenvorland*, 84–109. Mainz am Rhein: Verlag Philipp von Zabern.

Egloff, M. 1989. *Des premiers chasseurs au début du christianisme*. Hauterive: Editions Gilles Attinger.

Godwin, H. 1960. Prehistoric wooden trackways of the Somerset Levels: their construction, age and relation to climatic change, *Proc. Prehist. Soc.* 26, 1–36.

Hillam, J., Groves, C.M., Brown, D.M., Baillie, M.G.L., Coles, J.M. and Coles, B.J. 1990. Dendrochronology of the English Neolithic, *Antiquity* 64, 212–220.

Morgan, R.A. 1988. *Tree-Ring studies of wood used in Neolithic and Bronze Age trackways from the Somerset Levels*. Oxford: British Archaeological Reports 184.

Morris, G. 1984. Microwear and organic residue studies on Sweet Track flints, *Somerset Levels Papers* 10, 97–106.

Rackham, O. 1979. Neolithic woodland management in the Somerset Levels: Sweet Track 1, *Somerset Levels Papers* 5, 59–61.

Raftery, B. 1990. *Trackways through Time*. Dublin: Headline Publishing.

Weiner, J. 1992a. Eine bandkeramische Siedlung mit Brunnen bei Erkelenz-Kückhoven. In *Aus der Geschichte des Erkelenzer Landes*, 17–33. Schriften des Heimatvereins des Erkelenzer Landes 12.

Weiner, J. 1992b. Der früheste Nachweis der Blockbauweise. Zum Stand der Ausgrabung des bandkeramischen Holzbrunnens, *Archäologie in Rheinland 1991*, 30–3. Köln: Rheinland Verlag.

Weiner, J. 1992c. The Bandkeramik wooden well of Erkelenz-Kückhoven, *NewsWARP* 12, 3–11.

Weiner, J. 1994. Well on my back – an update on the Bandkeramik wooden well of Erkelenz-Kückhoven, *NewsWARP* 16, 45–17.

Whittle, A. 1996. *Europe in the Neolithic: the Creation of New Worlds*. Cambridge: Cambridge University Press.

Whittle, A., Rouse, A.J. and Evans, J.G. 1993. A Neolithic downland monument in its environment: excavations at the Easton Down Long Barrow, Bishops Cannings, north Wiltshire, *Proc. Prehist. Soc.* 59, 197–239.

20. Paths, Tracks and Roads in Early Ireland: viewing the people rather than the trees

Barry Raftery

Abstract: This paper considers some of the implications of trackway construction in Ireland, The Netherlands and Germany, including the decision-making process that led to the construction, the choice of materials, and the selection of a particular construction method. Particular attention is paid to trackways at Derryoghil, Co. Longford, and the variation between brushwood, hurdle and plank paths is considered. The great corduroy roads of the Iron Age (e.g. the massive Corlea 1) represent a further development. While communication between groups was undoubtedly one factor, it seems unlikely to have been the only one, given the scale of the operation and the lack of known settlement in the vicinity.

Over the last half century or so large numbers of trackways of prehistoric and early historic date have been discovered and investigated in the raised bogs of north-west Europe, notably in southern Scandinavia, in northern Germany and adjoining areas of the Netherlands, in south-west England and, in astonishing numbers, in the Irish midlands. The examination of these delicate wooden structures has been carried out on an increasingly detailed scale and, as John Coles more than anybody else has shown, they have opened up many new fields of information which are beyond the reach of dryland studies. Wetland archaeology, and the study of ancient bog trackways in particular, is now an established discipline in the wider field of archaeological research, with its own methodology, its own problems and its own research aims. Inevitably, of course, while yielding much new information, this field of archaeological enquiry has raised numerous questions which remain to be answered satisfactorily. The writer's own excavations in Co. Longford bogs in Ireland have made this point emphatically (Raftery 1996).

Research on the trackways, and the bogs in which they lie, informs us of the detailed fluctuations of past climates and of the changing nature of the physical environment in which the builders lived. We learn about their familiarity with the surrounding woodlands and their careful selection of suitable timbers for the various forms of trackway construction.

But there is more, much more. Examining the individual timbers in the tracks, we are constantly impressed by the pristine clarity of the axe- or adze-marks, so perfectly preserved in the waterlogged conditions, allowing us to distinguish between the blows struck by axeheads of stone and those of metal. We can often discern where an axehead jammed in the wood and we can recognise faults in the blade, a slight irregularity in the cutting edge, which leaves its distinctive signature on the wood. We can follow the chopping of a mortice and we can sometimes see where a mistake was made, the premature splitting of an intended mortice or a mortice begun and abandoned, to be recut nearer the end of a plank owing to its initial incorrect positioning. It is difficult to be unmoved by the essential humanity of such details which help to bring us closer to the long vanished builders of the ancient roads. For these ancient tracks are tangible witnesses to the aims and aspirations, to the needs and efforts, of early peoples. These are more than merely artifacts of wood preserved in the clammy embrace of the ancient peat. They are the physical embodiment of the thoughts and the cohesive actions of past communities.

Author's Address: Barry Raftery, Department of Archaeology, University College, Dublin

There is debate today about the theoretical frameworks within which archaeology may best develop. One of the paradigms currently under discussion is the cognitive-processual approach where the importance of the ancient mind is given prominence. Perhaps, in considering the bog tracks, aspects of the cognitive approach might fruitfully be adopted. Thus, the philosophical position of cognitive archaeology, recently enunciated by Colin Renfrew, seems to accord well with the fundamentals of trackway research. As he put it, "one conceives of the past as really existing in a physical world, much like the present, with human individuals living their lives, and interacting with each other and with their environment very much as we do today. In other words, the past really happened" (in Renfrew & Zubrow 1994, 10).

"Trackways represent dynamism, movement and change", as John and Bryony Coles wrote (Coles & Coles 1992, 43). They represent change from passive acceptance of bogs as a barrier to travel to an active determination to overcome that obstacle. And bogs must, indeed, have been formidable barriers to movement in ancient times. The vast stretches of raised bogs, up to 12 m deep in places and dangerously waterlogged, must have appeared as hazardous wastelands to the bog-fringing communities. Moreover, the physical dangers of the bogs might well have been magnified by the supernatural beings, not all of them benign, who were doubtless often perceived as lurking in the shadowy depths. We need only recall the first century Roman poet Lucan's evocative image of "a grove never violated during long ages, which with its knitted branches shut in the darkened air and the cold shade.... From the black springs water wells up and gloomy images of the Gods, rough-hewn from tree trunks stand there.... The people do not frequent it to worship but leave it to the Gods" (Raftery 1994, 186).

It is stating the obvious that the existence of a trackway in a bog is the final outcome of an initial decision that a trackway was to be built. But behind this basic decision a hierarchy of thoughts, needs and actions is implied. Was it an individual or a group of individuals who came together to decide that a track should be constructed and how was the decision arrived at? We can obviously never know but it might be that the differing dimensions of the trackways built, the varying complexity of their construction and the implied variation in the level of manpower required allow us to distinguish between what was of more localised agricultural significance and what was built in a wider, tribal context.

The decision had, however, first to be arrived at. There are varied reasons why a trackway should be built but in the final analysis the decision must be based on the premise that the effort involved in building the track was justified by the expected return, whether in economic, social or even, possibly, in spiritual terms. We must assume that the ancient agricultural communities did not have the luxury or the time to build follies! The construction of a trackway across a bog (assuming that military conquest was not a normal motivation) also presupposes that there was agreement between the peoples living on opposite sides of the bog on the desirability of the project. Again we might wonder if there was consultation between the two groups, whether some sort of formal acceptance was necessary and to what extent the work of building was shared.

Trackway construction, at any rate, represents communal effort. Clearly, the larger and more elaborate the track the greater the numbers involved and the greater the effort. For the building of a track requires organisation and planning – perhaps years ahead if forest management and the stockpiling of resources are taken into account. An efficient system of transport is also necessary, for the larger tracks at least, as timbers often had to be carried, or dragged, considerable distances. An intimate knowledge of the various available tree species is also implied. At times, too, woodworking skills of no small competence are also in evidence. Thus, in the differing scales of trackway construction, we may postulate degrees of communal effort ranging from the extended family to the tribe. They are, at any rate, indications of social cohesion with the common good being the motivating factor.

In some cases, as noted in the Netherlands and Germany, it is evident that trackways across bogs are part of wider, regional networks of communication (Hayen 1989, 68–9). This is scarcely possible to demonstrate with any conviction for Ireland, however likely it is that such must often have been the case. Abroad, however, the oft-quoted Trackway XLII in the Wittemoor in Lower Saxony, a 3 km long routeway of corduroy construction dating to 135 BC may well, as Hayen suggested, have been built to transport heavy loads of iron ores northwards to the navigable river Hunte along which the ores were further transported by boat to the river Weser and beyond (Hayen 1971a, b). There are indications, too, that trackway maintenance and repair were strictly regulated. Here the clear impression is that the track is an intrinsic element in a complex, integrated social and economic infrastructure.

A seventh century account, in Cogitosus' *Life of St Brigit*, illustrates well the tribal context of togher construction in early historic Ireland:

"Once an edict of the king of the country where she was living came into force throughout the *tuatha* and provinces which were under his jurisdiction and dominion, to the effect that all the peoples and *tuatha* should come together from all the territories and provinces and build a solid wide road. They were to lay a foundation of tree branches and rocks and some very solid earthworks in the deep and virtually impassable bog and in the sodden and marshy places through which a large river ran so that, when it was built, it could bear the weight of charioteers and horsemen and chariots and wagonwheels and the rushing of people and the clash of enemies from all sides..." (Connolly & Picard 1987, 23).

Comparable scenes might well have taken place in Ireland in the prehistoric period.

It is, nonetheless, reasonable to assume that most tracks across bogs had a more modest function and were to enable the local farming communities surrounding the bogs to communicate with one another for purposes of trade and exchange and for the varied acts of social intercourse. Commonest were the simple tracks of longitudinally placed brushwood bundles. Such constructions are virtually timeless, their form unchanging over the millennia. Brushwood was readily available, close at hand and easily harvested. A walking surface of tightly packed rods and branches of hazel or birch floated comfortably on the waterlogged bog and would, for a few years, have given a safe, dry walking surface for pedestrians and the more substantial examples would doubtless for a time have supported, in addition, the weight of animals.

Unusual in this regard is Trackway 19 at Derryoghil, Co. Longford, a trackway spanning the late second and early first millennia BC (Raftery 1996, 145ff.). Uniquely, this track had a large plank of ash, 45 cm in width and more than 2 m long, incorporated into its length (Fig. 20.1). At its surviving, carefully squared, end a pair of rectangular mortices was present. This plank was obviously not primarily intended to form part of a brushwood track. It may have come from a trackway of more substantial construction, or from some other structure. But it must have been conveniently available to the builders of the brushwood track who decided to use it in the more ephemeral structure however inappropriate this action might at first sight appear. Thus, in this instance, the individual preference of the builders overruled any perceived norms of orthodoxy or crude functionality which might have prevailed.

In some cases there are indications that rods for such tracks came from coppiced stands. While the problems associated with the recognition of true coppicing in the surviving record are well known, it is evident that where it can be reliably recognised it is an indication of organisation and planning on the part of the local inhabitants. It should not, however, be assumed that such coppicing was solely to produce the raw materials for trackway construction. Coppiced rods would have had a myriad of uses within the community, for fencing, for the wattle walls of houses, for baskets, fish-traps and other purposes.

Hurdle tracks (e.g. Raftery *op. cit.*, 158 ff.; 165ff.; 213ff.) were also often, though not always, constructed of coppiced rods. The advantages of a hurdle track over a simple brushwood example are not entirely clear though perhaps they were less liable to unravel and they would have been quicker to lay down once the hurdles were woven. Indeed, it is possible that their capacity for rapid dismantling in times of danger could have been an additional consideration in their construction. They were, at any rate, tough and durable with a surprising load-bearing capacity. Recent experiments have shown that hurdles placed on a wet bog could support the weight of a horse and rider (Raftery *op. cit.*, 457).

Plank footpaths involved a greater level of preparation than in the case of the brushwood tracks (e.g. Raftery *op. cit.*, 65ff.; 215ff.). Careful splitting of the timbers to provide the necessary planks was required, and substructural supports, and sometimes pegs, had also to be provided. Single plank paths must have been only for pedestrians but when two or more planks were placed together, such as the fine example from Meare Heath in Somerset (Coles and Coles 1986, 119, Fig. 29), or the elaborate examples excavated by Casparie in the Netherlands (e.g. Casparie 1986, Fig. 19), animals could have easily been accommodated, to say nothing of the increased security and ease of movement for travellers on foot.

Tracks of longitudinal poles, at their simplest, represent the most basic form of trackway construction. Some, such as the Middle Bronze Age example at Klazienaveen-Noord in the Netherlands (Casparie 1984) were of straight, regularly-laid poles, on transverse supports, carefully secured in position by lateral pegs. But some of the Late Neolithic/Early Bronze Age examples excavated in Derryoghil bog, Co. Longford in Ireland (e.g. Raftery *op. cit.*, Figs 207–8) seem so casually constructed as to demand very considerable feats of acrobatic balance on the part of those nimble and sure-footed people intrepid enough, and sober enough, to venture along them. Yet however flimsy and inadequate we consider such trackways today, these were conceived and constructed by prehistoric peoples in midland Ireland with a specific purpose in mind and were doubtless deemed adequate to fulfil that purpose.

Again and again in the trackways we encounter examples of human idiosyncracy, of the individual preference and choice of the individual mind. The well-known Sweet Track in Somerset is such an example (Coles & Coles 1986, 41–64). This, the oldest reliably dated trackway in the world, is a construction of very considerable technical sophistication which must represent the unique, unprecedented genius of a Stone Age farmer. Nobody else again attempted quite the same method of construction. An individual, too, was responsible for the planning and construction of Trackway 10 in Derryoghil, Co. Longford, dating to the mid-second millennium BC (Fig. 20.2; Raftery *op. cit.*, 132–6)). There the basic construction principle is corduroy, yet the rods employed, at least in most of the excavated section, were little more than brushwood rods carefully cut to the required lengths. Laying these edge-to-edge in transverse positions on a substructure of longitudinal brushwood was a far more laborious and time-consuming effort than would be the case of simply laying down brushwood in longitudinal bundles. The practical advantages of such a constructional approach seem only meaningful if wheeled transport is involved. Can we thus see Derryoghil 10 as evidence for precociously early wheeled transport in Ireland? Few, if any archaeologists, would favour such an explanation. We must thus view D10 as the decision of an individual builder to construct a more

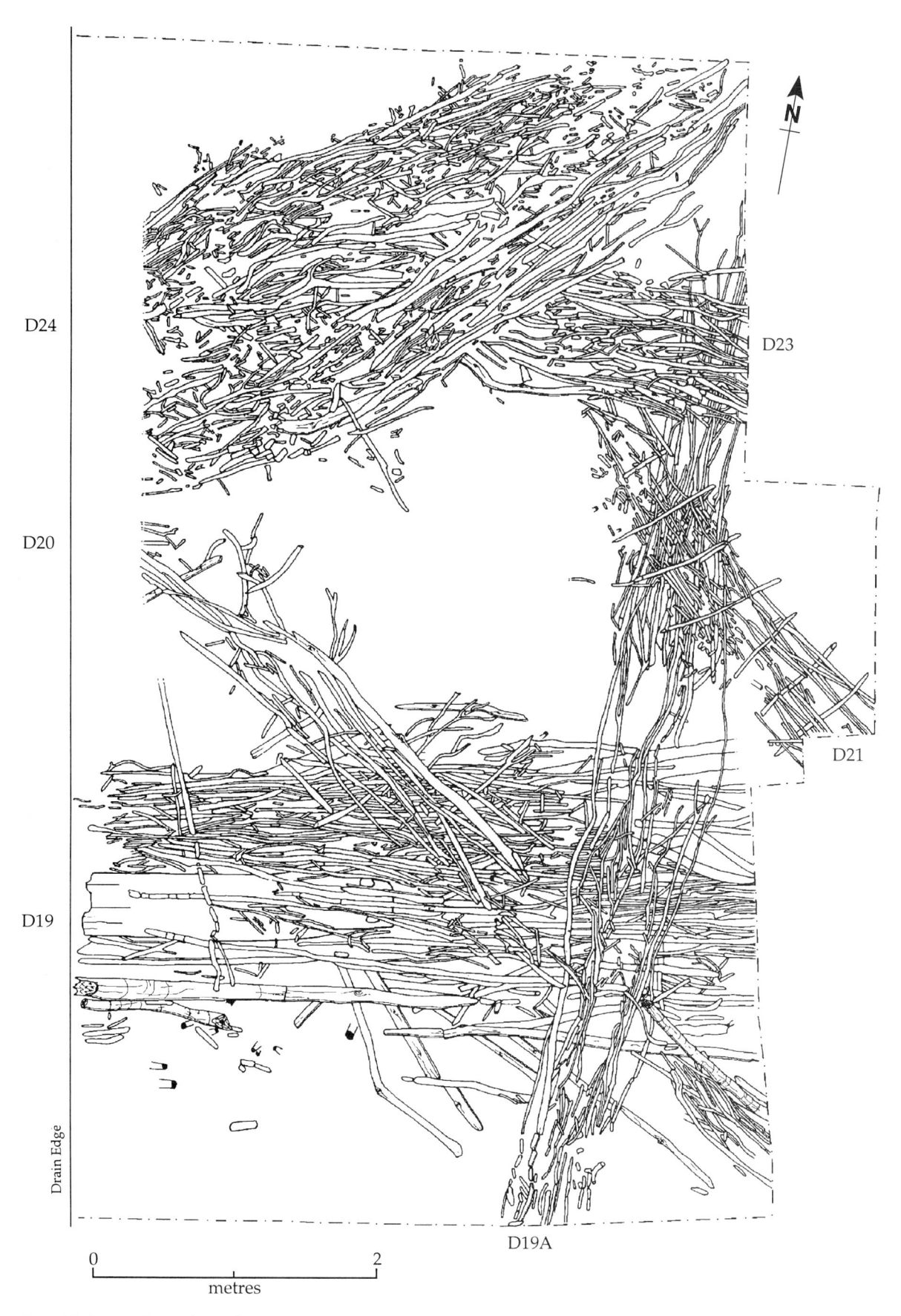

Fig. 20.1. Brushwood trackways, Derryoghil, Co. Longford. Mortised plank visible in western end of D19.

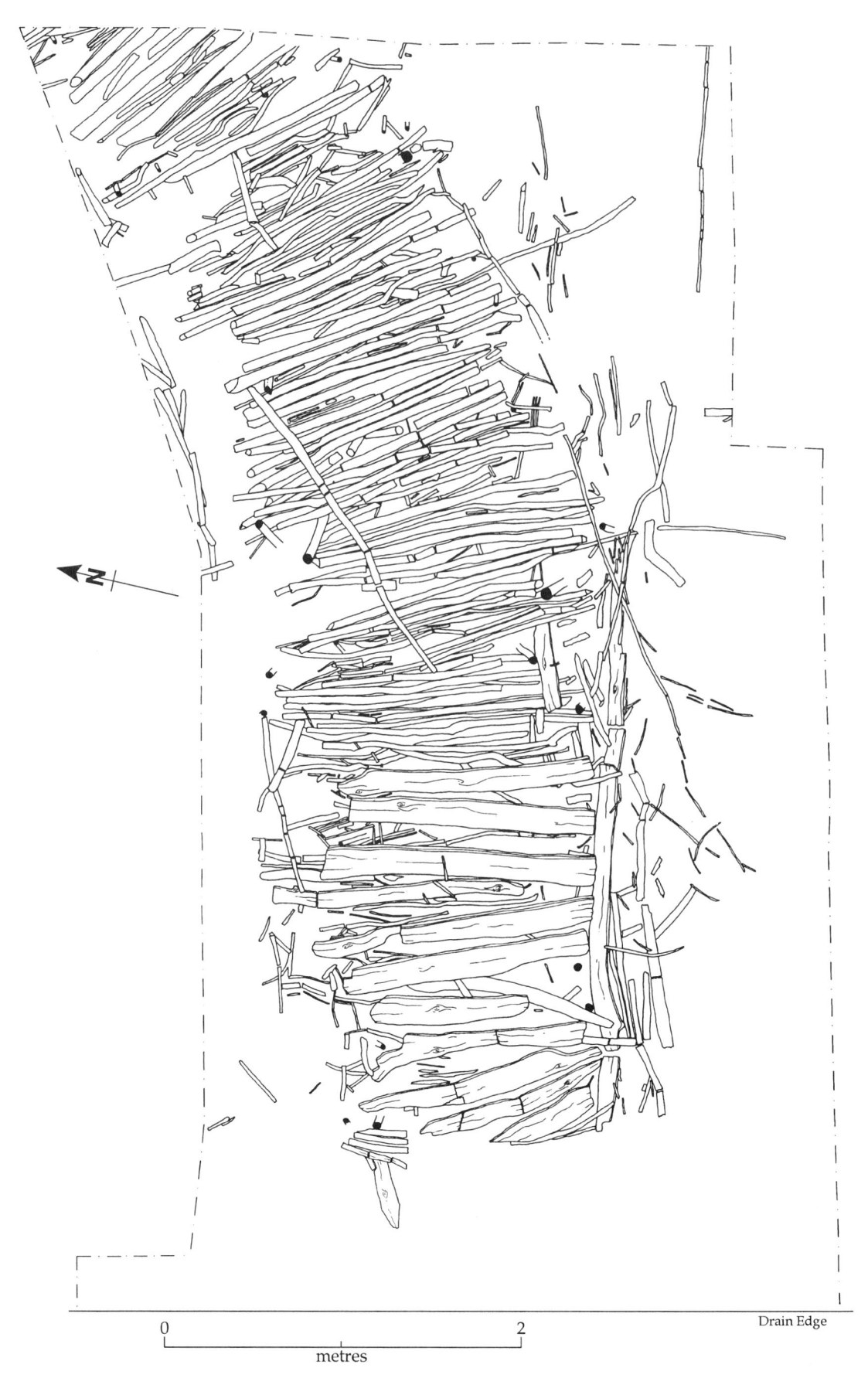

Fig. 20.2. Trackway 10, Derryoghil, Co. Longford.

elaborate and stylish trackway, perhaps to enhance his prestige and impress his neighbours.

The larger tracks of corduroy construction present us with different questions of function and purpose. As early as the late fourth and early third millennia BC, substantial trackways of this form are recorded from north Germany (e.g. Fansa & Schneider 1993) and there their purpose is clear. Associated wheels and fragments of carts indicate without question that these early constructions were built to bear the passage of vehicular transport. Indeed, Hayen argued plausibly that the subsequent development of the corduroy road in north Germany was directly associated with, and influenced by, the improvements which took place in wheeled transport there over the centuries (Hayen 1991). In the Netherlands, too, in the mid-third millennium BC, the Nieuw Dordrecht track, also a corduroy construction, was similarly built with carts in mind, for wheels were found in direct association with it (Casparie 1982).

But what of the early corduroy roads in Ireland? Cloonbony (Raftery *op. cit.*, 180 ff.) and Corlea 6 (Raftery *op. cit.*, 71ff.) were both third millennium BC constructions, while Derryoghil 1 (Raftery *op. cit.*, 107ff.) belonged to the tenth century BC. All three are significant trackways. All are 2 to 2.50 m in width. Cloonbony extended for a distance of 1 km across the bog, Corlea 6 was at least 750 m long and Derryoghil 1 was only slightly shorter. In each instance some 5 hectares of woodland were needed to provide the necessary timber. All three thus represent a very substantial expenditure of manpower, materials and time. But why build such large tracks? If we once more rule out wheeled transport – as surely we must at these early dates – what explanation remains to us? Pedestrians do not need such massive constructions. Are we to think of large-scale cattle herding across the bogs? This too seems an unconvincing argument, for such could have been easily facilitated by far less impressive tracks. Thus we are led to explanations in the sphere of status and prestige or perhaps even in terms of some ritual context impossible for us to understand today. Or should these sizeable tracks be viewed as expressions of power by tribal rulers seeking to proclaim their authority to the world in a visible and ostentatious way?

The latter certainly seems to be the case with the great Iron Age structure Corlea 1 (Raftery *op. cit.*, 7ff.). Here we have a huge trackway – in fact a road – almost 4 m wide and extending in all, over two stretches of bog, for a total of some 2 km. Clearly this must have been intended for wheeled vehicles, for the wheel was undoubtedly known in Ireland by this time. But wheels alone will not explain its prodigious size. This road was a massive undertaking which, for a period, must have drained the resources of almost an entire community. At least 375 mature oak trees, the produce of some 10 hectares of woodland, were needed to provide the timber for this road. The oak forests, some kilometres distant from the bog, must for a time have been filled with work teams felling the trees, cutting the great trunks to the required lengths, splitting them with mallets and wedges, chopping mortices in their ends and transporting the heavy timbers to the bog. Substructural roundwoods had also to be prepared and also the many thousands of sharpened pegs which were needed to anchor the oak sleepers in position.

This was the greatest prehistoric road in Europe, an ancient wonder. It was truly a colossus of roads. But why build it in the centre of Ireland, a small island clinging to the Atlantic fringe of Europe? Inevitably again, as with the earlier corduroy roads, it seems that explanations in terms of simple functionality will scarcely suffice. Ireland in the second century BC was in the throes of major cultural changes as a lengthy phase of seeming cultural stagnation was at last giving way to change and innovation. New influences from the world of the La Tène Iron Age were beginning to appear in the land. Not just new and spectacular metalwork was appearing but also there is evidence that a phase of major building was in train in these critical, final centuries BC. The construction of the impressive "40 metre" structure on the summit of Navan Fort in Co. Armagh took place at this time (Lynn 1986), as did the building of the great linear earthworks known as the Dorsey in south Armagh (Lynn 1982; 1989; Baillie 1988; Baillie and Brown 1989). Radiocarbon dates for an excavated stretch of the linear earthwork known as the Black Pig's Dyke in Co. Monaghan also indicate its erection in this period (Walsh 1987), and another stretch, the Doon of Drumsna in Co. Leitrim, was also broadly contemporary (Condit & Buckley 1989).

This is the context in which the Corlea road fits. Perhaps a phase of expansion and development was taking place, perhaps the development of tribal areas and the flexing of the muscles of strong rulers, jostling for power and anxious to proclaim, in tangible and monumental form, their claims to tribal greatness.

It is strange that there is virtually no evidence of human occupation in the Irish midlands contemporary with the Corlea road. There can be little doubt, however, that an entire tribe was involved in its construction. This mighty road thus gives us detailed insights into an otherwise invisible and forgotten people.

The construction of this Corlea road (and its extension in the neighbouring Derraghan bog) followed a consistent pattern along most of its length, but the excavation revealed frequent gaps in the superstructure. Sometimes the gap was the width of no more than one or two planks, but there were places where there were several metres devoid of any of the surface timbers. Not infrequently their former presence was marked by *in situ* pegs. How should we explain such gaps? Did differential rotting take place – which seems unlikely – or were individual timbers deliberately removed? And if so, were they removed for re-use elsewhere, or by enemy forces to damage communications or by the builders themselves to impede movement along the road by persons deemed to be unwelcome or hostile?

In two places the arrangement of the road timbers was particularly curious. In Cutting 14 there were very substantial gaps in the upper surface of the road and several of the partially surviving planks displayed evidence of extensive burning (Fig. 20.3). In addition, a number of plank sleepers lay together at one point in longitudinal rather than transverse positions. It is difficult to avoid the conclusion here that serious hostile action had taken place at some time not long after the construction of the road, rendering it impassable. There then followed an attempt to re-open the roadway for pedestrians by relaying some of the disturbed sleepers along the axis of the road.

Even more curious, and less readily explicable, is the situation encountered in Cutting 4 (Fig. 20.4). In the east of this cutting, a strange jumble of timbers was found which was otherwise unprecedented in the course of the modern excavations. Here layer upon layer of complete and fragmentary hewn oak planks were found, for the most part piled upon one another rather haphazardly in longitudinal arrangement. Many of these displayed traces of intensive burning. On top of these, also lying longitudinally, were long, straight roundwoods which can only have been intended as substructural runners. Along this heavily disturbed stretch there were very few pegs which might have marked the positions of regularly laid transverse sleepers.

What can we make of this anomalous stretch of Iron Age roadway? The burnt timbers suggest that deliberate destruction took place. But if this was so then there must have been an episode of systematic dismantling which was carried out with quite exceptional thoroughness. For, if this model is pursued, the positions of the timbers as revealed in the excavation would indicate that both upper and lower timbers were carefully lifted before being thrown back again casually into the bog, with the sleepers below and the original, substructural runners above.

Would people, however hostile was their intent, have gone to such trouble? If not, are there other explanations? Perhaps we should regard this curious stretch of road as indicating that the entire structure was unfinished, and here it is fascinating to remember that the famous description of the building of a large bog trackway in The Wooing of Étain, an eighth or ninth century Irish tale, ends with the road unfinished because of the disgruntlement of the workers (ÓhÓgáin in Raftery *op. cit.*, 359). This is thus a possible, but by no means an entirely satisfactory, explanation. Deliberate, systematic destruction, though it fails to answer all the questions, remains the least implausible answer.

Thus far consideration has been given to tracks which manifestly crossed from one side of a bog to the other. This is not, however, a universal phenomenon. The excavations in Co. Longford revealed a number of trackways which led from the dryland edge no more than 20 or 30 m into the bog before coming to an abrupt halt. This was particularly well illustrated in the two tracks at Annaghbeg (Raftery *op. cit.*, 165 ff.), especially in the stretch of trackway Annaghbeg 2, which was composed of three magnificently woven hurdles. In some cases this might be interpreted as resulting simply from a desire to cross the wetter zone fringing the bog, as has been noted elsewhere (e.g. Fansa 1992). The same principle is involved in the short discontinuous stretches of trackway which are not infrequently encountered within bogs, for these were surely intended to bridge particularly wet patches in otherwise passable bogland (e.g. Coles & Orme 1977, 11). The single hurdle Derryoghil 5 probably performed a similar function (Raftery *op. cit.*, 125ff.).

But at Derryoghil there was a remarkable concentration of trackways, at times as many as seven or eight in number, which were placed side by side, at precisely the same level in the bog and as little as 1 m or less distant from each other. There seems little doubt that these trackways, generally of longitudinal brushwood construction, were laid down at the same time (Figs 20.5, 20.6; Raftery *op. cit.*, 137 ff.). What motivated the builders of these tracks? Were they intended in some way to enable large numbers of people simultaneous access to the bog? Was there some ritual motivation involved? Or was there a more prosaic, mundane purpose behind the building of these multiple trackways? An answer to this problem is not readily apparent.

There are other areas of Europe where trackways extend deeply into, but not across, bogs. In the Netherlands, for example, Casparie has related the extension of the second century BC Emmerschans trackway into the middle of the Bourtanger Moor to the extraction of iron ore from the bog (Casparie 1986, 204–6), and he has regarded in a similar light a number of earlier structures one of which produced an iron chisel on its surface (Casparie 1984). Not so easily explained, however, is the Neolithic Nieuw Dordrecht trackway which ran for a distance of only 1 km into a 13 m wide bog. Was it simply unfinished or could it have served some unspecified votive purpose bringing people into the bog to carry out ritual acts? Yet again the question remains unanswered. Here we may call to mind, however, the so-called 'Römerstrasse' in southern Bavaria, a corduroy track of probable late Urnfield date (Schmeidl & Kossack 1967–68). It too led into, and not across, the bog, yet in this instance it was clearly evident that it had seen extensive use as there was a pronounced hollow worn centrally along its length. It appeared as if there had been heavy pedestrian traffic along it and the excavator wondered if its orientation on a small lake in the bog, known as the Weiher, might have been the destination of those using the roadway.

Equivocal, too, is the purpose of those trackways which do not extend across the width of the bog but rather run along its length. Several examples of this type were encountered in the course of the Co. Longford excavations. In each case only short stretches were uncovered, but these were, in every instance, deliberately and carefully constructed. Do they represent intra-bog communications, or links within the bog between stretches of more orthodox trackways? The strange complex of tracks D19 to D24 in Derryoghil bog (Fig. 20.1; Raftery *op. cit.*, 145 ff.)

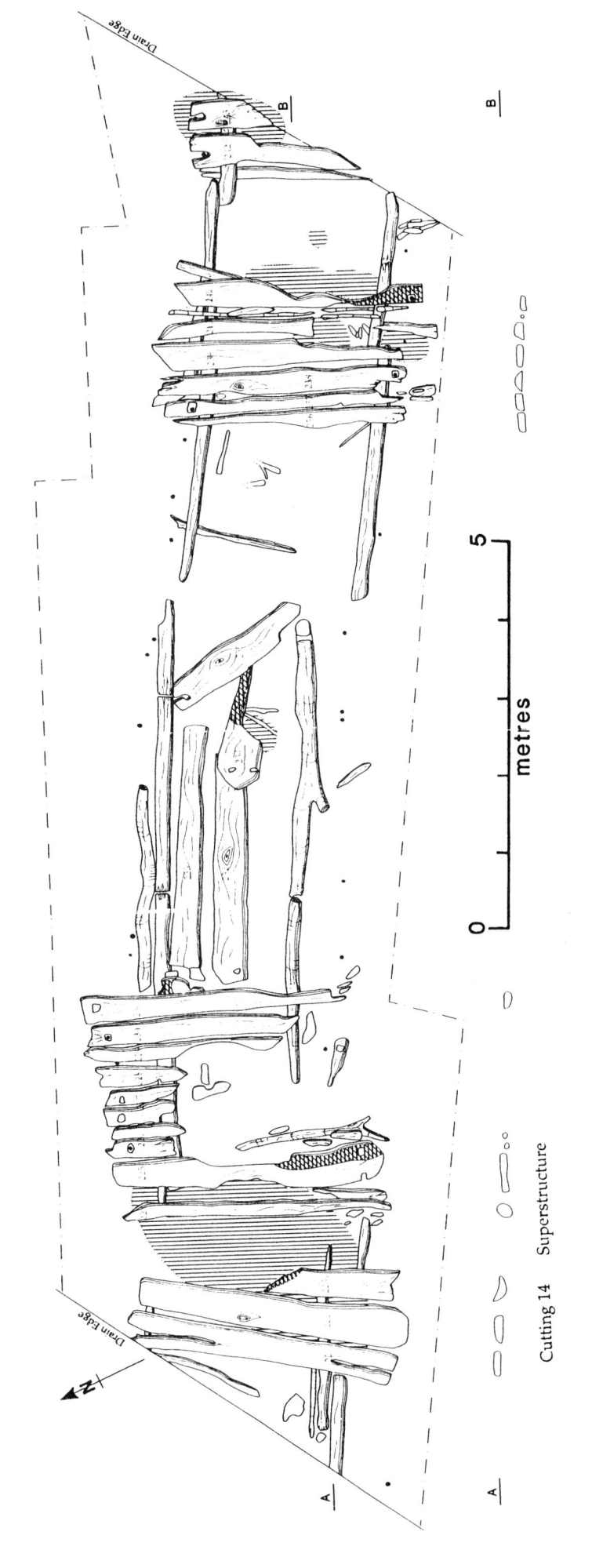

Fig. 20.3. Trackway 1, Corlea, Co. Longford. Heavily disturbed section in Cutting 14. Burnt zones are indicated by cross-hatching.

Fig. 20.4. Trackway 1, Corlea, Co. Longford. Heavily disturbed section in Cutting 4. Burnt zones are indicated by cross-hatching.

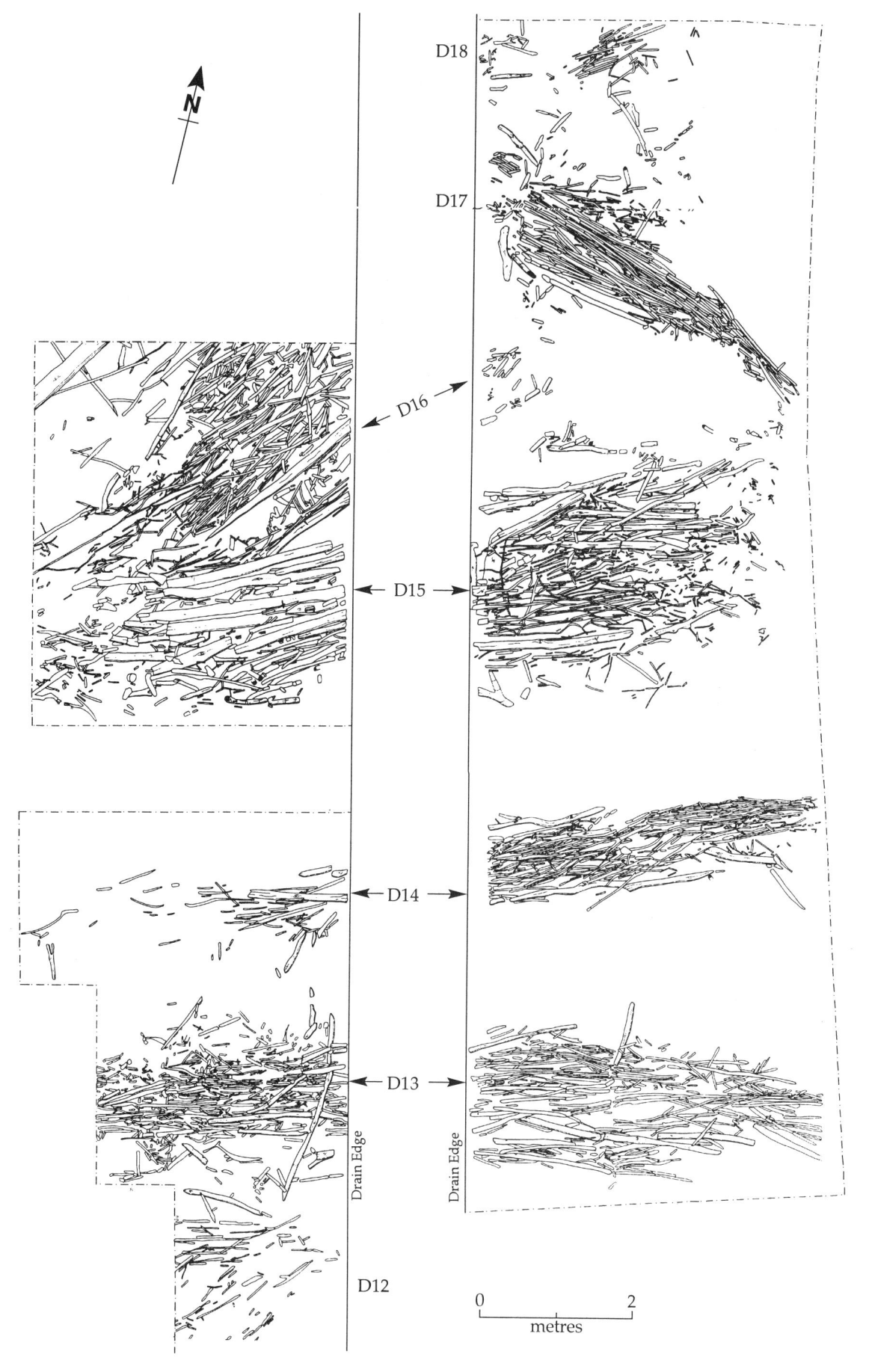

Fig. 20.5. Brushwood trackways, Derryoghil, Co. Longford.

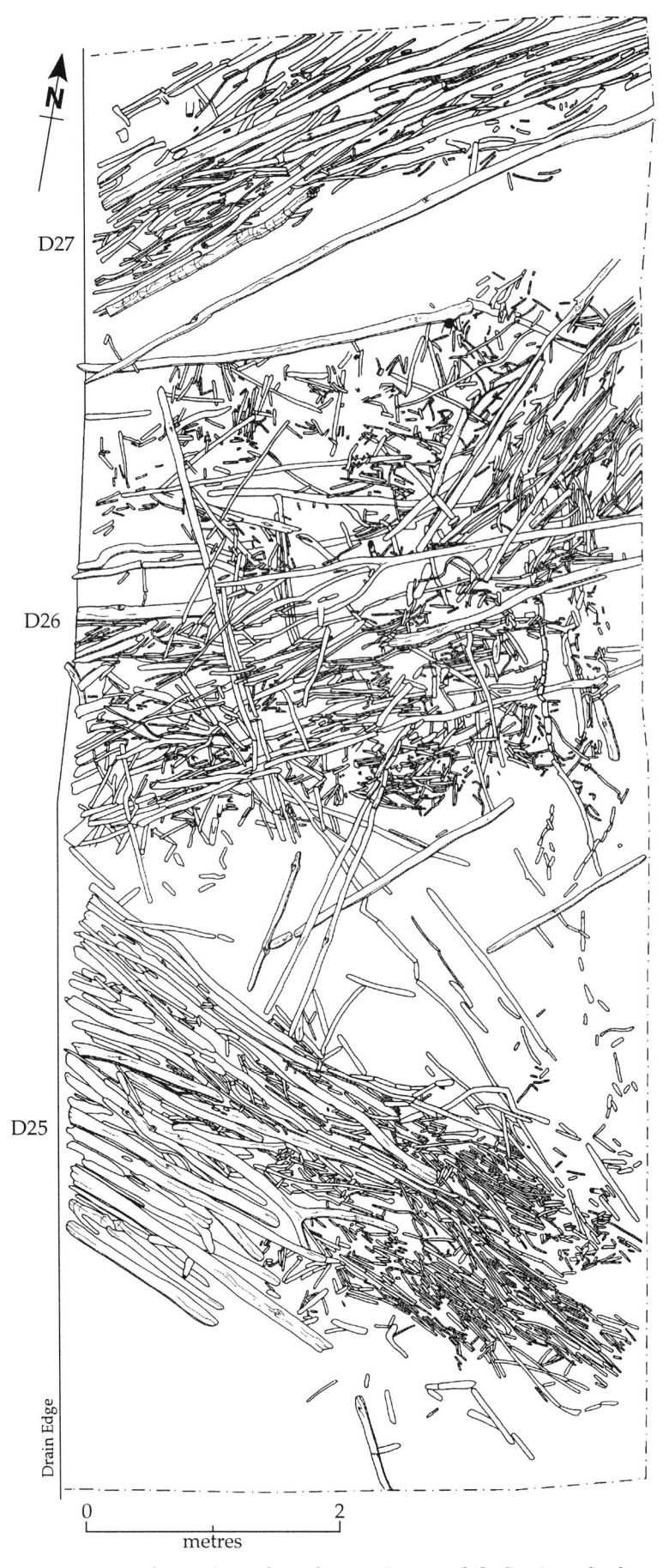

Fig. 20.6. Brushwood trackways, Derryoghil, Co. Longford.

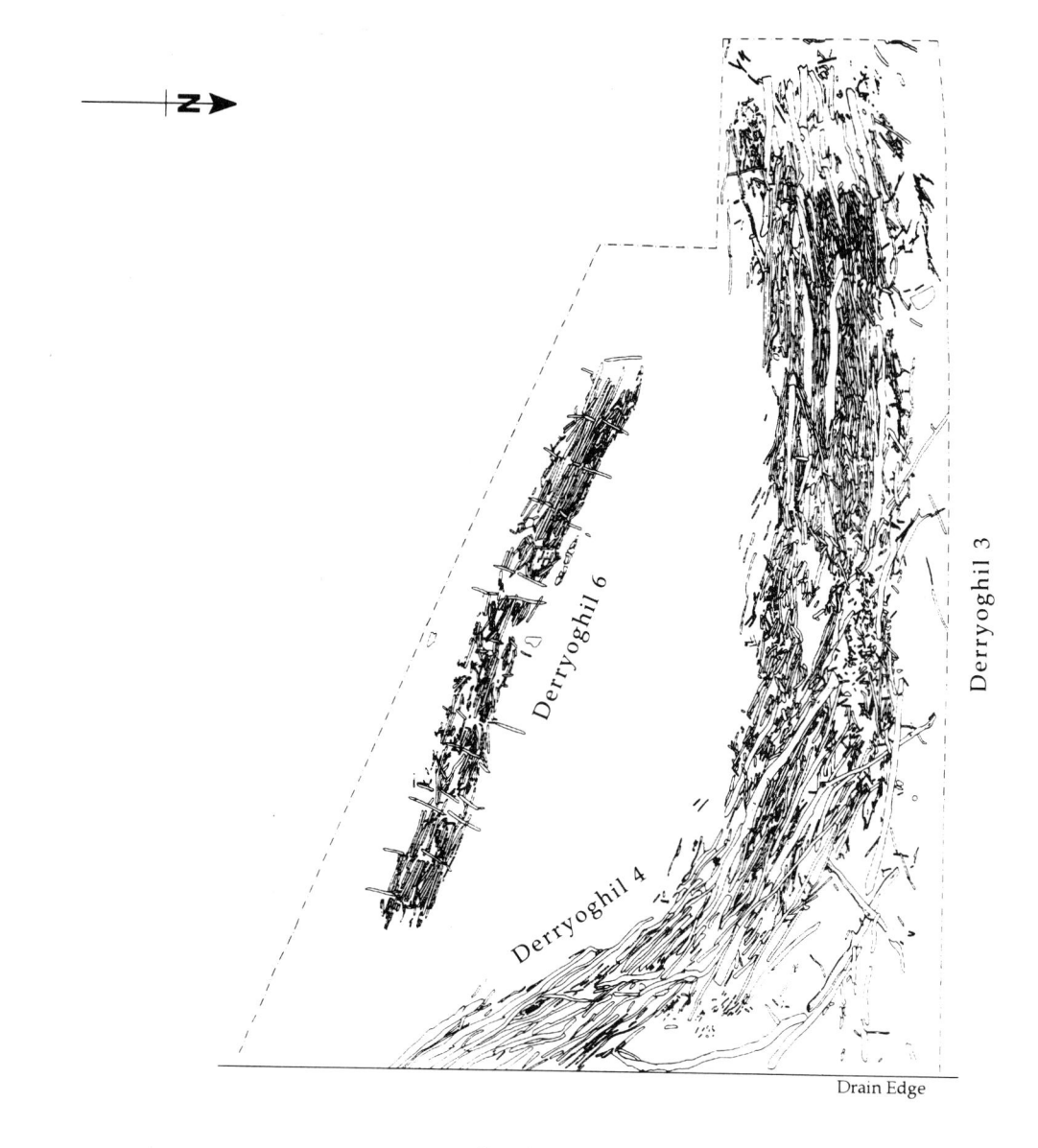

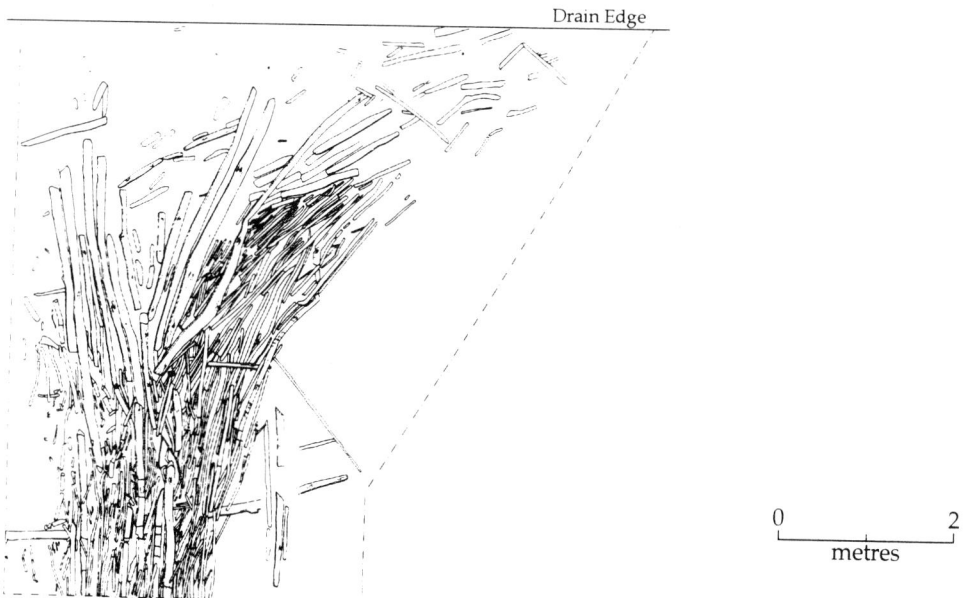

Fig. 20.7. Brushwood trackways, Derryoghil, Co. Longford.

represents a particularly intriguing concentration of structures. D19 is a perfectly normal brushwood track (apart from the incorporation in its structure, as earlier noted, of the double-mortised ash plank), running in a more or less east-west direction across the bog, and the trackways D23 and D24 are also of reasonably orthodox character. But what role do D20 and D21 play, both lying parallel to one another in north-west/south-east orientation? D20 had been placed directly on D19. Even more puzzling is D19a, a loose but deliberately laid arrangement of longitudinal brushwood rods, lying directly on D19 but overlain by D20. It extended in a north-south direction. Here we are clearly presented with a true conundrum.

In another section of Derryoghil bog a further intriguing arrangement of trackways was encountered (Fig. 20.7; Raftery *op. cit.,* 122 ff.). A major brushwood track D4, extending in the normal east-west direction across the bog, bent sharply at one point before continuing again in its east-west orientation. Was a deep pool encountered by the builders which they decided to circumvent by bending the track? Or did track builders from two sides of the bog find themselves not quite in line at the centre? Even more curious, however, is the presence within the bend of a straight length of trackway (D6) consisting of three hurdles laid end to end for a length of just over 7 m. This lay at precisely the same level in the bog as D4, and there can be little temporal difference between the two constructions. What was in the minds of the people who built D6? Was it a bypass, was it built at a time when D4 was becoming waterlogged, or was it just a product of man's innate compulsion to travel, wherever possible, the shortest distance between two points? At this remove, who can tell?

These are only a few of the intriguing questions which are posed by extended trackway research. In many cases answers are not readily forthcoming but the issues raised bring us face to face with the humanity of the builders and their at times random, idiosyncratic, responses to the continuous and varying challenges of trackway construction. To return to Renfrew again, for those involved in trackway excavation and research, it is easy to believe that "the past really did happen" (in Renfrew & Zubrow *op. cit.,* 10).

Bibliography

Baillie, M.G.L. 1988. The dating of the timbers from Navan Fort and the Dorsey, Co. Armagh, *Emania* 4, 37–40.

Baillie, M.G.L. and Brown, D.M. 1989. Further dates from the Dorsey, *Emania* 6, 11.

Casparie, W.A. 1982. The Neolithic wooden trackway XXI (Bou) in the raised bog at Nieuw-Dordrecht (the Netherlands), *Palaeohistoria* 24, 115–164.

Casparie, W.A. 1984. The three Bronze Age footpaths XVI (Bou), XVII (Bou) XVIII (Bou) in the raised bog of southeast Drenthe (the Netherlands), 26, 41–94.

Casparie, W.A. 1986. The two Iron Age wooden trackways XIV (Bou) and XV (Bou) in the raised bog of southeast Drenthe (the Netherlands), *Palaeohistoria* 28, 169–210.

Coles, J.M. and Coles, B.J. 1986. *Sweet Track to Glastonbury.* London: Thames and Hudson.

Coles, J.M. and Coles, B.J. 1992. Passages of time, *Archäologische Mitteilungen aus Nordwestdeutschland* 15, 29–44.

Coles, J.M. and Orme, B.J. 1977. Neolithic hurdles from Walton Heath, Somerset, *Somerset Levels Papers* 3, 6–29.

Condit, T. and Buckley, V. 1989. The Doon of Drumsna – gateways to Connacht, *Emania* 6, 11–14.

Connolly, S. and Picard, J.-M. 1987. Cogitosus: Life of Saint Brigid, *J. Royal Soc. Antiq. Ireland* 117, 5–27.

Fansa, M. 1992. Moorarchäologie in Niedersachsen, *Archäologische Mitteilungen aus Nordwestdeutschland* 15, 5–21.

Fansa, M. and Schneider, R. 1993. Die Bohlenwege bei Ockenhausen/ Oltmansfehn, Gde. Uplengen, Ldkr. Leer, *Archäologische Mitteilungen aus Nordwestdeutschland* 16, 23–43.

Hayen, H. 1971a. Hölzerne Kultfiguren am Bohlenweg XLII (Ip) im Wittemoor, *Die Kunde* 21, 1–36.

Hayen, H. 1971b. Hölzerne Kultfiguren am Bohlenweg XLII (Ip) in Wittemoor, Gemeinde Berne, Landkreis Wesermarsch, *Die Kunde* 22, 88–123.

Hayen, H. 1989. Bau und Funktion der hölzernen Moorwege: einige Fakten und Folgerungen. In H. Jankuhn, W. Kimmig and E. Ebel (eds) *Untersuchungen zu Handel und Verkehr der vor- und frühgeschichtlichen Zeit in Mittel- und Nordeuropa* 5, 11–82. Abhandlungen der Akademie der Wissenschaften in Göttingen, Phil.-Hist. Klasse. Göttingen: Vandenhoeck & Ruprecht.

Hayen, H. 1991. *Ein Vierradwagen des dritten Jahrtausends v. Chr.: Rekonstruktion und Nachbau.* Oldenburg.

Lynn, C.J. 1982. The Dorsey and other related earthworks. In B.G. Scott (ed.) *Studies on Early Ireland: Essays in Honour of M.V. Duignan,* 121–8. Belfast: [Association of Young Irish Archaeologists].

Lynn, C.J. 1986. Navan Fort: a draft summary of D.M. Waterman's excavations, *Emania* 1, 11–19.

Lynn, C.J. 1989. An interpretation of the Dorsey, *Emania* 6, 5–10.

Raftery, B. 1994. *Pagan Celtic Ireland.* London and New York: Thames and Hudson.

Raftery, B. 1996. *Trackway Excavations in the Mountdillon Bogs, Co. Longford, 1985–1991.* Transactions of the Irish Archaeological Wetland Unit 3. Dublin: Crannóg Publications.

Renfrew, C. and Zubrow, E.B.W. 1994. *The Ancient Mind: Elements of Cognitive Archaeology.* Cambridge: Cambridge University Press.

Schmeidl, H. and Kossack, G. 1967–68. Archäologische und paläobotanische Untersuchungen an der Römerstrasse in der Rottauer Filzen, Ldkr. Traunstein, *Jahresbericht der Bayerischen Bodendenkmalpflege* 8/9, 9–36.

Walsh, A. 1987. Excavating the Black Pig's Dyke, *Emania* 3, 5–19.

21. Underwater medieval sites on Lake Paladru (Isère, France): from rescue excavations to cultural project

Michel Colardelle & Eric Verdel

Abstract: This paper describes the rescue project which led to the preservation and presentation of the medieval settlement at Charavines on Lake Paladru, dating to around AD 1000. A rich collection of finds has been recovered, including wooden tableware, musical instruments, chessmen, riding equipment and weaponry. The question of the rise of fortified sites is considered, and the place of Charavines in this development is touched on.

Charavines, the subject of this paper, is a site in a very special position (Colardelle & Verdel 1993). It is a thousand year old settlement that was flooded by the waters of a mountain lake 35 years after its foundation, owing to a change of climate. This natural lake is in the south-east of France, between Grenoble and Lyon, near the alpine mountain of Chartreuse. It was necessary to carry out rescue excavations because the site, like the Neolithic example excavated by our colleague Aimé Bocquet, would have been destroyed by the building of a harbour and tourist facilities. All these projects have now been abandoned and, by saving the archaeological site, we have at the same time saved the natural shoreline with its reed vegetation, which is now protected. Such underwater digs require appropriate excavation techniques and procedures, and special equipment. One of the advantages of underwater sites is that thanks to the remarkable conservation of organic remains that are usually destroyed on dry-land sites, they contain exceptionally rich archaeological resources.

Covering an area of approximately 1300 m², the settlement was composed of three spacious buildings on oak footings (Fig. 21.1). Huge oak posts supported one or two storeys and reed-thatched roofs. These houses and their outbuildings, like stables for horses and workshops, were enclosed by a sturdy defensive palisade which gave it the look of a primitive castle. Defense was strengthened by the presence of the lake waters on three sides, and a marsh on the fourth, not easy for potential raiders to cross. A hypothetical reconstruction of the settlement shows the size of the middle building which, as we can judge from the domestic artifacts found, housed the leading family, masters of an agricultural domain of which the fortified *curtis* is the centre (Fig. 21.2).

Different scientific methods such as palynology and sedimentology showed that the inhabitants were colonists who came from a nearby region, probably the Rhône Valley. In 1003 they began to deforest the neighbouring hills to make space for agricultural land. The illustrations give some examples of their tools and domestic equipment (Figs. 21.3–21.5). The quality of our information about the daily life of these people in the eleventh century is exceptional. For example, there are axes, some complete with wooden handle, and we have found many agricultural tools, and the three most frequent are pick-axes, sickles, and pruning-hooks (Fig. 21.3, 8–13). Part of a plough is, for this period, unusual. In fields and meadows the farmers grew rye, wheat, oats, barley and millet and, probably in small gardens, a few peas, beans and lentils. Their meals were rounded off with the produce of orchards like

---

Authors' Addresses: Michel Colardelle, Conservateur général du Patrimoine, directeur du Musée National des Arts et Traditions Populaires – Centre d'Ethnologie Française, co-directeur des fouilles archéologiques de Charavines; Eric Verdel, Ingénieur de recherche au Musée Dauphinois - Conservation du Patrimoine de l'Isère, co-directeur des fouilles archéologiques de Charavines.

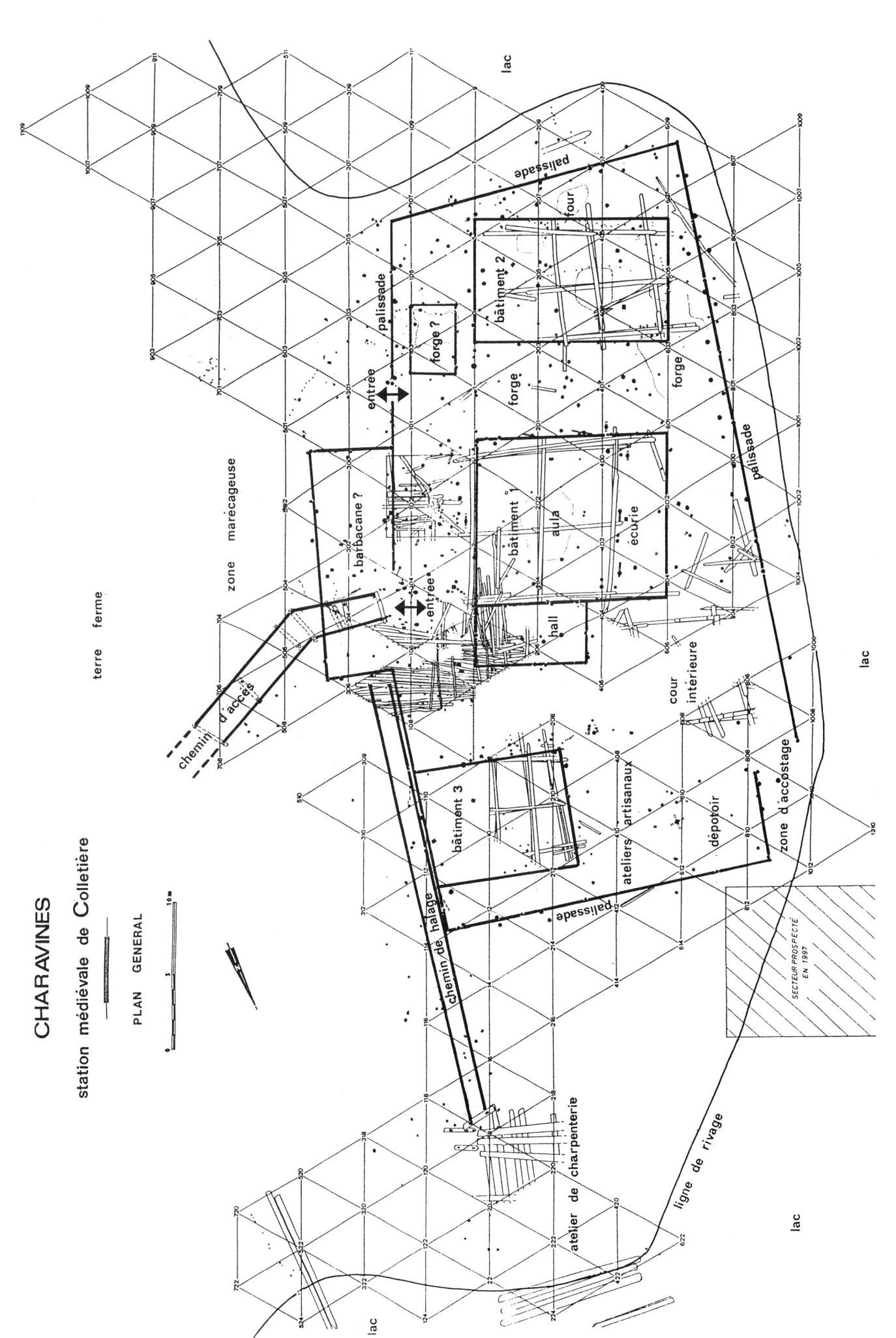

Fig. 21.1. General interpretation plan of the curtis of Colletière (Charavines)

Fig. 21.2. Hypothetical reconstruction model of the curtis *of Colletière (model by Lythos; photo Y. Bobin, Conservation du Patrimoine de l'Isère)*

walnuts, apples, cherries, peaches, plums, pears, and grapes for wine. They could also have had hazelnuts and chestnuts, and other wild plant species. They also placed importance on livestock: first of all pigs, which could have found a significant part of their food in the nearby woods, but also cows, used for meat, milk, leather, and for traction, for pulling carts and ploughs. They had horses, but not for work or for meat, as we shall see later. Goats and sheep, which gave wool, and poultry, were the other meat resources. Fishing must have played a greater role than hunting, and we found an oak dugout canoe, net-floats, harpoons, as well as bones and scales of perch, trout and roach. We have also collected all the cooking utensils and service dishes, wooden plates and spoons, pottery and knives, and we can tell what seasonal meals might have been cooked.

At the same time, the inhabitants of Charavines were good craftsmen. The frames of their buildings, and furniture such as chests, were made from the wood of forests and orchards. One of the nicest carpenter's tools we have found is a plane. They also carried out leather-work, specialising in shoes, harness or belts. Another craft practised by women was the weaving of hemp, linen and wool. Many weaving implements were discovered in houses, like spindles and fragments of looms. In a rural settlement, a forge was necessary; but here they had three forges, and the blacksmith was at the same time a farmer, making weapons as well as tools.

Probably they had an over-production of cereals, meat and crafts, and were able to sell the surplus. This is why they had silver coins of German kings, for we are in the Ottonian kingdom. And because of their wealth, they had locks and keys (Fig. 21.3, 7). Boxwood combs with a double row of teeth were used for hairdressing (Fig. 21.4, 9). Jewellery was of poor quality; it included clothing accessories like brooches, and some pins, pendants and rings (Fig. 21.4, 10–11).

During the Middle Ages, peasants and even farmers were not known to be rich; therefore their coins are surprising. But a greater surprise was the finding of a lot of musical instruments, flutes of elder wood or bone and little flageolets, a bagpipe chanter, clarinets, an oboe mouthpiece and bridges for hurdy-gurdies (Fig. 21.4, 12–14). The same is true for wooden or bone pawns and chessmen such as the queen, the bishop whose tiny protuberances on its head resemble the *alfil* or elephant of the Indian primitive game, brought across the sea by Muslims (Fig. 21.4, 1–6). Other playing counters belong to *trictrac*, the present-day backgammon (Fig. 21.4, 7). Most surprising of all is the discovery of various indications of writing, like a name engraved on a sickle blade; probably the owner of this tool was called Willelmus (William); the

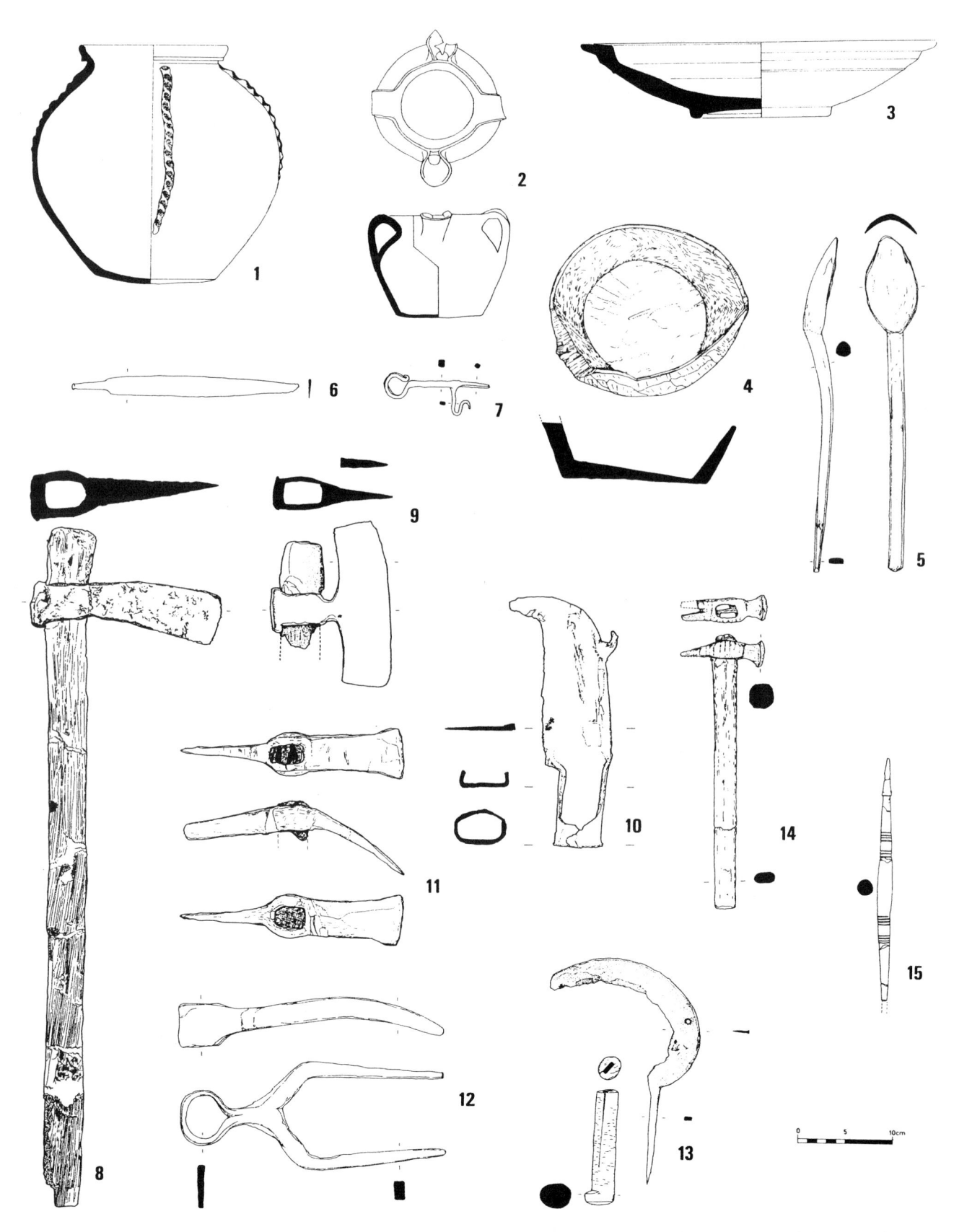

Fig. 21.3. Domestic pottery, wooden implements and iron tools from Colletière. 1. cooking pottery (80.91.158); 2. juglet (3366); 3. dish, ashwood (513); 4. plate of unidentified wood (2796); 5. spoon, boxwood (2479); 6. knife (1311); 7. key (563); 8. woodcutter's axe, ash haft (95); 9. carpenter's axe, ash haft (619); 10. pruning-hook (3360); 11. adze (4176); 12. hoe (89.46.19); 13. sickle, boxwood handle (3087); 14. blacksmith's hammer, ash handle (2751); 15. spindle, willow (2969).

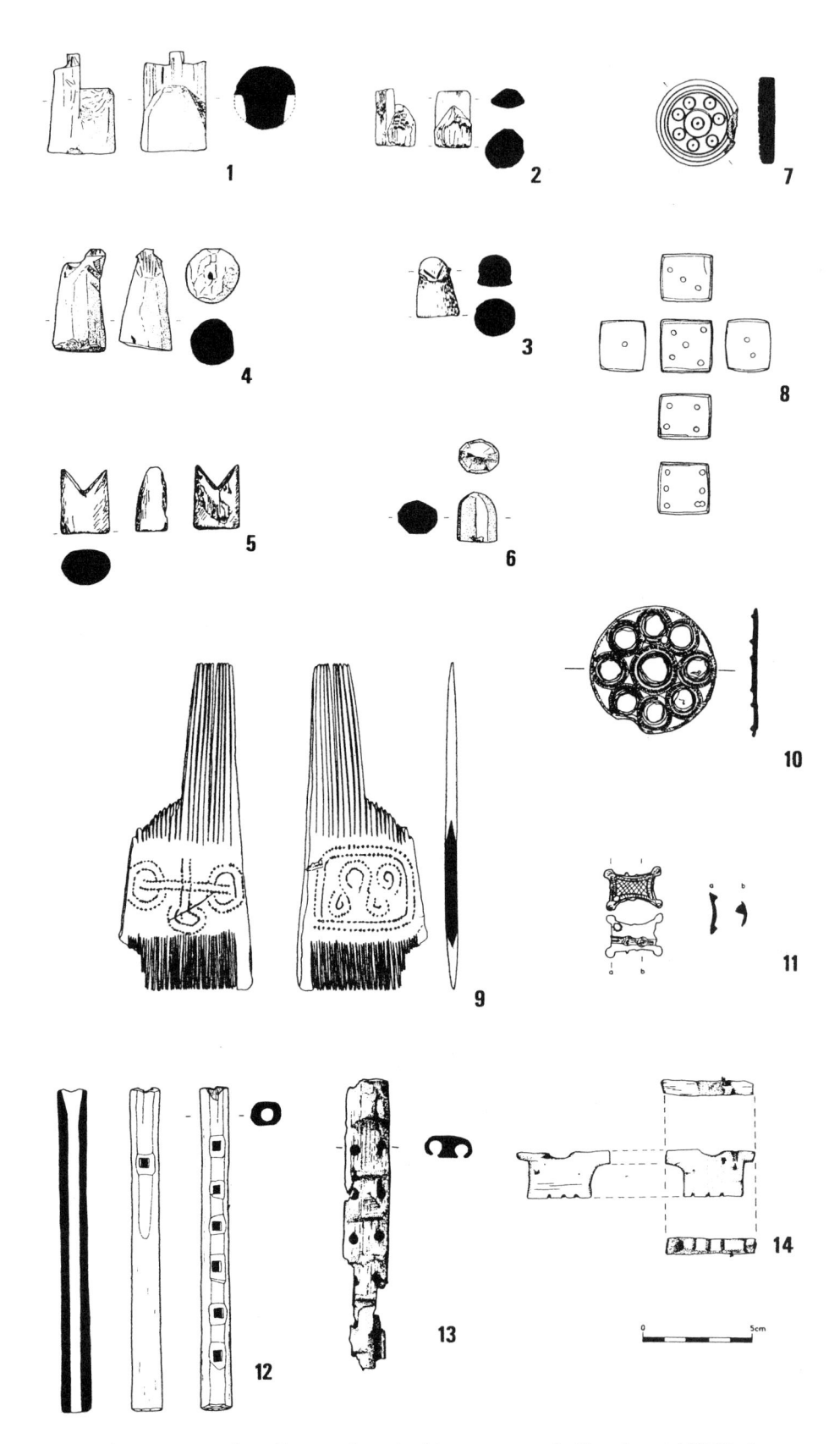

Fig. 21.4. Chessmen, gaming counters, jewellery and musical instruments. 1. king, hazel (4878); 2. queen, alder (2350); 3. bishop, hazel (84); 4. knight, walnut (4860); 5. rook, hazel (1815); 6. pawn, hazel (4274); 7. trictrac gaming counter, bone (4383); 8. die, yew (428); 9. carved comb, boxwood (3365); 10. circular brooch, pewter (65); 11. pendant brooch, pewter (4855); 12. flute, sambucus (1266); 13. bagpipe chanter of unidentified wood (280); 14. hurdy-gurdy bridge, willow (2402).

188   MICHEL COLARDELLE & ERIC VERDEL

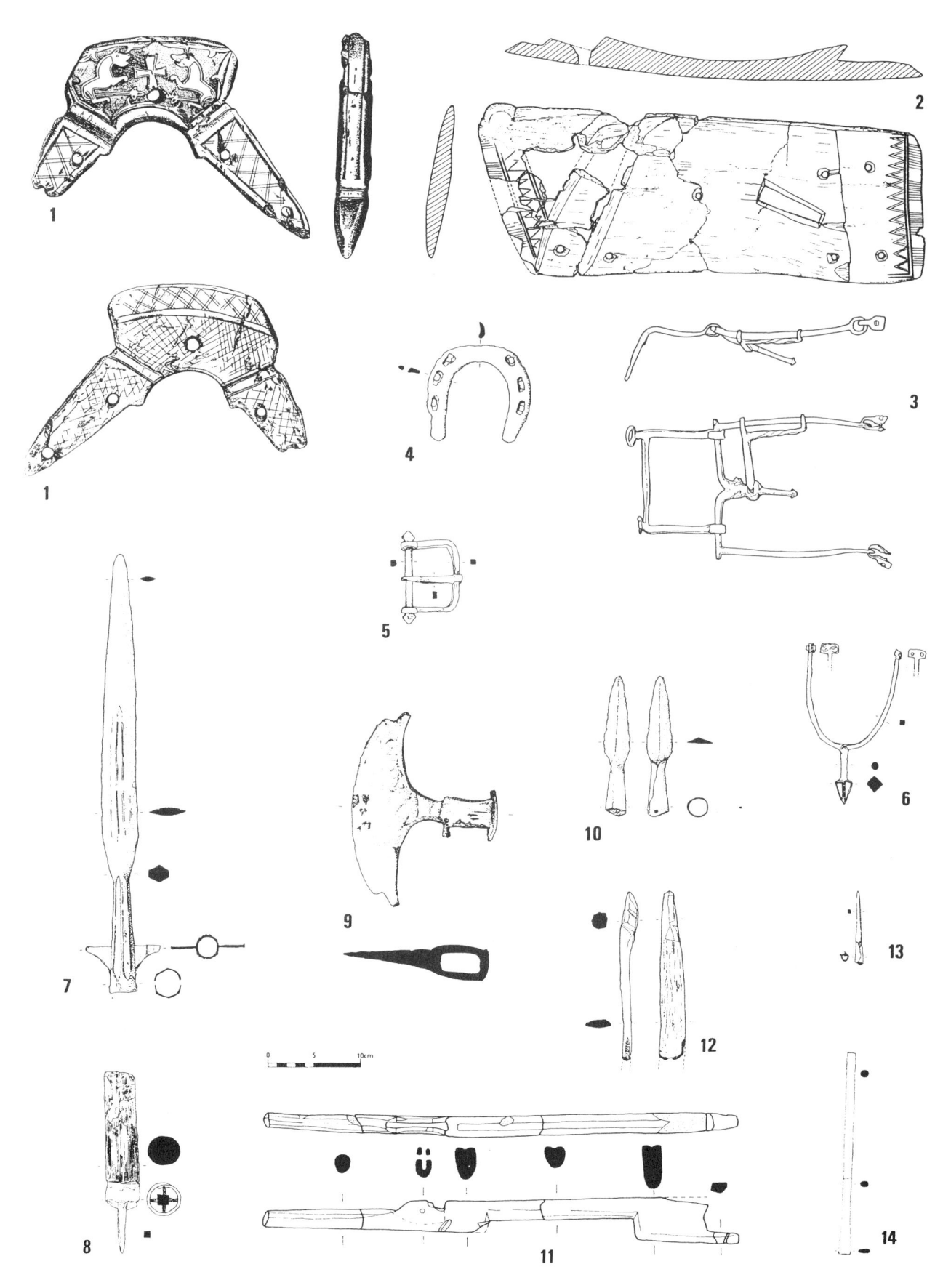

Fig. 21.5. Riding equipment and iron weapons. 1. saddle-bow, beech (4549); 2. saddle side, pomoideae *(1764); 3. bit (720); 4. horseshoe (3827); 5. saddlery buckle (2787); 6. spur (4784); 7. spear (4403); 8. spear heel, ash shaft (4749); 9. battle axe (3376); 10. javelin (4441); 11. crossbow tiller, beech (507); 12. bowstave, yew (395); 13. crossbow bolt-head (quarrel head) (840); 14. crossbow bolt-shaft, ash (1272).*

name is in the genitive and in abbreviated form: '*Wilmi*'.

Riding equipment was plentiful (Fig. 21.5). First, horseshoes, nails, and blacksmiths' hammers for driving and extracting nails (Fig. 21.3, 14). There were also spurs and buttons to attach them, double-bridle bits, particularly painful for horses and used for training or battle. An ornament (French *cocarde*) is for decorating a horse's headstall. It is a small embossed brass nail, with red and blue enamel plating. The rich wooden saddlery should also be mentioned: it is at present unknown on other sites. Examples include a fragment of a saddle-bow, decorated with geometric patterns, and above all an entire saddle-bow, recently discovered in the excavations, bearing an interesting and novel pattern: in the centre is a Christian cross, with on each side a fantastic animal which mixes the body of a lion and the head of a horse (Fig. 21.5, 1).

During the Middle Ages, especially in the early stages, horses were ridden for battle. And if weapons symbolized the social status of freemen during barbarian times, it is well-known that horses and weapons were the symbols of knights during the following period. In any event, horses were not used for ploughing or pulling carts before the twelfth century, because team shoulder collars were not invented until then. Farmers on the lake shores thus had many weapons: spears, javelins, battle-axes, and even crossbows and their iron bolts (Fig. 21.5, 7–14). The small crossbow that we found is the oldest currently known, and it seems, like the horseshoe, to be a new but very important accessory of the end of the tenth century.

The complete set of riding and battle equipment is known, and it is possible to reconstruct the appearance of the farmer-knights of Charavines. Only two things are missing: the helmet (it is not certain that they had them), and stirrups. Their appearance is very close to that shown on the Bayeux Tapestry. But Duke William's warriors were *vassi* and moreover belonged to the social class of knights. It is difficult to imagine Norman knights giving up their weapons during times of peace and using farming or craft tools. Work was, at that time, reserved for craftmen and peasants, in other words workers, in a three-class society: workers (*laboratores*), warriors (*bellatores*) and priests (*oratores*).

But the farmer-knights of Charavines were not lords. They seem to have been the actors of a mutated settlement, something between the old land-owners who were, during Gallo-Roman, Merovingian and Carolingian times, the upper social class, and the new class of knights. A few archives from other regions mention 'farmer-knights', particularly in the Pyrenees, and the settlers of Charavines were probably called this. It is interesting to note that it is always in the context of agrarian colonisation, which took advantage of a population explosion around the year 1000, that this intermediate social status appears. Demographic growth, the new distribution of wealth, the release of new energies, and agrarian conquests might have been the main reasons for social evolution, which was frequently encouraged by the official powers. For Charavines, there are a number of reasons for thinking that the colonization was undertaken by order of the Archbishop of Vienne who wanted to control the borders of his territory against the bishopric of Grenoble.

On the Bayeux Tapestry, Duke William supervises the building of a curious construction. His men are erecting an artificial hill, and on top there is a kind of tower named *castra*. This kind of castle, which is called a motte and bailey to differentiate it from stone ones, was an effective fortress during the eleventh century. Motte and bailey castles had dry or water moats, and a palisade on the top enclosing a keep. The motte itself was an earthwork, and the buildings in it of wood. It was easy to build in time of war, but it could also house a knight's family in time of peace.

It is a discovery of the last thirty years that we have in western Europe, particularly in France, thousands of motte and bailey castles. Excavations have produced many weapons on such sites. There is a big difference between these private fortresses and the fortified settlement of Charavines: here, knights lived in wooden towers on top of the motte, and craftsmen and peasants were below, under the fortification. Many mottes and baileys have been excavated in France, and some are very close to the *curtis* of Charavines and the two other fortified houses or small villages of the same period discovered on the shore of lake Paladru. They are probably the successor fortresses of our farmer-knights, who had abandoned their original site because of flooding, but it is impossible to prove this. They had deep moats, and excavations inside one of them, Le Châtelard in Chirens (Mazard & Colardelle 1993), showed there were three wooden buildings, the most important very similar to the main one of Charavines.

This model of private fortification is something very new. None is known before the end of the tenth century, and we think that in the middle of the eleventh century there were one or two thousand on the territory of present-day France. This phenomenon reveals a rising new social class of warriors, who usurped public rights that kings, dukes and counts, the official leaders, were unable to maintain. These castles were the starting point of the feudal system, because in these fortifications new lords of the manor could impose their power on kings, and also on the village inhabitants to whom they could offer protection. In exchange for this protection, for dispensing justice, and for policing the village, they demanded taxes from their people (called *malae consuetudines*, 'bad customs', because it was a new obligation and imposed by violence). In exchange for the right to keep their private castle, they recognized the law of their 'suzerain' and came out with their horses and weapons when war broke out. This agreement between the two parties, and the privatizing of public rights, is the principle of feudal organization.

What is the place of Charavines in this evolution? We think the excavations show two main things: one is the climatic change during the tenth and eleventh centuries: the fall in the water level of the lake is correlated with a drier and warmer climate for about fifty years, from 980 to 1030. Before this, oxygen isotope analysis of the rings of trees used for the buildings of Charavines shows, during the middle of the tenth century, the beginning of a hundred-year warm period (the medieval climatic optimum). For us it is certain that this climatic change is one of the main reasons for demographic growth during the period: better production of grain crops, better nutrition, better health, better perinatal survival.

The second phenomenon shown by Charavines is an unknown kind of society, something like a mutation. One of the hypotheses for the disorganized but very strong movement of social evolution – the birth of castles, and feudal society – is the agrarian colonisation which is a consequence of demographic growth. It must have been the perfect way to liberate personal energies, to change social status – it is the end of slavery, for example, and the beginning of new aristocratic families coming from *ministeriales*, a new distribution of power.

When we began the excavations, we thought that it would not be useful to create a site museum, because there was a large regional museum (Musée Dauphinois) in the nearest town, Grenoble. We therefore decided to give the local population and tourists open days in the summer. But it was difficult to organize such events, and we had too many visitors (2000 or 3000 in a single weekend). We changed our organisation ten years ago, and opened the excavations for two guided visits each afternoon. But this was not enough, because we could not show people the finds discovered in previous seasons. The local politicans then asked us to create a small site museum in the village hall. We have put on display here many of the finds (we have found about five thousand artefacts, and thus have enough items for both the regional and the site museum), and temporary exhibitions on regional archaeological or historical themes. But this museum is now too small for the number of visitors.

The success of the museum, which belongs to a collective organization of the Isère Département led by the Musée Dauphinois in Grenoble, is such that we proposed to bring in the different villages which formed the ancient feudal territory around the main castle near Charavines, Clermont. Private historical monuments were restored, and some (those that their owners could not maintain) were taken into public ownership. We organise school visits, tourist itineraries, exhibitions and concerts, providing considerable cultural interest in this rural area.

We now have a large-scale national and regional project for a museum and reconstruction site on the lake shore, with four main points of interest: Neolithic and medieval excavations, the earliest castles, pre-industrial and industrial local archaeology, and environmental and landscape evolution from the Neolithic to the present day. Twenty-one hectares have now been bought by the Isère Département, and we have received enough money from the State, the Region and the Conseil général to begin the building programme. The new museum and part of the experimental reconstruction will – we hope – be achieved in 2002 or 2003.

One of our main victories in this long battle is the fact that the 24 villages around the lake are today gathering together into a 'parish community', a new form of territorial administrative organisation; the backbone of this project is the museum, and people feel they belong to a historical community.

Acknowledgements

We are very happy to contribute to this volume in honour of our friend John Coles, who was always available when it was necessary, ready to think about our underwater excavations and to give us very useful assistance. He brought with him experience and precious advice on our methods, our goals, and on problems of preservation, in the perspective of the palaeoenvironmental studies which interested us. And at the official meetings of our Scientific Committee, he was the great wetland specialist, making very useful recommendations to disoriented dry-site specialists.

Bibliography

Colardelle, M. & Verdel, E. 1993. *Chevaliers-paysans de l'an Mil au lac de Paladru*. Paris: Errance – Musée Dauphinois.

Mazard, Ch. & Colardelle, M. 1993. Les fortifications de terre. In M. Colardelle and E. Verdel (eds), *Les habitats du lac de Paladru (Isère) dans leur environnement. La formation d'un terroir au XIe siècle*, 332–40. Documents d'Archéologie Française, 10. Paris: Editions de la Maison des Sciences de l'Homme.

Epilogue: Of weapons and wetlands

Timothy Champion

The conference on which this volume was based, and where the majority of the contributions were originally presented, was organised by the Prehistoric Society, and it was my role as the then President of the Society to make the closing remarks of the weekend. The conference had been arranged in honour of John Coles, who had served the Society as Assistant Editor, Editor, President and benefactor, and it was truly gratifying to see so many contributors and participants join with such enthusiasm in paying tribute to a colleague who had been such a long-term friend and supporter of the Society.

Summing up a conference is never easy. There is little time to reflect, you have a duty of sorts to be fair to all contributors, and the result inevitably, and rightly, reflects the mood of the moment. The only advantage of such a task is that it is ephemeral, soon forgotten by those who attended and unknown to the rest of the world. To translate those comments into the more permanent medium of the printed word is a very different challenge. The time elapsed since the conference allows more opportunity for profounder reflection, both on the individual contributions and on the occasion as a whole, but the switch from spoken to written word inevitably brings a loss of immediacy. What these comments can never fully convey is the atmosphere of this particular conference, remarked on both at the time and afterwards by many who were lucky enough to have been there. No one could remember a conference which had been so enjoyable and so stimulating intellectually, qualities which are not necessarily always found together. Pondering this general reaction in the months since the conference, I have become ever more convinced that it was not some random chance or lucky fluke, but due in no small measure to the qualities of the person in whose honour the event had been organised. John Coles has given much to archaeology and fellow archaeologists, as author, editor, colleague, teacher and friend, and his fellow archaeologists responded by creating a fitting tribute to the man and his work. Few who were there will forget the atmosphere of enjoyment and scholarship, nor the occasional surprising moments: as when a string of former undergraduates remembered their first encounter with John as an external examiner in their *viva voce* examinations, occasions recalled with rose-tinted fondness rather than horror or embarrassment; or when John typically stood in at short notice for an absent speaker, to give a paper on his rock art research; or the striking *coup-de-theâtre* when two Polish colleagues interrupted John's after-dinner speech to present him with a replica Bronze Age sword.

For the purposes of the original conference, five themes from John's research were selected as foci for the contributors: Scotland, the Bronze Age, wetlands, rock art and experimental archaeology. How many other archaeologists could claim to have made such contributions to so many different fields of research? And yet it did not do justice to the full breadth of his output, and several other areas were not properly celebrated. His work on early prehistory was in particular neglected, though duly reflected in this publication by the papers by Paul Mellars and Jean Clottes. The textbook, *The Archaeology of Early Man*,[1] may now seem, like its title, somewhat outdated, but it was a well-thumbed book in its time. John's work on the Mesolithic of Scotland, however, as Roger Mercer reminds us, will hold a lasting place in the study of early human settlement there. And what of the Iron Age? Though his work in that period has been 'only' about the Somerset lake villages, our knowledge of these important, if rather specialised, sites is now on a much firmer basis: the unparalleled range of evidence from Bulleid's classic excavation at Glastonbury has provided the basis for repeated attempts to develop models of Iron Age society, and the reappraisal of the fundamental record of the original investigations (1995),

---

Author's Address: Timothy Champion, Department of Archaeology, University of Southampton, SO17 1BJ

as well as the substantive publication of the first excavations at Meare Village East (1987), will enable all such concepts to be more reliably founded, while the new excavations at Meare Village East (1983) and West (1981) have shed much new light on the environmental setting and economic organisation of these marginal sites. We may wonder where the study of the Iron Age would now be if it had been more central to John's research, but in view of his well-known penchant for tackling only those problems where good returns can be expected for hard work, perhaps his concentration on the earlier periods of prehistory is actually telling us something about the nature of Iron Age studies.

As a rapid survey of John's enormous output will show, the majority of his publications have been devoted to the Bronze Age. Many of the strands of thought now current in Bronze Age research owe something to his earlier writings, and the sheer breadth of his scholarship can be seen in his contribution to *The Bronze Age in Europe* (1979), a work which at the time of writing nearly twenty years later is still an unsurpassed survey of the period and has stood the test of time remarkably well. These wider concerns for the nature of social and economic organisation in the Bronze Age are at the core of the papers here by Henrik Thrane and Graeme Barker. But the breadth of John's vision was based on a detailed knowledge of the material evidence. His studies of the Bronze Age metalwork of Scotland (1962, 1966, 1970) were carried out at a time when the framework of metalwork typologies and chronologies was being sorted out by archaeologists such as Colin Burgess, George Eogan and himself, and those classic works have remained fundamental to all later research on the period; despite the inevitable revisions in the light of further discoveries and new research methods, they are still the backbone on which the chronology is constructed, and the development of more recent interest in the social use of bronze would have been largely impossible without them. Though studies primarily concerned with typology and chronology are less fashionable today, there is still much to be learnt, and the papers by Andrew Lawson and Roger Thomas show how careful documentation and analysis of the primary data can still reveal striking spatial and temporal patterns in the deposition of bronze which need appropriate explanation.

Current interests in the production, circulation and deposition of Bronze Age metalwork are, however, clearly foreshadowed in some of John's own work. The analysis of the gold objects of the 'Wessex Culture' (1970), for instance, raised questions of craft skill, production and distribution which are at the heart of current research, problems reflected in the papers here by Joan Taylor and George Eogan. John's early papers on musical instruments (1963) and shields (1962) also went beyond questions of chronology to investigate the social context of their use, which, as Anthony Harding reminds us with reference to Bronze Age armour, are still unresolved debates. One paper I remember reading with particular excitement was the short note on the Dowris hoard in Ireland (1971), for it raised the possibility that so-called hoards might not be unitary assemblages, but the result of multiple and repeated acts of deposition, thus putting the question of structured deposition firmly on the agenda long before it became a hot topic in Bronze Age circles.

John's move to Edinburgh to study with Stuart Piggott was a blessing not just for the Scottish Bronze Age, but for the whole of Scottish prehistory. There is a long and impressive tradition of prehistoric research in Scotland, and John occupies a significant place in the story. Both in fieldwork and in artifact studies he helped to lay the foundations for the growth of modern research methods and programmes, and, as the papers by Roger Mercer, Graham Ritchie, Gordon Barclay and Alison Sheridan all demonstrate, the tradition is continuing with a lively programme of investigations which owe much to John's inspiration.

Perhaps any country to which John turned his archaeological attention would feel itself enriched. As Bo Gräslund points out, it is ironic, but entirely typical of John, that he should have established himself as one of the few experts on Swedish rock art, and as the author of guidebooks to the most important sites. He has found his own special niche in this rather esoteric field of enquiry, with an emphasis on the empirical problems of recording the art and of placing it in a physical and social landscape, and also in a human context. Richard Bradley's contribution here explores similar problems in coming to terms with this attractive but intractable material.

In research on the Bronze Age, on Scottish prehistory and on rock art, John Coles built on the work of earlier scholars, but in two fields he will surely be remembered as the pioneer who laid the very foundations of modern research. In experimental archaeology and in the archaeology of wetlands, John has played a quite extraordinary role, which is very fittingly reflected in the international flavour of the contributions on those themes in this volume.

The potential of experimental archaeology has had obvious attractions for many exponents, but it required a serious synthesis to give it academic credibility, and that is exactly what John's books have done (1973, 1979); as Peter Reynolds argues, it is now an established method of enquiry with its own disciplinary logic. From a focus on the more obvious inorganic materials such as stone and metal, attention has spread to inorganic resources, which survive less commonly, but probably played a far larger part in the technologies of most prehistoric societies. As the papers by Ole Crumlin-Pedersen, Wojciech Piotrowski and Graeme Lawson all show, experimental work on wood and bone can reveal not just the technological processes practised so skilfully by past societies, but also something of the society which used their products.

But it is with the theme of the archaeology of wetlands that the name of Coles will be most readily and most firmly associated throughout the world. John and Bryony Coles have played an absolutely unique role in demonstrating the archaeological potential of the world's wetlands and the imminent threats that beset them, and in mobilising the resources to exploit them while they still survive. It is no exaggeration to say that, without their pioneering efforts to preach the gospel of the wetlands, the discipline of wetland archaeology, now flourishing internationally, would simply not exist. When the history of British archaeology in the late twentieth century comes to be written, the Somerset Levels Project will, I am sure, be seen as one of the critical events of the period. The results there, and John's enthusiastic involvement with and support for similar work elsewhere, were instrumental in securing further generous sponsorship from English Heritage for major programmes in the Fenlands, and in the Humber and North-west Wetlands. John and Bryony's interests and influence spread much wider, however, as we can see from the contributions by Barry Raftery from Ireland and by Michel Colardelle and Eric Verdel from France. Wetland archaeology is undoubtedly difficult and expensive, but the results are frequently spectacular (so much so that one sometimes wonders why we bother at all with degraded dryland sites), and we have surely only just begun to realise the full potential of this resource.

As we have seen, the conference contributions were arranged to reflect some of the major fields of archaeological research which John had influenced by his own work, but it is important that we should not forget some of the other, perhaps less obvious, ways in which he has served the discipline well. He has been a powerful advocate for the preservation of archaeological sites, and a source of wise advice, not least in his role as a member of the Royal Commission on the Ancient and Historical Monuments of Scotland. As a teacher, John inspired generations of Cambridge students, many of whom went on to become colleagues, and some indeed contributors to this volume. As Editor of the *Proceedings of the Prehistoric Society*, he undertook the very necessary but frequently unrecognised task of seeing other people's work into print, and many archaeologists are indebted to him for his help in getting their contributions into a shape fit for publication. I can clearly recall one typical piece of advice John gave me when I was taking over from him as Editor: I had asked about the policy on the maximum length of papers, and he replied, "Twenty pages. If you can't say it in that, it probably isn't worth saying".

It was a particular pleasure for the Prehistoric Society to play host to the assembled participants in the conference, and to be the medium through which John's contribution to archaeology could be so memorably celebrated. We thank him for providing us, through his own work and through his generous support of the work of others, with the opportunity and the excuse for meeting in such convivial circumstances. With our eyes firmly fixed on the past, we archaeologists may not be the best people to predict the future, but I have a vision of our successors in another ten years' time on the Council of the Prehistoric Society, surveying recent progress in the discipline and saying, "That man Coles has done rather a lot of important new things in the last few years. Shouldn't we have a conference to celebrate his achievements?" I am sure they will be right on both counts.

Notes

1 For references to works of John Coles mentioned here, please refer to the full Bibliography that follows this Epilogue.

J.M. Coles – A Bibliography

1960
A bronze sword from Douglas, Lanarkshire, *Proc. Soc. Antiq. Scotland* 91, 1957–58, 182–86 (with R.G. Livens).[1]

1961
Scottish swan's-neck sunflower pins, *Proc. Soc. Antiq. Scotland* 92, 1958–59, 1–9 (Chalmers-Jervise Prize Essay).

1962
Scottish Late Bronze Age metalwork, *Proc. Soc. Antiq. Scotland* 93, 1959–60, 16–134.
The Salta Moss rapier, *Trans. Cumberland & Westmorland Antiq. & Arch. Soc.* 61, 16–24.
European Bronze Age shields, *Proc. Prehist. Soc.* 28, 156–90.

1963
Environmental studies in archaeology. In *Science in Archaeology. A comparative survey of progress and research* (eds D. Brothwell & E.S. Higgs), 93–98. London: Thames & Hudson.
Irish Bronze Age horns and their relationship with northern Europe, *Proc. Prehist. Soc.* 29, 326–56.
Archaeology by experiment, *Illustrated London News* 1963, 299–301.
A flat axe from Chatteris Fen, Cambs, *Proc. Cambridge Antiq. Soc.* 61–62, 5–8.
The Hilton, Dorset, gold ornaments, *Antiquity* 37, 132–134.

1964
New aspects of the Mesolithic settlement of south-west Scotland, *Trans. Dumfries & Galloway Nat. Hist. Antiq. Soc.* 41, 67–98.
A Late Bronze Age vessel from Flaxby, Yorks, *Yorks Arch. J.* 41, 184–90 (with P. Addyman & C. Hartley).
A Late Bronze Age find from Pyotdykes, Angus, *Proc. Prehist. Soc.* 30, 186–98 (with H. Coutts & M. Ryder).

1965
The Archaeology of the Cambridge Region: prehistory. In *The Cambridge Region 1965* (ed. J.A. Steers), 112–25. Cambridge: [Local Executive Committee for] The British Association for the Advancement of Science.
Scottish Bronze Age weapons, *Ancient Scottish Weapons. The Scottish Art Review* 1965, 3–7.
The archaeological evidence for a 'bull cult' in Late Bronze Age Europe, *Antiquity* 39, 217–9.
The Torran hoard, *Proc. Soc. Antiq. Scotland* 96 (1962–63), 352–4 (with M. Campbell).
The Late Bronze Age hoard from Peelhill, Strathavon, Lanarks, *Proc. Soc. Antiq. Scotland* 96, 1962–63, 136–44 (with J.G. Scott).
Bronze Age metalwork in Dumfriesfries and Galloway, *Trans. Dumfries & Galloway Nat. Hist. Antiq. Soc.* 42, 61–98.
The excavation of a Neolithic round barrow at Pitnacree, Perthshire, Scotland, *Proc. Prehist. Soc.* 31, 34–57 (with D.D.A. Simpson).
A rock-carving from south-west Ireland, *Proc. Prehist. Soc.* 31, 374–5.
Reconsideration of the Ambleside hoard and the burial at Butts Beck quarry, Dalton-in-Furness, *Trans. Cumberland & Westmorland Antiq. Arch. Soc.* 65, 38–52 (with C. Fell).

1966
Scottish Middle Bronze Age metalwork, *Proc. Soc. Antiq. Scotland* 97, 1963–64, 82–156.
The excavations at McNaughton's fort, Kirkudbrights, *Trans. Dumfries & Galloway Nat. Hist. Antiq. Soc.* 43, 73–9 (with J. Scott-Elliot & D.D.A. Simpson).
Flere Forsøg, *Skalk* 1967 no.1, 26–30.
The Plzeň shield: a problem in nordic and east Mediterranean relations, *Archeologické Rozhledy* 19, 352–5.

1967
Some Irish horns of the Late Bronze Age, *J. Royal Soc. Antiq. Ireland* 97, 113–7.
A rapier and its scabbard from West Row, Suffolk, *Proc. Cambridge Antiq. Soc.* 60, 1–5 (with B. Trump).
The Plzeň shield, *Germania* 45, 151–3.
Studies in Ancient Europe. Essays presented to Stuart Piggott. (eds. J.M. Coles & D.D.A. Simpson). Leicester: Leicester University Press.
Ancient man in Europe. In *Studies in Ancient Europe*, 17–43.

1968
A Neolithic god-dolly from Somerset, *Antiquity* 42, 275–7.
Experimental archaeology, *Proc. Soc. Antiq. Scotland* 99, 1966–67, 1–20.
Prehistoric roads and tracks in Somerset, England: 1. Neolithic, *Proc. Prehist. Soc.* 34, 238–58 (with F.A. Hibbert).
The 1857 Law Farm hoard, *Antiq. J.* 48, 163–74.
The god-dolly from Somerset, *Illustrated London News* 1968, 32–3.
A Mesolithic site at Low Clone, Wigtownshire, *Trans. Dumfries & Galloway Nat. Hist. Antiq. Soc.* 45, 44–72 (with W.F. Cormack).

1969
The Archaeology of Early Man. London: Faber & Faber (Penguin, 1976). 454 pp. (with E.S. Higgs).

Metal analyses and the Scottish Early Bronze Age, *Proc. Prehist. Soc.* 35, 330–44.

A hermaphrodite wooden figure from the British Neolithic, *Archeologické Rozhledy* 21, 231–2.

Man before history. In *The Awakening of Man*, The Hamlyn History of the World vol. 1 (ed. J. Coles), 9–13. London: Hamlyn.

1970

Neolithic and Bronze Age trackways in Somerset, England. In *Actes du VIIe Congrès International des Sciences Préhistoriques et Protohistoriques, Prague 1966* (ed. J. Filip), 528–30. Prague: Academia.

The Wessex culture: a minimal view, *Antiquity* 45, 6–14 (with J.J. Taylor).

Scottish Early Bronze Age metalwork, *Proc. Soc. Antiq. Scotland* 101, 1968–69, 1–110.

Prehistoric roads and tracks in Somerset, England: 2. Neolithic, *Proc. Prehist. Soc.* 36, 125–51 (with F.A. Hibbert & C. Clements).

The bull cult in the Bronze Age of western Europe. In *Britain – a study in patterns* (ed. M. Williams), 12–16. London: Research into Lost Knowledge Organization.

1971

The early settlement of Scotland: excavations at Morton, Fife, *Proc. Prehist. Soc.* 37, 284–366.

Bronze Age spearheads with gold decoration, *Antiq. J.* 51, 94–5.

A Neolithic wooden mallet from the Somerset Levels, *Antiquity* 46, 52–4 (with F.A. Hibbert).

Dowris and the Late Bronze Age of Ireland: a footnote, *J. Royal Soc. Antiq. Ireland* 101, 164–5.

Contributions to prehistory offered to Grahame Clark (ed. J.M. Coles), *Proc. Prehist. Soc.* 37, ii.

1972

Field Archaeology in Britain. London: Methuen. 267 pp.

1973

Archaeology by Experiment. London: Hutchinson. 182 pp.
(*Archeology by Experiment*, New York: Scribners, 1974; *Experimentele Archeologie*, Groningen: H.D. Tjeenk Willink, 1975; *Forsøg med Fortiden*, Højbjerg: Wormianum, 1975; *Erlebte Steinzeit*, Munich: Bertelsmann, 1976; *Arquelogia Experimental*, Lisbon: Tempo Aberto, 1977; *Archeologia doświadczalna*, Warsaw: Panstwowe Wydawnictwo Naukowe, 1977; [*Archaeology by Experiment*], Tokyo: Gakushi, 1977; *Archeologia Sperimentale*, Milan: Longanesi, 1981).

Later Bronze Age activity in the Somerset Levels, *Antiq. J.* 52, 269–75.

The Somerset Levels, *Current Archaeology* 38, 70–4 (with B. Orme).

The excavation of a midden in the Culbin Sands, Morayshire, *Proc. Soc. Antiq. Scotland* 102, 87–100 (with J. Taylor).

Prehistoric roads and tracks in Somerset: 3. The Sweet Track, *Proc. Prehist. Soc.* 39, 256–93 (with F.A. Hibbert & B. Orme).

1974

A jade axe from the Somerset Levels, *Antiquity* 48, 216–20 (with B.J. Orme, A.C. Bishop & A. Woolley).

1975

The Somerset Levels. In *Recent Work in Rural Archaeology* (ed. P.J. Fowler), 12–26. Bath: Adams & Dart (with F.A. Hibbert).

Archaeology in the Somerset Levels, *Somerset Levels Papers* 1, 5–8.

The Honeygore Complex, *Somerset Levels Papers* 1, 8–19 (with F.A. Hibbert).

The Eclipse Track, *Somerset Levels Papers* 1, 20–28 (with B. Orme & F.A. Hibbert).

Withy Bed Copse, *Somerset Levels Papers* 1, 29–40 (with B. Orme, F.A. Hibbert & R. Jones).

Tinney's Ground, 1974, *Somerset Levels Papers* 1, 41–53 (with B. Orme, F.A. Hibbert & R. Jones).

Timber and radiocarbon dates, *Antiquity* 49, 123–5 (with R. Jones).

Archaeology in the Somerset Levels, *Archaeology* 28, 148–156.

The 1857 Law Farm hoard: an addition, *Antiq. J.* 54, 128.

1976

Forest farmers: some archaeological, historical and experimental evidence relating to the prehistory of Europe. In *Acculturation and Continuity in Atlantic Europe, mainly during the Neolithic period and the Bronze Age. Papers presented at the Fourth Atlantic Colloquium, Ghent 1975* (ed. S.J. de Laet), 59–66. Dissertationes Archaeologicae Gandenses.

Experiments in Prehistory. In *Festschrift für Richard Pittioni zum siebzigsten Geburtstag, I. Urgeschichte* (eds H. Mitscha-Märheim, H. Friesinger & H. Kerchler), 7–22. Wien: Deuticke.

Art of the Ancients, *Collier's Encyclopaedia 1976*, 48–53.

Archaeology in the Somerset Levels 1975, *Somerset Levels Papers* 2, 4–6.

The Abbot's Way, *Somerset Levels Papers* 2, 7–20 (with B. Orme).

The Sweet Track, Railway site, *Somerset Levels Papers* 2, 34–65 (with B. Orme).

A Neolithic hurdle from the Somerset Levels, *Antiquity* 50, 57–61 (with B. Orme).

Lifting the Walton hurdle, *Current Archaeology* 52, 143–7 (with B. Orme).

The origins of metallurgy in the British Isles. In *Les débuts de la métallurgie*, Colloque XXIII, *Union International des Sciences Préhistoriques et Protohistoriques, IX Congrès, Nice 1976*, 15–27.

The Meare Heath track: excavation of a Bronze Age structure in the Somerset Levels, *Proc. Prehist. Soc.* 42, 293–318 (with B.J. Orme).

1977

Archaeology in the Somerset Levels 1976, *Somerset Levels Papers* 3, 4–6.

Neolithic hurdles from Walton Heath, Somerset, *Somerset Levels Papers* 3, 6–29 (with B. Orme).

Experimental investigations in hurdle-making, *Somerset Levels Papers* 3, 32–38 (with R. Darrah).

Rowland's hurdle trackway, *Somerset Levels Papers* 3, 39–51 (with B. Orme).

Garvin's tracks, *Somerset Levels Papers* 3, 72–81 (with B. Orme).

Conservation of wooden artifacts from the Somerset Levels 1. *Somerset Levels Papers* 3, 87–89 (with B. Orme).

Experimental archaeology: theory and principles. In *Sources and Techniques in Boat Archaeology* (ed. S. McGrail), British Archaeological Reports S29, 233–243.

Parade and display: experiments in Bronze Age Europe. In *Ancient Europe and the Mediterranean. Studies presented in honour of Hugh O. Hencken* (ed. V. Markotic), 50–58. Warminster: Aris and Phillips.

1978

The Somerset Levels: a concave landscape. In *Early Land Allotment in the British Isles* (eds H.C. Bowen & P. Fowler), 147–8. British Archaeological Reports 48.

Music of Bronze Age Europe, *Archaeology* 31, 12–21.

Man and landscape in the Somerset Levels. In *The Effect of Man on the Landscape: the Lowland Zone* (eds S. Limbrey & J. Evans), 86–89. CBA Research Report 21.

Tree ring studies in the Somerset Levels. In *Dendrochronology in Europe* (ed. J. Fletcher), 211–222. British Archaeological Reports S51 (with R. Morgan & B. Orme).

Archaeology in the Somerset Levels 1977, *Somerset Levels Papers* 4, 4–9.

The Meare Heath track, *Somerset Levels Papers* 4, 11–39 (with B. Orme).

Multiple trackways from Tinney's Ground, *Somerset Levels Papers* 4, 47–81 (with B. Orme).

Structures south of Meare island, *Somerset Levels Papers* 4, 90–100 (with B. Orme).

Bronze Age implements from Skinner's Wood, Shapwick, *Somerset Levels Papers* 4, 114–121 (with B. Orme).

The Somerset Levels Project, *Rescue News* 15, 4–7.

The use and character of wood in prehistoric Britain and Ireland, *Proc. Prehist. Soc.* 44, 1–45 (with V. Heal and B. Orme).

1979

The Bronze Age in Europe. An Introduction to the Prehistory of Europe c 2000–700 BC. London: Methuen. 581 pp. (with A.F. Harding).

Experimental Archaeology. London: Academic Press. 274 pp.

Archaeology in the Somerset Levels 1978, *Somerset Levels Papers* 5, 4–6.

Meare Lake Village West: a report on recent work, *Somerset Levels Papers* 5, 6–17 (with B. Orme & C. Sturdy).

Conservation of wooden artifacts from the Somerset Levels: 2, *Somerset Levels Papers* 5, 52–43.

The Sweet Track: Drove site, *Somerset Levels Papers* 5, 43–64 (with B. Orme).

An experiment with stone axes. In *Stone Axe Studies* (ed T.H. McK. Clough & W.A. Cummins), 106–107 CBA Research Report 23.

Excavations of Late Bronze Age or Iron Age date at Washingborough Fen, *Lincs History & Archaeology* 14, 5–10 (with B. Orme, J. May & N. Moore).

1980

Prehistory of the Somerset Levels. Cambridge: Somerset Levels Project (with B.J. Orme). 64 pp.

Archaeology in the Somerset Levels 1979, *Somerset Levels Papers* 6, 4–6 (with B. Orme).

The Baker site: a Neolithic platform, *Somerset Levels Papers* 6, 6–25 (with A. Fleming & B. Orme).

The Abbot's Way 1979, *Somerset Levels Papers* 6, 46–49.

Tinney's Ground, 1978–1979, *Somerset Levels Papers* 6, 60–68.

Tinned axes, *Antiquity* 54, 228–229 (with J. Close-Brooks).

Presidential Address: the donkey and the tail, *Proc. Prehist. Soc.* 46, 1–8.

1981

Prehistoric brass instruments, *World Archaeology* 12, 280–86 (with P. Holmes).

Archaeology in the Somerset Levels 1980, *Somerset Levels Papers* 7, 4–6 (with B.J. Orme).

The Sweet Track 1980, *Somerset Levels Papers* 7, 6–12 (with B. Orme).

Meare Village West 1979, *Somerset Levels Papers* 7, 12–69 (with B.J. Orme, A.E. Caseldine & G.N. Bailey).

Conservation of wooden artifacts from the Somerset Levels: 3, *Somerset Levels Papers* 7, 70–79.

Meare, *Current Archaeology* 77, 189–190 (with B.J. Orme).

Reconciling tree-ring sampling with conservation, *Antiquity* 55, 90–95 (with R.A. Morgan, J. Hillam & S. McGrail).

Metallurgy and Bronze Age society. In *Studien zur Bronzezeit. Festschrift für Wilhelm Albert v. Brunn* (ed. H. Lorenz) 95–107. Mainz: v. Zabern.

1982

Ancient woodworking techniques: the implications for archaeology. In *Woodworking Techniques before A.D. 1500* (ed. S. McGrail), 1–6. National Maritime Museum, Greenwich; British Archaeological Reports International Series 129.

Archaeology in the Somerset Levels 1981, *Somerset Levels Papers* 8, 4–9 (with K.R. Campbell).

The Eclipse track 1980, *Somerset Levels Papers* 8, 26–39 (with A.E. Caseldine a R.A. Morgan).

Beaver in the Somerset Levels: some new evidence, *Somerset Levels Papers* 8, 67–73 (with B.J. Orme).

The Somerset Levels: a waterlogged landscape. In *Proc. ICOM Waterlogged Wood Working Group Conference, Ottawa 1981* (eds D.W. Grattan & J.C. McCawley), 129–40. Ottawa: ICOM.

The Somerset Levels project goes public, *Current Archaeology* 84, 25–27 (with B.J. Orme).

The Bronze Age in north-western Europe: problems and advances, *Advances in World Archaeology* 1, 265–321.

Prehistory in the Somerset Levels 4000–100 BC. In *The Archaeology of Somerset. A Review to 1500 AD* (eds M. Aston and I. Burrow), 29–41. Taunton: Somerset County Council.

1983

Archaeology, drainage and politics in the Somerset Levels, *The Royal Society of Arts Journal* no. 5320, vol.131, 199–213.

A BGC pipeline transect at Morton, Fife. In *Young Archaeologist. Collected unpublished papers, contributions to archaeological thinking and practice* [by M.S. Gregson] (ed. K.W. Ray), 193–207. Cambridge: privately published.

The Fenland Project, *Antiquity* 219, 51–52 (with D. Hall).

Archaeology in the Somerset Levels 1982, *Somerset Levels Papers* 9, 5–6 (with B.J. Orme).

The Sedgemoor survey 1982, *Somerset Levels Papers* 9, 6–8 (with B.J. Orme).

Prehistoric woodworking from the Somerset Levels 1: Timber, *Somerset Levels Papers* 9, 19–43 (with B.J. Orme).

Meare Village East 1982, *Somerset Levels Papers* 9, 49–74 (with B.J. Orme and R.J. Silvester).

The site record and publication, *Conservation on Archaeological Excavations* (ed. N.P. Stanley Price), 65–77. Rome: ICCROM.

Homo sapiens or *Castor fiber*? *Antiquity* 57, 95–102 (with B.J. Orme).

1984

The Archaeology of Wetlands. Edinburgh: Edinburgh University Press. iii + 111 pp.

Archaeology in the Somerset Levels, *Somerset Levels Papers* 10, 4.

Ten excavations along the Sweet Track, *Somerset Levels Papers* 10, 5–45 (with B.J. Orme).

A reconstruction of the Sweet Track, *Somerset Levels Papers* 10, 107–109 (with B.J. Orme).

Prehistoric roads and trackways in Britain: problems and possibilities. In *Loads and Roads in Scotland and Beyond: Land*

Transport over 6000 years (eds A. Fenton and G. Stell), 1–21. Edinburgh: John Donald.

Lost British opportunities? *Quarterly Review of Archaeology* 4, 4, 1983, 3–4.

Comments on Archaeology and Experiment, *Norwegian Archaeological Review* 16, 79–81.

Foreword, *Fenland Research* 1, 1983–84. Fenland Project.

Introduction, to *Prehistory, priorities and society: the way forward.* Prehistoric Society policy document.

One swallow, one summer? A comment on a wooden stake in Kenn Moor, *Somerset Arch. & Nat. Hist.* 128, 31.

1985

Découvertes archéologiques dans les terres basses des Somerset Levels, Angleterre, *L'Anthropologie* 88, 109–113.

Excavations at Kilmelfort Cave, Argyll, *Proc. Soc. Antiq. Scotland* 113, 11–21.

Prehistory of Denmark, *Annuaire souvenir Normand* 1984, 5–8.

Archaeology in the Somerset Levels 1984, *Somerset Levels Papers* 11, 5–6.

Prehistoric woodworking from the Somerset Levels, 2: Species selection and prehistoric woodlands, *Somerset Levels Papers* 11, 7–24 (with B.J. Orme).

Prehistoric woodworking from the Somerset Levels, 3: Roundwood, *Somerset Levels Papers* 11, 25–50 (with B.J. Orme).

A Neolithic jigsaw: the Honeygore complex, *Somerset Levels Papers* 11, 51–61 (with B.J. Orme, A.E. Caseldine and R.A. Morgan).

Third millennium structures on Walton Heath, *Somerset Levels Papers* 11, 62–68 (with B.J. Orme, A.E. Caseldine and R.A. Morgan).

Godwin's track: a Bronze Age structure at Sharpham, *Somerset Levels Papers* 11, 69–74 (with B.J. Orme, A. E. Caseldine & R.A. Morgan).

A Later Bronze Age complex at Stileway, *Somerset Levels Papers* 11, 75–79 (with B.J. Orme, A.E. Caseldine and R.A. Morgan).

Radiocarbon dates: fifth list, *Somerset Levels Papers* 11, 85 (with B.J. Orme).

1986

Sweet Track to Glastonbury. London: Thames and Hudson (with B. Coles). 200 pp.

Archaeology in the Somerset Levels 1985, *Somerset Levels Papers* 12, 5–6 (with S.D. Loxton).

Meare East 1932–1956: an introduction, *Somerset Levels Papers* 12, 27–30.

Archaeology. In *Radiocarbon Dating: 1975–1985. A review of the contribution to quaternary research by the NERC radiocarbon dating laboratory over the last decade* (eds D.Q. Bowen and D.D. Harkness), 26–27. London: Natural Environment Research Council.

Conference: the exploitation of wetlands, *NewsWARP* 1, 9–10.

1987

European Wetlands in Prehistory (eds. J.M. Coles & A.J. Lawson). Oxford: Clarendon Press. xix + 299 pp.

Preservation of the past: the case for wetland archaeology. In *European Wetlands in Prehistory*, 1–22.

Meare Village East. The excavations of A. Bulleid and H. St George Gray 1932–1956 (= *Somerset Levels Papers* 13). 254 pp.

Precision, purpose and priorities in wetland archaeology, *Antiq. J.* 66, 1986, 227–247.

Preservation of the Past, in *Theoretical Approaches to Artefacts, Settlement and Society* (eds G. Burenhult, A. Carlsson, A. Hyenstrand and T. Sjövold), 53–63. Oxford: British Archaeological Reports, International series 366.

Irish Bogs: the time is now, *North Munster Antiquarian J.* 26, 3–7.

The preservation of archaeological sites by environmental intervention. In *In Situ Archaeological Conservation* (ed. H.W.M. Hodges), 32–55. Los Angeles: Getty Conservation Institute and Inst. Nacional Antrop. Historia.

Conference: wet-site archaeology, Florida, 1986, *NewsWARP* 2, 15–16.

Alpine settlements of the Neolithic and Bronze Age: a review, *NewsWARP* 2, 8–10.

Conference: wood and archaeology, Louvain-la-Neuve, October 1987, *NewsWARP* 3, 13–16.

1988

A wetland perspective. In *Wet-Site Archaeology* (ed. B.A. Purdy), 1–14. Caldwell: Telford Press.

The peat hag. In *Wet-Site Archaeology*, 43–53.

An assembly of death: bog bodies of northern and western Europe. In *Wet-Site Archaeology*, 219–235.

Commentary and conclusions. In *The Exploitation of Wetlands* (eds P. Murphy and C. French), 369–371. British Archaeological Reports 186.

Archaeology in the Somerset Levels 1986–1987, *Somerset Levels Papers* 14, 5–6.

The Meare Heath Track 1985, *Somerset Levels Papers* 14, 6–33 (with B.J. Coles, R.A. Morgan and A.E. Caseldine).

Some Neolithic brushwood structures, *Somerset Levels Papers* 14, 34–43 (with A.E. Caseldine and R.A. Morgan).

A Neolithic hurdle on Franks' Ground 1984, *Somerset Levels Papers* 14, 44–49 (with A.E. Caseldine and R.A. Morgan).

Excavations at the Glastonbury Lake Village 1984, *Somerset Levels Papers* 14, 57–62 (with B.J. Coles and R.A. Morgan).

Radiocarbon dates: sixth list, *Somerset Levels Papers* 14, 91 (with B.J. Coles).

Tools of the trade: the angle indicator, *NewsWARP* 4, 22–23.

An archaeological wood survey of European and American projects, *NewsWARP* 5, 5–16 (also published in N.T. Nayling, *The Archaeological Wood Survey*, 12–20. London: English Heritage 1989).

1989

People of the Wetlands. Bogs, Bodies and Lake-Dwellers. London: Thames and Hudson (with B.J. Coles). 215 pp.

The Archaeology of Rural Wetlands in England, Proceedings of a Conference sponsored by WARP and English Heritage (eds J.M. Coles & B.J. Coles). Exeter & London: WARP & English Heritage.

Archaeological survey in the Somerset Levels. In *The Archaeology of Rural Wetlands in England*, 10–14.

The organisation of wetland archaeology in the English countryside. In *The Archaeology of Rural Wetlands in England*, 51–54.

The Fenland evaluation project, *Fenland Research* 6, 1–4.

The peat hag. Twelfth Beatrice de Cardi lecture. *CBA Report* 38, 68–73.

The Somerset Levels Project 1973–1988, *Somerset Levels Papers* 15, 5–14.

Prehistoric settlement in the Somerset Levels, *Somerset Levels Papers* 15, 14–33.

Somerset Levels Project catalogue of finds, *Somerset Levels Papers* 15, 33–61.

Index to site reports, *Somerset Levels Papers* 15, 70.

Index to subjects, *Somerset Levels Papers* 15, 71–72.

A bibliography of the archaeology and prehistory of the Somerset Levels, *Somerset Levels Papers* 15, 72–78.

The world's oldest road, *Scientific American* vol. 260, no. 11, 100–106.
The archaeology of wetlands: post-mortem methods, *NewsWARP* 6, 24–25.

1990

Images of the Past. A guide to the rock carvings and other ancient monuments of northern Bohuslän. Vitlycke: Hällristningsmuseet (also as *Bilder Vergangener Zeiten* and *Bilder från forntiden*).
Excavations at Grandtully, Perthshire, *Proc. Soc. Antiq. Scotland* 120, 33–44 (with D.D.A. Simpson).
Green in the Somerset Levels, *Antiquity* 64, 145–147.
Waterlogged Wood. Guidelines on the recording, sampling, conservation and curation of structural wood. London: English Heritage. 21 pp.
Waterlogged Wood. The recording, sampling, conservation and curation of structural wood: proceedings of a conference sponsored by WARP and English Heritage (eds J.M. Coles, B.J. Coles and M.J. Dobson). Exeter & London: WARP & English Heritage. v + 49 pp.
Guidelines on waterlogged wood. The recording, sampling, conservation and curation of structural wood. In *Waterlogged Wood*, 39–49.
Tools of the trade: the pin, *NewsWARP* 7, 19.
Pfahlbauland, *NewsWARP* 8, 2–3.

1991

From the waters of oblivion. C.J. Reuvens-Lezing 2. Assen: Stichting voor de Nederlandse Archeologie.
Wet-site Excavation and Survey (eds J.M. Coles & D Goodburn). London: Museum of London, Nautical Archaeology Society and WARP.
Survey and excavation in rural wetlands, and the preservation of waterlogged sites: strategies and logistics. In *Wet-site Excavation and Survey*, 2–9.
Elk and Ogopogo. Belief systems in the hunter-gatherer rock art of northern lands, *Proc. Prehist. Soc.* 57, 129–147.
Un chemin de bois pour dater le néolithique britannique, *La Recherche* 231, 494–495 (with B.J. Coles) (also as Un camino de madera para datar el Neolitco Britanico, *Mundo Cientifico* 114, 672–673).
Sex on the rocks. Mamligt, kvinnligt, mänskligt, *Fynd, Tidskrift för Göteborgs Arkeologiska Museum* 2/91, 20–30.

1992

Arthur Bulleid and the Glastonbury Lake Village 1892–1992 (with S.C. Minnitt and A. Goodall). Taunton: Somerset County Council Museums Service and Somerset Levels Project. 79 pp.
Passages of time, *Archäologische Mitteilungen aus Nordwestdeutschland* 15, 29–44 (with B.J. Coles).
The dying rocks, *Tor* 24, 65–85.
The wetland revolution: a natural event. In *The Wetland Revolution in Prehistory* (ed. B.J. Coles), 147–153 (with B.J. Coles). Exeter: WARP & the Prehistoric Society.

1993

A Spirit of Enquiry. Essays for Ted Wright (eds J.M. Coles, V. Fenwick and G. Hutchinson). London: National Maritime Museum, Nautical Archaeological Society, WARP.
Boats on the rocks. In *A Spirit of Enquiry*, 23–31.
Indskrifter og helleristninger Guidebillede. In *Arkaeologisk felthåndbog*. Copenhagen: Rigsantikvariens Arkæologiske Sekretariat.

1994

Fenland survey. An essay in landscape and persistence (with D. Hall). London: English Heritage. 170 pp.
Images of the Past. 2nd edition. Skrifter utgivna an Bohusläns museum och Bohusläns hembygdsförbund, 32. Uddevalla: Bohusläns museum. 96 pp. (also in German and Swedish).
Rock carvings of Uppland: a Guide. Occasional Papers in Archaeology, 9. Uppsala: Societas Archaeologica Upsaliensis. 98 pp. (also in Swedish 1995).
Japanese wetland archaeology, *NewsWARP* 15, 3–8 (with B.J. Coles).

1995

"Industrious and fairly civilized". The Glastonbury Lake Village. [Somerset]: Somerset County Council Museums Service & Somerset Levels Project. 213 pp. (with S. Minnitt).
Rock art as a picture show. In *Perceiving Rock Art. Social and Political Perspectives* (ed. K. Helskog and B. Olsen), 181–199. ACRA: the Alta conference on rock art. Oslo: Novus forlag: Instituttet for sammenlignende kulturforskning.

1996

Enlarging the Past. The contribution of wetland archaeology. The Rhind Lectures for 1995. Edinburgh: Society of Antiquaries of Scotland. (with B.J. Coles).
The Lake Villages of Somerset. Glastonbury: Glastonbury Antiquarian Society, Somerset County Council, Somerset Levels Project (with S. Minnitt).
Life and death in the wetlands: discoveries 1893–1993. In *Water and Archaeology* (eds. G. Barber and T. Barnett), 83–94. Bristol: Wessex Water and Bristol University.

1997

The Fenland Project: from survey to management and beyond, *Antiquity*, 71, 831–44 (with D. Hall).
John Grahame Douglas Clark 1907–1995, 1996 Lectures and Memoirs, *Proc. British Academy* 94, 357–87.
Wetland worlds and the past preserved. In *Hidden Dimensions: The cultural significance of wetland archaeology* (ed. K. Bernick), 3–23. Vancouver: UBC Press.
Experimental archaeology. In *Proc. First International Symposium on Wood Tar and Pitch* (eds W. Brzezinski & W. Piotrowski), 307–12. Warsaw: State Archaeological Museum.

1998

Changing Landscapes: the Ancient Fenland. [Exeter]: WARP and Cambridgeshire County Council. iv + 92 pp. (with D. Hall).

Editorial work

Proceedings of the Prehistoric Society, 1970–79.
Somerset Levels Papers, 1975–79.
NewsWARP, 1987–present.

Note

1 Articles in the *Proceedings of the Society of Antiquaries of Scotland* are listed here by year of appearance. During the 1960s, this journal appeared two or three years after the 'session' to which it referred, and both dates or sets of dates appear on cover and title page. Elsewhere in this volume, the articles in question are referenced by the date of the session, with the date of appearance in square brackets.